KILLING AT ITS VERY EXTREME

DUBLIN: OCTOBER 1917–NOVEMBER 1920

DEREK MOLYNEUX
& DARREN KELLY

MERCIER PRESS

To

Lieutenant James 'Kruger' Smithers, B Company, 3rd Battalion, Dublin Brigade, Irish Volunteers

and

Captain James Molyneux, C Company, 4th Battalion.

MERCIER PRESS
Cork
www.mercierpress.ie

© Derek Molyneux and Darren Kelly, 2020

ISBN: 978 1 78117 754 9

A CIP record for this title is available from the British Library.

This book is sold subject to the condition that it shall not, by way of trade or otherwise, be lent, resold, hired out or otherwise circulated without the publisher's prior consent in any form of binding or cover other than that in which it is published and without a similar condition including this condition being imposed on the subsequent purchaser.

No part of this publication may be reproduced or transmitted in any form or by any means, electronic or mechanical, including photocopying, recording or any information or retrieval system, without the prior permission of the publisher in writing.

Printed and bound in the EU.

Contents

Introduction	5
Prologue	9
1 New Leaders Emerge	13
2 Planned Assassinations	28
3 Shootings at Soloheadbeg and the First Dáil	47
4 Escape from Lincoln and Collinstown Arms Raid	63
5 G-Division Penetrated and Tensions Escalate	78
6 Shootings, Ambush and Assassination	99
7 Formation of the 'Squad'	115
8 G-Division Under Pressure	137
9 War Declared, Elections and Raids	160
10 G-Division Decimated and British Intelligence Pummelled	176
11 The Black and Tans Arrive	195
12 New Players at Dublin Castle	220
13 Intelligence War Intensifies	238
14 Shootings, Reprisals and Auxiliaries Deployed	256
15 Auxiliaries take on IRA and Propaganda Disasters for Britain	274
16 Peace Offerings and Tragedy for the Dublin Brigade	296
17 Increased British Pressure and Propaganda Disasters	318
Epilogue	335
Endnotes	337
Bibliography	353
Acknowledgements	362
Index	365

INTRODUCTION

This book is the first of two that deals with the War of Independence in Dublin. It is also the third book of four whose subject matter is the 1916–21 period and the momentous events that took place in Ireland's capital during those tumultuous years, seen through the eyes of those from both sides who endured them.

In this sense it is a successor to our previous works: *When the Clock Struck in 1916: Close Quarter Combat in the Easter Rising* (The Collins Press, 2015), and *Those of us Who Must Die: Execution, Exile and Revival After the Easter Rising* (The Collins Press, 2017). It picks up where the latter left off and carries on, bringing the reader on a continuation of the incredible journey embarked upon by a great number of our ancestors, many of whom did not survive.

We have divided our War of Independence work into two volumes. This is because it would have been impossible to inject the level of information and vivid detail that this story deserves into one. Our first two works introduced a diverse tapestry of compelling characters whose experiences were recounted equally expressively. Many of them continue to feature here and we could not have done them justice if their stories were diluted and compromised simply for expediency.

The timeline featured here is from October 1917 until November 1920. We initially explore the build up to the conflict: the aftermath of Thomas Ashe's funeral, the reorganisation of Sinn Féin (meaning 'We Ourselves' in English) and the Irish Volunteers under the growing influence of Éamon de Valera, the Conscription Crisis and the German Plot of 1918. This took place in conjunction with the arrival of Ireland's new uncompromising lord lieutenant; the man who represented the British crown in Ireland, Sir John French, and the ensuing plot to assassinate the British War Cabinet. We then touch on the effects of the end of the Great War in Dublin, the Spanish Flu epidemic, the monumental 1918 general election and the subsequent inauguration of Dáil Éireann set against the Soloheadbeg killings that laid down an ominous marker for what was to follow. This leads us to the onset of armed struggle, of offensive actions being taken by Volunteer General Headquarters (GHQ) run by predominantly young formidable men such as Richard Mulcahy and Dick McKee, underpinned by a growing intelligence network under the charismatic and meticulous control of Michael Collins, and bolstered further by adept propagandists.

The reader will then see events throughout the spring, summer and early autumn of 1919 in Dublin when, soon after the departures of De Valera and his trailblazer Harry Boland to the United States (USA), the 'Special Duties Units' – later known as 'The Squad' – were formed against the backdrop of an audacious police boycott. These units were formed to neutralise those officers who refused to back away from their investigations into Sinn Féin, Dáil Éireann and the Volunteers. So began the first assassinations. Following the banning of the Dáil, the later autumn months saw the further gunning down of detectives on Dublin's streets by the now officially named Irish Republican Army (IRA). The intelligence war escalated. IRA intelligence had a particularly advantageous head start gained from a clandestine overnight visit paid to a prominent city police station the previous April by Collins and a comrade. They amassed a great deal of information to help seal the fate of some of the same detectives who had cruelly tormented the surrendered Volunteers three years earlier after the Easter Rising and who, despite warnings, still refused to curtail their pursuit of political enemies.

Winter 1919–1920 then saw, amid the shifting sands of escalating political and military conflict, the culmination of several attempts to assassinate Lord French at Ashtown in north-west Dublin in a daring and game-changing attack. Things then really heated up as the war entered a new phase. In conjunction with sweeping military round-ups and internments, a succession of intelligence officers were dispatched by the crown to infiltrate both the military and the financial wings of the Irish republican forces. When these proved consistently futile – not to mention fatal for the officers – desperate measures were undertaken.

The notorious 'Black and Tans' and 'Auxiliaries' arrived in the country during the spring and early autumn of 1920 alongside a new wave of undercover agents, as did military reinforcements, all while the Dublin Castle administration was also overhauled. Yet the insurgents met each successive strategy with their own counterpart and maintained the initiative, aided in no small part by organised labour. Assassinations and arms raids continued, as did countermeasures and reprisals from both the police and their undisciplined quasi-military reinforcements.

All the while the republican government formed in early 1919 continued to assert itself. It gained significant control of local government, administered

INTRODUCTION

its own courts and, accordingly, cemented its own credibility among the populace. A growing number of people were driven further to support them by the escalating atrocities of the 'Tans' and Auxiliaries who were, inadvertently, doing most of the republicans' propaganda work for them in instilling hatred towards the police and military – a striking case in point being the sacking of Balbriggan, which is explored here in some detail.

Then, in the wake of this atrocity the capacity of the British government for public relations own goals reached a new zenith in the capital with the first of numerous executions since the Rising – that of Kevin Barry – taking place on a particularly notable religious holiday, All Saint's Day. This was also the day after Ireland had buried its most famous hunger striker, Terence MacSwiney, who had brought Ireland's struggle to the front pages of newspapers throughout the world. These all occurred against a backdrop of frenetic gun-battles happening almost daily in Dublin, while in the background, peace feelers were being set in play.

We conclude for now in the immediate period following Barry's execution. It came hot on the heels of a series of pivotal events that saw the transition of the war into its next phase. British agents had successfully established themselves in Dublin and, in conjunction with a police and military offensive, were carrying out their own extra-judicial killings. In doing so they were laying the foundations for unprecedented counter-measures that we explore in a similarly visceral style in our next work.

Ireland's War of Independence is the subject of numerous works. It has not, however, in our opinion, been covered in such a detailed and comprehensive manner, one that immerses the reader into Dublin's turbulent and lethal streets. Here we seek to do precisely this; we aim to convey the sense of initial zeal and continued adventure that accompanied the reorganisation of the revolutionary forces. We then display how it evolved into a pitiless state of terror, as illustrated by the multitude of stalkings, killings and reprisals that characterised that period. We strive to embed the reader into Dublin's smoggy thoroughfares and squares, where filth and squalor clashed with salubrious splendour, and where urban guerrilla warfare was mercilessly perfected. It was also necessary to make numerous references to and explorations of wider developments throughout Ireland as well as abroad. Little in war happens in isolation.

Like our previous works, we employ graphic depictions of the violence that is all too often glossed over, while simultaneously warning the reader that significant parts of this work are not for the faint-hearted. As we stated in both our previous books, it is only by endeavouring to convey the ferocity, the pain, the terror, the hunger and the anguish involved that authors can do justice to the conditions faced by those from both sides who risked everything and paid an appalling price.

Harsh lessons learned from 1916 and its aftermath were employed by the men and women who continued the fight that is depicted within these pages. Their dogged tenacity in the face of new challenges and opportunities inspired hundreds of thousands of their countrymen and women, millions of foreigners and the worldwide Irish diaspora. The Volunteer army's strategies and tactics – as they sought to defend the increasingly effective counter-state – were admired by world figures who later gained prominence in Latin America, North Africa, India, the Middle East and South-East Asia. It was, of course, not supported in all quarters, but no such conflict is.

To the historian, however, it represents an incredible and moving account of Ireland's relentless and steadfast refusal to accept what was felt to be a detrimental rule by the greatest empire in the known world. It has, again, been a privilege to walk among them, to study their gripping accounts from one of our principal sources – Ireland's Military Archives – which, among other sources, has frequently allowed us to feel breathless at the boldness of these figures, while also being greatly aware of the personal price paid by so many ordinary men and women.

The war was, indubitably, fought with considerable cruelty from both sides. Its ruthlessness was, however, punctuated with the same acts of humanity that characterise the human spirit in all wars. Conflicts such as this unleash the full spectrum of human behaviour – good and bad – and from all sides. We prefer not to cast judgement, but merely to facilitate the readers' immersion into what is a gripping story, which, once again, we hope to have done some justice to.

DEREK MOLYNEUX and DARREN KELLY

PROLOGUE

'Fill the jails and break the system'

St Patrick's Day fell on Sunday in 1918. To mark the occasion, Brigadier Dick McKee – now addressed as such following a recent promotion and, consequently, was soon due to depart from Irish Volunteers 2nd Battalion's command – led its several hundred-strong ranks on manoeuvres for one last time in the Coolock area of North Dublin. Among the battalion's ranks were 1916 veterans such as Oscar Traynor, Frank Henderson, Vincent Byrne, Paddy Daly, Martin Savage and Harry Boland – to name but a few.

They were tailed by a detachment of policemen. Standard procedure for the Royal Irish Constabulary (RIC) was to follow such columns on bicycles. Most of the Volunteers were itching to confront them, infuriated at the idea of men they considered traitors following the battalion and keeping tabs on its officers, non-commissioned officers (NCOs) and men.[1] However, a standing order was in place from General Headquarters (GHQ) that the RIC and Dublin Metropolitan Police (DMP) were not to be challenged by Volunteers on parade.

With it being a holiday, the policemen had correctly anticipated a higher than usual turnout of Volunteers. Therefore, their own ranks had also been bolstered to match an adversary they had, since 1916, learned not to underestimate. McKee oversaw a brief foot-drill while watching the police. He noticed reinforcements arrive on bicycles. After further mustering of the distinctive dark-green uniformed policemen a middle-aged officer, County Insp. Andrew Roberts, strode to their front. He glared at McKee, standing out among his battalion at over six-feet-tall with broad shoulders and a distinctive stooping posture. McKee had a striking and tireless looking face, a long and slightly hooked nose, thin moustache, thick jet-black hair, and piercing, determined eyes.

Insp. Roberts knew of McKee's rank – at least his most recent one. The RIC acted as the eyes and ears of Dublin Castle – the nerve-centre of British rule in Ireland – and missed little in intelligence gathering. From a safe distance and with his men forming a phalanx just behind him, batons at the ready, he called on McKee to cease drilling his men. McKee refused. His nearest fellow officers hot-footed to his side, expecting trouble. The battalion's companies and sections continued marching in step. Insp. Roberts, however, realising his men were vastly outnumbered, and fearing a riot, ordered his men to withdraw; but not before loudly remarking that McKee was a 'cheeky fellow,' much to the sudden amusement of Volunteers within earshot.[2]

Soon afterwards, the 2nd Battalion resumed their march towards the city until twenty-year-old Lt Martin Savage, commanding its advance guard, ordered a halt, observing the same county inspector with what now looked like an increased number of RIC men forming a hedge-to-hedge cordon, six-to-eight ranks deep, and shoulder to shoulder at a crossroads in Beaumont.[3] He then saw military lorries speeding towards the crossroads. A runner was dispatched to the main force moments before the lorries screeched to a stop. Lt Savage expected soldiers to emerge from the vehicles. To his surprise, however, the rapidly alighting cargo turned out to be additional police reinforcements. Moments later, the rest of Savage's battalion arrived.

A standoff ensued until McKee stood forward accompanied by Oscar Traynor, Patrick Sweeney, and McKee's 2nd Battalion's replacement commandant, Frank Henderson. Insp. Roberts quickly identified these officers to a nearby superintendent. Their arrests followed, resulting in fury from the Volunteers. Tensions escalated as the four were wrenched away. Curses filled the air, stones and rocks were hurled at the vehicles, clashing noisily against their metal and wooden hulls and tearing at their canvas cargo coverings. Volunteers surged forward until a sudden succession of sharp commands from their remaining officers jolted them, reminding them of the standing order regarding the police, and adding that their strategy, in any case, was to fill the jails and break the system from the inside.

McKee and his fellow officers spent St Patrick's night in the dank cells beneath bridewell police station in Dublin's Chancery Street. They were later joined by two comrades, Eddie O'Mahony and Christie Lynch, who had been arrested following the battalion's continued march into Dublin. Their other cellmates consisted of drunks.

The following morning saw the same half-dozen weary Volunteers brought before the criminal courts charged with 'illegal drilling'. Their appearances were brief. McKee spoke with a laconic Dublin accent, and on behalf of all the accused, refused to recognise the court.[4] The court's response was equally swift. McKee, Traynor and Sweeney each received three-month prison sentences while Henderson, Lynch and O'Mahony were handed down two-months. They were then transferred to Mountjoy Prison on Dublin's North Circular Road. McKee's role as brigadier had gotten off to a bumpy start. However, he had just taken the helm in a campaign in Dublin that was set to revolutionise the art of guerrilla warfare.

1

NEW LEADERS EMERGE

'To resist conscription by the most effective means'[1]

By early March 1918 a major reorganisation of the Irish Volunteers had been set in motion. It was almost two years after the Easter Rising had seen central Dublin go up in flames, and less than a year since the last of those interned and imprisoned throughout England and Wales for participating in it had been released and returned home. Now, under new leaders they were once again gearing up for war, and in doing so, preparing for a conflict that would eventually shake the British Empire to its foundations.

Those who had returned home from the prisons and camps had, in the main, been battle-hardened from the rigorous ordeals of the Rising, during which they had held out against overwhelming odds until escalating civilian casualties had compelled their leader, Pádraig Pearse, to order their surrender. They had also been tempered by its demoralising aftermath, which had seen them corralled in cruel, unsanitary and grossly overcrowded conditions in Richmond barracks and Kilmainham Gaol. It was in Kilmainham that fourteen of their leaders had been shot over a ten-day period in May 1916 by firing squad before being hastily interred in a communal quicklime grave in Arbour Hill; another leader had been executed in Cork.

Their subsequent deportations to similarly comfortless conditions in prison and internment regimes across the Irish Sea – where despair, cold, rat and lice proliferation, gnawing hunger, and repeated solitary confinements had tested the sanity of many – had ultimately served to further inure them. Eventually, while in captivity, emerging leaders such as Éamon de Valera, Richard Mulcahy, Michael Collins, Dick McKee and numerous others formulated future political and military strategies.

Now that they were back in Ireland, most had re-immersed themselves in the Volunteers. Reorganisation had been vigorous. They represented a formidable core from which they sought to expand and assimilate the growing numbers of truculent young men and women flocking daily to their ranks, eager to get to grips with their colonial masters. The next four years would ensure that those young men and women and their more seasoned mentors would not be disappointed.

Autumn 1917 had seen pivotal events transpire in Dublin that illustrated the revolutionaries' resurgence. Most prominent was the death of one of their most charismatic and respected emerging leaders, Comdt Thomas Ashe, on 25 September from a gruesome force-feeding incident while on hunger strike in Mountjoy Prison. Ashe's grisly death set the scene for a monumental gathering at his funeral in Glasnevin Cemetery five days later. The attendance of large numbers of uniformed Volunteers, Fianna, and Cumann na mBan members, combined with volleys of rifle-shots over his grave showcased the reinvigorated spirit among these organisations.[2] It was the first large-scale public gathering of their uniformed members since the Rising. The tens of thousands of civilians who paid respects while Ashe's body had lain in state in City Hall, and the funeral's enormous civilian turnout, also highlighted the greatly increased public support for the radical nationalists that had manifested since the executions of May 1916.

The backlash from Ashe's cruel and unnecessary death drove thousands to the Volunteers and far greater numbers of ordinary men and women to support Sinn Féin. Ashe had been imprisoned for making a seditious speech. This was considered no greater a charge than the gun-running offences openly committed several years earlier in Ulster during the Home Rule crisis by senior unionists who were now serving as prominent British government officials.[3] Ashe appeared, simply, to have been on the wrong side.

Then, in the month following Ashe's funeral, two additional key events had transpired. The first was the Sinn Féin Convention (Ard-Fheis), which met on 25–26 October 1917. Held at the Mansion House in Dublin's Dawson Street and attended by over 1,700 delegates and supporters, its fundamental objective was to establish the party's constitution and seek international recognition for the Irish Republic. It was deemed that once this was established a referendum would follow to allow the country's citizens determine what precise subsequent form the government would take. During the proceedings De Valera was unanimously elected as party president, facilitated by its founder, forty-six-year-old Arthur Griffith, stepping aside to become joint vice-president alongside Fr Michael O'Flanagan.[4]

The Ard-Fheis had also been employed to mask the second key event – the equally significant Volunteer Convention. Its purpose was to put the Volunteers on a proper military footing and to organise nationwide resistance to British rule.[5] It convened on 27 October in the far less stately Gaelic Athletic Association (GAA) grounds on Jones' Road Drumcondra (Croke Park). Attended by over 1,100 Volunteers of all ranks, they sat throughout the park's pavilion on bales of hay and planks of wood while armed guards patrolled the area, keeping watch for police or the military.

During the Volunteer Convention two committees had been set up: a twenty-member national executive and a seven-member resident executive. The former was to strategically co-ordinate the Volunteers throughout the country, while the latter was a subcommittee whose members, as a requirement, were residents of Dublin. Notably, De Valera was also elected as national executive president, highlighting the nominal unity of Sinn Féin and the Volunteers. Given his position as leader of both the political and military wings of the separatist movement, in conjunction with the recent death of the Irish Republican Brotherhood (IRB) president – Thomas Ashe – De Valera had become the undisputed man in charge. The IRB was the oath-bound secret society founded originally in 1858 to overthrow British rule in Ireland by force. De Valera was not a member. He had been, but had left the organisation after the Rising.

Éamon de Valera, the undisputed man in charge following the Sinn Féin and Volunteer conventions of October 1917. (*Courtesy of Kilmainham Gaol Museum OPW, KMGLM 2012.0139*)

A mathematics teacher by profession who had grown up in Co. Clare, De Valera was the methodical, calculating and uncompromising thirty-five-year-old commandant who, during Easter 1916, had led the 3rd Volunteer Battalion against the British before narrowly avoiding his own death sentence following his capture. His distinctive aloofness frequently gave way to boyish geniality and a warm smile. He had returned to Ireland in June 1917 from imprisonment in England, where he had expressly established his leadership credentials, and was one of the year's four by-election winners for Sinn Féin. He represented East-Clare and had won the election in July. He lived in Greystones with his wife, Sinéad, and five children.

The resident executive was placed under the chairmanship of forty-three-year-old Cathal Brugha, another Easter Week veteran. His exploits during the fighting had bestowed him with an unyielding reputation that belied his modest physical stature and more austere civilian profile. He was a director of Lalor Candles in 14 Lower Ormond Quay. Brugha had been spared court martial, execution and prison following the insurrection, as he had been so badly wounded during the intense fighting for the South Dublin Union that the British had not expected him to survive; they then effectively ignored him. His recovery since had been astonishing. A non-smoking teetotaller, he had been a passionate athlete. He had overseen the reconstitution of the Volunteers in late 1916 despite suffering greatly still from his wounds. He lived in Rathgar with his wife and six children. Both De Valera's and Brugha's towering personalities would become paramount in the coming struggle.

Several months later, during early spring 1918, morale within the Volunteers flourished. Training and recruitment accelerated. This impelled the national executive to propose and oversee the election of a GHQ staff to provide the nationwide organisation with a central focus.[6] GHQ was established at existing Volunteer headquarters (HQ) – 44 Rutland Square (Parnell Square), close to battle-scarred Sackville Street in central Dublin and adjacent to the Rotunda buildings.[7] It was within the Rotunda's walls that their organisation had been originally formed in 1913, and from which several hundred battered and weary Volunteer and Irish Citizen Army (ICA) combatants had been held and mistreated appallingly by the enemy following the Rising.

In early March, the night before the GHQ elections had been scheduled to take place, a meeting of Volunteer officers was convened at 44 Rutland Square to select names to be put forward as its staff. Two salient names were initially nominated for chief of staff: Richard Mulcahy and Michael Collins. Both were already resident executive members and would soon be at the forefront of a new and unforgiving form of warfare in Ireland.

Mulcahy, a thirty-one-year-old medical student at University College Dublin

(UCD), and former post office engineer, was tough, physically unimposing and reserved, but radiated an affable smile that belied the remorselessness he both possessed himself and extolled to others as a fundamental requisite in any forthcoming war. From Waterford, he was a formidable, articulate officer with a proven track record as a leader during the Rising. During the Battle of Ashbourne, which took place between Comdt Ashe's 5th Volunteer Battalion and the RIC on Friday 28 April 1916, Mulcahy's critical intervention had swung the brutal engagement in favour of the Volunteers and landed them with their only decisive victory. The RIC had suffered dozens of casualties.

Collins, on the other hand, was an extrovert, gregarious, mischievous, convivial, charming and at times brooding, but always ruthless when required. He was twenty-seven-years-old, almost six-feet tall with dark hair, brown eyes and a square-jawed commanding presence underscored by a comprehensive command of foul language. Born and raised in West Cork, his previous career had seen him studying at King's College and working for the post office in a clerical capacity in London. He was also an administrator for the GAA there, as well as a ferocious player. His time in London was followed by a short period working with financial firm Craig Gardner in Dublin.

Collins, compared to Mulcahy, however, remained untested up to that point. He had participated in the Rising but in a much less critical role. His uncompromising, straight talking charisma had nonetheless become prominent during his internment in Frongoch in Wales, as well as since their release. He had been particularly influential in imprisoned Volunteer Joseph McGuinness' crucial South Longford by-election victory in May 1917, and a conspicuously short but rousing graveside speech he had delivered at Thomas Ashe's funeral had spellbound the assembled crowds. His influence was clearly on the rise Ultimately, however, after some deliberation, it was agreed between the meeting's attendees that Mulcahy – who had furthered his own credentials in Frongoch to an even greater degree, not to mention at Ashe's funeral, when as commandant of the Dublin Brigade he had taken charge of the event's military direction – would be the position's sole nominee.

Later that night, following the selection of the other GHQ nominees, of whom there were to be five, Mulcahy departed the four-storey building accompanied by one of the five. This was another officer whose prominence was rapidly growing: twenty-four-year-old Comdt Dick McKee, also an Easter

Rising veteran. As both spoke and walked through the city centre, a great deal of it still in ruins, McKee confided his relief, to Mulcahy's surprise, that the latter was now the only name being put forward as chief of staff. Collins – in spite of his charm, growing profile, and herculean ability for administration – had, nonetheless, developed a disconcerting reputation among McKee and some of his fellow Volunteer officers for play-acting and volatility. McKee elaborated that this, combined with his comparatively untested track record as a leader, did not mark him out for such a senior position. Like numerous others among the organisation's officers, McKee was wary of entrusting Collins with complete control.[8] On the other hand, they trusted Mulcahy implicitly. Both then parted ways.

The following night, the walls of the same ground floor room in Rutland Square witnessed, amid a cloud of tobacco smoke, the formal approval of Mulcahy's nomination. Accordingly, Mulcahy commanded the entire underground army. Another well-known veteran officer, Austin Stack, was elected as Mulcahy's deputy. Collins was elected to two GHQ positions: director of organisation, which overlapped with his resident executive brief, and he now took the additional role of Volunteer adjutant-general. McKee was appointed director of training. Seán McMahon – another veteran officer – became its twenty-four-year-old quartermaster general (QMG). McMahon had his work cut out; rifles were so pitifully lacking that many Volunteers were forced to drill using broom-handles as substitutes. Rory O'Connor, also a resident executive member, took the title of director of engineers. O'Connor, thirty-three years old, assumed the additional rank of officer commanding (O/C) operations in Britain, where the Volunteers and the IRB maintained a strong presence. Eamonn Duggan became its director of intelligence.

Michael Collins, the equally imposing and unrelenting Volunteer director of organisation and adjutant general.
(Courtesy of Mercier Archive)

Within days another meeting was convened at GHQ. With Mulcahy's

NEW LEADERS EMERGE

Richard Mulcahy, the Irish Volunteers formidable and ruthless chief of staff. (*Courtesy of National Library of Ireland* INDH 40)

responsibility for the whole country, a new brigadier was required specifically for Dublin's 2,000 strong contingent. McKee then filled the gap when he was unanimously elected by the various delegates as Dublin Brigade commandant, while also retaining the GHQ director of training role. McKee, also an IRB member, had joined the Volunteers in 1913 and greatly impressed his comrades both before and after the Rising when he had been instrumental in the reconstruction of the Dublin Brigade. He had already, the previous autumn, followed Mulcahy's footsteps into his former role as O/C 2nd Battalion. He previously held a captain's rank and was a compositor by trade. He worked at M. H. Gill & Son publishers and booksellers in Sackville Street.[9] He was a keen sportsman, and lived in Finglas. His second-in-command would be vice-brigadier Michael Lynch.

McKee would, however, not be at large for long under his new rank. On 17 March he and several of his fellow Volunteer officers were arrested for illegal drilling in Beaumont in north Dublin. The following morning saw him and the others imprisoned; this was on the same day that news arrived in the capital of the death of Volunteer Thomas Russell in Co. Clare from an RIC bayonet charge during a similar incident. After a brief initial stint in Dublin's Mountjoy Prison,

McKee and the others were transferred to Dundalk Gaol where significant numbers of republicans were incarcerated for similarly seditious offences. McKee, the highest-ranking prisoner, ensured their time there was not wasted. Dundalk Gaol mirrored, on a smaller scale, Frongoch internment camp – where many evenings had been spent debating future tactics and strategies – by becoming, effectively, another 'Republican University'. Under the guise of Irish language classes, McKee oversaw a series of lectures that would have a momentous influence in the coming months and years.[10]

Dick McKee was elected as commandant of the Dublin Brigade in March 1918. McKee, a gifted strategist and tactician, he became an inspirational leader at the very forefront of Dublin's War of Independence. (*Courtesy of Kilmainham Gaol Museum OPW, 19PC-3N12-14*)

Meanwhile, four days after McKee's arrest, unforeseen developments in the still-raging Great War – which, since 1914, had repeatedly acted as a catalyst to inflame Ireland's revolutionary spirit – took a monumental turn. Events unfolded on a mammoth scale and drew in the eyes of the entire war-weary world. Their ripple effects soon propelled McKee to the cutting edge of the unfolding struggle in Dublin, as well as irrevocably altering Ireland's turbulent political landscape.

***

Following the Treaty of Brest-Litovsk between Bolshevik Russia and Germany on 3 March 1918, dozens of German fighting divisions were rapidly redeployed from the eastern to the western front, paving the way for the 'Ludendorff Offensive' on 21 March.[11] A major component of this was 'Operation Michael', which resulted in the rapid breakthrough of German forces along the British front line to the east of the city of Amiens following an apocalyptic artillery bombardment.[12] For the first time since the late autumn of 1914 the surging Germans succeeded in radically buckling the British front lines.[13] Soon another offensive aimed at the Channel ports – 'Operation Georgette' – was opened. Additional offensives were also directed to the south against French armies to the east and north-east of Paris. Panic took hold. Casualties were colossal. British divisions were routed by wave after wave of German shock troops.

The Westminster cabinet's reaction to these developments as far as Ireland was concerned was unprecedented and disastrous. Conspicuously, in public relations terms, the backlash against the measures they were about to take to try and shore up their lines would dwarf the indignant reaction to the 1916 executions and scupper any lingering prospect of stability.

Six weeks before the offensive had been unleashed, on 6 February 1918, a bill had been passed through parliament relating to existing conscription parameters. These parameters had originally been enacted in January 1916 and amended the following May, and decreed that men aged between eighteen and forty-one years were liable for conscription, with notable exceptions such as widowed fathers and clergymen, as well as specialised industrial workers. The purpose of the new February 1918 bill, however, was to cancel such exemptions and to conduct a further trawl for manpower, and replenish the army's interminable losses on the western front.[14] To increase the overall potential trawl, the director of national service, Sir Auckland Geddes, had constituted the bill to – among its numerous other functions – raise the military service age to fifty-one, if required. Additionally, clergymen would henceforth be drafted under the proposed legislation, regardless of denomination, and would have to take their places amid the carnage.

The bill also looked in one other direction to replenish the military's dwindling forces: Ireland. Ireland had thus far remained untouched by conscription despite the protestations of the war cabinet that considered such a policy wasteful of a valuable potential resource, not to mention an open sore among existing conscripts who considered it unfair and unjust. Irish fighting qualities were tremendously regarded by the high command, as well as equally respected by their enemies. Over 200,000 Irishmen had volunteered to fight in the Great War so far. They had fallen in their multitudes. Nevertheless, as far as the cabinet was concerned, there appeared to be plenty more where they had come from, particularly given the fact that emigration of young men from Ireland had stalled since the war's outbreak.

Under the new bill, conscription would also be extended to Ireland. This latter fact raised eyebrows among the British cabinet. The prime minister, fifty-four-year-old David Lloyd George, a Liberal Welshman who had succeeded Herbert Asquith into office in December 1916, was among several who expressively doubted the wisdom of this.[15] Conscription's introduction in mainland Britain in 1916 had caused protest and resistance. Further afield, it had proved impossible to introduce by the Australian government. In 1917, the prospect of conscription in parts of Canada had provoked civil unrest. The fact that Ireland was a far more turbulent part of the British empire did not bode well. On the other hand, the Unionist and Conservative cabinet members insisted that, regardless, it needed to be implemented in Ireland.

The issue had been carefully weighed, until it was eventually resolved to link conscription to the painstaking process of implementing Home Rule for Ireland. This had already been a long-standing promise set to follow the war. Now, using the carrot and stick approach, they planned to piggy-back conscription into the country by dangling the carrot of accelerated Home Rule. A committee to oversee this was set up under the reluctant chairmanship of the sixty-four-year-old colonial secretary and former chief secretary for Ireland Walter Long. He, however, like other vociferous unionists, favoured conscription, but without the *quid pro quo* of Home Rule.

Home Rule's application had originally been suspended in September 1914 by a government who, ironically, had seen the war's outbreak as an unexpected respite from the political minefield of reconciling the intractable, decades-old issue. Then the Rising had bludgeoned it back onto their agenda. Following the Rising, however, despite strenuous efforts to reconcile the trenchantly opposing positions of Sir Edward Carson and John Redmond – the former being the staunch and formidable unionist at the helm of Ulster resistance to Home Rule, the latter the equally tireless but more moderate pro-Home Rule Irish Parliamentary Party (IPP) leader – progress had proved elusive.

In the aftermath of failed talks between Carson and Redmond, the Irish Convention had been orchestrated in Trinity College, commencing on 25 July 1917. Its government-sanctioned purpose had been to sideline radicals, and instead provide a forum to facilitate a scheme for Irish self-government with the onus for achieving this placed firmly upon Irish shoulders.[16] It had recently been making modest headway. Up to early March, Lloyd George had hoped such fragile progress might at least help keep the IPP onside if, and when, conscription was set in play. He was wrong. John Redmond passed away unexpectedly on 5 March. Meanwhile, the start of the German offensives drove it home that procrastination was not a luxury the British government could afford. On 25 March, in the wake of the offensives, the decision was finally taken to introduce conscription into Ireland.

Two weeks later, 9 April 1918, the Military Service Bill was introduced to parliament with the proviso: 'His Majesty the King may by order in council extend conscription to Ireland'. By then intelligence had already reached Volunteer GHQ of its pending announcement. Lloyd George issued a simultaneous invitation to parliament to pass a measure of self-government to Ireland, hoping to placate John Dillon – the sixty-six-year-old Member of Parliament (MP) and now, as the late John Redmond's successor, leader of the IPP. This was futile. Dillon, as well as his fellow Irish MPs, was aghast at the prospect of conscription for Ireland. They soon walked out of parliament to return home and campaign against it. Nevertheless, the bill was expedited through both the Houses of Commons and Lords, receiving royal assent on 18 April.

Thursday 18 April was also the date selected by Dublin's lord mayor, fifty-four-year-old Laurence O'Neill – himself also a former post-Rising internee – to hold an anti-conscription conference at the Mansion House that was attended by a cross-section of political parties and trade unions. The conference saw the formation of the Irish Anti-Conscription League. De Valera, representing Sinn Féin and mirroring the antagonistic Ulster Covenant of 1912 that had threatened armed resistance to Home Rule and organised a mass signed pledge, now drafted their own anti-conscription pledge. Aware that the quickest conduit to the Irish populace was via the Catholic church, the pledge was quickly prepared for delivery to the Catholic bishops conference that was taking place the same day in St Patrick's College Maynooth, Co. Kildare – the centre of ecclesiastical power in Ireland. It read:

> Denying the right of the British Government to enforce compulsory service in this country, we pledge ourselves solemnly to one another to resist conscription by the most effective means at our disposal.[17]

With no time to waste, a delegation that included De Valera, Arthur Griffith and the lord mayor sped by car to Maynooth from the Mansion House. First to address the bishops was the mayor, followed by De Valera, who laid it on the line, stating that if conscription was enforced it would be resisted by physical force. John Dillon even added a comment that flew in the face of his party's previous stance, asserting that resistance to conscription by all means was necessary.

The Catholic church in Ireland, notwithstanding its overall disinclination towards republicanism, had become more aligned with Sinn Féin since the Easter Rising, particularly among its younger members and especially in more recent months.[18] When the bishops eventually divulged their outright agreement with – and on the face of it – their unequivocal moral sanction to Sinn Féin, it was then decided that the pledge would be made available to be taken at every Catholic church door in the country the following Sunday, 21 April. Bishop O'Dea of Galway was then heard to assert – regarding the proposed conscription of priests and their male flock – 'If the Pope himself came over to this country and told the boys to enlist they wouldn't go'.[19] Two million people signed the pledge that Sunday.[20]

Delegates from the Labour movement ratcheted up resistance to conscription at the All-Ireland Trades Conference at the Mansion House on Saturday 20 April, calling for a one-day general strike for Tuesday 23 April. Labour and Sinn Féin had, since 1916, formed an accord based upon mutual good faith and broadly comparable aspirations. The strike was comprehensively supported throughout the country but with notable exceptions: north-east Ulster and the cities of Belfast and Derry – the two largest in Ulster.[21] On the day in question, with the late-spring sun blazing, the rest of Ireland, excepting some government buildings, came to a virtual standstill. It marked the first fundamentally successful general strike in Ireland's history.

The crisis deepened each passing day. Sinn Féin – founded in November 1905 by the more moderate yet indomitable Arthur Griffith, to originally pursue a 'Dual Monarchy' political strategy – saw its support ascend at the expense of the IPP, which was becoming redundant.[22] Sinn Féin boasted over 1,200 branches countrywide and over 120,000 members. Sinn Féin had always opposed the Great War. The party had not in any way orchestrated the 1916 Rising; it had been a force for moderation. Yet its brand had become synonymous with the insurrection when the authorities in Dublin Castle had erroneously blamed those they mistakenly referred to as 'Sinn Féin Volunteers' for coordinating it. The Rising was referred to afterwards as the 'Sinn Féin Rebellion', a fact that inadvertently saw the party's popularity increase proportionately with the growing exaltation of the rebellion's recently executed and exiled leaders.

Griffith, a strait-laced working class Dubliner, abhorred violence for political ends, but this had not prevented his own incarceration in Reading Gaol following the rebellion, a move which brought him into close contact with his more radical fellow internees. He saw the Great War as an unnecessary catastrophe, nothing to do with Ireland. Griffith had for many years advocated for a constitutionally achievable devolved parliament for Ireland, albeit under the British crown. Sinn Féin had been invited to participate at a marginal level in the Irish Convention – the principal reason for the release of the republican prisoners in June 1917 – but had boycotted it. Sinn Féin, under its new leaders, sought far more than what the Convention could offer.

Sinn Féin founder Arthur Griffith. Griffith had originally formulated Sinn Féin as a non-violent nationalist force for change. The party's inadvertent association with the 1916 Rising had, however, radically increased its popularity, and, therefore, its usefulness as a ready-made political vehicle for revolutionary republicans to align themselves with. (Courtesy of *Mercier Archive*)

When the Rising had failed it soon became clear to those at its forefront that to further the republican cause henceforth would require a democratic mandate that would, if necessary, run alongside a future military campaign. The Sinn Féin brand's unexpected sudden rise in popularity represented a ready-made political vehicle to drive this, justifying the subsequent amalgamation – despite some glaring ideological differences – of the moderate and radical, the latter of which were ensured to be at the wheel. Two additional electoral victories followed those of 1917 – in April and June 1918, albeit following three conspicuous earlier defeats.[23] The June victory saw Griffith elected by a significant majority to the East Cavan constituency.

The strategic political direction soon to be pursued by the republicans was straightforward: if the Westminster government would not accede to an independent parliament, then they would simply set up their own – and preserve it by whatever means necessary. Those means soon saw the Irish Volunteers put to a prolonged and ruthless test in a conflict to defend what became, effectively, an elected Irish government in exile within its own country. This war soon drew in the eyes of the entire civilised post-war world and tested the British empire in a way that it did not see coming during the tumultuous months of early 1918. Meanwhile, the Irish Volunteer ranks continued to swell.

Michael Collins, who was to become a close political associate of Arthur Griffith's, had spent a significant part of the early spring months of 1918 dispatching officers throughout Ireland to reorganise the force. Collins was well suited to his director of organisation role. His aptitude for this had been recognised by Kathleen Clarke – the insuperable widow of executed Rising leader Tom Clarke – when she had previously appointed him as secretary of the Irish National Aid and Volunteer Dependants' Fund (INAVDF). The fund consisted of £28,000 – the seeds of which had been entrusted to Kathleen by her late husband. Its office was in 10 Exchequer Street, and subsequently 32 Bachelors Walk. Notably, she also provided Collins with the IRB's entire records. One such officer dispatched by Collins in his role as director of organisation was twenty-two-year-old Dubliner Seán McLoughlin. McLoughlin, as well as being an IRB member and Volunteer, had also been an officer of the Fianna – the boy-scout styled force founded in 1909 and committed to subverting British rule. Like most of his fellow Volunteer officers who had fought during the Rising having come up through the Fianna ranks, his rigorous training and tactical dexterity had stood out at a critical time. In his case, it had led to his field promotion to commandant-general, a rank he held briefly before his garrison's disbandment following the surrender. His quick thinking, when an unexpected opportunity to slip through a police identification procedure was exploited, had then facilitated his escape from the attentions of DMP Det. Johnny Barton in Richmond barracks and seen him deported rather than court-martialled. Following his return from Frongoch he was eventually assigned to the Fianna in Belfast with the rank of commandant-general for the entire organisation. However, following the issuing of a warrant there for his arrest, he was reassigned by Collins to Tipperary as both an official organiser for GHQ and O/C Southern Area. Politically he was an avid socialist.

Never the type to waste his abundant energy, McLoughlin set about his tasks in the Munster county with a zest that, on the one hand, alienated some of his more laid back rural comrades, but on the other, resonated with the aspirations of many who could not wait to get to grips with the authorities. Some of them got to such grips soon enough – with colossal consequences.

McLoughlin quickly gained respect in the region as an organiser and tactician. Several weeks after his arrival a meeting of Volunteer officers from Tipperary itself, east-Limerick and north-Cork was held in Galbally, on the Limerick/Tipperary border. Top of the agenda was the conscription issue and, more importantly, what they could do to combat its pending enforcement given their meagre supplies of weapons. This problem had already manifested itself with lethal consequences in Co. Kerry on 13 April when two Volunteers – John Browne and Richard Laide – were shot dead by RIC men during an arms raid on Gortatlea barracks outside Tralee.

McLoughlin's solution was simple: somewhat reluctantly, he issued an order: 'all arms in the hands of private individuals should be seized'.[24] He knew such an order would be unpopular among the agrarian populace they would be relying on for support, but felt they had no choice given the pressing urgency of the circumstances. Additionally, once hostilities commenced they would avoid fighting in larger brigades, and instead, engage the enemy in small guerrilla bands – or flying columns – each consisting of roughly forty men. If inadequate supplies of arms were available for all forty or so, those unarmed would be detailed with first aid, quartermaster, or demolition duties. Attending the meeting was twenty-four-year-old Lt Liam Lynch, who proposed that the same units should also feature Cumann na mBan members. Cumann na mBan had been founded in April 1914 as a female auxiliary to the Volunteers; in 1918 it was undergoing significant reorganisation along systematic military lines. McLoughlin readily agreed.

Following the meeting, McLoughlin felt satisfied that, given what was expected, his proposed deployment of flying columns represented the appropriate strategy. Accordingly, he detailed a report of this to GHQ in Dublin. It did not go unnoticed by Mulcahy and McKee. Flying columns eventually formed the bedrock of the Volunteers on the run in Ireland's provincial areas – particularly in Tipperary and the rest of Munster – and wreaked havoc upon the enemy as the republicans and crown forces eventually grappled for control of the country.

2

PLANNED ASSASSINATIONS

'With all the subtlety of a cavalry charge'

At a meeting in London's Horse Guards building on 5 May 1918, Lord Alfred Milner, of Lloyd George's war cabinet, approached Field Marshal Viscount John French in the latter's office with a proposal from his prime minister.

French was the British army's sixty-five-year-old commander-in-chief (C-in-C) of the home forces. Comparatively short, he was a distinguished cavalry officer with an uncompromising reputation. Regarded as kind and charming by associates, he came from an aristocratic Anglo-Irish family and had recently purchased a country estate, Drumdoe House, in Roscommon with the intention of retiring there.

He had held the rank of C-in-C of the British Expeditionary Force (BEF) on the western front until his resignation had been demanded by Lloyd George's predecessor, Prime Minister Asquith, following the catastrophic Battle of Loos in autumn 1915; French had been accused of vacillation during a crucial point in its opening stages. It was not the first time his resignation had been compelled: in 1914 he had been forced from his position as chief of the imperial general staff (CIGS) over the Curragh Incident in Ireland.[1] In his role subsequent to C-in-C, French had dispatched General Sir John Grenfell Maxwell to Ireland during the Easter Rising's latter stages. Maxwell's actions in overseeing the post-Rising executions had proved a disastrous own-goal. Those who were shot by Maxwell's firing-squads rapidly became martyrs and their deaths turned the tide of public opinion radically in favour of the revolutionary nationalists, some of whom were very soon gearing up to strike at the heart of Britain's government. French was a dyed in the wool cavalryman and strode with a bow-legged gait. His previous reassignment, considered a demotion, had done little to undermine his irrepressible energy.[2] When addressed by Lord Milner, Ireland was on the agenda. French, typically outspoken, had conveyed previously to Lloyd George as to how Ireland should be governed – with a cast-iron hand. French's attitude given the current situation was uncomplicated: governmental authority should be categorically re-established, Home Rule implemented, and any clandestine relations between Irish rebels and Germany stamped out once and for all. Two years earlier it was the admission of such relations by the late 1916 Rising leader Pádraig Pearse that had, in the minds of the government, justified its subsequent contentious executions policy.

Field Marshal Viscount John French, commander-in-chief of Britain's home forces, soon to be dispatched to Ireland as lord lieutenant. (*Courtesy of the National Library of Ireland*)

Milner offered the office of the crown's representative – the lord lieutenancy – to French, in the prime minister's name.[3] He accepted on the basis that his role would be quasi-military.[4] Ireland, notably, would now have a soldier lord lieutenant.[5] French replaced Lord Wimbourne, the current occupant of the Phoenix Park's magnificent vice-regal lodge (Áras an Uachtaráin).

French then went straight to the war office where he sought out his superior, fifty-four-year-old Field Marshal Sir Henry Wilson, the Longford-born CIGS. French had two specific arrangements in mind: firstly, he sought to replace General Sir Bryan Mahon, the Galwayman who had succeeded General Maxwell as C-in-C Ireland, with fifty-six-year-old Major-General Sir Frederick Shaw, currently serving as chief of general staff home forces. Secondly, and more tellingly, he desired for Ireland to be removed from the home forces authority and placed under the control of the war office. Wilson, a fellow Curragh Incident conspirator, staunch unionist, and vociferous advocate of conscription in Ireland, had earlier written that Ireland resembled 'a mine which may go up at any minute'. He promptly saw to both requests.

***

Back in Dublin that same afternoon, the ground floor of 44 Rutland Square was the setting for another Volunteer conclave. Unlike previous GHQ meetings this was an operational affair. Those summoned included Joe Good, a twenty-three-year-old London-Irish electrician. He had fought in the Rising with the 'Kimmage Garrison' of Volunteers drawn primarily from Ireland's British diaspora, before being deported, and subsequently returning to Dublin. Like so many comrades he had struggled to find work and frequently had to exist on whatever could be afforded from the Volunteer Dependants' Fund. At this time, however, Good was working in the huge munitions factory in Parkgate Street next to Kingsbridge (Heuston) railway station, where he employed his engineering prowess to sabotage British artillery shells.

Also included in the meeting were Matt Furlong, who worked alongside Good, as well as Sam Reilly, James Mooney, John Gaynor, William Corcoran, Patrick Murray and Peadar Clancy. Another youthful Volunteer and similarly struggling 1916 veteran, William Whelan, also attended, along with a handful of others. Good and Whelan conversed briefly when they arrived. Whelan was curious why they had been summoned. Good, on the other hand, had a remarkably accurate inkling.

When Good was directed to a room with Richard Mulcahy and Cathal Brugha, the latter addressed him from behind a small baize-covered card table and revealed: 'You have been recommended as one likely to go on a dangerous mission'.[6] Brugha elaborated that the enterprise would necessitate GHQ looking after his dependants', if he had any; at best for the mission's duration, or at worst, permanently. In other words, he would be lucky to get back.

To Mulcahy's and Brugha's surprise, Good replied that he had already considered the increasing likelihood of such a hazardous mission. He was then asked who he had been speaking to. He responded 'no one', but then calmed their suspicions: he had recently been ordered by superiors to observe what kind of supplies the British Army were bringing into Ireland, particularly any unusual equipment that might indicate an escalation of operations that might in turn betray the imminent implementation of conscription. A subsequent ten-day trip around the country indicated plenty: the army was stockpiling sandbags and railway sleepers – far more of the latter than necessary for routine maintenance. He had seen similar employment of sleepers as barricades during the Rising. It appeared to him that the military were preparing to isolate the country's villages and towns and round up their young men.

Good then confessed to having considered that if members of the British cabinet were assassinated it might force the remainder to reconsider conscription. Brugha radiated a half smile before telling Good to consider the matter and if he was of the same mind report back in a week.[7]

When Good left the room, Whelan entered. Similarly, Brugha disclosed to him, without revealing specifics, that there was a dangerous job pending and asked if he was prepared to volunteer for it. Whelan said yes. Outside the room, the other summoned Volunteers sat smoking and speaking quietly, awaiting their turns to enter.

The secretive operation was expedited. Several days later the selected men were summoned again and informed of its approval by GHQ. Given the ominous probability of it becoming a one-way trip, they were asked if any had reconsidered. When this was cleared up with an unequivocal 'no' they were informed of the plan itself: the mission, as Good had correctly speculated, was to assassinate members of the British war cabinet. A brief silence followed as the rest of the Volunteers absorbed the thunderbolt. Brugha then scanned each man's face for reactions that might expose misgivings. There were none.

Satisfied, he expanded: they would travel to London in two-man teams with each provided with a lodging address. Whelan and Good would act as an advance party, travelling almost immediately to ensure each address was secure and suitable. Following confirmation of this, the remaining units would be dispatched and given £5 per man to tide them over until established. They were then dismissed having been ordered to maintain a low profile and stay away from haunts frequented by policemen and enemy agents until contacted with further orders. Before they left, Cathal Brugha told those assembled with a sense of fatherly assurance: 'I will be with you and in charge of the party'.[8]

Good and Whelan arrived in London within days.

***

Travelling in the opposite direction on the night of 10 May, Field Marshal French and his staff crossed to Dublin on the mail boat from Holyhead.[9] He was sworn in as lord lieutenant of Ireland the next day. Then, with the formalities aside, he set his mind to his tasks, establishing a scaled-down HQ within the vice-regal lodge. His chief aide was Edward Saunderson, an uncompromising unionist and confidant of Walter Long. French's immediate aim was to destroy Sinn Féin in order to create an environment in which Home Rule could safely be granted.[10] With the imminence of Home Rule then established, the authorities could implement conscription. To him it was that straightforward. He had, however, been impressed upon by propaganda-conscious Lloyd George of 'the necessity of putting the onus for first shooting on the rebels' if and when both sides crossed swords.[11]

French already felt assured he had enough evidence to circumvent any Sinn Féin counter-moves, basing some of it on obsolete links between the 1916 leaders and Germany. However, he also believed that he had a far more compelling ace up his sleeve in the form of thirty-three-year-old Joseph Dowling. Dowling had served with the Connaught Rangers before being captured by the Germans in 1914. While a prisoner of war (POW) he had joined Roger Casement's Irish Brigade – an endeavour undertaken by the diplomat and humanitarian to recruit British POWs to assist Ireland's planned insurrection.[12]

Dowling had been landed from a U-boat off the coast of Clare on the 12 April 1918 with the intention of re-establishing communications between the German High Command and Irish Volunteers.[13] Following his subsequent capture and arrest, however, he was transported to London. There, under interrogation by Basil Thompson, Metropolitan Police Assistant Commissioner in New Scotland Yard he had confessed his reason for landing. This saved Dowling from execution but had far-reaching unforeseen consequences. French was then egged along with prominent politicians, including Chancellor of the Exchequer Austen Chamberlain, Edward Carson, and Walter Long, and by Assistant Commissioner Thompson and the director of Naval Intelligence Admiral Sir William Hall, into believing that Sinn Féin were equally culpable as conspirators, and that this was sufficient to justify a move against its leading members. He finally made this move on the night of 17–18 May with all the subtlety of a cavalry charge.[14] Ironically, in doing so he ultimately paved the way to achieving precisely what the Germans, and Dowling, had hoped – to tie up tens of thousands of British troops – albeit far too late to be of any use to the former.

French was unaware that intelligence had leaked from Dublin Castle concerning his intended swoop. Det. Sgt Eamon (Ned) Broy, employed as a confidential clerk with the DMP's 'G-Division' – the detective unit based in the Central Police Station in Great Brunswick Street which had been keeping tabs on the Irish Volunteers and Sinn Féin since 1913 – had made a copy from Dublin Castle of the list of those to be arrested over the supposed plot. Broy, thirty-years old, from Rathangan in Co. Kildare – an area still harbouring a bitter legacy from the 1798 Rebellion – was sympathetic to the Volunteers. Having become disillusioned with the Home Rule debacle and subsequently inspired by the Rising, he had been passing valuable intelligence since 1917. He had passed the list to Volunteer Patrick Tracy, a husband of his cousin. Tracy had then forwarded it to Harry O'Hanrahan, brother of the late Michael who had been executed following the Rising. O'Hanrahan subsequently delivered it to Michael Collins. Another sympathetic member of G-Division who too was set to become an invaluable asset to the IRA, Joseph Cavanagh, had also leaked word to Dublin Brigade Intelligence officer Thomas Gay that a round-up of prominent 'Sinn Féiners' was imminent. This had also been relayed to Collins.

On the evening of Friday 17 May, as French was poised to strike, the Sinn Féin executive along with several high-ranking Volunteer officers, including Richard Mulcahy and Michael Collins, had assembled for a conference in Croke Park. Collins, in his conspicuous West-Cork accent, informed everyone present as to who was to be arrested that very night. His exhortation to all was to go on the run. To his astonishment, however, the consensus among most was instead to sit-tight in their homes and await arrest. This was for two reasons: the political backlash from their incarceration would constitute a propaganda coup; additionally, they feared that becoming fugitives *en masse* risked forcing the Volunteers into premature active resistance.[15] The more military minded among them, on the other hand, considered otherwise and feared no such thing.

Collins, Mulcahy and Harry Boland quickly made themselves scarce. Collins himself was fresh from a three-week stint on remand in Sligo Jail. Bail had been posted to free him to await a trial for sedition but he later neglected to attend; with conscription imminent, Collins would be no use to GHQ behind bars. Cathal Brugha also departed the gathering and caught the earliest boat to Holyhead. He had a job to oversee in London.

French's soldiers, accompanied by policemen and detectives, struck as planned throughout that night and the following early morning. Seventy-three prominent Sinn Féin members – including Kathleen Clarke and Maud Gonne, who was also the widow of an executed 1916 leader, John MacBride – heard the abrupt knocks of rifle butts and pistol handles on doors. De Valera was taken, as were William Cosgrave, Arthur Griffith and Joseph McGuinness. Countess Markievicz, the forty-nine-year-old Anglo-Irish aristocrat turned radical socialist, and former prisoner following the Rising, was also arrested, as were scores of other Volunteer officers and members. This was done under Regulation 14B of the Defence of the Realm Act (DORA).[16] Laughably, it was observed that some of those arrested had pre-packed suitcases, apparently in anticipation of a 'trip'. Luckily for their Castle insiders, the authorities read nothing into this staggering 'coincidence'.

Collins and Boland stayed the night in Volunteer Secretary Seán McGarry's house in Mountjoy Street after it was raided and McGarry arrested, considering it, consequently, to be the safest house in Dublin.

News of the round-ups travelled fast. On the morning of 19 May Joe Good and William Whelan, now established at their London lodgings, sat to eat their meagre breakfasts; food rationing was biting hard there. Their jaws gaped when they saw the newspaper headline: French had struck in Ireland.

French, meanwhile, was jubilant; he was convinced that his trawl had succeeded in decapitating Sinn Féin. He had no idea of the consequences of what had just been set in play. The arrests had in one swoop cleared most of the moderates from the party at large and left the way clear for its more militant members. He published his evidence to justify the arrests on 25 May, confident that it would be received well. It was not.

The backlash was instantaneous. Much of the evidence of clandestine communications between the Germans and Sinn Féin's leaders was alleged to have been based within the time frame when the majority had been in British prisons after the Rising. Worse, more than a few more liberal British government members confessed to being unconvinced by any of it. Searching questions were asked in the Houses of Lords and Commons, voicing dissent over the fact that not a single case had been before a judge. French's predecessor, Lord Wimbourne, was among those who complained about the scant proof to justify such widespread round-ups.

Ireland's population at large viewed the 'German Plot', as it quickly became known, with suspicion. In public relations terms it drove yet another nail into the coffin of the dwindling support for those whose sentiments towards the British government were more dispassionate than those of the radicals. It represented the latest in a litany of monumental oversights by the government since the Easter Rising. Sinn Féin was seen as the driving force behind the anti-conscription campaign and it appeared that the British were simply taking its leadership out of circulation.[17]

Yet there was more to come: widespread implementations of special juries and judges – in the faces of those *in situ* who were seen as sympathetic to Sinn Féin – announced under the Criminal Law and Procedure Act on June 14 further escalated national indignation, as did increased arrests under DORA for attending anti-conscription gatherings, and for even condemning the war.[18] Sinn Féin gained further ground and support, a clear example being Arthur Griffith's 20 June by-election victory, which was notable because it was the first by-election since the Plot arrests and laid down a critical marker underpinning party support.

***

9 June 1918 saw a one-day nationwide protest by Ireland's women. 'Lá na mBan' (Women's Day), when women's organisations such as the Irish Women's Workers Union (IWWU), Cumann na mBan and the Irish Women's Franchise League – of which Lord French's seventy-four-year-old sister, Charlotte D'Espard, was an active member – signed their own anti-conscription pledge at pre-arranged nationwide locations. They were followed in turn by women who did not belong to such organisations but who also wished to pledge

their resistance. Over 2,400 IWWU members, led by 700 Cumann na mBan members, led, in turn by – among others, thirty-five-year-old 1916 ICA veteran Helena Molony – assembled in a deluge of rain outside the IWWU headquarters in Great Denmark Street and marched to City Hall to sign their names.[19] This pledge which, like April's, also echoed the Ulster Covenant, read:

> Because the enforcement of conscription on any people without their consent is tyranny, we are resolved to resist conscription of Irish men. We will not fill the places of men deprived of their work through enforced military service. We will do all in our power to help the families of men who suffer through refusing enforced military service.[20]

Tens of thousands of women signed the pledge despite torrential rain throughout the day. The demand to sign it was so strong that venues remained open during the following days to accommodate numerous latecomers.

The same month saw Brigadier McKee back on Dublin's streets after his three-month stretch in Dundalk Prison. Top of his agenda was a visit to his twenty-five-year-old sweetheart, Cumann na mBan member May Gibney. He then quickly threw his abundant energy into the fight against conscription. His previous career at Gill & Sons was not resumed; his salaried position as brigade commandant now required full-time attention. With this in mind, his first move was to convene a brigade council meeting at GHQ with his commandants: Tom Byrne for the 1st Battalion, Frank Henderson – 2nd, Joseph O'Connor – 3rd, and Edward Kelly – 4th.

During the meeting thirty-eight-year-old Comdt O'Connor presented a plan he had been working on since advised by GHQ to consider all potential measures to resist conscription. O'Connor had proven himself a capable commander during Easter 1916 when, under De Valera, he had overseen the tenacious defence of the Boland's Bakery and Mill area, turning it into a stronghold that proved impervious to its assailing forces. He had inadvertently escaped the courts martial that followed the Rising and was sent to Frongoch. When McKee saw O'Connor's plan, he sanctioned it before applying some finishing touches. He then officially submitted the plan to his fellow GHQ members; it was approved.

Without time to waste, GHQ then issued a general order that any Volunteer carrying arms was to henceforth resist any arrest attempts. A previous standing order to 'fill the jails' no longer applied. Following this, McKee recalled the Dublin Brigade O/Cs to another council where he, O'Connor and the others, finalised their plan. They were aware that the English king, George V, could sign the Conscription Act at any time; even during the middle of the night should it prove opportune, and if this transpired it was likely that Dublin's inhabitants could wake to discover the British Army had already surrounded the city and cordoned off its populous areas for clearance, employing the railway sleepers and other materiel spoken of by Joe Good to do so. However, if the British Army were getting ready, the Volunteers would also be prepared.

McKee then instructed the commandants that it had been recognised that during the Rising too many men had been deployed together in small areas.[21] John MacBride – executed in Kilmainham Gaol in 1916 – had exhorted to those under his command shortly before the surrender of Jacob's biscuit factory: 'If it ever happens again, take my advice and don't get inside four walls'.[22]

In future the city would remain divided by the same general battalion demarcation areas as before. Their command structure consisted of: commandant, vice-commandant, adjutant, quartermaster, lieutenant of engineers, chief of signallers, chief of medical service and chief of scouting and cycling.[23] Each comprising six-to-eight companies of fifty-to-150 men under the overall command of an elected captain, each of which were sub-divided into four sections under lieutenants and NCOs and other specialists respectively. Each chosen area in turn would be subdivided into blocks varying in size depending on the number of houses or buildings needed to form one isolated rough square or parallelogram. A census was to be taken of Volunteers living within each designated block. A block commander would then be chosen for each separate one and he in turn would make a list for his quartermaster of weapons, ammunition and available tools such as shovels, crowbars and picks. He would maintain contact with neighbouring block commanders. Architects, tradesmen and engineers would then survey each block to determine where communication tunnels and lines of retreat would be best situated. Recent Volunteer recruits were formed into separate companies; it was suspected that many had only joined to avoid conscription. Until they could prove otherwise, the integrity of existing companies was not something GHQ were willing to risk compromising.

Each block in an area would act as a separate fortification.[24] Once engaged by the enemy its garrison would fight tooth and nail until it became untenable. At that point they would disengage to predetermined positions or to the next block, which would then re-engage. McKee also initiated plans for an attack on Dublin's Custom House – the headquarters of the Local Government Board – by 2nd Battalion.

Eventually if necessary, the entire city would be evacuated block by block towards the country.[25] 1st and 2nd Battalions would redeploy to the north, 3rd and 4th to the south. The brigades of the surrounding counties, Wicklow, Kildare and Meath, meanwhile, would simultaneously converge upon the city and engage the enemy's rear while preventing their reinforcements from entering the city. If the British insisted on compelling Irish men to fight – then fight they would: for every house on every street in every district in every suburb. It was estimated that for every man conscripted it would cost the British five. The British authorities had, however, unbeknownst to Volunteer GHQ, already factored losses such as these and were prepared for them. They were aware that the vastly widened trawl for conscripts under way closer to home would simply not be acceptable to the affected English, Scottish and Welsh men – far superior in number – and their families, if they knew their burden was not being shared in Ireland, forcefully or otherwise.

Each Volunteer battalion commander then got to work. Arms and ammunition procurement were given priority, as well as first aid equipment and parcels of edible rations. There would be no respite for QMG Seán McMahon overseeing this. A munitions factory soon operated out of 10A Aungier Street – a premises run by 3rd Battalion Volunteer Séamus Donegan. Engineers made improvised grenades from gelignite left over from the Rising; pipes and sawn-off gun barrels were filled with the gelignite, experimental Mercury fulminate detonators, caps and fuses were then fitted. Many of these were tested at the Hellfire Club in the Dublin Mountains, often under surveillance by the Royal Air Force (RAF). Astonishingly, chemical weapons were experimented with for defensive deployment in the event of their use by the British Army, as were masks and goggles to protect Volunteers from them.[26]

A company of engineers was formed under GHQ's direct control, to carry out explosive sabotage of communications, comprising four sections – one for each battalion. GHQ also operated a smaller-scale munitions factory. Lectures on demolition, train derailment, destroying bridges and felling trees were given in C Company 3rd Battalion HQ in 34 Lower Camden Street. Additionally, shopkeepers within the city were asked to order extra stocks of non-perishable food to feed the populace. Lack of food had become a grave problem during the Rising – this would not happen again.

Soon afterwards McKee inspected every such block in the city, adapting the plan to include advantageous strong points. Buildings at intersections dominating the gates of the city's numerous army barracks were ideal. Small groups of Volunteers would hold these, delaying actions and inflicting maximum casualties before displacing to stronger supporting positions.

As the days and weeks passed every aspect to this strategy was put in place. Nightly meetings took place in Cullenswood House, 4 Oakley Road in Ranelagh where McKee, Mulcahy and others updated and adapted plans. By the summer of 1918 Dublin city had been transformed into a potential nightmare for the British military: a multi-layered defence in depth. Such defences had already proven their worth during the Rising. The British had suffered hundreds of casualties in protracted battles where the employment of defence in depth had seen assault after assault driven off. While all this was in play the National Defence Fund raised over £250,000 – a huge sum – from church gate and doorstep collections.

While Dublin prepared, Volunteers in Tralee on 14 June upped the ante by opening fire on the two recently promoted RIC men who had killed their comrades in Gortatlea in April. One of the policemen was wounded.

Meanwhile, Cathal Brugha, having long since established himself close to Regent's Park in London, was also busily preparing for the proposed assassinations. On one balmy Sunday afternoon he cycled into the park only to be stopped by a solitary policeman informing him that cycling was forbidden there. Brugha promptly dismounted and walked with his characteristic limp to an unoccupied bench and sat down. Brugha had limped since the Rising; in fact, it was joked that he rattled when he walked with so many bullets and shrapnel pieces lodged in his body. The policeman moved on.

Brugha had earlier sent word out via twenty-seven-year-old Matt Furlong, his second-in-command, that all fourteen mission operatives were to assemble in the park, and to maintain a line of sight with the gate through which he had just entered. Doing their best to remain inconspicuous, individually and in clusters, each then approached Brugha, while keeping a discreet look out for any other policemen. Some of them were carrying .38 revolvers in case of any attempted arrest. As the first of them reached him, Brugha held out his hat. The first man, soon followed in turn by the others, pulled a small piece of paper from the hat with a name on it. Brugha then ominously told each of them to: 'Get familiar with the movements of this man and execute him when the time comes. Matt Furlong will deliver your final orders.'[27]

Joe Good was the last to pull a name. His target would be Andrew Bonar Law, the fifty-nine-year-old Conservative Party leader. William Whelan remained at Brugha's side for what would without doubt become a suicide mission: they would assassinate as many MPs as possible in the House of Commons, taking aim from the public gallery while parliament sat. Their primary target would, however, be none other than Prime Minister Lloyd George. Leaving nothing to chance, John Gaynor, twenty-one-year-old captain of the Balbriggan Volunteers, travelled to Gwynedd in North Wales, ready to pounce if Lloyd George went to his home there.

The summer days and weeks passed tortuously for those who had volunteered for the planned assassinations. Apprehension took its insidious toll as, employing their £10 per-week allowance, they shadowed their targets to and from Westminster, to picture palaces, theatres and operas, grappling with incessant dread.[28] Almost every movement the politicians made was monitored by their prospective killers – frequently astonished at their lack of security measures – as they awaited word to proceed, shuddering at the thought of committing the unpalatable and perilous act while longing to conclude their tension-filled days and nights in the bustling but lonely metropolis. They saw little of one another, which aggravated intermittent periods of self-doubt, but groups of young able-bodied men congregating out of military uniform would have attracted unwanted attention. However, occasional rowing trips on the river Thames near Kew were organised to maintain fitness and to let off steam, one of which almost drowned Brugha after his boat capsized, providing precious amusement to all.

On more than one occasion William Whelan and Matt Furlong flanked Brugha, seated in the House of Commons visitors' gallery. Ironically, Brugha was helped into the cramped gallery by the parliamentary ushers, who, owing to his pronounced limp, assumed he was a wounded war veteran. On one such occasion Brugha had whispered to Whelan that when the time came he was to:

'Keep the people away until I have finished the firing'.[29] On another occassion, as haughty exclamations of 'Order! Order!' and 'Here! Here!' erupted from the chamber below, Whelan discovered to his shock that Brugha had a Mauser semi-automatic pistol concealed down the leg of his trousers. Whelan, who had been unarmed at the time, whispered alarmingly to Brugha: 'Are you going to start?' Brugha replied covertly with a cold smile: 'No, I am not going to start: I only want to get the feel of this thing here in the gallery'.[30]

As matters transpired, however, their growing talents for assassination plotting would not be of use for some time: contrary to all expectations, the threat of conscription in Ireland began to dissipate over the summer months.

The German Ludendorff offensive had by that time lost its momentum.[31] To add to this loss of inertia the Kaiser's army then lost over half-a-million soldiers to sickness. An unanticipated pandemic, Spanish Flu, swept across Europe during the spring and summer, killing and debilitating *en masse*. Then, the British military, its ranks also thinned by disease, but bolstered by reinforcements from its dominions, recent enlistments and conscripts, and from other since-settled theatres, launched a series of hugely successful counter-offensives, as did its allies.[32] What followed became known as the 'Hundred Day Offensive' at the end of which the surviving Germans were reeling behind their spring start-lines, battered beyond belief.

The Germans were not the only ones receiving a battering. On 22 September a women's protest in Dublin's Foster Place against the continued imprisonment of the German Plot internees – particularly the females – was met with a vicious baton-charge from large numbers of uniformed DMP who, having initially surrounded the protesters, converged lashing out with truncheons. Josie McGowan, a twenty-year-old Cumann na mBan member, was severely beaten about the head. Taken to an aid station in Ticknock, she died a week later.

Meanwhile, the growing stream of daily news boasting of Allied victories as the autumn days shortened eventually convinced Cathal Brugha to dispatch his squads incrementally back to Dublin. No heroic welcome awaited them, however; instead they returned to near destitution. Most were tradesmen but had lost their jobs, and some their lodgings, while away. Joe Good was eventually forced to seek a personal loan from Michael Collins to tide him over until Collins eventually reassigned him to Mayo as a paid Volunteer organiser.

***

KILLING AT ITS VERY EXTREME

On Monday 11 November 1918, the guns on the western front finally fell silent. The Great War was over and the conscription threat had finally passed in Ireland. It was a political disaster and a military failure.[33] Ultimately, Dick McKee's block system, while an excellent source of training, and weapons and ammunition procuring exercise, would not – to the disappointment of some of McKee's fellow planners – be called upon. Volunteer recruitment began tapering downwards and many recruits to recently formed companies left. Nonetheless, some who remained proved equally worthy to their cause in the coming months and years as the most seasoned veterans.

However, as the war ended, Ireland's latest conflict was only just beginning. A riot that took place outside the Sinn Féin offices at 6 Harcourt Street on Armistice night was just one further harbinger of the fact that there was fighting ahead, and that it would be up close and personal. Harry Boland and many others under twenty-seven-year-old 3rd Battalion Adjutant Simon Donnelly drove away a frenzied mass of unionist Trinity College students with batons and hurley sticks. Scores of attackers, having marched up through Grafton Street and Stephen's Green waving Union Jacks, pelted the building with stones, bottles and tried to set fire to it. Thirty-one-year-old Boland – combustible, gregarious and hugely popular – was also a proficient hurler who had played for Dublin; the contest did not end well for many of the building's assailants who had to be hospitalised, though casualties were plentiful on both sides. The same fracas also saw the wife of thirty-five-year-old Joe Clarke – the building's caretaker – conducting a desperate, almost medieval defence, standing alongside her husband upstairs and throwing lumps of coal and pouring boiling water out of the window at the attackers. Ironically, Edward Carson's former home was just two doors away in No. 4.

Elsewhere in Dublin that night, including outside the Mansion House – where earlier in the day Sinn Féin had met to initiate its campaign for the forthcoming 1918 general election – similar clashes had seen people maimed. Liberty Hall, the battle-scarred building that had spawned the 1916 insurrection, was attacked by soldiers in a melee that saw the structure successfully defended by hard-pressed remnants of the ICA. On the other hand, soldiers and policemen were also attacked throughout the city – draped throughout in red, white, and blue victory flags and buntings – by Volunteers under the direction of Peadar Clancy, some being seriously injured.

Rioting mobs returned to Harcourt Street, as well as the rest of the city over the following nights, but were beaten off from Sinn Féin headquarters again by Boland, Donnelly and Volunteers under Capt. Paddy Flanagan from the 3rd Battalion's C Company. The last raid resulted in the heart attack and death of the thirty-eight-year-old writer and editor of Sinn Féin's *Nationality* newspaper Séamus O'Kelly. His funeral became another republican rallying point.

Throughout 1918, Volunteer attacks on RIC barracks and on members themselves had escalated all over the country, as had small-scale arms and ammunition raids. Counter-measures in the form of police raids also intensified. Casualties occurred on both sides, as well as calamities; for example, September saw the accidental death of Seamus Rafter in Co. Wexford from explosives he was manufacturing. In Dublin in November, the bullet-riddled Royal College of Surgeons – which had been ICA HQ during the Rising – was infiltrated by 1st Volunteer Battalion members hoping to acquire its huge stock of Officer Training Corps (OTC) rifles. The weapons, however, had been moved. A more successful raid, on the other hand, was carried out by the ICA under forty-three-year-old Capt. Christopher 'Kit' Poole. In this instance, a large consignment of small arms and ammunition was systematically removed from the US Navy freighter USS *Defiance* while she was berthed in Dublin Port under the noses of its US marine complement.

As tensions mounted, infantrymen stood guard in Dublin Castle alongside armoured cars as barbed wire entanglements were constructed by sappers both above ground and beneath the numerous manholes leading to the subterranean River Poddle.[34]

By and large, any and all means of obtaining weapons for the republicans had been exploited, including purchasing them from British soldiers. Capt. Liam O'Carroll, also of the 1st Battalion, employed his father's shop in Manor Street as a drop-off point for soldiers to sell their weapons cheaply. Harry Boland's tailor shop in 64 Middle Abbey Street served a similar purpose. Alternatively, prostitutes – a bustling trade – were employed to help steal them. Feminine charms were also applied to lure soldiers into the clutches of Volunteers waiting to relieve them of their weapons, employing violence if necessary.

The training and drilling of Volunteer companies and battalions intensified as ranks swelled and GHQ extended its tentacles, as did those of Cumann na mBan. Many Cumann na mBan members – at least those over the age of thirty – now had the right to vote for the first time. This was since the passing of the Representation of the People Act the previous February, which had given the vote to enough women of such age to make them account for thirty-six per cent of the new electorate.[35] Support for Sinn Féin continued to grow despite a proclamation from Lord French in July prohibiting unauthorised public assemblies of – now declared 'dangerous' – Sinn Féin members and supporters, as well as Irish Volunteers, Cumann na mBan and even the ostensibly apolitical Gaelic League and GAA. The prohibiting of the latter organisation had resulted in tens of thousands of defiant crowds and players assemble on 'Gaelic Sunday' on 4 August for a host of concurrent nationwide hurling and football games.

Such political support was unsurprising among women considering that John Redmond, as head of the IPP, had for years opposed female suffrage. Now too, all men over twenty-one years could vote regardless of status, as well as younger war veterans. The electoral franchise throughout Britain and Ireland had nearly trebled, introducing legions of younger male and not-so-young female voters with no prior allegiance to the IPP to burden them as they flocked to cast their votes in the general election – the first in eight years – held on Saturday 14 December. This was in no small measure conducted under the control of the Volunteers and Cumann na mBan, who in many regions policed meetings and election booths despite Lord French's July proclamation to constrain them.

The election was a game-changer. It was a resounding victory, with 46.9 percent of the overall vote, and seventy-three seats won from a total of 105 for Sinn Féin, whose manifesto heralded two particularly noteworthy pledges: to withdraw its representatives from Westminster and set up a functioning government within Ireland, and to use any means available to render Britain's rule impotent. The IPP, by comparison, won just six seats. Ironically, its withdrawal of members from Westminster during the conscription crisis provided indirect vindication for Sinn Féin's proposed abstentionist policy. Michael Collins, Harry Boland, Cathal Brugha and Richard Mulcahy won seats, underpinning the hard-line military conviction that was to the forefront of the party considering the number of more moderate Sinn Féin candidates still languishing in prisons since the May arrests. The election also saw equally belligerent Countess Markievicz elected as the first ever female MP – representing Dublin St Patrick's – while she was still imprisoned in Holloway in North London. The IPP was all but wiped out and never recovered.

December 1918 also saw shots fired over the grave in Glasnevin Cemetery of twenty-eight-year-old Volunteer Capt. Richard Coleman in another stage-managed funeral on a smaller scale to that of Thomas Ashe but at the far more opportune time of the election. Coleman, from Swords in Co. Dublin, had fought at the Mendicity Institution under the late Seán Heuston in the Rising, been imprisoned following his court martial, repatriated and ultimately re-arrested during the German Plot. He became gravely ill during early December in Wales' Usk Prison. He was diagnosed with Spanish Flu and died on 9 December, his skin having turned blue and his lungs filled with fluid as his agonising demise progressed. However, when word got out that his medical treatment had been withheld, the public outpouring of sympathy reflected that which had followed Ashe's horrific death the previous year. More than 15,000 attended his funeral after a far greater number had paid their respects while his remains lay in St Andrew's church in Westland Row. Dick McKee oversaw the funeral's extensive military preparations.[36]

Capt. Richard Coleman's death in Usk Prison resulted in widespread public indignation towards the British at the time of the 1918 general election. (*Courtesy of Kilmainham Gaol Museum OPW, KMGLM 2019.0043*)

Broadly speaking, the arrival of Spanish Flu – the world's worst pandemic since the Bubonic Plague – inadvertently helped to justify the decision of the Sinn Féin members who had allowed themselves to be arrested and imprisoned over the German Plot. As the pandemic cut a swathe through British and Irish prisons, the refusal of the authorities to release them for their own safety horrified voters and further alienated them from the establishment and, ultimately, propelled them in huge numbers towards Sinn Féin.

Politically, 1918 had seen the waning of the influence of moderate nationalists in favour of the radical republicans, set against the tumult of the final throes of the Great War and the arrival during autumn of the flu pandemic that killed just as indiscriminately in Ireland as it had in France, Belgium and elsewhere. Many blamed the Great War for the pandemic as its victims thronged to the already over-burdened hospitals where coffins were soon stacked by the dozen.[37] Cumann na mBan members such as Annie Cooney, former sweetheart of the late Con Colbert – executed in 1916 – dedicated their efforts and risked their lives nursing flu-victims throughout the city's burgeoning slums. Dr Kathleen Lynn, Sinn Féin's joint director of health, on the run since the German Plot arrests, returned to her home to set about helping flu victims. When subsequently arrested she was promptly released, as doctors were desperately needed.

1919 saw the continued ascent of the republicans as they began to wrestle power from Westminster. This was set against an escalating and increasingly pitiless conflict, soon to become known as Ireland's War of Independence, for which Dublin formed the cornerstone.

3

SHOOTINGS AT SOLOHEADBEG AND THE FIRST DÁIL

'We are now done with England'

On 7 January 1919 the newly elected Sinn Féin representatives and the higher echelons of the party – excluding those in prison or on the run – held a private meeting in the Mansion House. Several meetings had been held since December's election, both in the Mansion House and at City Hall. Following their victory, they were keen to decide their next course of action. Taking their Westminster seats when parliament was due to sit early the following month was out of the question; instead, a date was set when their own parliament – Dáil Éireann (Assembly of Ireland) – would convene its inaugural meeting. A committee was put together to oversee this and they were then charged with drafting the Dáil's provisional constitution, democratic programme, declaration of independence, and a message to the free nations of the world.

Attending the meeting was thirty-eight-year-old Piaras Béaslaí, recently elected Sinn Féin MP for East Kerry. A journalist raised in Liverpool, Béaslaí had held the rank of vice-commandant and fought in 1916 alongside Comdt Edward Daly – executed following the Rising. A talented propagandist, but markedly edgy, Béaslaí was now Volunteer director of publicity. During the summer of 1918 Michael Collins and Richard Mulcahy had tasked him with editing a bi-monthly newspaper called *An t-Óglách* (The Volunteer), which was to be printed by Dick McKee on a Linotype machine at the Gaelic Press in 30 Upper Liffey Street. Its first edition had been published on 15 August 1918. It soon became a vital conduit for communicating information, tactical and technical instructions, and propaganda from GHQ to Volunteer units throughout Ireland.

Béaslaí was a fluent Irish speaker and writer and, at the meeting, was asked to translate the drafted inauguration documents into Irish. He also became responsible for the event's choreography. Following his agreement to this, his own subsequent action was to propose that Cathal Brugha acted as chairman (*ceann comhairle*) of the Dáil proceedings. When this was accepted, it was also agreed to invite to the Dáil all those recently elected for Irish constituencies, including unionists, and the survivors of the decimated IPP.[1] Harry Boland and fellow party secretary Thomas Kelly took responsibility for this. The date for the first sitting of Dáil Éireann was set for Tuesday 21 January 1919.

Lord French, meanwhile, in the wake of a nationwide protest on 5 January against the continued German Plot internments, had been busy with his brief.[2] Lamentably aware now that the solution to the country's political problems was not just a simple matter of decapitating Sinn Féin, his latest enterprise was to invite to Ireland his friend, sixty-two-year-old former Lord Chancellor Viscount Richard Haldane, for an informal consultation on the state of Ireland at the viceregal lodge.[3] Lord Haldane, a heavy-set Scotsman with a rounded face and stern expression, accepted. A liberal by disposition, he was an exceptional administrator and before the Great War he had overseen significant reforms within the British Army that underpinned the creation of the British Expeditionary Force.

Haldane, familiar with Ireland from previous administrative visits, arrived in Dublin on 16 January. He was quick to deliver candid revelations to French: the Dublin Castle administration – top-heavy with officialdom and currently preparing to welcome Ireland's combative new chief secretary, Ian Macpherson – was in disarray in the face of Sinn Féin.[4] One of the factors that seemed to dumbfound the castle's civil servants was their inability to grasp that Sinn Féin was not run by typical politicians, with characteristic vulnerability to the pursuit of power and material wealth rendering them susceptible to leverage; on the contrary, the party was run by far less malleable idealists; worse, they felt no fear of imprisonment, or even death so relying upon such traditional methods of influence was useless. Compounding French's difficulties was the fact that Sinn Féin's more radical tentacles were penetrating every class of society, apart from those in the staunchly unionist northern regions. It was also infiltrating local authorities and this trend needed to be urgently curtailed.

Haldane's proposed solution to French represented a significant overture: Sinn Féin and the Irish public would be offered 'self-government on the status of a dominion under the Crown'. Significantly, he felt certain that this would disarm Britain's critics abroad. Furthermore, the British government would provide generous financial provisions, as well as providing general assistance to help form a new Irish government. A critical prerequisite would be for Sinn Féin to ensure that violence did not erupt before the necessary negotiations could be concluded.

However, Haldane warned French of two hurdles: the inevitability that Ulster's more forceful unionist protagonists, not to mention the die-hards in the Conservative and Unionist Party, would – given previous form – reject any such proposal outright; secondly, it would be difficult convincing Sinn Féin that such an offer was genuine, given their knowledge of such trenchant unionist stances. Ultimately, however, Haldane felt that these could be overcome by creating a three-man committee to attain a platform of consensus. consisting of a unionist, a Sinn Féin member, and a neutral. He then proposed that to display goodwill all interned political prisoners should be immediately released, adding that the Sinn Féin committee member would have to be De Valera, considering that the party's currently incarcerated president would undoubtedly become prime minister in an Irish parliament.[5] French eventually told Haldane that he would need to consult with other members of the Irish Executive before responding.

French did not take long. When he later informed Haldane that the proposals were provisionally acceptable – at least to him – he requested that Haldane would chair his proposed committee. Haldane agreed on one condition: he insisted on consulting with Sinn Féin first. Meanwhile, French instructed Haldane that he would formulate a plan to convince Edward Carson, James Craig and Lloyd George that the enterprise was worthy. Then, Haldane slipped out into the winter darkness to contact Sinn Féin through some back channels.

Haldane was expeditious and by the late afternoon of 17 January, he already had his response from Sinn Féin. They had declared through intermediaries that they 'would not pull the house down on his head' if he would set himself to work out a meaningful plan on dominion status and agree to release their prisoners.[6] Satisfied, he went straight to Lord French. French, however, notwithstanding his similar satisfaction, was simultaneously formulating a more 'drastic and extensive' solution if the proposed talks failed.[7] He would have been equally happy to convert his proverbial cast-iron hand into a fist.

French then updated Walter Long of the developments. Long, phlegmatic faced, bald and with a distinctively thick hanging moustache, was a die-hard unionist – he had formerly led both the Irish Unionist and Ulster Unionist parties – and was contemptuous of the enterprise. He also mistrusted Haldane, considering him to have been a German sympathiser during the war.[8] French did, however, persuade him to at least hear Haldane out.

***

Shortly after midday two days later, on Sunday 19 January, far from the salubrious heated rooms of the vice-regal lodge, roughly forty Volunteers from C Company 3rd Battalion, under Capt. Flanagan, were tucking into rations following musketry and field telegraphy practice, as well as general manoeuvres on icy cold Three Rock Mountain near Stepaside in South Dublin. When Flanagan, twenty-seven years old, acting as lookout, spotted three RIC officers approaching, he quickly alerted his men but ordered them to remain where they were and allow the police to approach. When they did Sgt Lawson, in charge of the policemen, went to arrest Flanagan. The captain, however, pulled his revolver, pointed it at the sergeant and retorted: 'I don't recognise your authority and I am placing you under arrest'. The surrounding Volunteers then set about the officers, roughing them up, disarming them and, much to their chagrin, tying them up with their own trouser-braces. Flanagan, suspicious that an informant had alerted the police, then ordered his men to depart the area before reinforcements arrived. Cyclists soon scouted out their escape route. A short time later, three miles towards Rathfarnam, they spotted six lorry loads of police moving out towards Three Rock Mountain.[9] Flanagan re-directed his men. A few hours later, as darkness was descending, the police reinforcements found their bound, shivering and much-relieved colleagues.

When RIC County Insp. Andrew Roberts heard of this incident he was appalled. It appeared that the Volunteers had lost any fear of the police and he expected that the situation would only get worse. Within two days his misgivings proved correct.

One hundred miles from Dublin, on the cold misty morning of 21 January 1919, nine Volunteers of the 3rd Tipperary Brigade took up ambush positions just outside Soloheadbeg quarry, five miles north of Tipperary town.

Eight were lying in wait, another acting as lookout. Among them were Dan Breen, Seán Treacy, Seán Hogan and Séamus Robinson. Seán McLoughlin had recently been reassigned from the southern area, having completed his organisational duties in the region with vigorous training exercises and a stirring speech to over 1,000 Volunteers during which he had declared, while holding up a revolver, that arms were the only thing preventing the British from making slaves of the Irish. The gesture did not go unnoticed by the RIC. Michael Collins had since reassigned McLoughlin to Wicklow until a bout of influenza hospitalised and nearly killed him.

The same nine men had been lying in ambush for five days, taking up positions before daylight and dispersing after dark. This allowed them to avoid detection from passers-by as their meagre rations dwindled daily. In late December they had received intelligence of a large cargo of explosive gelignite and detonators that were to soon be delivered by horse and cart from the local RIC barracks to the nearby quarry on or around that date. Their wait would soon be over.

Dan Breen was the twenty-four-year-old brigade quartermaster (BQM). An uncompromising republican regarded by some as hot-headed, his youth had been spent in rural poverty among his family of eight siblings and peers who harboured bitter memories of the recent land agitations. Breen, as a youngster, had witnessed a brutal eviction by the RIC – at a landlord's behest – of a nearby tenant who had subsequently died by the roadside. A fervent nationalist from his school years, he had joined the IRB aged eighteen and the Irish Volunteers soon after its inception. Having been frustrated by the advent of Eoin MacNeill's countermand order's effect on his locality during Easter 1916 he then felt great resentment at the subsequent executions. The killing of nationalist leaders who had risen under arms – set against the embrace bestowed by the same authorities upon unionist leaders who had flirted with treason two years earlier by threatening war in Ulster – betrayed to him where he and his fellow countrymen stood in the eyes of Dublin Castle. He yearned to strike back. Armed with a handgun, and with a handkerchief ready to cover his fearless-looking face, he was about to.

Seán Treacy was the brigade vice-commandant. More dispassionate than Breen, with dashing features and a dry sense of humour, he was almost twenty-four years old. He and Breen had been close friends for years. Treacy, no less patriotic, had joined the IRB in 1911. In fact, he had sworn Breen into the brotherhood. Both had been raised in the area within which they were preparing to strike. Having been picked up in the round-ups after the Rising, Treacy had eventually returned home. Both men then acted as bodyguards for Éamon de Valera during his 1917 by-election. Treacy had been imprisoned afterwards in Mountjoy and participated in the same hunger strike that claimed the life of Thomas Ashe. He then served time on two separate occasions in Dundalk Gaol, the latter stretch being spent alongside Dick McKee, Oscar Traynor and Frank Henderson. There, McKee's frequent lectures were not wasted on his marginally younger comrade. He was released alongside the others in June 1918. Like Breen, Treacy was impatient at what he saw as an overly moderate Volunteer movement. He galled at seeing the spirit of resistance that had underpinned the anti-conscription movement tapering away and strove to reignite the hostilities he and his men saw as inevitable. He held a Winchester repeating rifle at his position at the gate to Cranitch's Field, overlooking the fourteen-foot wide stone and clay roadway along which the explosive cargo would pass.

Séamus Robinson was the thirty-one-year-old Belfast-born brigade commandant. He had recently been transferred to the area and elected to his command the previous October under Richard Mulcahy's direction. He was a veteran of the Rising and had fought in Sackville Street and the General Post Office (GPO).

The rest of the ambush party consisted of Seán Hogan, Tim Crowe, Michael Ryan, Patrick McCormack, Jack O'Meara, and their lookout Patrick O'Dwyer. Hogan, seventeen-years-old, had provided his comrades with a tin shed within which to make and store their weapons and explosives, and which they had returned to each day.

They were unsure of the size of the RIC guard complement but expected it to number between two and six officers. They had determined while planning the ambush that they would shoot without warning if there were six. Otherwise they would demand a surrender before firing if necessary. Gags and ropes to silence and tie up the policemen had been hidden in the quarry to deal with the latter contingency.

When breathless Patrick O'Dwyer arrived back at their position and alerted them that the target was approaching and the guard consisted of two policemen accompanied by two civilian workers they made ready. The endless waiting had played havoc with their nerves but the nine men readied weapons and steeled themselves. In the clear air they heard the sounds of the horse's hooves and the rumbling of the heavy cart, which grew louder as the cart came into view.[10] Patrick Flynn, a council worker, and the driver, James Godfrey, led the horse and cart with its explosive cargo stacked upon it carefully in sealed wooden boxes. Two constables: James McDonnell and Patrick O'Connell, armed with Lee-Metford rifles, strode along in rain-smocks behind. Both sported Prussian-styled moustaches, common among RIC men. McDonnell smoked his pipe. Both were popular locally. McDonnell, from Mayo, was known for his quirky sense of humour and was a fluent Irish speaker. He was forty-seven years old, a widower, with seven children. O'Connell was a thirty-year-old bachelor from Cork. Neither had any political leanings. It would not save them.

Both were members of what was seen by radical nationalists as a force of enemy occupation, none more so than the men about to attack them. The 9,300-strong RIC were an armed force, unlike the DMP, trained in basic military tactics, who operated from barracks – 1,400 in total countrywide – and whose principal operations included funnelling local knowledge of separatist agitators to the agents of the crown. Conversely, most RIC members considered themselves nationalists, albeit with no time for revolutionaries. Many joined up simply to attain secure pensionable employment in what was generally regarded as an esteemed profession. A select few had actually been persuaded the previous year by GHQ members to remain within the force as insiders when they had threatened to resign during the conscription crisis.[11] The force's broad rank and file had shared the public indignation during the crisis, but nonetheless, trusted in the authenticity of longer-term government pledges to settle Irish matters once and for all. On the other hand, others – particularly higher ranks – shared far more unionist leanings.

When the cart drew level with the field gate Breen and Treacy sprung to its side from the left, their cocked weapons trained, shouting 'Hands up!' Robinson and O'Dwyer jumped in front while simultaneously Hogan and the others appeared behind, shouting the same command and pointing their guns. In a split-second of instinct, and pumping suddenly with adrenalin, the policemen worked their rifle bolts, even as O'Connell rushed for cover and McDonnell fumbled desperately to ready his weapon.

Treacy fired his rifle, Breen, Robinson and Crowe shot their revolvers. The muzzles cracked and shattered the surrounding stillness. The policemen jerked and spun as the bullets tore through them. They collapsed to the earth, oozing blood. McDonnell was shot in the head and the arm, killed instantly. O'Connell was hit through the side and perished within seconds. O'Dwyer grabbed hold of the panicked horse's reins to steady it. Treacy kissed his rifle; then Hogan, Breen and him leapt onto the cart and sped away.[12] The remainder, under Robinson, collected the dead policemen's rifles and equipment before making their escape. The workmen, still frozen to the spot, looked on, horrified as blood seeped into the clay around the two lifeless bodies. The acrid smell of cordite dissipated in the still winter air.

Moments later, as the unsprung cart raced down the rough and bumpy roadway, Treacy spoke. He looked back at their sixty-kilogram cargo of gelignite and detonators and said alarmingly to Breen: 'Do you remember, Dan, when we were reading about explosives? The books said they were not to be jolted!'[13] Breen looked from Treacy to the cargo. They could not stop now. Hogan whipped the horse on.

***

Back in Dublin that same afternoon, Dawson Street's 200-year-old Mansion House was the setting for a dinner hosted by the Dublin Women's Unionist Club and the POW Committee to welcome home 400 recently repatriated POWs from the Royal Dublin Fusiliers. Most had been captured by the Germans during the war's early stages, and since supplied by the committee with donations of food parcels and clothing. The ceremony listed to follow illustrated the political polarity pervading the country: at 3.30 p.m., Dáil Éireann's inauguration would commence in the grandiose setting of the building's ninety-eight-year-old Round Room, which could hold up to 3,000 people.

Thousands of Irishmen had served with the Dublin Fusiliers. The regiment had an exemplary record and was regarded by friend and foe for its fighting qualities. Some of its units had engaged the republicans during Easter 1916 and fought valiantly. Within minutes walking distance from the Mansion House stood the Fusilier's Arch in St Stephen's Green, built in 1907 as a tribute to the regiment's bravery during the Second Boer War, now pockmarked with bullet-holes from the Rising. Some Fusiliers had shown brutality towards their prisoners following their surrender in the capital. The regiment had by that time been battle-hardened beyond the comprehension of the rebels, whom many of the Fusiliers' privates and officers considered to be subverting their own blood sacrifices in British uniforms. They had been assured that the introduction of Home Rule after the war would justify their countless casualties and this was why many had joined up. For many others who had enlisted during the 1913 Lockout, simple survival had compelled them to join. Many of their relatives had subjected the surrendered 1916 insurgents to an appalling tirade of abuse, for a variety of reasons. Others from the regiment had shown mercy towards their republican prisoners following their surrender in 1916.

As the Fusiliers dined together, some of their comrades' former prisoners were outside, standing on the steps under the building's metal and glass portico, acting as ushers for the upcoming Dáil – a ticketed event. A queue had formed along the entire 200-yard incline of Dawson Street, adorned ironically with Union Jack flags and buntings to celebrate the earlier arrival of the Fusiliers. As the crowds increased in size, the cobbled recess in front of the Mansion House became thronged. The excitement was palpable. One Volunteer was heard by one of the scores of journalists wedged by the thickening mass to joyously ask a comrade, 'Did you ever think you and I would live to see this day?'[14] Volunteers from the 3rd Battalion – under Adjutant Simon Donnelly, overseeing security – were also deployed in the surrounding streets armed with revolvers and semi-automatic pistols collected from an arms-dump in Volunteer Michael O'Flanagan's fishmonger's in nearby Wexford Street, a conduit for smuggled arms from Liverpool and Glasgow. A few others carried hand-grenades, ready to hurl the fist-sized bombs at hostile forces should they arrive in strength. Unarmed lookouts patrolled Nassau Street, Kildare Street, Grafton Street and Stephen's Green, ready to bolt and alert their armed comrades at the first sight of the military. Notably, the previous day, Lord French's proclamation from the previous July banning such unauthorised assemblies had been reversed by Dublin Castle; the ban was finally recognised as having been a public relations fiasco.

Directly opposite the Mansion House sat the Royal Irish Automobile Club (RIAC). Monitoring the proceedings from the sash windows of the club's upper floors were the DMP's less joyous chief commissioner, Col Walter Edgeworth-Johnstone, and the RIC's Insp. General Byrne. Each of its front windows was filled with G-Division detectives with notebooks ready to record names of anyone they recognised. The DMP had raided the Sinn Féin headquarters on the night of 11 January. Numerous drafts of documents seized had provided them with thorough intelligence of the Dáil's intentions. Sgt Lawson, 'arrested' at Three Rock Mountain, also studied the crowd with probing eyes alongside another colleague from the incident, as they hoped to recognise faces from that day. One such face was Capt. Flanagan, now a wanted man.

Shortly after 2 p.m. a military band playing the British anthem 'God Save the King' heralded the march in step of the Dublin Fusiliers as they left the Mansion House to attend a variety show and Charlie Chaplin film at the Theatre Royal in Poolbeg Street. They passed lines of bemused-looking Sinn Féin supporters as ushers parted the crowd for them. The irony that many of the Fusiliers had also been members of the Volunteers before the organisation's split just after the war had started was not wasted on observers, or on many of the marchers.[15]

At 3 p.m. the Mansion House's doors opened. Those with tickets entered while those without braved the cold to witness the historic moment from as close as they could. Soon the Round Room's open chamber and balconies were thronged with Sinn Féin members and supporters, administrators, clerks, journalists – many from overseas – and spectators; fifty priests attended, as did two US Navy officers. Other Volunteers patrolled the building, providing armed security and ensuring routes to facilitate escape were clear in case of a raid by the military, the police, or both.

Just before 3.30 p.m., to resounding applause, two-dozen of the elected members of the new assembly entered the chamber, led slowly along its centre aisle by Count George Noble Plunkett – seventy-year-old father of executed Rising leader Joseph – and fifty-two-year-old Eoin MacNeill, both of whom walked with marked gravitas. When they reached the front row of upholstered seats facing the platform upon which stood the speaker's chair, Count Plunkett – representing Roscommon North – took a seat to the left, MacNeill – representing National University of Ireland and Derry City – to the right.[16] Otherwise the front row remained unoccupied, purposely highlighting the enforced absence of so many through imprisonment. The short procession of Dáil deputies who had followed took their seats behind, sitting upright, knowing the eyes of the world were upon them. Their comparative youth marked them out from similar national forums, typically the preserve of more grey-haired and wrinkled legislators.

When the accompanying hum had tapered off Count Plunkett stood up and from the lectern, above which hung a recently raised tricolour flag to replace the Union Jack from the earlier ceremony, formally moved that Cathal Brugha – elected to represent Co. Waterford – took the chair as *ceann comhairle*. Then, having done this, Brugha called upon Fr O'Flanagan – the forty-one-year-old vice-president who was effectively in charge of Sinn Féin in De Valera and Griffith's absence – to deliver a prayer amenable to all Christian denominations in Ireland. The entire audience stood up. Following this, Brugha rose again and called for a roll to be taken of the 104 men and one woman – Countess Markievicz – who had, in total, been recently elected. A momentary silence ensued, as if everyone was absorbing the unfolding spectacle with awe. Then, as each name was called it was answered 'Present! (*Í láthair*)' if that member was in attendance.

The six IPP and twenty-six Unionist MPs who had also been elected did not recognise the Dáil. As far as its members were concerned, however, this was now the legitimate parliament of Ireland. Accordingly, invites had been dispatched to all elected TDs (*Teachtaí Dála*) as they were to be addressed officially as members of the new assembly. Only one unionist, Sir Robert Woods, the surgeon representing Dublin University, had responded, stating that he would be unable to attend. It fell to twenty-nine-year-old veteran Volunteer Seán Nunan, acting as a Dáil clerk, to call out 'Absent! (*As láthair*)' when such names were called. When Edward Carson's name was called out the occasion's solemnity gave way as laughter erupted throughout the entire chamber at the very notion of

21 January 1919: Dáil Éireann TDs in attendance at Mansion House for its inaugural meeting.
(*Courtesy of Kilmainham Gaol Museum OPW, KMGLM 2011.1156*)

his attendance. It took a minute to restore the decorum to resume the roll call. Carson, having been elected for the Belfast Duncairn constituency, had, like the other seat winners, received his invitation, but kept it instead as a souvenir. The list carried on. By the time Nunan had reached its conclusion less than thirty members had been marked present. Scores of names were called out in rapid succession as, 'Jailed by a foreign enemy!' (*Fé ghlas ag gallaibh*), or, 'Deported by a Foreign Enemy' (*Ar díbirt ag gallaibh*).

Michael Collins and Harry Boland – the former representing South Cork and the latter South Roscommon – had each been marked both present and absent. This was done to confuse the authorities if they managed to get their hands on the attendance roll afterwards.

After some further notices and articulations Cathal Brugha once again stood up. He drew a deep breath and looked around intently. He then read the constitution, followed by the declaration of independence: broadly adapted from the 1916 Proclamation and promising equality for all citizens regardless of age, status or gender, and a share in the country's resources. Sinn Féin's party members, despite many of their incompatible differences of opinion regarding its vehemently egalitarian characteristics, not to mention their apprehensions at the distaste such components might foster among their financially well-heeled supporters, repeated the words after him. In a deal brokered by Harry Boland, the Labour Party – under Thomas Johnson and William O'Brien – had facilitated Sinn Féin's recent election victory by not forwarding any candidates, and now, accordingly, ensured its more equitable influence was felt. This was particularly important as the party would soon be dispatching delegates to the International Socialist Conference in Berne, Switzerland; it was hoped that international credibility here would bolster the Dáil's worldwide profile, and, eventually, Labour's with it.

This, in turn, was followed by readings of the democratic programme and the address to the free nations of the world, the former delivered in Irish by Piaras Béaslaí, and in English by Richard Mulcahy – TD for Dublin Clontarf – and the latter was read by the bespectacled thirty-seven-year-old Robert Barton, who was the TD for Wicklow West. These were eventually delivered by various speakers in Irish, French – the language for international diplomacy – and lastly, English. Journalists and reporters scribbled frenetically in shorthand as proclamations such as Brugha's 'We are now done with England!'

resonated.¹⁷ Soon afterwards, the address to the free nations was brought to France, via a delegation under thirty-seven-year-old Seán T. O'Kelly, TD for College Green. They strove to present Ireland's case at the Peace Conference in Versailles, which had commenced three days earlier.

Roughly half of the attendance was made up of women, and one of them, twenty-seven-year-old Máire Comerford, a Sinn Féin activist from Wexford, welled up with tears, and reflected on the fact that there would be no going back. Once again, as in the Rising she had participated in, they were crossing the Rubicon, albeit in a constitutional fashion this time around – at least for now.

Barton's reading of the address to the world acted as a cue for Collins and Boland to slip out of the Mansion House into the descending darkness. They had a mail boat and a train to catch to Manchester. Preparations were under way to spring De Valera from Lincoln Prison. Collins and Boland were pivotal to this, having received orders from Cathal Brugha to oversee the mission. The Dáil finally adjourned at 5.20 p.m. As far as its members were concerned, the day's work had been nobly done.¹⁸ A dinner was hosted by Count and Countess Plunkett afterwards in the Mansion House's Oak Room in honour of visiting journalists, while another function took place in the Supper Room.¹⁹

Dublin city's restaurants, hotels, pubs and cafés were filled that evening and night despite people's concerns about the Spanish Flu. Journalists and reporters, intellectuals, merchants, tradespeople and observers from all walks of life discussed the momentous day's events. US President Woodrow Wilson's previous year's declaration of his idealistic '14 Points' focusing on the principles of an acceptable peace following the Great War, and their theoretical application to Ireland, were the topic of lively debates. Point number five referred to adjustments of colonial claims being henceforth based upon equity of interests between governments and the governed. National aspirations were to be respected. Self-determination was taken to mean precisely that, and people were only to be governed by their own consent. People spoke comparatively of countries such as Poland, Estonia, Lithuania and Czechoslovakia, which had recently declared their own independence. However, they were neglecting one ominous notable point: none of these countries had seceded from any of the Great War's victors.

'Throughout the city there was celebration, many speaking of the sacrifices of

1916 bearing fruit. However, there was also apprehension and condemnation. Many unionists were averse to the idea of independence, having prospered under the crown. The maintenance of the status quo was viewed by significant numbers of Ireland's unionist inhabitants as essential for reasons such as mutual security, land and property ownership, preservation of their own power base, tradition, trade, and the British empire's perception as a liberal and benevolent influence that rewarded those with a sense of duty towards it. This was set against a fear of, on the one hand, Bolshevist infiltration of Sinn Féin, and on the other – particularly among many non-Catholics – of the potential emergence of an antagonistic Roman Catholic theocracy in the empire's absence. The attendance of so many Catholic priests in the Mansion House did little to alter this sentiment.[20]

Also added to the celebrations and condemnations that night was a sense of ambivalence. To tens of thousands of the city and county's 480,000-or-so inhabitants, like any other winter's day, the harsh realities of life in pestilent flu-ravaged slums remained their primary focus. Meanwhile, the Dublin Brigade battalions received orders to 'stand to' in case full-scale hostilities broke out as a result of the day's events. From 8 p.m. they converged upon their various company HQs.

Also widely spoken of that night were the declaration of independence and the democratic programme. However, printing them in the following day's press was another story. Both domestic and foreign journalists were heavily censored and forbidden to print either the wording of the documents or the content of related speeches. This did not deter the underground or 'Mosquito Press'; free from the censor, their printers pounded for days.[21]

Lord French spent the evening of 21 January awaiting a briefing on the day's Dáil proceedings from George Moore, one of his two intelligence agents who had infiltrated the assembly. Earlier in the day French had asserted to Walter Long that: 'These seventy-three devils will soon go bag and baggage over to Westminster,' referring to those recently elected.[22] Long had laughingly agreed that they would soon see the error of their ways when they discovered that they could not draw their annual £400 salaries in Dublin.[23] Moore, however, emphasised to French that the apparent integrity of the Mansion House proceedings had been impressive. When French appeared dismissive, Moore protested to his lord lieutenant that he needed to understand that, regardless of any of their predispositions, the Dáil represented the general feeling in the country.²⁴

By the time Moore had briefed French, word had already reached the viceroy about the Soloheadbeg killings. Portentously, they were later confirmed as the actions of Irish Volunteers. By late in the night, the growing talk of the shootings threatened to eclipse the Dáil's inauguration. Richard Mulcahy was exasperated at the unauthorised shootings, given their timing. Volunteer raids were systematic at that point, and the 'arrest' of Sgt Lawson and his two colleagues by Capt. Flanagan at Three Rock Mountain days earlier further showcased the growing hazards of police work. However, Mulcahy felt that the country still needed convincing of the justification for war and the inevitable deaths of crown forces, military and police; this would take time, and methodical persuasion. The Soloheadbeg killings risked plunging the country into conflict at a far-less-opportune juncture. He feared that all the work that had gone into the Dáil's meticulous stage-managing would be overshadowed by the backlash that would come from both the national and international press for these killings. Sinn Féin and the Irish Volunteers political and military strategy was founded upon a proverbial three-legged stool, representing: effective governance, military efficacy underpinned by robust intelligence and, critically, propaganda. They needed public support. It appeared to the chief of staff that the latter – and most important leg – had just been kicked out from under them.²⁵

Luckily for Sinn Féin, the following day, the British press – while dismissive of the Dáil's formation – largely separated their accounts of both events. However, not in all cases. Some claimed that the Dáil members were unable to manage their own physical force men.

County Insp. Roberts expressed profound regret to French that it appeared his predictions of three days earlier were indeed coming true. Lord French wrote to since-departed Viscount Haldane on 22 January, informing him of his findings relating to the attack and the deaths of the policemen, stressing that it was pointless to proceed with their plans. He decried the shootings as an outrage that had occurred on the very day that they had felt reason to hope secret influences were being brought to bear to prevent such instances.²⁶ He was also conscious that the British press would be comprehensively scathing of the killings, as well as anyone dealing with the forces connected to them – political or otherwise. A fork in the road had been reached between a potentially agreeable settlement, and a unilaterally enforced one. As far as French was concerned, the latter course would now be pursued.

On 22 January, a private meeting of the Dáil took place in the Mansion House's Oak Room. Eager to ensure that the assembly was taken seriously, its first provisional ministers were assigned, pending the anticipated return of the German Plot internees. Cathal Brugha was appointed acting president of the first ministry. Four additional portfolios were assigned: Richard Mulcahy – defence; Count Plunkett – foreign affairs; Michael Collins, who had ceased working for the Volunteer Dependants' Fund – home affairs and Eoin MacNeill – finance.

Lord French moved fast. On 23 January South Tipperary was designated a Special Military Area under DORA following the killings. So began a pattern that would eventually be replicated throughout Ireland. Both policemen were buried the following day: McDonnell in Tipperary and O'Connell in Cork.

Then, on 31 January, following a meeting of the Volunteer National Executive, *An t-Óglách* carried a statement to the effect that since the Dáil's formation, soldiers and policemen acting for the crown now constituted armed enemy forces and would be treated in the same manner as an invading force by a defending national army, providing – at least ostensibly – some retrospective justification for the fateful blood-letting of ten days earlier.

Meanwhile, two men who, among others, would have been happy with Lord French's belligerent conclusions to the events of 21 January – Michael Collins and Harry Boland – had successfully made their planned sea crossing.

4

ESCAPE FROM LINCOLN AND COLLINSTOWN ARMS RAID

'We who have waited, know how to wait'

Monday 3 February saw the culmination of several months of planning to rescue Éamon de Valera from Lincoln Jail. He and others had been transferred there from Gloucester Prison the previous June following their May 1918 arrests. His escape would constitute a propaganda coup and an opportunity to humiliate the British authorities. Since 21 January, Michael Collins and Harry Boland, taking advantage of relaxed post-war travel controls, had travelled back and forth from Dublin, making further transportation and safe house arrangements to facilitate his escape. Both were now regular travelling companions, sharing food, beds when necessary, and their passions for skulduggery.

Boland came from an intensely republican background. His father, Jim, had been a prominent IRB member and Harry himself had joined in 1904 at the age of seventeen. In 1909, while living in London, Boland, having met Collins through the London GAA, introduced him to IRB leader Sam Maguire, who subsequently swore Collins in. Boland had participated in intense fighting in Sackville Street and Moore Street during the Rising, deployed in the same area as his brother Ned; his other brother Gerry fought in Jacob's biscuit factory. Harry had been court-martialled in Richmond barracks, then deported to prison in England, before returning home in June 1917. Throughout his incarceration he became an intractable thorn in the side of the prison authorities. He stirred up trouble at every opportunity, but at the same time winning over many guards and even a prison governor with his irrepressible stoicism and audacity, while also providing an invaluable diversion to his fellow inmates. Assuming the role of IRB president the previous May, he had since won the

Harry Boland, Sinn Féin's ebullient and irrepressible party secretary. (*Courtesy of Kilmainham Gaol Museum OPW, KMGLM 2012.0138*)

seat for South Roscommon in December's election following an industrious year at the spearhead of Sinn Féin's militant wing. His political leanings veered towards democratic socialism. His home was in Clontarf, which had previously been the home of Bram Stoker of *Dracula* fame. Looking the part of a tailor, five-foot-ten and dapper, with meticulously combed dark hair, his blue eyes were quick to brighten with a disarming smile from a strong, full face that could just as quickly wither a wanting assailant.

Lincoln Jail sat a mile east of its ancient town centre. Several ingenious attempts had been already made to fashion copies of its master key; each had failed. Eventually, a blank copy and a file were sent in, encased within a cake which one of the prisoners – Peter DeLoughry, a locksmith – was then able to cut to the required size using the file.

Behind the jail was a large field enclosed by barbed wire. Collins, Boland and Frank Kelly, who had spent several weeks beforehand preparing the ground locally for the escape, cut their way through this around 7.30 p.m. doing their best – unsuccessfully – to remain silent; Boland protested that the wire snapping could be heard half-a-mile away. They then crept slowly in the pitch darkness of the still night towards an iron gate in the rear wall where the link-up had been prearranged. When Kelly became unexpectedly separated and disorientated he was forced to make his way back out of the field. Collins and Boland, with no time to spare, pressed on.

Then, at 7.40 p.m., as the low moon began to brighten the sky, Boland took a torch from his coat pocket and switched it on. This was the signal for which De Valera had been waiting. But then, to everyone's sudden alarm, the torch would not switch off. Meanwhile, De Valera lit a handful of matches in his cell window as his return signal while Boland cursed profusely, banging and shaking the torch before shoving it into his pocket to shield its glare.

De Valera untied his copy of the master key from his trouser braces. He then made his move, accompanied by two accomplices: former IRB president Seán McGarry and Seán Milroy. Time was of the essence. They had an hour-and-a-half before the prison warders would check the prison, its cells and lock each cell door. McGarry and De Valera, both wearing distinctive narrow-rimmed spectacles, had pulled socks over their shoes to stifle the sound of their feet on the flag-stoned prison passages. Milroy, a forty-two-year-old journalist, had neglected to do this, concluding his own soft-soled shoes would not require damping. Then, to his perplexity, one of the soles suddenly tore away from the upper and flapped noisily.[1] Whispering obscenities he did his best to muffle the sound as he and his two palpitating comrades sped along.

Passing through a succession of heavy doors and narrow corridors, De Valera methodically locked each door behind them to avoid causing an alarm. Outside, meanwhile, Collins and Boland crept to the outer wall gate. Collins took a key from his pocket; a similar key to the ones that had been sent to the prison originally. When he turned it in the gate lock, it snapped. He swore. Weeks of meticulous planning were unravelling with the most ridiculous of mishaps. Both his own and Boland's minds raced to their back-up plan: a rope ladder that Boland had carried in a haversack. Collins then suddenly heard the three prospective escapees shuffling on the gate's far side. He whispered anxiously through the keyhole: 'I've broken a key in the lock, Dev.'[2]

De Valera's uncharacteristically colourful choice of language at this revelation echoed that of Collins, but the Sinn Féin president quickly gathered himself. Reluctant to use a rope ladder, he inserted his key into the lock from the inside and, muttering prayers, managed to push out the broken one before successfully turning his own. Then, to momentarily disbelief and relief, the gate swung open on its rusty hinges, making a grating noise. Each man grimaced at the prospect of alerting the guards. Luckily, no alarms were raised.

De Valera and McGarry removed their socks from outside their shoes. The five then hurried back across the field through the cut section of barbed wire and eventually began their mile-long walk to their waiting transport, but not before Boland had thrown a second-hand ladies fur coat he had also carried in the bulging haversack around De Valera's shoulders to disguise him as a woman in the darkness; not an easy task considering De Valera was six-foot-three. He then linked his own arm through that of the man he referred to as

'Chief' to emphasise the disguise as they passed some soldiers from the military hospital across the road. Fortunately for them, the soldiers were preoccupied with female companions. Boland, dauntless as ever, wished the soldiers 'good night, chums', as they hurried along Wragby Road towards a waiting taxi parked outside the Adam and Eve tavern in the town centre.[3]

Paddy O'Donoghue, leader of the Manchester Volunteers and a close friend of Collins, was standing by at the taxi, which was to take him and the escapees the twenty-five miles to Worksop. When the five arrived outside the rustic tavern, Collins and Boland, having said their farewells to the escapees, set off together on foot catch the London train. Their exuberance increased with every stride despite their continued concerns for Frank Kelly whom they assumed had made his own way away from the prison.

When the taxi arrived in Worksop, Fintan Murphy, recently travelled from Dublin with Collins and Boland, was waiting at a hotel with another cab to take the escapees on their next leg – a further twenty miles to Sheffield. When the driver protested that the distance would breach petrol restrictions still in place from the war and suggested getting a train that was available later that night, Murphy insisted that they needed to catch another train in Sheffield and so could not wait for the Worksop one. The driver, satisfied, soon had them on their way.

Liam McMahon, another of the escape's architects, waited in Sheffield to take the fugitives on the last leg to separate safe houses in Manchester. Meanwhile, back at Lincoln Jail, at 9.30 p.m., the alarm was raised, but it was too late.

The three former prisoners arrived in Manchester around midnight; roughly the same time Collins and Boland's train steamed into King's Cross Station in London. From there they soon made their way back to Dublin.

***

Days after the escape, GHQ met in Dublin for the first time since the Dáil's inauguration. The news of De Valera's escape, and the fallout from the Soloheadbeg killings, topped the agenda. During some animated discourses, Cathal Brugha professed to supporting the actions of Breen, Treacy, Robinson, Hogan and the others, insisting that as Volunteers they were members of the army of a lawfully elected government, and accordingly, were entitled to slay the officials and agents of a foreign invader, as well as what he called: 'the spies and informers waging war on the elected government of Ireland'.[4] Despite this, it was subsequently agreed that the Volunteers, for now, would maintain passive resistance ostensibly but covertly adopt a war footing.

Also discussed were events 100 miles to the north. An unprecedented general strike was taking place in Belfast, instigated initially by shipyard workers but quickly spreading to electricity and gas workers. Nationalists and unionists were united in their pursuit of a forty-four-hour working week. The potential for exploitation of this unlikely alliance was not wasted on Brugha, Mulcahy, McKee, McMahon, O'Connor, Duggan and Collins. Meanwhile, Mulcahy's deputy, Austin Stack, was personally feeling the strike's effects in Belfast's Crumlin Road Prison, where he had been incarcerated since the previous May for wearing a Volunteer uniform.

After the meeting Brugha prepared to travel once again to England – this time Manchester. He wished to keep De Valera abreast of the overall situation in Ireland, and discuss a plan already in play – at De Valera's behest – to spirit the holed-up Sinn Féin president to the USA. Once there, financed by the Friends of Irish Freedom (FOIF), he would drum up support for the Irish cause and place as much pressure as possible on President Wilson – a tall order carefully weighed during his incarceration in Lincoln. Brugha sought to persuade him to return to Ireland first.

His mission was a success. At 1 a.m. on Thursday 20 February the former hospital ship SS *Cambria* steamed into Dublin's smoggy docks. After it docked on North Wall Quay, De Valera, disguised as a priest, stepped onto the quayside with his fellow passengers. His charade worked. He received no acknowledgement other than typical deference to his white clerical collar. Awaiting his 'chief' was Harry Boland, who initially employed similar propriety until they were inside a waiting motorcar. Boland's ebullience returned as the car trundled through the dark streets to a safe house, 5 Merrion Square, belonging to gynaecologist Dr Robert Farnan. The following morning De Valera, rested and fed, provided an interview to American journalist Ralph Couch who had been driven blindfolded to the four storey Georgian residence. The interview – in which De Valera asserted that the Dáil was ready to take over the country's administration with immediate effect, but more ominously, was prepared for violence if necessary – was to be published by 700 American newspapers.[5]

Couch was not the only American to take part in such clandestine conferences with Sinn Féin representatives. Collins and Boland also conferred with influential journalist and public relations visionary, forty-two-year-old George Creel, dispatched to Ireland by President Wilson. Following the discussions, Creel – like Viscount Haldane the previous month – concluded that dominion status, with discretionary options for Ulster's counties, would reconcile the Irish question, but he was also concerned that if the issue was not settled expediently it would result in an unyielding posture being adopted by Sinn Féin, the Dáil, and more precariously, the Irish Volunteers. The following month he presented this conclusion to his president. By then, however, dominion status was firmly off the table.

Milroy and McGarry also safely returned to Ireland, having both disguised themselves and mixed with the Irish crowds returning from the Waterloo Cup coursing meet in Lancashire.[6]

The following Sunday, 23 February, Boland drove De Valera, the two beginning to form a bond, to the archbishop's palace in Drumcondra. When Boland had seen him safely into the palace's gate-lodge, De Valera hinted to Boland of his plans to travel to the USA. Boland, however, had no idea at the time that he would soon act as De Valera's pathfinder on the same trans-Atlantic journey.

As the search continued for the three Lincoln fugitives the escape's propaganda value quickly became clear. De Valera's whereabouts became a worldwide sensation. In Paris, he was widely spoken of by Peace Conference delegates. Described as towering in height, thin and sallow-faced, bespectacled and scholarly, he had, apparently, been seen in cities throughout Europe. An arrest warrant was issued for him in Holland following an alleged sighting. One magazine took it further, publishing a competition jokingly titled: 'Find De Valera' which contained maps of Ireland, Britain and France. Nearly 1,000 people submitted entries.[7] In Ireland, meanwhile, the anticipation of his whereabouts reached fever pitch. Boland boasted on one occasion while addressing a crowd of onlookers outside Dublin's Gresham Hotel, dressed in a typically chic suit and trilby hat, that at least they all knew where De Valera was not to be found: in jail. Laughter erupted. He then announced to a roar of applause that De Valera 'was strong, happy and perfectly safe'.[8]

Two days after the Lincoln escape, Chief Secretary Macpherson attended a cabinet meeting in London's Downing Street during which he conveyed Lord

French's advice that all the German Plot prisoners be released, considering the Great War's armistice had long since been signed. It was not received well. Several cabinet members, including the Secretary for War Winston Churchill, feared being seen to pander to the advent of Dáil Éireann.

Four weeks later, however, on 6 March, the death from Spanish Flu in Gloucester Jail of thirty-four-year-old Pierce McCan, TD for East Tipperary, became the last straw. Dr James Bell, the prison doctor, declared that the prison could not cope with an influenza epidemic. Macpherson, acting in French's place – who had himself been debilitated by the sweeping pandemic – advised the cabinet of the growing unrest over the internments. Fearing further escalation, it was decided to release all the German Plot prisoners.⁹ This began on 9 March. Pierce McCan's remains were shipped from Holyhead to Dublin, where both Collins and Boland helped carry his coffin through the packed city on its way to Kingsbridge station and its eventual destination, Tipperary. Over 10,000 people attended his funeral. McCan had been a mentor of Seán Treacy's.

Pierce McCan TD, whose death in Gloucester Jail from Spanish Flu on 6 March 1919 prompted the release of the German Plot prisoners. *(Courtesy of Mercier Archive)*

The prisoners were free men. De Valera, however, having escaped, was technically still a fugitive, although his arrest was deemed unlikely. He spent as much time as he could with his family while preparations were made among some of Sinn Féin's leaders to stage a civic reception for his triumphant return at Mount Street Bridge for 26 March, followed by a ceremony hosted by the mayor in the Mansion House. De Valera was to be handed the keys to the city. Mount Street Bridge, and adjacent Northumberland Road, was the same idyllic location straddling Dublin's Grand Canal that had proved disastrous to the British infantry three years earlier and cost the lives of four Volunteers under De Valera's command, one of whom – Lt Michael Malone – had contributed to the hundreds of enemy casualties with De Valera's own weapon which had been loaned to him. De Valera prepared a fiery speech for his homecoming, which was to be presented as, effectively, the welcoming of a returning sovereign at the gates of the city. This would be seen as treasonous by Dublin Castle, particularly as the last such welcome in Ireland had been extended to Queen Victoria.

General Shaw, accordingly, issued a proclamation banning the ceremony, along with any other seditious gathering to welcome the man whom he referred to as 'the escaper'. De Valera, Griffith and the lord mayor became fearful, after some deliberation, of civilian casualties that would probably result from an inevitable confrontation should they proceed. Michael Collins, on the other hand, became aghast at what he saw as the party leaders' unexpected acquiescence. As far as he was concerned, the potential propaganda value of a violent British reprisal outweighed the risk of attendant casualties. De Valera settled the matter with a letter urging composure containing the words: 'We who have waited, know how to wait.'[10]

Nevertheless, the escape from Lincoln, as well as an earlier lower profile one from Usk Prison in South Wales, had become powerful public relations coups, not to mention a source of huge embarrassment to the authorities. His IRB comrades jokingly referred to Collins as the 'Director of Escapes'. Further breakouts were set to happen very soon, this time in Dublin.

***

Less content with waiting for action than the imperturbable Sinn Féin president were the Volunteers from the 1st Battalion's A and F Companies. At 10 p.m., Wednesday 19 March, twenty-five of them assembled at GHQ for the Dublin Brigade's first high priority offensive operation since the Dáil's inauguration. Their pending mission was daunting: an arms raid at the RAF base at Collinstown Aerodrome (Dublin Airport), six miles north of the city. Arms raids – nothing new to the Dublin Brigade – had in more recent months dramatically increased in frequency, but they were smaller scale and more opportunistic, not to mention haphazard. Eight days earlier a civilian, Alfred Pearson, had been shot dead in Richmond Road, Drumcondra, when one such raid for rifles and pistols had gone tragically wrong. A nearby attempt to hold up an arms train at Newcomen Bridge at North Strand had also failed.

In command of the Collinstown mission was twenty-two-year-old Lt Patrick Holohan, a steadfast officer from Dublin who was no stranger to daring commando-style raids. He and several others, including his equally unwavering older brother Garry, had, as Fianna members, spearheaded the ruthlessly executed raid on the Magazine Fort in the Phoenix Park on Easter Monday 1916. This had been planned as the act to herald the Rising. Holohan had subsequently taken acting command of the last of the vastly outnumbered 1st Battalion to surrender the following Sunday after a brutal thirty-hour battle. He had since suffered deportation and further imprisonment soon after his return. Now, almost three years after the Rising, he was officially leading his first mission as a Volunteer officer.

The mission had been postponed twice previously; initially when Vice-Brigadier Lynch had been unable to secure transport for the expected haul of weapons and ammunition, and then as a result of De Valera's anticipated arrival in Dublin following his escape. GHQ had feared that the authorities would watch the country's roads and ports afterwards for fleeing Volunteers if the arms raid went wrong – or on the other hand – if it was successful and they were suspicious that arms from the haul were being moved by car, truck or boat. Such surveillance would have jeopardised De Valera's return.

The aerodrome was one of several airfield sites surveyed in May 1917 by the Royal Flying Corps.[11] In March 1919 construction was still under way and over 800 civilians were employed there, Patrick Holohan among them. Collinstown was home to the RAF's 24th Training Squadron, specialising in day bombing.

Most of those assembled for the raid had, for the sake of secrecy, been unaware of the details of their mission before final assembly. Lt Holohan and his second-in-command, 2nd Lt Peadar Breslin – also employed at the aerodrome – set to detailing them of the location, the objective, and the type of weapons required: handguns and trench-knives. When Holohan and Breslin began placing the trench-knives and pistols on the table in front of them they were awestruck at the menacing sight of the knives. They were quickly picked up and examined. Each had a 'knuckle-duster' attachment to the handle of its seven-inch blade. Ropes and sledgehammers were also distributed among the wide-eyed men who were pulsating at the prospect of offensive action.

Brigadier McKee, hearing initially of the proposed raid weeks earlier from Cmdt Tom Byrne, and recognising its potential, had lent his full support and designated it a brigade affair – which meant that, if necessary, all Dublin battalions would participate and immersed himself in its planning. When he appeared suddenly in the room, he summoned Holohan and Breslin to his side before asking Holohan if the operation's preliminaries had been put in place. Holohan confirmed that they had, adding that he and his thirty-two-year-old comrade Seán Doyle had taken care of an unpalatable contingency: giving a lethal dose of morphine to the aerodrome's two Airedale Terrier guard dogs.[12] He then reassured McKee that recent observations had confirmed the airfield's guards were lax. McKee, Holohan and Breslin then approached the table. The rest of the Volunteers stood attentively. McKee spread a large detailed map of the objective across its wooden top and covered the plan.

The raiding party was to be split in two. Members of A Company, under Lt Breslin and George Fitzgerald, would approach the guardhouse's rear entrance. Holohan would simultaneously lead F Company to approach the front and overcome the sentries. Then, both sections on Holohan's command would storm both entrances. With the guardhouse secured, Holohan would then lead a small group with sledgehammers to the nearby motor pool. This would compensate for their shortage of cars. Vice-Brigadier Lynch had originally estimated the need for nine cars. So far, he had only requisitioned three. Another was being acquired while the briefing was underway. McKee, adapting, instructed Holohan to use appropriate manpower to commandeer two military vehicles from the motor pool as transport and disable the remainder.

Each man was then issued with an identification number; no names were to be used. Holohan and Breslin were not the aerodrome's only employees participating – the last thing they wanted was their names being inadvertently divulged to the guards. A final point driven home by McKee was that while everyone on the raid had a particular task, independence of action where appropriate was authorised.[13]

McKee then identified every approach route to the aerodrome and locations where trouble was most likely.[14] He emphasised stealth, pointing out the threat posed by the 500-strong enemy garrison of Gordon Highlanders billeted close by – they had a fearsome reputation. McKee asked if every man had brought a mask to conceal his face. Nervous chuckles erupted when fiery red-head Dan McDonnell pulled one of his mother's 'long-john' stockings from his pocket with eye slits cut out of them. The others had scarves. Then, the twenty-five increasingly nervous men were divided into their raiding parties. McKee and Lynch shook hands with each of them. Wishing them luck, McKee urged them to strive for a bloodless victory. Finally, as the men prepared to leave, Holohan, Breslin, Fitzgerald and two others changed into British army uniforms, Holohan and Fitzgerald disguising as officers.

Following the arrival of the fourth requisitioned car, the vehicles departed Rutland Square at 11.30 p.m. in two pairs. The first pair made their way towards Collinstown via the Swords Road and the others via the Naul Road. Their planned rendezvous was near the Blanchford Arms public house just north of Collinstown where the soft-surfaced roads were so narrow that only one car could pass at a time.[15] Their way was lit by a bright moon, greatly increasing their difficulties in approaching unnoticed. All went well initially until one car broke down and had to be repaired, delaying matters. The moon was high by the time the cars reached the muster point north of Dardistown Cross behind schedule. The raiders primed themselves, gripped by tension as Lt Holohan issued his final instructions.

Meanwhile, just north of the city, teams of Volunteers from B company 2nd Battalion, acting in support and armed with revolvers and semi-automatic pistols, were patrolling the routes between Whitehall and Santry recently taken by the raiders. They were ready to open fire on enemy transports that might threaten the operation.

Twenty-four-year-old Lt Joseph Lawless – seconded from the Fingal Brigade, which operated from the countryside north of the capital – was acting as a driver along with Owen Cullen, Patrick McCrea and Vincent Purfield. All were familiar with the surrounding roads. Lawless, from close to Swords, was another Easter Rising veteran, along with his brother and father. He had lost the little finger on his right hand following an accident in Richmond barracks. Following his return from internment he had been among the firing party at Thomas Ashe's funeral. The previous month he had acted as one of De Valera's drivers. His motoring skills were augmented by an engineering aptitude that saw him helping run a bomb factory from the basement of his cycle repair shop in Great Britain Street. He and the other three drivers watched nervously in the cold night as the special force, their faces masked, moved off slowly in file, crouching in the shadows of hedgerows on either side of the road towards the camp's entrance.[16] Within moments they lost sight of them. They then waited in the dead silence, listening for any sound that might signal success, or alternatively, disaster.

Some of the Volunteers who were approaching the aerodrome became jittery when it appeared in sight. As Lt Holohan's group approached the front of their objective, one man stopped suddenly, overcome with fear. Dan McDonnell, following just behind, prodded his spooked comrade in the back with his revolver and, cursing profusely through his mother's long johns, told him to get a move on. The file of men moved ever closer to the guardhouse.

Lt Breslin's section had to crawl across open ground for 200 yards to get to the guardhouse's rear. Creeping slowly across the cold damp grass George Fitzgerald, in front, kept his eyes trained on a lit window, fearing if a soldier looked out they would be sitting ducks. The distance narrowed. Eventually, to Fitzgerald's relief, they reached the target undetected. Fitzgerald then stood, dusted down his officer's uniform, the elbows and knees wet from the grass, and galvanised himself before the final assault. Suddenly, to his horror, the two guard dogs bounded towards him. The poison administered earlier had apparently not had the desired effect. He reached for his trench-knife and prepared to slash and stab with it, but since he was in uniform, they did not attack. Fitzgerald observed with some relief, however, as he then petted them that they were too groggy to notice the men still creeping up behind him. Satisfied, the dogs turned and ambled away.

Meanwhile, at the front entrance, Tom Merrigan monitored a sentry marching to and fro across the building's entrance until he reached the furthest point from it. He then sprang to his feet, and with lightning speed overpowered him. The cold razor-sharp steel of the trench-dagger cutting into his neck accompanied by an equally sharp warning not to resist or make any noise convinced the stunned sentry to comply.

At this point Lt Holohan stood, looked around, expecting to see another guard, but he was nowhere in sight. He waited cautiously, unaware that the second sentry was actually warming his feet by the fire inside the guardhouse alongside his corporal who was already in bed, surrounded by the rest of the guards in various states of dress, smoking pipes and cigarettes. Holohan crept around momentarily in his officer's uniform, searching for the sentry. His men looked on, gripping the handles of their knives, ready to pounce. Finally, Holohan lost patience and issued the order: 'Ah! Come on, lads!' They launched the attack.[17]

Dan McDonnell was first in. He burst through the door of his allocated room and caught the dozen soldiers there completely off guard. Pointing his handgun, he ordered them to put their hands up before Mick Magee and P. J. Ryan raced in with ropes to tie them up. Tom Merrigan hustled the sentry he had subdued into the room.

George Fitzgerald, hearing the attack from the front, rushed in from the rear, bursting suddenly into another room. Lounging soldiers jumped up smartly to salute the uniformed officer, until the situation dawned on them. Masked men in civilian dress with trench-knives poured in, surrounding them. One soldier muttered that they would be in trouble now. They offered no resistance and were brought to the room where Magee and Ryan were tying up their comrades. Ryan called out: 'More rope!' when he saw them and noticed an unforeseen opportunity presented by the roof trusses.[18] When the rope arrived moments later Ryan and Magee ordered the soldiers onto their backs. They then tied each man's hands and feet before hoisting his legs into the air with the ropes tied around the trusses, calling again and again: 'More rope! More rope!' as they went from man to man. Chuckling comrades told Ryan that 'more rope' would now become his nickname.

The sentry who had been warming his feet then appealed to the Volunteers, fearing disciplinary action for having not resisted; he was then brought outside, roughed up, and rolled about in mud and dirt. Then he too had his legs tied up in the air. As if to add to the sense of farce, another soldier, feeling the cold, asked if he could have a blanket thrown over him.[19] A nearby Volunteer obliged. Meanwhile Dan McDonnell and several others hammered and smashed at the padlocks to the rifle racks, while others disabled telephones.

Lt Holohan, sensing that everything was going to plan, sharply called out the identification numbers for the section to deal with the military vehicles. He then led them at the double to the aerodrome's garage. Once there, however, frustratingly, they could not start the vehicles, so the sledgehammers were used against their engines. Rags were employed to muffle the strikes and blows. As the men hammered and smashed, Holohan, improvising, dispatched Patrick O'Connor to the initial rendezvous point to inform their own four drivers that they urgently needed two of their cars to transport their haul.

Back at the rendezvous point, Joseph Lawless spoke with trepidation to his fellow drivers as they waited. Something appeared wrong. The complete silence and the growing time lapse since their comrades had set off perturbed them.

Eventually, they drew their handguns and made their way on foot towards the aerodrome until they caught sight of its entrance where, to their relief, they met O'Connor. He informed them of Holohan's recent order. They turned around. Then as soon as they had returned Cullen and McCrea jumped into their cars and drove them with their lights off into the aerodrome. They backed them up to the guardhouse and loaded them with seventy-five Lee-Enfield rifles and bayonets and over 4,000 rounds of .303 calibre ammunition. Their haul also included boxes of Very lights (signal flares) and soldiers' kits. Soon both cars suspensions creaked under the weight: almost half-a-ton each. Then, with their mission accomplished, Holohan ordered the cars to withdraw to the rendezvous point. A handful of men ran alongside the cars, the remainder quick-stepping behind as soon as Holohan had issued them with the order to withdraw. When the two cars arrived back, Lt Lawless was confounded at the crushing strains visible on their chassis, springs and tyres.

Soon afterwards the two empty cars were packed with Volunteers and sped to the city, their tyres rubbing off their mud-wings under the weight of their passengers. Each car took a different direction and dropped men off *en route*, their drivers desperate to reach the city as soon as possible, expecting the enemy, once alerted, to react quickly with roadblocks.

The vehicles laden with the night's haul also split up. One was driven with similar haste and difficulty into 44 Rutland Square where Patrick Lawson waited to unload it, while the other was driven northward on muddy roads by Owen Cullen towards The Naul a dozen miles away. There, two Fingal Brigade Volunteers, Vice-Comdt Michael Rock and Quartermaster William Rooney, waited in the freezing cold at a prearranged point on the road to guide the car to their arms dump close to Walshestown. However, things went wrong: when one of the tyres blew out under its payload on the narrow twisty and pitted road, the car became almost impossible to drive. Cullen persevered nonetheless and eventually made the rendezvous, struggling to retain control. However, the car could travel no further under the weight of its cargo so it was unloaded. Rock and Rooney sped away on foot to fetch a horse and cart to transport the rifles and ammunition. They soon returned, the bright moon lighting their way. Cullen and his comrades, anxious to return to the city, turned the car and nursed it to Springhill near Swords, where it had to be abandoned. They walked the rest of the way into the city, worn out by the time they arrived after sunrise.

ESCAPE FROM LINCOLN AND COLLINSTOWN ARMS RAID

Dick McKee and Michael Lynch waited nervously at Rutland Square until the weapons, ammunition and other materiel were safely unloaded and all the mission's men accounted for. McKee was delighted with the night's work, particularly by the absence of casualties, and congratulated the raid's participants who were present, adding that they had paved the way for similar missions. Before they were finally dismissed Lt Holohan called some of them aside and, ordering them to attention as he spoke, instructed them to consider themselves henceforth on active service and added that they were to ensure that they could be contacted easily. The instruction was welcomed wholeheartedly on the back of the mission's success by the weary but elated men.

Within hours of dismissing his men, Holohan and the other members of the raiding party also employed at the aerodrome reported for work. Grappling exhaustion they observed their captives from the previous night being marched away under a heavy military escort. They were wary of any suspicion that might be directed their way as the day wore on. However, in the aerodrome itself, nobody suspected a thing. The same could not be said of General Shaw, who soon afterwards ordered that all civilian workers be dismissed from Collinstown.

The captured arms that had been transported to Walshestown were, aside from a small amount retained for the Fingal area, eventually delivered into the city in small batches to various dumps in a motorcycle-sidecar combination by twenty-nine-year-old 2nd Battalion Quartermaster Mick McDonnell. This was after police and army units had combed the entire area unsuccessfully around where the abandoned car was discovered. McDonnell suffered several close calls with the authorities as he rode to and from the city. Most of the haul was eventually redistributed outside the capital. Future engagements within the city were anticipated to take place at a proximity that would favour pistols and bombs over rifles. Ominously, Volunteer GHQ were laying the groundwork for such close quarter attacks in the capital. Things would soon heat up.

5

G-DIVISION PENETRATED AND TENSIONS ESCALATE

'I'm a poor lonesome whore'

Soon after Collinstown, on 29 March, with small victories coming thick and fast, another daring prison escape was orchestrated. This time in Dublin, the second within a two-week period from Mountjoy Prison.

The first had taken place on the night of Sunday 16 March. Recently imprisoned Robert Barton had escaped using a file to saw through his cell bars, then a rope ladder to scale the outer wall.

Barton came from a wealthy Anglo-Irish family from Annamoe in Co. Wicklow. He was a cousin of Erskine Childers, who had shipped the consignment of German Mauser rifles into Howth Harbour in July 1914 aboard his yacht The *Asgard* as a response to the Ulster gun-running. These had been used later by republicans during the Rising. Barton had joined the Volunteers in 1913 but when the Great War broke out he accepted a lieutenant's commission in the Dublin Fusiliers. However, following the Rising, he had been appalled at the cruelty meted out to many of the insurgents by his army comrades in Richmond barracks. Collins and others had observed the kindness he had displayed towards them while prisoners there. The stoicism displayed by the surrendered men and women under the terrible conditions at both the barracks and Kilmainham Gaol had impressed Barton. As a result, he eventually resigned his commission and threw in his lot with Sinn Féin.

Barton had travelled to London in December 1918 with Collins, Seán T. O'Kelly and George Gavan Duffy in an attempt to present their case to President Wilson on his way to the Paris Peace Conference. When the president refused to meet them Collins had proposed kidnapping him. His fellow delegates dismissed this outright as a brash, ill-founded suggestion.

G-DIVISION PENETRATED AND TENSIONS ESCALATE

A month after his landmark address at the first Dáil, Barton was arrested following another event at the Mansion House and charged with speaking seditiously at an earlier proclaimed gathering in Wicklow. He had asserted during the same speech that if he were imprisoned he would successfully escape.

Collins, and Sinn Féin, had developed a great regard for Barton and his potential value to them. While Barton was remanded in Mountjoy, Collins made contact with Joe Berry, a warder. Through Berry it was arranged for Richard Mulcahy to visit Barton, posing as a solicitor's clerk offering advice for his upcoming court martial. Mulcahy then smuggled in the file that Barton was able to conceal in his riding breeches which he still wore in prison.

On the night in question, Barton, having sawed through his window bars with the file, rigged up a dummy in his bed to fool the warders on their night inspections. Ever the gentleman, and with a sense of humour, he also left a note addressed to the prison governor saying he felt compelled to leave as the uncomfortable surroundings were not to his taste, while saluting the overall good conduct of the prison's warders. He then escaped into a yard and, upon the prearranged signal – a bar of soap thrown over the twenty-five-foot wall – Rory O'Connor, who was in position beyond with a section of Volunteers, threw a weight over the same section of wall attached to a rope ladder. Barton scaled the wall using the ladder and, unable to reuse it for his descent with no one inside the wall to hold it, jumped from the wall to be caught outside by several Volunteers using a stretched out rug to soften his fall. They quickly retrieved the rope ladder and escaped in the darkness, minus Barton's spectacles, which he lost when he fell.

A few streets away he was met and congratulated by a buoyant Michael Collins who brought Barton to the home of his friend Batt O'Connor at No. 1 Brendan Road in Donnybrook. When both men arrived at the red-bricked dwelling, O'Connor's wife was initially confused at the sight of Barton. The last time she had set eyes upon this well-spoken man was as an enemy officer – albeit a kindly one – in Richmond barracks three years earlier when her husband had been detained before being deported with the other prisoners.

Pivotal to the second and even more ambitious escape operation planned for 29 March was thirty-year-old father-of-four Paddy Daly, a formidable Volunteer officer under whose command Patrick Holohan had cut his teeth in action at Easter 1916.[1] Daly, from Clontarf, had been wounded during the Rising and subsequently deported to Frongoch, where he had taken part in numerous protests, including a two-week hunger strike. Upon returning, he took up the revolutionary baton again with B Company 2nd Battalion. In January 1919, as Company O/C, he was arrested overseeing training in Company HQ at Clonliffe Hall in Drumcondra, following which their HQ had to be relocated to 35 North Great George's Street. Refusing to recognise the court at his trial – standard practice among Volunteers – he was subsequently sentenced to six months hard labour.

Also recently incarcerated in Mountjoy were Piaras Béaslaí, Seán McLoughlin and twenty-five-year-old Pádraig Fleming. Béaslaí had been arrested in Dublin's College Street on 4 March for sedition and possessing incriminating documents. He was court-martialled and sentenced to two years' imprisonment. Accompanying him on his way to prison that day had been McLoughlin who, after more or less recovering from Spanish Flu and since making several lucky escapes from G-Division detectives, had been arrested in Dublin, then charged and convicted over his more recent Tipperary speeches and activities.

Pádraig Fleming had been transferred to Mountjoy from Maryborough (Portlaoise) Prison. He was incarcerated several times since his involvement in the Rising in Queen's County (Laois) during which his unit had derailed a train and severed the Waterford-to-Dublin line. He suffered terribly under a punishing regime in Maryborough, which saw him stripped naked and left on a bare floor after smashing up his cell. He was repeatedly subdued by eight prison officers at a time for refusing to wear prison clothes and was once clamped in a straight-jacket, which he wrestled free from and set fire to. He was nicknamed 'Samson' as a result. Too much of a handful for the prison authorities, he was eventually transferred. The move did little to alter his behaviour.

Fleming had disclosed an escape plan to Daly upon the latter's arrival into Mountjoy. Michael Collins, typically immersed in such conspiracies, and flying high on the back of Barton's escape, asserted to Batt O'Connor that Fleming and Béaslaí would be next. Having Béaslaí – such an effective propagandist – at large was particularly important, but Collins also had great admiration and concern for Fleming. Communications flowed to the prisoners from outside, again via Joe Berry and some colleagues. To facilitate the plan, Fleming's protests, which had recently seen himself and several others confined to their twelve-by-six-foot cells for twenty-four hours a day, ceased.

Daly's wife Daisy was gravely ill which presented a justifiable cause to apply for parole to visit her. Despite Barton's earlier escape, which Daly feared would scupper his application, it was, to his surprise, approved. Then, while he was out, Daly approached Peadar Clancy, who subsequently arranged a meeting between himself and Richard Mulcahy at Cullenswood House – Mulcahy's residence – to discuss the proposed break-out.

A Saturday evening was eventually selected as being most suitable for the attempt as there would be fewer warders on duty. Daly met with Clancy before his re-incarceration to cover the plan's specifics, involving the re-employment of the same rope ladder as had been used during Barton's escape. Daly had decided not to escape, as it would render future visits to his dying wife impossible if forced into hiding.

It was eventually agreed that as many prisoners as possible would be sprung, but three would be given priority: Béaslaí, Fleming, and the fiery Sinn Féin TD for Cork City, thirty-nine-year-old J. J. Walsh.

On the evening in question with everything in place, Daly took a position at the end of C-wing to the prison's north-east overlooking the Royal Canal. Observing a party on the canal towpath adjacent to Whitworth Road, which he surmised was Peadar Clancy and his men, he signalled them by waving a handkerchief. The signal was returned. It then took the same length of time for Clancy's unit, with three bicycles, to cross the canal and take positions next to the prison's canal-facing wall as it did for Daly to get to the exercise yard where a game of football was under way. The weather was biting; snow fell. Within moments a stone to which a rope was attached was hurled over the prison wall, crashing to the ground inside. Fleming quickly grabbed it and yanked the attached rope ladder over. Several other inmates, seeing this, quickly overpowered the three guards, and at one point used large spoons wrapped in handkerchiefs to appear like revolvers to keep them in check.[2] Two of the guards were compliant, but asked their 'assailants' to rough them up for the same reason as the guard in Collinstown: fearing disciplinary action if they were recognised as accomplices, willing or otherwise. A twenty-five-year-old comrade and close friend of Daly's, Joe Leonard, happily obliged. One less cooperative guard was punched in the jaw and offered no further hindrance.

Piaras Béaslaí was first to scramble over the wall, grappling with the slippery rope ladder and struggling to maintain his balance at the top. Time was of the essence. He was followed by Fleming, who clambered with similar haste, then Walsh, and seventeen others, including 1916 veterans Liam Tannam, who was a highly respected Volunteer captain, and Ned Lyons.

The escapees quickly dispersed in small groups towards Drumcondra Road where look-outs posted earlier stood ready with whistles to alert their comrades if police or military arrived in the area. Because the original plan had been for three men to break out that number of bicycles had been brought along, one of which had developed a flat tyre but was, nevertheless, used by Tannam to get to a safe house in Baggot Street.

That night, one of the men under Clancy's command for the breakout, twenty-five-year-old Cork man Joe O'Reilly – Michael Collins' confidential courier and aide-de-camp – having helped oversee the safe delivery of the original three planned escapees to various city centre houses, reported to Collins that – effectively – the entire prison had broken out, while Collins sat awaiting news in Wicklow Street's Wicklow Hotel, which was his regular haunt. Collins, jubilant, rushed to find and congratulate Fleming, and then spent the remainder of the night in his basement office with some associates in Cullenswood House, erupting into spontaneous fits of laughter at the day's unexpected result. Hot on the heels of Usk, Lincoln, and Barton's earlier escape, it resulted in further humiliation for the authorities. Unfortunately for Liam Tannam, he was eventually rearrested and charged with escaping, to which he humorously claimed instead to have merely taken 'French leave'.[3]

As a result of the escape, Paddy Daly was, with several others, placed in solitary confinement. Then, to add to his burden, his wife's condition rapidly deteriorated and she died two days later. Nevertheless, despite the escape, the prison governor, Major Charles Munroe, placed an application for additional parole to allow Daly attend her funeral. It was granted. Daly attended, heartbroken but grateful, then returned to Mountjoy. Seán McLoughlin was released soon after the escape. His health had begun to deteriorate again following a recent hunger strike. Meanwhile, Pádraig Fleming was spirited to Queen's County before being smuggled to the USA to recuperate from his recent ordeals. Béaslaí quickly returned to his Dáil and, crucially, his propaganda duties.

***

G-DIVISION PENETRATED AND TENSIONS ESCALATE

Three days after this escape, Tuesday 1 April, as Dublin's youngsters relished in April Fool's Day pranks, the Dáil's first ministerial sitting since the wholesale prison releases in March took place. Béaslaí and Barton, having both had their backs slapped to congratulatory remarks about making fools of the prison authorities, sat among the fifty-two attendees looking on as Éamon de Valera was nominated by Cathal Brugha to be elected president (*príomh aire*) of Dáil Éireann's Second Ministry.⁴ The title would further bolster De Valera's status on his pending US mission.

For security reasons, unlike the Dáil's inauguration nine weeks earlier, members of the public were not permitted to attend this particular gathering. Seán T. O'Kelly was chosen as *ceann comhairle* (chairman/speaker).

At a subsequent sitting the following day De Valera selected his cabinet: Arthur Griffith took over home affairs, Count Plunkett remained at foreign affairs, Cathal Brugha took over defence.⁵ He soon operated the ministry from his business premises, but remitted his minister's salary of £350 to Richard Mulcahy, clearing a path for the latter to devote his full-time energies to assisting him as his deputy.⁶ Mulcahy's medical studies had already been postponed owing to GHQ demands. Nevertheless, he managed to maintain an office in UCD's chemistry corridor in Earlsfort Terrace. However, its purpose was far from academic; he employed it solely to facilitate his duties as commander. Countess Markievicz was appointed Minister for Labour, but only after she threatened to defect to the Labour Party if overlooked because of her gender. She then established an office in North Frederick Street cloaked as a letting agency and piano school. Eoin MacNeill took on industry; William Cosgrave, thirty-eight-years-old, took local government, with offices established in 18 Clare Street 'under the pretence of a private business concern', and later 29 Wicklow Street.⁷ Michael Collins adopted the pivotal portfolio of finance, initially operating between two addresses in Mary Street, Nos 5 and 22, and an additional office above the Sinn Féin headquarters.⁸ Michael Noyk, a solicitor and regular counsel to arrested republicans, as well as a long-standing associate of Griffith's and high-level advisor to the Department of Finance, took care of obtaining leases where necessary. Four non-cabinet directorships were also created: Laurence Ginnell – publicity, Robert Barton – agriculture, Ernest Blythe – trade and commerce and Seán Etchingham – fisheries.

Foremost on the list of discussion topics of Tuesday's first sitting had been the allocation of expenses for deputies attending from outside Dublin. When another meeting took place on Friday 4 April similarly leaden issues topped the agenda, one example being Griffith's questioning by Seán O'Mahony about the setting up of public courts of arbitration and appeal in order to supplant those of the crown. Griffith asserted that a committee was expected to report imminently on the issue. Soon afterwards, however, attentions became focused on more dramatic concerns: Brugha was asked if a motion would be forwarded to reposition his ministry away from its official posture of passive resistance towards more blatant militant subversion. He responded tactfully, professing that the ministry believed they would not at that time be justified in calling on the country to carry out such proposals.[9] Brugha was aware that an offensive disposition at this time could frustrate Ireland's position at the peace conference.[10] He then changed the subject, proposing a pressing financial motion to fund the counter-state: the authorisation of republican bonds to be issued to the value of £250,000.[11] This was seconded by sixty-seven-year-old Laurence Ginnell and subsequently passed. Collins now had his work cut out overseeing this as finance minister. Then, finally, it was agreed that the next Dáil would convene in public. The date was set for Thursday 10 April.

During spring 1919 Collins had, unofficially – though with Mulcahy's approval – been feverishly building up a full-time intelligence department to replace the part-time one already in place under Eamonn Duggan. Duggan, forty-three years old, ran a legal practice in Dame Street. He and his assistant Chris Carbery had been struggling with the growing workload of information passed to them by Dick McKee's numerous intelligence officers. Collins, meanwhile, via a web of IRB and Volunteer intelligence officers from both the Dublin Brigade and beyond, was piecing together a vast network of agents both in Ireland and throughout England. They comprised everyone from sailors, dockers, postal-clerks, maids, and government typists. Among the latter was Elizabeth 'Lily' Mernin, Piaras Béaslaí's cousin and shorthand typist within Dublin Castle. Astonishingly, Collins' second cousin with whom he was very close, Nancy O'Brien, was employed in the castle's posts and telegraphs office decoding messages for none other than Sir James MacMahon, the fifty-four-year-old under-secretary for Ireland. More incredibly: MacMahon had sought her for the position. Consequently, he was not the sole recipient of the decoded information and rarely the first. Barmen were recruited, hotel and theatre

G-DIVISION PENETRATED AND TENSIONS ESCALATE

workers, and crucially – policemen and members of G-Division. Collins soon established personal contact with any policeman willing to pass information to the Dublin Brigade, or to Sinn Féin.

Ned Broy was one such policeman. His official workload centred around typing and filing incoming reports. During a recent meeting where he was introduced to Collins at Michael Ó Foghludha's suburban residence at 5 Cabra Road, both men, gauging one another at first, discussed the RIC, the DMP and its detective division. Broy, marginally taller than Collins and speaking with his deceptively cultured accent, was then able to provide the increasingly attentive Collins with a detailed breakdown of the detective units' inner workings, as well as a broad picture of how to strategically undermine the police.

Broy initially broke the DMP structure down to seven divisions – listed A to G. The force was overseen by its chief commissioner and his assistant chief commissioner. Immediately under these was the chief superintendent, followed in turn by a superintendent for each division. Overall, twenty inspectors, 100 sergeants and 1,000 constables made up the rest of the force.

As a national strategy Broy advocated attacking RIC barracks in smaller rural towns. This would force their occupants to retreat to more secure urban barracks and, effectively, decollate the king's writ throughout swathes of the countryside. Simultaneously, policemen involved in political work in towns and cities would be harassed and attacked to the point of forced retirement. Those who refused would be exposed as the hard-core to be dealt with ruthlessly. He emphasised, however, that only those involved in political work should be attacked; the majority of policemen – particularly uniformed DMP members – did not see themselves as crown forces, and there was no sense alienating a potentially valuable resource in terms of men who could surely be brought on side. Another recommendation from steely-faced Broy was more obvious: Dublin Brigade Volunteers should stop wearing military attire; they were far too easy for the authorities to spot.

Both men grew more impressed with one another at the meeting. Broy's quirky sense of humour was disarming. Nevertheless, levity aside, it became apparent to Broy that Collins did not understand the complete background of the detective organisation.[12] To surmount this both men decided radical action was called for: Collins would need to gain access to G-Division's offices and examine their reports and files for himself.

By this time Collins was also assuming the official role of director of intelligence. At his side were trusted men: Joe O'Reilly, Tom Cullen, Thomas Gay and Liam Tobin. When, eventually, Eamonn Duggan side-stepped to the less taxing role of intelligence staff officer, Collins set about constructing an intelligence network that would rival any enemy operation.

On 6 April Broy and Collins met again in Cabra. They then set up their audacious plan: to meet the following night at the DMP offices in Great Brunswick Street where their political files were stored. Broy would be on duty from 10 p.m. to 6 a.m. Collins was to telephone first in case of last-minute shift changes and ask for a man named 'Long' – Broy's codename. Collins, masking as an informer, would be codenamed 'Field'.

Tom Cullen and Liam Tobin standing to the left and right of Michael Collins respectively. Cullen and Tobin were at the forefront of Dublin's intelligence war. *(Courtesy of Mercier Archive)*

In the meantime, Cathal Brugha's determination to maintain the ostensible posture – at least for now – of non-violent resistance did not prevent G-Division's zealous detectives from escalating their long-established practice of harassing and frustrating Volunteer and Sinn Féin members. The growing volatility of the situation, particularly since Collinstown and the most recent prison escapes, was further aggravated by the shooting of another two policemen on the same day in Limerick. Const. Martin O'Brien was shot dead and a colleague badly wounded in a rescue attempt to free hunger-striking Volunteer prisoner Robert Byrne, himself also killed in the melee. A socialist local government – or Soviet – was soon declared in Limerick as an imaginative, and for a time successful, reaction to the area's subsequent declaration as a Special Military Area.

In the capital every move the republicans made was monitored as the mosaic put together in Brunswick Street and Dublin Castle of the workings of both Sinn Féin and the Volunteers was enhanced. Homes, pubs, theatres, cinemas and workplaces were watched. Some of those shadowing British cabinet members the previous year felt the irony of similarly relentless surveillance measures against themselves, albeit with less calamitous objectives in play – for now. Republicans were followed through the streets, on trams, and at ports and train stations by plain-clothed officers frequently displaying arrogant disregard for their own concealment. In response, Brigadier McKee assigned four men to shadow G-Division members involved in political work.

Finally, as the pressure intensified, Mulcahy, McKee and Collins dispatched instructions to Volunteers to – upon receipt of orders – accost detectives where possible on the streets or in buildings and to issue them with 'friendly' warnings to cease political work, but inform them to feel free nonetheless to continue everyday police work. Officers who could not be found on patrol instead had letters sent to their homes, warning that they would henceforth be shot if they refused to comply.

***

The following night at an IRB gathering in a regular haunt – Vaughan's Hotel at 29 Rutland Square – Seán Nunan was asked by Collins to remain behind after the meeting. Nunan agreed. Both men already knew one other from London several years before the Rising and from Stafford and Frongoch afterwards. Then, at midnight Collins made a call. Nunan then heard Collins ask the question: 'Field here. Is that Long?'[13] Ned Broy, at the other end, replied abruptly: 'Yes, and bring a candle', and hung up.

Then Broy, half a mile away in Central Police Station, nervously prepared himself for his anticipated visitor. He hoped Collins would be carrying a gun. Insp. Daniel Barrett, in charge of B-Division – which shared the station – was less inclined than other inspectors to give G-Division a wide berth. Broy knew he would not think twice about investigating an unexpected light coming from his G-Division colleague Insp. McFeely's office in the middle of the night.[14] The semi-circular room's blinds only partially covered its windows. If discovered, Collins might have to shoot his way out.

Back in Vaughan's, Collins turned to an increasingly curious Nunan and suggested that they should go for a walk. They then set off, taking a detour through side-streets, re-tracing their steps at times to ensure they were not being followed. Collins then informed Nunan about what they were going to attempt. Nunan's momentary apprehension brought forward Collins' gruff reassurance that he had a man on the inside who would be the only detective in the station until 6 a.m. He emphasised the potential value of what they might find there. Nunan did not need further convincing.

Arriving soon afterwards at the Dickensian castle-like building, constructed just over three years earlier in Scottish Baronial style with a granite exterior, they were ushered inside by a jumpy-looking Det. Broy. They were quickly detailed with the building's layout, including their proposed escape route: a wooden door onto Townsend Street. Then, suddenly, to their shock, they heard the crash and clatter of breaking glass. Broy quickly shoved both men into the shadows close to a nearby door and rushed to investigate: a drunken British soldier had hurled a rock through one of the station's windows and was being arrested by a constable just outside the Brunswick Street door. Relieved that the situation appeared under control, Broy returned to the men in the shadows, quickly explaining what had happened and asking Collins if he had brought candles. Collins, surprised, replied: 'No, I thought you were joking!' Broy quickly fetched some matches and candles from the storeroom, then sneaked the two men upstairs.

On the way, using a master key, he quietly locked the hall door leading to the dormitory on the top floor where the station's unmarried detectives slept. Then, trembling, he opened McFeely's office. Collins and Nunan stepped inside and followed him towards what looked like a large safe built into a wall. Broy unlocked and opened its door. Collins and Nunan were wide-eyed at the Aladdin's cave of files suddenly before them – precisely what they had come for.

Broy then left them and returned to the station's main desk, preparing to gather up the broken glass strewn about the flag-stoned floor. He then suffered the abrupt shock of banging on the main door. When he opened it, the constable from earlier stood unexpectedly before him and asked how much it would cost to replace the smashed window. Broy, aghast at the absurdity, dismissed him with a rough estimate and returned to his desk, wondering in exasperation if anything else could go wrong. An avid reader, he then distracted himself with a book.

Meanwhile, Collins and Nunan began rummaging through the files by candlelight. As the small hours slipped past Collins accumulated a detailed picture of the workings of G-Division and the RIC, their agents and informers, and what they knew about Sinn Féin and the Volunteers. Collins laughed briefly at one point when he came across his own file, before checking himself when Nunan looked at him uneasily. Their present location demanded silence. Collins read that he came from a farming family of moderate means and good intellect.

Soon afterwards, he discovered a bound file which left him gaping at its contents: a detailed list of all the telephone calls and messages received by the DMP during and immediately after Easter 1916, mostly from known loyalists informing on rebel positions, but also, and more strikingly, from certain individuals currently masquerading as republican sympathisers.

Just after 4 a.m., to Nunan's relief, Collins concluded that they had gathered all the intelligence they needed. It would only be a couple of hours before the station's detectives, including those slumbering in its dormitory, reported in. On their way out Collins took with him the 1916 file. Moments later, standing on Brunswick Street, drawing deep breaths as dawn rose, Collins felt like an enlightened man. He had an unprecedented weapon in his arsenal: the entire modus operandi of RIC and G-Division intelligence and could now tailor his own network to rival the British.[15] Equally importantly, he also had a comprehensive list of enemy spies and informers, as well as precise knowledge of detectives involved in the suppression of the separatists. The two men walked away, leaving behind Broy, tremendously relieved as he furtively unlocked the dormitory door and quietly settled back at the main desk, re-immersing himself in his book while awaiting his relief by the morning shift.

Collins had little sleep after his night's work. There was an Ard-Fheis to attend to at the Mansion House, as well as an urgent meeting with Mulcahy. At the meeting Collins sought authorisation from Mulcahy to provide Dublin Brigade's most trusted Volunteers with the names of the relatively low-profile detectives forming the core of his growing web of double-agents. This was to avoid them becoming inadvertently caught up in Brigadier McKee's next move: the final issuing of a list of police targets already supplied to McKee by Collins, to Dublin's relevant battalion commandants. Orders were to be issued to proceed against those listed commencing the following day – 9 April. Collins, for security reasons, had purposely waited until the last moment to disclose the double agents' identities. With no time to waste Mulcahy authorised this and Collins hastened to contact the relevant Volunteers.

Across the city over the ensuing days policemen involved in political work and their informers – following confirmation of their identities – were accosted and man-handled by small teams of Volunteers practising shadowing techniques that soon were refined by their most daring and ruthless members into an efficient killing system. For now, however, killing was not their business.

Det. Denis O'Brien became one among many on the receiving end of a less lethal but nonetheless hostile warning. He had been seen on numerous occasions observing and shadowing Volunteers and Sinn Féin members.[16] He had a particular interest in those from his home county of Cork, including Collins, whom he had helped apprehend on Bachelors Walk the previous year before Collins' three-week incarceration in Sligo. One night Det. O'Brien was grabbed and manhandled by a group of armed Volunteers who tied him to a set of railings close to his home near Mountjoy Prison, gagged him and, finally, warned him that if he continued his duties there would be no mercy shown next time.[17]

Det. Sgt Halley's home, situated in nearby Norfolk Road, was also raided, but Halley, from Tipperary, drew his revolver, a shot was fired, and the matter quickly ended in the policeman's favour. O'Brien's far-less-glorious episode was eventually concluded when he was unbound by a sympathetic passer-by. He then sped on foot to Dublin Castle where Superintendent Owen Brien – a long-standing officer and formidable superior – berated the breathless O'Brien for 'allowing himself' to be tied up. O'Brien, aghast, demanded that his superior advise him as to what he could have done to prevent his assailants humiliating him in such a way. When the superintendent eventually left the room, O'Brien turned to Ned Broy, who had witnessed the discourse and, with look of relief on his face, said unexpectedly: 'They were damned decent men not to shoot me, and I am not doing any more against them.'[18]

Elsewhere within the Castle, however, another detective – Sgt Patrick Smyth – who had received such a warning letter, expressed contempt. He was heard to say: 'I'm not letting any young scuts tell me how to do my duty.'[19] He had also participated in Collins' arrest the previous year alongside O'Brien and their colleague Johnny Barton. Smyth's attitude soon set him on course for a fate far worse than public humiliation. Fate was also set to close in on Barton.

***

As the pursuit of G-Men and informers was set under way, the Dáil met publicly again on the morning of Thursday 10 April. After a roll-call of TDs, Seán T.

G-DIVISION PENETRATED AND TENSIONS ESCALATE

10 April 1919, TDs assembled for Dáil Éireann's first public sitting since the release of the German Plot internees. (*Courtesy of Kilmainham Gaol Museum OPW, KMGLM 2018.0068*)

O'Kelly instructed the Mansion House's packed public gallery that there was to be no applause or demonstration during proceedings. He then called on the president to issue a statement. De Valera stood momentarily, poised, employing the descending silence to underscore his position's distinction, setting it against some of the ridicule that had succeeded that Dáil's inauguration, which he had been unable to attend. He addressed the house with a ministerial statement of policy. He spoke slowly and clearly, his soft-pitched, craggy accent stating to all that his duty as president was to make it clear to the world the position that Ireland was in. He followed this by stating: 'There is in Ireland at this moment only one lawful authority and that authority is the elected government of the Irish Republic. Of the other power claiming authority …' He paused, then carried on: 'The authority of that power is no lawful authority. Therefore in soul and conscience the Irish people owe that authority neither respect, nor attachment, nor obedience.'[20]

He then informed the house that Dáil representatives would be sent to the Paris Peace Conference and to the soon-to-be-formed League of Nations; ambassadors were also to be dispatched to prominent receptive countries. He then spoke to the transfixed audience on trade matters, the National Loan whose target was doubled to £500,000 – half of which would be raised abroad – and agriculture. He concluded with the assertion that the Minister of Defence was in close association with the voluntary military forces, which formed the foundation of the national army.[21]

Following the president's speech, questions and answers flowed back and forth. Cathal Brugha stood up to address the house. He had an important point to articulate under his own brief: that the government's defence forces were stronger than ever. He voiced his hope that Ireland would get the best it could from the conference in Europe, but confidently insisted nonetheless: 'Know this, the defence forces are ready, and ready if they need to be used.'[22]

The point was received.

During the afternoon session, after initial discussions fluctuated between a proposed message that would be sent to the Irish diaspora, and the continued hardships being endured by republican prisoners, De Valera rose to speak. Once again, all eyes turned towards him as silence descended. Brugha's earlier stagecraft was about to be eclipsed.

De Valera then, echoing January's *An t-Óglách*, spoke of the RIC, heralding: 'I rise to propose that members of the police forces acting in this country as part of the British occupation and as agents of the British Government be ostracised socially by the people of Ireland'.[23] He justified this colossal proposition by charging that the police were the main instruments in keeping Ireland in subjection, that the force worked solely for the British government and were, simply, spies in their midst – the eyes and ears of the enemy. He then added, 'They are no ordinary civil force as police in other countries. The RIC, unlike any other police force in the world is a military body armed with rifle and bayonet and revolver as well as baton.'[24] He then reminded the members of the Dáil, and the stunned public gallery, of the RIC's record as landlord enforcers in the land wars. He also spoke of more recent outrages, like the brutal treatment of many of their comrades, some of whom, such as Thomas Ashe, had perished in jails around the country, contending that their comrades were only imprisoned in the first place because of the RIC. When he pleaded that the motion be passed it was quickly seconded by Eoin MacNeill, and subsequently approved.

The police now, as official Dáil policy, suffered ostracisation within their communities. The groundwork had been laid for a protracted national campaign that eventually claimed the lives of hundreds of its officers, on top of prompting mass resignations within the force, while simultaneously hamstringing recruitment.

Since 1916, those same police authorities had been taking extensive security precautions during Easter in case the period sparked another rising. 1919, particularly with recent tensions, saw a particularly volatile atmosphere descend over the city in the two weeks following De Valera's momentous speech. Throughout the country, main access roads to prominent towns and cities were barricaded, while battle-ready troops were tactically deployed. Dublin was in lock-down in the days leading to and following Easter Sunday, 20 April, while military garrisons and police throughout the city remained on high alert. The only notable action, however, was an arson attack at the tax offices in 32 Nassau Street by Volunteers.

Shortly after Easter, Harry Boland was appointed by De Valera as the special envoy from the elected government of the Irish Republic to the United States. On 4 May Boland, having crossed the Irish Sea nursing a debilitating hangover from his 'American wake' at Vaughan's Hotel, set sail from Liverpool on the transatlantic crossing, posing as a stoker, to pave the way for the president himself whose departure to drum up support for the Irish cause became more imminent by the day. Collins had lamented the departure of his enterprising, entertaining, and resolute colleague and comrade, protesting his own pending status to him lyrically during the 'wake' with: 'I'm a poor lonesome whore'.[25] Collins had helped ensure the occasion – traditionally convened to mark the parting of emigrants unlikely to return – was a riotous affair. Boland appreciated the light-hearted sentiment but in the coming months regularly felt far more lonesome and isolated than Collins, given his remoteness from the city he revelled in, despite the adventurous life of an envoy. His subsequent replacement as party secretary by forty-two-year-old pacifist Hanna Sheehy Skeffington exasperated and infuriated Collins.

Dublin's police in the subsequent weeks were itching to hit back at the Dáil and Volunteers whenever they could. On 9 May they had a golden opportunity to apprehend Collins, who was still on the run following the issuing of a bench warrant over the trial for sedition for which he had failed to turn up the previous year. Collins was recognised by detectives as he strode into the Mansion House shortly before lunchtime. He was there to speak on economic matters and of grievances such as disproportionate taxation rates at a reception presented by the lord mayor for three American political delegates – Frank Walsh, Edward Dunne and Michael Ryan – who would then attempt to persuade President Wilson to receive a Dáil delegation at the peace conference.

Reinforcements were quickly summoned by the detectives to raid the building. Luckily for Collins, Det. Broy got word of the raid. He quickly left the station and called the house where he knew De Valera was staying from an untapped public telephone. Then, when De Valera's voice sounded at the other end, Broy, still fearing eavesdropping telephone exchange operators, voiced his warning in French, of which he was a fluent speaker. De Valera, however, was not. Luckily Piaras Béaslaí was with him, who was.

Soon Béaslaí, risking capture considering he too was on the run since his prison escape, rushed to the Mansion House where he warned Collins. Collins appeared unperturbed. Instead, to Béaslaí's astonishment, he remained seated and prepared to tuck into his lunch. Joe O'Reilly, meanwhile, having just finished his own lunch at a nearby vegetarian restaurant, had to sneak past the rapidly growing police and military cordon to warn Collins what was happening in the streets. A 200-strong British Army company struggled through the surrounding streets, teeming with converging crowds of civilian onlookers, with an armoured car, trucks and machine gun sections. The Volunteers outside had already disappeared from sight when they arrived. Then, to coarse commands of NCOs, the soldiers quickly surrounded the Mansion House, deploying around Molesworth Street, Schoolhouse Lane and Dawson Street. Alarm spread within the Mansion House. The American delegates inside were spellbound.

Soon after the cordon had been secured, a section of police and soldiers led by G-Division Det. Daniel Hoey approached the Mansion House's back door in Schoolhouse Lane. The back door was set into a twenty-foot high wall at a bend in the laneway that completely shielded the Mansion House and adjoining buildings. Hoey, thirty-one years old and with nine years' service, detested republicans, and had behaved with cruelty and spite in Richmond barracks after the Rising. He had unrelentingly pursued Seán MacDermott before and during his court martial and gloated at the imminent prospect of his execution in front of a firing squad. He had also arrested Austin Stack before his imprisonment in Belfast. He was hated and feared by the Volunteers.

As they prepared to effect entry, Collins, attempting to escape out the back and checking to see if the coast was clear, spotted them through the same door's keyhole. Behind Collins stood fellow fugitive Robert Barton, as well as Comdt Edward Kelly and Joe O'Reilly, whose eyes quickly fell upon a ladder placed on the ground nearby. The four then used it to scramble up and over an adjacent wall, pulling the ladder up through an elongated building behind them. They eventually made their way into a nearby yard surrounded by windows behind which onlookers stared out, gaping in curiosity. O'Reilly shook his fist at them in a warning not to give them away. Meanwhile Hoey and his men forced the back door and stormed in, narrowly missing the four. The high wall had prevented them seeing their escape.

The detectives at the Mansion House's front door waited for the lord mayor to open it before rushing into the building, which was then thoroughly searched along with its occupants. However, they failed to find Collins, Barton, or anyone else on their wanted lists, including Béaslaí, who remained undetected in the building. Outside meanwhile, when the thousands of civilians now gathered began singing the anthem 'The Soldier's Song', a British soldier, trying to re-assert authority, fired a warning shot into the air. The measure backfired, however, as the cacophony only increased.

Eventually, when the policemen left the Mansion House empty-handed, to the mocking taunts of the burgeoning crowd, Collins, coming out of hiding with his companions and sensing an unforeseen opportunity, dispatched O'Reilly to fetch his Volunteer officer's uniform from the Munster Private Hotel a mile away in 44 Mountjoy Street – his main residing address. Three hours later, with the American delegates still in the Mansion House, and De Valera having since arrived by limousine to great fanfare alongside Countess Markievicz and William Cosgrave, Collins reappeared in the reception in dashing fashion, fully uniformed and to rapturous applause. The delegates relished the gesture as Collins, his 'Scarlett Pimpernel' persona now riding high, instructed them as to what they had just witnessed: the naked subjugation of the elected government by a hostile army of occupation.[26]

Béaslaí was not at large for long, however; he was re-captured within days and dispatched to prison in England. Meanwhile, another in the area who had escaped the detective's attentions, Seán McLoughlin, a fugitive again, had made his way during the fracas to a building in Molesworth Street where he found shelter with Richard Mulcahy and his fiancée Min Ryan, former sweetheart of the late Seán MacDermott. McLoughlin was subsequently dispatched for three months to Kiltyclogher in Co. Leitrim as an organiser and instructed to stay at the MacDermott family home.

***

Five days after the raid, on 14 May, GHQ received word of an incredible rescue the previous evening of a Volunteer formerly under McLoughlin's watch. Seán Hogan, one of the Soloheadbeg ambushers, was liberated from the clutches of a four-man RIC escort by train in Knocklong, Co. Limerick. Dan Breen, Seán Treacy and Séamus Robinson – all still on the run and assisted by five others – rescued Hogan, who had been arrested near Thurles the previous day and was being transported to Cork Prison. Two policemen were mortally wounded. Four Volunteers were wounded, Breen seriously. Following the rescue, widespread arrests were made in the region.[27] Lord French, still reeling from illness, was horrified, as was Chief Secretary Macpherson. French's revulsion would, by the year's end, prove well founded. Hogan, Breen, Treacy and Robinson remained at large and, within months, became major players in the capital, and would make several close-run attempts on his life.

Det. Hoey's near capture of Collins was not the policeman's only near miss that May. Soon after the Mansion House raid, the moustachioed King's County (Offaly) man spearheaded a raid on Heron and Lawless' cycle and engineering shop on 198 Great Britain Street. Situated at the junction of King's Inns Street, the shop was the recently set-up front for the bomb-making factory in its basement run by Joseph Lawless and Archie Heron – the Fingal Brigade's vice-commandant. The factory was under the overall command of Vice-Brigadier Lynch. A furnace was operated while sand-casting, turning, drilling and milling machines fabricated hand-grenades and mortar bombs. Some of these were then tested in Aungier Street in a sealed cast-iron bath covered in sand-bags, while others were brought to the Hellfire Club to be tested. Upstairs, a more benevolent façade preoccupied with wheel repairs, general overhauls and other rudimentary metalwork was presented. The only way in and out of the basement was via the ground floor.

The factory was in full flow when a dozen policemen barged in one afternoon. A warning light system was in place to alert those working in the basement when there was trouble overhead. During the raid, however, a detective stood in the way of Lawless flicking its activation switch – disguised as a lamp-switch. Two men downstairs, Matt Furlong and Thomas Young, remained obliviously consumed in their noisy work as the detectives swarmed above. Lawless tried desperately to get to the switch without drawing suspicion but could not. He then began berating the detectives, protesting that they were impeding the work of loyal and honest businessmen, concluding that a veneer of such indignation would bolster his protestations of innocence. The ruse worked. He was then able to brush past the switch and flick it discreetly after the policeman obstructing it had finally stood aside.

Lawless' subsequent refusal to direct the policemen to the basement entrance bought precious minutes for Furlong and Young, having now seen the warning, to mask their illegal endeavours as the production of harmless axle boxes. When the policemen eventually discovered the sulphurous-smelling basement and descended its rickety steps, the Volunteers completed their masquerade by bewildering them with a verbal diatribe of technical jargon. It worked until, to Lawless' horror, a sack full of Very lights from the Collinstown raid was discovered. Scrambling for a pretext, he tried to pass them off innocently as fireworks. However, he soon found himself interrogated by Det. Hoey in Dublin Castle, then the bridewell.

Lawless had been quicker on his feet than anticipated by Hoey, however. He had slipped the keys to his Richmond Road home to another employee who was not under arrest. When the home was subsequently ransacked that night Lawless' Volunteer uniform and some other incriminating weaponry and ammunition had been safely moved elsewhere. Lawless was released the following day without charge; astonishingly, the police could not prove any connection between the Very lights and the Collinstown raid.

Ominously for Det. Hoey, his unrelenting pursuit of Volunteers was becoming a thorn in the side that would, within months, be plucked once and for all.

Meanwhile, on 24 May, Lord French, having considered and approved a novel idea recently conveyed to him by Walter Long, relayed it to Secretary Macpherson: as a proposed response to the recent escalation of tensions and the body blows being suffered nationwide by the RIC, they would bolster the force's ranks with former soldiers. The decision sowed the seeds for mayhem throughout the country.[28]

Long's suggestion was, nonetheless, telling. By May 1919, both the RIC's and the DMP's authority was being successfully usurped by increasingly active, albeit unofficial, Volunteer police units. In Dublin these went after petty criminals and more organised gangs such as the 'Moore Street Gang,' also known as the 'Sons of Dawn', who were keen to capitalise on the growing sense of disturbance. Businesses like Woolworth's on nearby Henry Street had engaged the Volunteer units to protect them.

Meanwhile, General Shaw was becoming increasingly perturbed at the escalating trouble brewing throughout the country. Forebodingly, in spite of almost 100,000 soldiers drawing salaries in Ireland, less than 10,000 battle-ready troops were available for internal security duties due to pending overseas deployments, long-term hospitalisations and demobilisations. Consequently, he summoned reinforcements that would more than double his fighting strength. These consisted of five infantry battalions, one machine gun battalion, cyclist units, and, strikingly, four tanks.[29] Soon Dublin's quays bustled with the disembarkation of troops and vehicles whose numbers suggested, tellingly, that they were an expeditionary force making its way to war.

6

SHOOTINGS, AMBUSH AND ASSASSINATION

'We will go down in history as a laughing-stock'

On 17 May, after the recently published draft of the Versailles Treaty suggested Ireland's claims to independence would be ignored, the Dáil dispatched a letter to the peace conference signed by Seán T. O'Kelly and George Gavan Duffy – another of the original delegates dispatched to Paris in January. The document repudiated the right of the British plenipotentiaries in Paris to speak for Ireland. It also contained a respectful exhortation that any future agreement signed by those plenipotentiaries would not be seen by the Dáil as binding on Ireland's people.[1]

On 26 May, another letter was sent, this time from De Valera, Arthur Griffith and Count Plunkett. This drew the conference delegates' attentions to the fledgling League of Nations' position on the rights of small nations. It asserted, among other things, that lasting post-war peace could not be secured without preserving the rights of one such small nation – Ireland.[2]

Then, on 1 June, De Valera left his wife Sinéad and their children – now numbering six – at their home in Greystones and finally set sail for Liverpool where he would subsequently make his way to the USA as a ship stowaway. Ironically, he shared his preceding Irish Sea crossing with Sir James MacMahon. The Roman Catholic under-secretary for Ireland was, coincidentally, a former pupil of Blackrock College where De Valera had in more recent years worked as a teacher while regularly indulging his passion for rugby. De Valera, with the help of Liverpool IRB, eventually boarded White Star Line's SS *Lapland* on 14 June disguised as a sailor, avoiding attentions of detectives conducting a murder hunt for a local man as he boarded. The company enjoyed by the Dáil president in the cramped, murky and interminably noisy disused tank that formed his lodgings consisted of a small plague of rats. Having initially helping themselves to his sandwiches the creatures tormented him incessantly. He spent a great deal of the tortuous eight-day journey to New York – the city of his birth to an Irish mother and Spanish father – switching on and off a flashlight to frighten his unwelcome fellow travellers. He became very ill for a time on the voyage.[3] Seán Nunan also travelled to New York to assist De Valera's mission, and to ship small arms to Ireland whenever possible. He posed as a ship's fireman on board RMS *Aquitania*, departing Liverpool on 6 June, and found the trip far less gruelling despite the back-breaking work involved.

Arthur Griffith became acting Dáil president in De Valera's absence. Collins added weekly visits to De Valera's home to support Sinéad and the children to his frenetic schedule. None of them knew how long De Valera would remain away.

Conspicuously, on the day Nunan departed, and while De Valera crossed the Atlantic ahead of him, the US Senate passed a resolution asking for the Dáil delegates to be afforded a hearing at the Paris Peace Conference.

Meanwhile, trouble had brewed again at the Mansion House. On the evening of Thursday 5 June, to celebrate what would have been the forty-ninth birthday of the late James Connolly – executed at Kilmainham Gaol in 1916 – a concert was organised by the Socialist Party of Ireland. The ICA – reorganised since the Rising, albeit in far less potent form – had been asked to marshal the event. Under the command of Comdt James O'Neill – Connolly's successor – several dozen members, including twenty-four-year-old veteran Frank Robbins, clashed with the DMP, who formed a cordon outside to stop the event.[4] They also patrolled the surrounding streets and laneways in force. The ICA had little regard for the DMP as it had been formed originally to defend strikers and agitators against the brutality displayed by the DMP during the 1913 Lockout. Josie McGowan's death following the Foster Place baton-charge the previous September provided further evidence to them of the violent predilections of many of its hated rank and file towards them. The feeling was mutual; the ICA had shot dead two unarmed DMP members during the Easter Rising as they had sought to disrupt their mobilisations, one a mere 200 yards from Dawson Street.

At one point, when a detective went to apprehend Capt. James O'Shea, the ICA man drew his pistol and fired half-a-dozen shots. Several comrades

SHOOTINGS, AMBUSH AND ASSASSINATION

then joined in. This was followed by frantic screams and shouts as a stampede of over 2,000 concert goers and onlookers desperately sought cover from the echoing rounds. Moments later, Dawson Street was clear. Five policemen and one female civilian sat and lay wounded, groaning in agony. Ambulances and police reinforcements rushed there. The concert was eventually abandoned and took place instead later that night in Capel Street's Trades Hall, and was, in turn, followed by another tense stand-off with the DMP. Capt. O'Shea went on the run afterwards.

Capt. Flanagan, of C Company 3rd Battalion, himself still a fugitive since he had been identified outside the Mansion House in January, had been spending more recent days and nights at a Volunteer field camp at Glendoo in the Dublin Mountains. Early one June morning he awoke to find an RIC sergeant standing over him in his tent. The RIC had been closing in on the camp for some time; the previous week had seen an attack by the 3rd Battalion members on a British military field kitchen in nearby Ticknock. On their overnight trek to Glendoo the policemen had succeeded in wounding 2nd Lt Séamus Grace – a thirty-year-old veteran of the Rising's Battle of Mount Street Bridge – as he made his way to a nearby Fianna camp. Grace, shot in the leg, was taken to Royal City of Dublin Hospital in Baggot Street.[5] In wounding Grace, a handful of policemen had succeeded where two battalions of British infantry had failed three years earlier.

When Capt. Flanagan saw that the sergeant had managed to get his hands on his own pistol from beneath his makeshift pillow, he propelled himself from his bedding to escape, wearing nothing but a shirt and some undergarments, the former of which he wriggled out of as the sergeant grappled to apprehend him. He then bolted from the tent, past an unwary constable outside, and scampered away barefoot past several other policemen through some adjacent fields. He then glanced behind to find, to his relief, no one in pursuit. He eventually scrambled over a gate onto a roadway, only to then come face to face with a passing farm-girl. Startled and terrified, she ran away, screaming that there was a madman on the loose. Flanagan, embarrassed and bewildered, quickly collected himself and continued his escape, fearing that the girl's screams would draw the policemen. Cursing the fact that the RIC had reached his tent undetected, he eventually made for a nearby farmhouse where he received a set of replacement clothes from a sympathiser, as well as a welcome breakfast. Soon afterwards, the camp was moved several miles west to Bohernabreena.

In a far less slapstick episode than that suffered by Capt. Flanagan, the same month saw the setting up of the Dáil civil service in a motion presented by Arthur Griffith and seconded by Cathal Brugha. Also decreed was the establishment of the national arbitration courts, following the recommendations of the committee spoken of by Griffith in April.[6] Additionally proposed was the resources and industries commission, aimed at estimating national productivity in terms of industries, minerals and agriculture, as well as fisheries. Another crucial development was the replacement of Laurence Ginnell as director of publicity following his arrest; thirty-one-year-old Desmond Fitzgerald succeeded him on 17 June. Fitzgerald had overseen rations for the GPO garrison in 1916. His frugality there had won him few friends. While the rebel HQ had been pummelled by British artillery suggesting the imminent need for evacuation, he had continued to administer to half-starved Volunteers portion sizes more appropriate to a month-long siege. Now, he would begin to play a role far better suited to his talents and connections, which soon became pivotal.

During the latter part of June, the Volunteer 1st Battalion was back in action again with trench-knives and pistols to hand for another arms raid – this time at Ashtown, a wayside railway station near Castleknock five miles north-west of the city. Its primary purpose was servicing the nearby vice-regal lodge and the Phoenix Park races. Joseph Lawless provided some of the cars for the mission in which he acted again as driver, along with a team that included Owen Cullen and Patrick McCrea from the Collinstown raid. Lawless, fearing surveillance following his recent arrest, had since sold his share in the legitimate end of his cycle shop/bomb factory in Great Britain Street to a front acting on behalf of Vice-Brigadier Lynch, and re-established himself with the proceeds and some borrowed funds as the owner of a car rental company on St Ignatius Road near Drumcondra – a convenient cover from which to organise Volunteer transport.

Thirty men converged on the station to prepare their assault at 6.00 a.m. one bright morning, having arrived earlier using different routes to avoid attracting the authorities' attention. A train was expected from Mayo carrying an alluringly large quantity of weapons and ammunition to the Army Ordinance Depot in Islandbridge barracks. It was due to stop on its way through at 6.30 a.m. This time around, unlike Collinstown, they had more than enough vehicles to transport the anticipated haul.

As soon as the cars had been concealed, the Volunteers mustered and took up positions to the east of the station's level-crossing. Lt Patrick Holohan rushed to the nearby signal cabin with pistol at the ready to hold up the signal officer. The plan was to force him to stop the train, then assault it from both sides of the tracks and overwhelm the guards. Assuming resistance was minimal, any soldiers or policemen would be tied up while the weapons and ammunition were unloaded; failing that, more ruthless measures would be employed.

Holohan crept up the wooden steps to the cabin, then rushed its door. The signalman was startled, but then, realising what was happening, identified himself to Holohan's surprise as a fellow Volunteer, citing his battalion and company as proof. He then protested that they could have saved themselves a lot of trouble if they had let him in on their plans beforehand. He then added the dispiriting revelation that the train they sought, which ran on an unreliable timetable, had passed the station twenty minutes earlier – they were too late.

Dick McKee, leading the raid and sensing a setback, quickly made his way to the cabin to hear the same bad news. He and Holohan were then alerted that another passenger train full of troops was due within minutes, prompting McKee to rush back out to warn the Volunteers, primed to assault and concealed in cover, not to attack it. The train soon stopped and passed, its windows full of soldiers looking out. Then, frustrated and cursing the haphazard timing, McKee ordered the unit back to the city, where the vehicles, dispersing again separately, blended with the early traffic. It would not be the last Volunteer mission at Ashtown to go wrong.

***

23 June saw trouble brewing in Tipperary again with the gunning down of RIC Dist. Insp. Michael Hunt in Thurles. Hunt had been assiduous in the pursuit of Volunteers in the area, particularly since Knocklong. He was shot at close range during a fracas in the packed town square following a race meeting. What was particularly noteworthy of this shooting was the indifferent response of the crowds: no one went to the mortally wounded inspector's aid, a fact that was not wasted on GHQ as they laboured over the potential public relations ramifications of similar shootings they were soon to order in the capital. A

proclamation the following day from the Catholic bishops in Maynooth underscored their growing confidence that public opinion was veering in their favour. The bishops proclaimed words to the effect that Britain ruled Ireland by the sword in a manner unsuited to a civilised nation and, accordingly, such misrule was the root cause of the country's escalating violence.

Within weeks all Sinn Féin organisations were banned in Tipperary. Lord Haldane, still abreast of developments in Ireland, expressed horror at such bluntness. He correctly foresaw such reactive measures spreading throughout the country, sowing the seeds of lost opportunities for dialogue with Sinn Féin moderates who, as far as he was concerned, were 'far from murderers'.[7]

The Dáil and GHQ maintained a low profile in Dublin during celebrations leading to and following the signing of the Versailles Treaty on 28 June 1919, when revellers took to the capital's streets in force to mark the official end of the Great War. Union Jack flags hung from unionist-controlled buildings. Sinn Féin's long-suffering headquarters was attacked by loyalist civilians and raided yet again by the police. Rioting took place throughout the city. Shots were fired, causing casualties. It also marked a clear vindication in the strategy of preparing for armed conflict – at least as far as Sinn Féin's more hawkish protagonists were concerned. They regarded their castigation of the party's moderates as having been justified, given that the peace conference had yielded nothing to Ireland's claim to self-determination.

On the same date as these celebrations Michael Collins was elected as IRB president, replacing Harry Boland. However, given the Dáil's recent investiture, the secretive 'organisation' was viewed as increasingly obsolete, not to mention threatening by De Valera and Cathal Brugha, among others, who decried its lack of transparency. Its proponents, on the other hand, still extolled the virtues of having such a clandestine structure in the background given the precarious existences of both Sinn Féin and the Dáil, which operated with far less motility. Ominously, this discord set the scene for a growing chasm within Sinn Féin as the time passed. Lord French was not unaware of such fault-lines.

A week-or-so following these events, Vice-Brigadier Lynch was summoned to Volunteer GHQ to receive some unexpected news from his close friend Brigadier McKee: a recent conference between McKee, Mulcahy and Collins had resulted in the conclusion that the time had come to wipe out G-Division, marking a momentous shift in the Volunteers' official strategy.[8]

SHOOTINGS, AMBUSH AND ASSASSINATION

Lynch remained silent when initially struck with McKee's bombshell. McKee then referred to Mulcahy's frustrations at the round-the-clock scrutiny the Volunteer and Dáil leadership were being subjected to by G-Division. This, combined with the evidence of their intentions obtained by Collins and Nunan the previous April during their overnight visit to Central Police Station, as well as the rapidly growing quantity of intercepted police mail, suggested they were preparing to pounce. The GPO – relocated to the Rotunda after the Rising while its Sackville Street headquarters was being rebuilt – was by now, at least among its clerical staff, infested with republican sympathisers. Leaks there had revealed further intelligence underpinning their fears of an imminent swoop. This risked costing the Dublin Brigade their officer corps, as well as the entire Dáil. The loss of an arms dump to the police on Lower Stephen Street on 1 July provided further urgency. McKee looked Lynch straight in the eye and said: 'Michael, if this happens we will go down in history as a laughing-stock.'[9] Lynch nodded in agreement as McKee then added: 'They have been warned already to stop or receive a bullet, we have to proceed at once!'

Lynch, however, despite agreeing in principle with such measures, could not reconcile himself with carrying them out. Grappling with this he eventually professed that it was a job he simply could not do; therefore, he could not reasonably subordinate such a task. He then requested that when men were selected for such missions that he would be left out.[10] McKee was surprised. Nonetheless, he accepted that proposed warfare such as this was not for everyone.

As an afterthought Lynch felt compelled to warn McKee that Cathal Brugha would raise hell over such controversial measures should they be undertaken without his own official prior sanction, particularly given his position as Defence Minister and chairman of the Volunteer Resident Executive – which meant he was still nominally in charge of Volunteer policy. McKee responded, shrugging his shoulders: 'Whether Brugha approves or not we are going ahead. I am making arrangements to have Smyth shot'.[11]

He was referring to the same Det.. Smyth who had dismissed the Volunteers' earlier warnings. Smyth, fifty-two-years-old, with twenty-eight-years experience, was nicknamed 'the Dog'. A father of seven from Longford, he was detested by republicans, and his interminable barrage of insulting and offensive remarks to them in Richmond barracks in 1916 ensured the feeling was mutual. He was also unpopular with his colleagues, seen as arrogant and bullish. As a detective he was tenacious and resolute. Among his transgressions as far as GHQ was concerned was his arrest of and subsequent testifying against Piaras Béaslaí, leading to the latter's two-year sentence that had only been interrupted by the mass escape during March. Ironically, Smyth's younger brother, Eugene, had acted as an agent for the IRB in Dublin Castle before the Rising, and had also helped leak warnings the previous year of the German Plot arrests.

McKee continued: 'At the next meeting of GHQ, Cathal will ask under whose orders was Smyth shot and I will say by mine'.[12] He added that he would probably, at that point, be suspended by Brugha and subsequently court-martialled for exceeding orders. This, he asserted, would necessitate Lynch taking over as brigadier. Lynch, however, bolstered McKee with the promise that he would, in such an event, tell Brugha that he too had approved the operation, and would surrender his rank if McKee were reprimanded. McKee smiled at this.

Following this, McKee sought out Quartermaster Mick McDonnell, trusted unreservedly, to put together a list of men to carry out the intended assassination and ensure adequate weapons. McDonnell, originally from Wicklow, with a receding hairline and a markedly composed, pouting expression at odds with his frequently rigid personality, was a close associate of both McKee and Collins. He had a contact in Islandbridge barracks as one source of weapons and ammunition, another was a public house on Parkgate Street; messengers would call there and ask if there was 'any message for Mick Mac'.[13] He had seen first-hand the harsh treatment meted out by Smyth and his more enthusiastic colleagues in Richmond barracks three years earlier, and had since advocated shooting them given their unrelenting pursuit of Volunteers since. When asked to officially by McKee, unlike Lynch, he needed no further persuasion.

Meanwhile, on Saturday 19 July, the political polarity still pervading the capital registered once again in a victory parade to honour British Army units such as the Irish Guards, Royal Horse and Field Artillery, Gordon Highlanders, Royal Dublin Fusiliers, Machine Gun Corps, Royal Army Medical Corps, Women's Legion and Women's RAF, as well as a parade of armoured cars followed in turn by the Tank Corps, the latter a huge novel attraction. Lord French was due to take their salute.[14]

Overlooking College Green, a huge Union Jack flag hung proudly above Trinity College. Since early morning the vehemently loyalist university's rooftops were thronged with well-dressed students, civilians and former soldiers and officers who congregated on the north-eastern rooftop where the flag fluttered in the warm breeze. The event was, notably, boycotted by the Nationalist Ex-Servicemen's Association. The occasion also provided an outlet for a great many of the flu-weary populace to enjoy widespread street-celebrations less constrained by the dreadful pandemic whose effects were abating dramatically.

It also afforded the Volunteers 3rd Battalion an opportunity to plan French's assassination with pistols and grenades as he stood on a platform erected within the grounds of the old Parliament buildings, now the Bank of Ireland. GHQ eventually called off these plans, however, following explicit instruction from Cathal Brugha, due to the inevitability of civilian casualties in the densely packed streets. Such a prospect would not have sat well either with Desmond Fitzgerald, particularly as at the same time he was setting up a weekly mimeograph publication condemning acts of crown aggression against innocent civilians.

Meanwhile, by the time Lord French had basked in the salute, Mick McDonnell had compiled his list of possible men to take the fight to G-Division. Within days a large group of initially selected Volunteers, mostly 2nd Battalion, assembled at 35 North Great George's Street, a four-storey Georgian house. There, McKee and McDonnell moved between them, picking men out here and there and directing them to an inner room.

McKee and McDonnell then dismissed those left over and addressed the selected men assembled at attention in the inner room. McKee got straight to the point, asking if any of them had any objection to shooting enemy agents.[15] As expected, some did, and were duly dismissed. Then, the remainder were asked again – individually. James Slattery, a twenty-two-year-old Clareman, was the first to affirm that he was prepared to obey such orders, followed by McDonnell's half-brother, Tom Keogh, a twenty-year-old railway fitter who regularly plied his trade making hand-grenades in Great Britain Street. Keogh was followed by twenty-seven-year-old docker, Tom Ennis, originally from Enfield in Co. Meath and a close associate of McKee's. When the remainder had also confirmed their agreement, McKee instructed them that they were to form a 'Special Duties Unit' of the Dublin Brigade. When their time came to be called, they would get their orders from McDonnell; for now they were to lie low.

The first three unit members: Slattery, Keogh and Ennis, were not long awaiting their first target: Det. Smyth. They were soon summoned before McDonnell and Mick Kennedy, who had also been selected and knew Smyth by sight. McDonnell then gave the order to Slattery, Keogh and Ennis. They would strike as the sergeant made his way from Botanic Avenue in Drumcondra, where he alighted the tram from work to walk the short distance to his home in 51 Millmount Avenue. This was to be done at the earliest opportunity. Slattery himself lived just off Botanic Avenue, in 9 Woodville Road. Kennedy lived in nearby Ballybough.

For four consecutive evenings following these orders, and with Smith and Wesson five-shot .38 revolvers at the ready, the four prospective assassins, following a quick reconnaissance of the area, waited fruitlessly at the corner of Millmount Avenue and Drumcondra Road for their target to appear on Drumcondra Bridge over the twenty-yard wide River Tolka. Then, on the fifth evening, as the sun began to set, Mick Kennedy, looking towards the bridge from Millmount Terrace, suddenly jolted his comrades: 'I think this is Smith [sic]', he declared as he noticed above the bridge balustrades a tall dark-haired man with a distinctively thick moustache striding in their direction.[16] As pulses quickened Slattery told him to make sure, but Kennedy could not be certain without a closer look that might alert the target. The tension escalated as the four began arguing in heated whispers whether or not it was him.

Taking charge, Slattery readied them, saying: 'if he turns down Millmount Avenue we will shoot him'. However, Smyth – for it was indeed him – instinctively attuned to the abnormality of the four nervous looking men, became suspicious. Instead of turning left as normal onto Millmount Avenue he carried straight on and instead took the next left onto Millbourne Avenue, a narrow uphill side-street running parallel a dozen yards beyond, checking over his shoulder to see if he was followed. From there he could get home by circling the block. Slattery became momentarily concerned that they had almost shot the wrong man. Kennedy, however, keeping his eyes trained firmly on the target as the others conferred, saw him take the left turn. He was certain this was their man; but now it was too late – he was out of effective pistol range.

The frustrated and desperately anxious gunmen argued quietly amongst themselves again, the strain of the situation showing. Suspecting that Smyth would probably look out of his window in their direction as soon as he got

SHOOTINGS, AMBUSH AND ASSASSINATION

home, they remained in place for thirty minutes to offset any suspicion from the detective other than what would be customarily afforded to four unfamiliar men congregating in the diminishing light. To avoid further suspicion they postponed the mission for a few more days.

Then, on the warm night of 30 July the unit was back in position on Millmount Terrace, having once again performed the same area reconnaissance and ensured their getaway routes were unobstructed. Soon their prey appeared, highlighted by street lamps as he walked northbound across the bridge. Gripped with tension and dread but eager to have the grim task behind them, they steeled themselves, their eyes instinctively darting between the target and potential dangers in the immediate area. Smyth, who – unusually – was unarmed, observed them again but his suspicion had abated. Seeing no reason for another detour he eventually turned left in front of them onto Millmount Avenue. It was the wrong move: as soon as he did, the four men's sweating hands drew their revolvers from their coat pockets, cocking their hammers. Their revolving cylinders turned, making soft metallic clicks as index fingers rested on triggers. Then they opened fire.

In the still twilight the dry cracks of the shots reverberated along the gardenless red-bricked terraces. Smyth's body jolted forcibly with the impacts of two bullets, one in his back and the other in his right leg. Half-a-dozen more had missed, ricocheting from brick, concrete and railing further into the street. To the assassins' astonishment, however, Smyth remained upright and bolted desperately for his home less than 150 yards away on the street's northern side. Shouting that the men behind him were cowards, half-staggering, he began traversing the road.

Slattery and Keogh, petrified but pumping with adrenalin, quickly gave chase, concluding that their guns were not powerful enough. They would need to finish him off up close. Smyth cried out desperately for help as he continued his teetering run, his front door coming into tantalising view. Slattery and Keogh, quickly catching up, fired their pistols from just behind. They did not miss. Three more bullets tore into their victim.

One of Smyth's sons, fifteen-year-old Thomas, alerted by the shots, raced from No. 51 to his father's aid. Within seconds his equally horrified younger brother bolted from the house, shouting that he would 'catch those who shot Dada'.[17] Slattery and Keogh never even noticed the youngster then giving chase as they turned and sprinted to link up with Kennedy and Ennis back towards Drumcondra Road. Smyth, half-delirious, wheezing, groaning and with blood soaking his bullet-holed clothes, was helped into his home. Stunned neighbours quickly came out along the terraces, some to help, others looking on.

Joseph Lawless had heard the distant shots while speaking to a neighbour on Richmond Road. When the neighbour suggested the shooting came from close to where Det. Smyth lived, he made his way there.[18] Soon, Lawless observed clusters of inquisitive civilians darting and ambling apprehensively from the bridge and from the upper end of Drumcondra Road. He soon saw a Fire Brigade ambulance turn from the bridge onto Millmount Avenue. Then, mingling with the onlookers, he arrived outside No. 51 just in time to see the unconscious detective being carried out on a stretcher. Then to his surprise, he recognised the ambulance driver – Joseph Connolly of the ICA. Struck by the irony of this, Lawless manoeuvred himself next to the ambulance. Connolly, recognising Lawless straight away and referring to his recently loaded passenger, remarked: 'I don't think he is dead yet'.[19] Connolly sounded disappointed. His brother Seán's death in action during the Rising had been maliciously gloated at by a colleague of Smyth's – Johnny Barton. The ambulance then revved up and drove to the Mater Hospital a mile away. Lawless had a feeling that a discernible line had just been crossed. He was right.

When Smyth was examined in hospital soon afterwards five bullets were detected in his body; four in the upper leg and hip area and one in his back which had pierced his lung. When he had regained consciousness, he managed to give a colleague, Sgt Lynch, a detailed statement. Recovery looked probable.

The following morning Mick McDonnell, aghast that Smyth was still alive and determined to investigate, made his way hurriedly to James Slattery's house. Slattery had barely slept. Throughout the long night the prospect of himself and his comrades being identified by the detective if he did survive had plagued him. His own predicament was particularly alarming, living as he did within two minutes' walk from Millmount Avenue. His disquiet was aggravated by the endless repetition of the shooting playing itself out in his mind. Shooting a man up close in the back as he desperately ran away was not something that lent itself well to the conscience of a young man valuing the sanctity of human life, notwithstanding the fact that he had been the first to volunteer for it; killing in combat, and from a distance that entailed a rifle was one thing – up close was another. The fact that it happened within yards of the victim's family intensified his revulsion. Nevertheless, he was a Volunteer, and orders were orders.

McDonnell's visit was almost a welcome respite from his mental whirlwind. Slattery's red-bricked home was the first on the left as McDonnell strode into Woodville Road, a small cul-de-sac. The area was deathly quiet. As McDonnell, a tough taskmaster by nature, entered the hallway his tone was characteristically unforgiving. He spat the words in his unusually high-pitched voice: 'You made a right mess of that job!'[20] Slattery's endless hours of pent up tension then vented with the protestation that the .38 calibre revolver was obviously not a powerful enough weapon for this type of job. McDonnell, caught by the response, then listened to Slattery's agitated account of the shooting. Eventually both concluded, pragmatically and ruthlessly, that more powerful .45 calibre ammunition would be necessary for similar future operations.

***

The next GHQ meeting took place hot on the heels of the shooting dead of two more policemen by Volunteers during an ambush close to Ennistymon in Co. Clare on 4 August. Among the meeting's attendees were Vice-Brigadier Lynch and Brigadier McKee, both waiting apprehensively for Cathal Brugha's expected adverse reaction to Smyth's shooting. Lynch, as pledged, stood ready to side with McKee.[21] However, their concerns were soon assuaged; as soon as discussions commenced, Brugha fired out the question: 'Who shot Smith [*sic*]?' When McKee replied: 'Certain members of the Dublin Brigade', Brugha, to their unexpected relief, responded approvingly: 'A damn good job!'[22] However, he then added that they were to hold off on further such shootings for the time being. He had recently dispatched a correspondence to De Valera in the USA asking how the American public would react if they started an onslaught against the military and police here in Ireland. He was still awaiting his answer.

Brugha was not the only one waiting. McKee's ears were also pricked in anticipation of the public reaction, as were Mulcahy's and Collins'. A week after the shooting that response so far mirrored the Thurles shooting in June – noticeably reticent. However, Smyth still lived. If, on the other hand, he died and there was a substantial backlash they would then know that the general population were not ready for war. Mulcahy also had his attentions focused on what moves the British authorities would make if Smyth died. His conclusion was that should they attack Sinn Féin and the Volunteers, then the movement had every right to defend itself; therefore, the Volunteers would need to be ready.

Moves were indeed being made by Dublin Castle. On 7 August, Chief Secretary Macpherson introduced the Constabulary and Police (Ireland) Bill to parliament, aimed at improving pay and conditions within the force whose morale, and numbers, were plummeting. A gratuity would also be provided to the police, pending the legislation's enactment. Meanwhile, that same day it was announced in the House of Commons that the exasperating cost of Ireland's military garrison was almost equal to the country's entire annual pre-war revenue. The response, a week later, was noteworthy: it was asserted that within a year, a bolstered police force should pave the way for a normal sized, and far-less-costly military garrison. The speaker – Winston Churchill – could not have been more wrong.[23] Nonetheless, it was an ominous harbinger of what the eloquent and bellicose secretary for war had in mind in terms of a bolstered police force, considering what was to come. It was also an indication that the attentions of powerful, capable and ruthless men such as Churchill were turning towards Ireland given that the Versailles Treaty was now signed.

Back in Dublin's Mansion House, on 15 August, Sinn Féin's national executive convened a meeting to have the details of the National Loan made public. Also confirmed was a definitive target for De Valera's fund-raising enterprise in America – five million dollars. Copies of the loan prospectus – printed at Dollard's on Wellington Quay along with the bonds – signed by De Valera and Collins, were distributed. IRB members were soon busily soliciting those considered likely to support the venture.[24] Bank accounts were quickly set up in the Munster & Leinster Bank and Hibernian Bank throughout their Dublin branches, diminishing the risk of discovery. They were opened under the names of individuals sympathetic to Sinn Féin and Dáil members. Others were set up in fictitious names. Facilities were put in place to deposit gold on the premises of Corrigan Undertakers in 5 Lower Camden Street, while a solicitor and 1916 veteran bearing the same surname, William, made preparations to employ his practice in 3 St Andrew Street as a clearing house for funds.

On 20 August, at a subsequent Dáil meeting, Brugha, to bring the Volunteers under the Dáil's direct control and away from the IRB's, forwarded a motion that the Volunteers, along with the Dáil deputies and clerks, should swear allegiance to the Dáil and the Irish Republic, which as far as he was concerned, were one and the same. For many Volunteer IRB members on the other hand, this represented a conflicting conundrum: they held the IRB's Supreme Council as the real government of the Irish Republic, and the Dáil as an administrative body established effectively by that government, but nonetheless a subordinate entity that could, if required, be abrogated – particularly if it fell short on its republican principles. The oath read:

> I ... do solemnly swear (or affirm) that I do not and shall not yield a voluntary support to any pretended Government, authority or power within Ireland hostile and inimical thereto, and I do further swear (or affirm) that to the best of my knowledge and ability I will support and defend the Irish Republic and the Government of the Irish Republic, which is Dáil Éireann, against all enemies, foreign and domestic, and I will bear true faith and allegiance to the same, and that I take this obligation freely without any mental reservation or purpose of evasion, so help me, God.[25]

Within days of this the Irish Volunteers assumed the official title of the IRA, and became the standing army of Dáil Éireann. Collins worked expeditiously in the shadows to ensure the oath was accepted among hard-line IRB members.

Meanwhile, throughout the country, things were heating up. In Dublin during late August an IRA section were engaged by a military party in Deansgrange. The soldiers were driven from the area by superior fire, but there were no casualties on either side. Back in Co. Clare on 23 August, fifteen-year-old Fianna scout Francis Murphy was shot dead sitting by the fire in his home by soldiers acting in revenge for the shooting of the two policemen in the county earlier in the month.

Then, forebodingly, on 27 August, General Shaw announced that, owing to a continued lack of trained men despite recent reinforcements, the army would soon not be able to provide support to the police in many areas. Insp. Gen. Byrne was horrified at this unexpected thunderbolt. As a solution Shaw – echoing Lord French, Walter Long, and Churchill – advocated bolstering the RIC with a special force of ex-soldiers, who would be armed by the military but employed by the police.[26] Byrne's response was a prophetic warning of the negative effect such a strategy would have on overall discipline. Byrne's influence was, however, rapidly waning. Then, to add further to his increasing woes, on 2 September, Tipperary was in the headlines again when two RIC members were shot – one dead – by IRA men in Lorrha, close to the Galway border at Portumna.

Five days later, in Fermoy, Co. Cork, on the morning of Sunday 7 September, Liam Lynch, accompanied by local IRA commander Michael Lynch, led an audacious attack by twenty-five IRA members from the North Cork Brigade against seventeen infantrymen from the King's Shropshire Light Infantry. This marked the first planned ambush of British soldiers in Ireland since the Rising. The attackers were armed with only six handguns, while most carried clubs concealed under their jackets. Nonetheless, despite such crude handicaps the well-orchestrated attack outside the town's Wesleyan Methodist church resulted in the capture of thirteen rifles and five military casualties, including one dead infantryman – Private William Jones. He was shot while swinging a rifle butt at Lynch, who himself was shot in the shoulder. The IRA unit's escape was equally well-executed. The following night, in retaliation, scores of soldiers broke out of their barracks and looted the town. They returned two nights later with similarly vengeful intent, only to be driven back to their barracks by huge angry crowds of the town's residents and traders.

Meanwhile, back in Dublin's Mater Hospital Det. Smyth finally succumbed to his gunshot wounds on 8 September, dying of multiple organ failure five weeks after the shooting. He was buried three days later in Glasnevin Cemetery.

Dublin Castle's reaction to these milestones was rapid. Sinn Féin, Cumann na mBan and the Gaelic League were banned in Cork on 10 September. Then, early on 12 September, a far more momentous step was taken; Dáil Éireann was declared a dangerous association under the Criminal Law and Procedure Act 1887 and outlawed. Its existence was intolerable as far as French and Macpherson were concerned. No more Dáil meetings could be held publicly and its members risked arrest. Arthur Griffith was aghast, sensing that, crucially, the Sinn Féin moderates were completely side-lined. He declared in disgust that Dublin Castle had 'proclaimed the whole of the Irish nation as an illegal assembly'.[27]

There would be no going back – it was war.

7

FORMATION OF THE 'SQUAD'

'You'll die for this tonight'

The Dáil's banning presented an opportunity for G-Division's more zealous detectives to quickly flex their muscles. They did not intend to squander it. Numerous raids took place throughout the city immediately afterwards, one of which was a large-scale onslaught directed at Sinn Féin's offices backed up with two lorry loads of soldiers in battle-dress.[1]

The building was positioned at the bottom of Harcourt Street on its western side. It was a four-storey Georgian house with a large arch over its front door. Two sash windows sat to the left of the front door, above which hung a sign: 'Sinn Féin Bank Ltd'. The bank had been incorporated in 1908 as a co-operative dedicated to supporting Irish enterprises and industries. It had established offices in Harcourt Street in 1910, leasing the upper floors to Sinn Féin itself. Dáil Éireann based its Trustees' account there and Collins' Department of Finance operated from its upper floors. This was the raid's primary target given Dublin Castle's pressing exigency of throttling the Dáil Loan. Information leading to the destination accounts of loan subscriptions was given the highest priority.

Collins was seated in a second-floor office at the building's front with a close IRB associate, twenty-seven-year-old Dáil cabinet secretary and IRA Director of Communications Diarmuid O'Hegarty. Raised in Skibbereen in West Cork, O'Hegarty shared Collins' Herculean administrative skills and, having toiled relentlessly to reorganise the Volunteers following the Rising, had worked alongside Collins at the Volunteer Dependants' Fund. Also upstairs was IRA assistant director of training thirty-one-year-old Jeremiah J. O'Connell, nicknamed 'Ginger' due to his fiery red hair. O'Connell had lived in the USA and served in its army for a time.

At 10.30 a.m. O'Connell entered Collins' office, leaving a door open, only to suffer Collins' quick-tempered castigation for doing so. Collins' secretary, Eithne Lawless, sister of Joseph, got up from her desk to shut the door. Then, to her alarm, she spotted a uniformed policeman standing on the step next to the railings outside. She then saw the lorries disgorging khaki-clad infantrymen, wearing steel helmets, fixing bayonets and sealing the street. They shouted with English accents at pedestrians and drivers to clear the area. She turned sharply to warn Collins while quickly closing the door. Knowing she would not be searched she then took Collins' revolver from him and hid it in her stocking. Other women in the room similarly rushed to grab whatever weapons or incriminating documents were within their grasp.

When the police and military entered, they quickly dispersed throughout the ground floor and sealed the building's rear, locking the front door behind them. To the sound of boots on varnished timber floors they then began systematically searching from the ground floor and basement upwards, inadvertently providing time for the women to conceal as much paperwork as they could. Collins, having got to his feet and seen what was unfolding and realising they were cornered, declared: 'We are caught like rats in a trap and there is no escape'.[2] He then sat back down at his desk and waited for the detectives to arrive. He still had one potential ace up his sleeve: he knew the last person the DMP would expect to find working, in the bearing of calm detachment he was about to project, was Michael Collins.

His luck held. Det. Hoey, coordinating the search and one of the first to enter the building, would have instantly recognised Collins. As chance would have it, however, Hoey focused his own initial attentions and those of his equally earnest colleague Insp. Love on searching the ground floor and the basement, leaving the upper floors to Insp. McFeely, a far less zealous Sinn Féin adversary. When McFeely, fifty-one-years-old and originally from Donegal, stepped into Collins' office, the latter, recognising him, saw his chance. Det. Broy had previously informed Collins that McFeely was an ardent 'Home Ruler'. His family had been forced to leave Donegal in 1881, victims of mass evictions. Collins pounced at the opportunity to unbalance him with a tirade of derisive remarks aimed at the inspector's apparently conflicting loyalties, adopting the same strategy that had worked for Joseph Lawless during the bomb factory raid – feigning serene disregard, which was hardly the demeanour of a fugitive. Seated, composed, with one of his crossed legs swinging casually, he venomously spat the words:

What sort of legacy will you leave to your family, looking for blood money. [*sic*] Could you not find some honest work to do?'³ The tactic worked. Unsettled, and assuming Collins was just an irate clerk, the inspector quickly left to search the caretaker's room on the top floor. Once this was completed, McFeely and his accompanying section of officers moved back down to the lower floors. Collins, with the women keeping watch, rushed to hide in the caretaker's room; it would hardly be searched twice.

Det. Hoey, meanwhile, probing James Kavanagh's office, picked up a tray of paperwork. Sinn Féin activist Brian Fagan looked on. Fagan had been crippled during the Rising and had to use leg-braces to walk. His acerbic wit had suffered from no such impediment, however. Hoey was jolted enough to replace the tray without further inspection when Fagan declared ominously at him: 'Hoey, the last man to handle that tray of papers was Sergeant Smyth'.⁴ Hoey and Love were soon upstairs rummaging around in Collins' office, but finding no one or nothing of interest, they quickly departed. Soon the search was over. Those arrested included TDs Patrick O'Keefe and Ernest Blythe. As soon as the front door was shut behind the departing officers Collins returned to his work, despite the pleadings of Eithne Lawless to leave the building for his own safety. Moments later, as the three-ton Dennis truck carrying O'Keefe and Blythe trundled away past bystanders and spectators on the cobblestones next to St Stephen's Green, O'Keefe leaned across to Det. Hoey and scoffed: 'Hoey you'll die for this to-night [*sic*]'.⁵ Det. Hoey ignored the comment, but it was prophetic – Hoey had just hours to live.

Richard Mulcahy decided the time had come as the suppression of Dáil Éireann was a declaration of war. It was time to hit back – and fast. Collins quickly sent the names of those who had led the earlier raid in Harcourt Street to the IRA C-in-C. Then, Mulcahy, acting equally expeditiously and ruthlessly, dispatched orders to Brigadier McKee: the Special Duties Unit was to strike again. He also provided him with its target – Det. Hoey. McKee then passed the order straight away to Mick McDonnell.

During the early evening, McDonnell returned to James Slattery's house in Drumcondra, instructing him that they had a job on. He spoke of the earlier raid, alluding to Collins as the 'man we want to guard', and pointing out how close the police had come to capturing him.⁶ He then spoke of their target: the detective force's 'rising star' – Hoey. Being a creature of habit, Hoey's movements were known to IRA intelligence. The two men soon set off on foot, collecting three pistols *en route* to Tom Ennis' home on Lower Oriel Street; Ennis completed the three-man unit. The preceding weeks had hardened the resolve of both Ennis and Slattery since their shooting of Smyth; the line was already crossed. Future such missions were no less unsavoury, not to mention dangerous, but the growing familiarity of what was to come, coupled with the necessity of such extreme measures under the relentless pressure of growing counter-measures, quickly seasoned these young assassins.

Armed with Colt .45 semi-automatics, they made their way to Townsend Street, which flanked the northern side of Central Police Station. McDonnell had briefed both men on the route that Hoey would be taking on foot once he came off duty at 10 p.m. He lived in the barracks' single quarters. Tensions again mounted as they approached the area. Stomachs churned, hearts raced, eyes darted nervously from position to position. Deep down within each man was an unwelcome, overpowering urge to be anywhere else. Cigarettes were inhaled deeply as they initially scouted the area surrounding D'Olier Street/College Street/Westmoreland Street, trying not to draw attention from passers-by or policemen on foot patrol.

Finally, at 10 p.m. Hoey approached the police station from College Street, his tall height marking him out. Slattery, his mouth dry with tension, asked 'is that him?' McDonnell was unsure but instructed Slattery and Ennis that if he went straight to the door of the building, 'We will go after him'.[7]

They closed in on Hoey, from a safe distance, and still glancing around for danger. Then Hoey entered Townsend Street but unexpectedly walked past the police station until he entered a milk bar situated just before the junction of Tara Street. McDonnell, suddenly remembering that the detective always went for a glass of milk when coming off duty, muttered in satisfaction: 'It is Hoey all right'.[8]

The three then quick-stepped back to the corner of Hawkins Street and lurked in the shadows from the surrounding lamp-posts, waiting for their target to re-emerge 100 yards away. Their hearts palpitated. Pistol chambers were loaded, the well-oiled parts sliding and snapping into place.

Moments later Hoey was back in view, stepping across the narrow roadway, making his way along the pavement to the station, completely oblivious to the intentions of the three men pacing intently in his direction. The distance between

FORMATION OF THE 'SQUAD'

the hunters and the hunted closed until Hoey reached the station's eight-foot-wide garage door close to the College Street end of the building. Then, before the detective could react, three pistols – their safety switches clicking off almost in unison – appeared, each with fingers resting on triggers, held with hands struggling to steady their aim. The cracks of three shots suddenly pierced and echoed in the air as two eleven-millimetre bullets ripped into his torso at 300 metres-per-second, the first of which shattered his watch chain, driving in additional sharp metal flecks along with the bullet and clothing fragments.[9] Another bullet tore into his neck, exiting explosively from the far side. Blood and tissue from the exit wounds spattered the station's granite wall as Hoey was hurled backwards under the force of the rounds before buckling and crumpling helplessly under the merciless assault. Ejected bullet cartridges tinkled to the pavement.

The three-man unit, assured they had done their job, quickly made their escape, bolting into Hawkins Street, pistols at the ready. They quickly became breathless, but luckily for them, they were able to obscure themselves in the crowds of weekend picture house and theatre goers as well as others coming to and from the public houses surrounding O'Connell Bridge and Sackville Street.

Police and detectives rushed from the barracks, one remarking later that the

Det. Daniel Hoey's height marks him out in this photo (*second from right*). It also helped mark him out for his killers. Det. Sgt Smyth, shot on 30 July in Drumcondra, is visible in the centre of the picture with his distinctive moustache. (*Courtesy of Mercier Archive*)

shots were so quick it sounded like someone running a cane across a railing.[10] They were horrified to find their colleague slumped in a growing pool of blood with his life ebbing. Wafts of smoke rose from the scorched bullet-holes in his overcoat and waistcoat. As curious and horrified onlookers gathered in the area to the shrills police whistles, he was rushed by ambulance to Mercer's Hospital a half-mile to the south-west but was pronounced dead on arrival.

The IRA had sent a clear message to G-Division by shooting dead its second detective. Meanwhile, McDonnell oversaw the dumping of their weapons for cleaning, before ensuring Collins was immediately informed of the shooting. Hoey, ironically, had been due to transfer shortly to Scotland Yard in London.[11] He was buried in King's County (Offaly).

***

Within days, Collins met with Mulcahy, McKee and Brugha at GHQ. McKee, hot on the heels of Hoey's killing, was pushing for an expansion of the Special Duties Unit to maintain the offensive. The conclusion was that a full-time squad would be needed to deal equally ruthlessly with spies, informers and G-men. It would report to GHQ Intelligence. The intelligence department itself would select future assassination targets, which would then be sent to Brugha for final sanction before the squad carried them out. McKee, as brigadier, would select candidates to expand the unit into such a squad.

McKee wasted no time. Foremost on his mind were Paddy Daly and Joe Leonard. The additional men – apart from Slattery, Keogh and Ennis, who had been told to lie low at July's meeting – would be held in reserve for now. Daly and Leonard had both been released from Mountjoy Prison early the previous month. Leonard, originally from Co. Mayo, headstrong and square-jawed, was another 2nd Battalion 1916 veteran with an uncompromising temperament backed by a withering and pitiless stare. At Thomas Ashe's funeral two years earlier, he had almost shot an impatient British Army truck driver threatening to barge through the cortege in his overheating truck. Leonard's aggressive intervention at pistol point on the day had quickly persuaded the driver to see sense. He had recently overseen the holding up of a mail lorry and the subsequent collection of its valuable intelligence.

Daly and Leonard were soon summoned to GHQ, where McKee detailed to them what was proposed. Then, neither having expressed any qualms about

FORMATION OF THE 'SQUAD'

such duties, Daly suggested that another IRA man, Ben Barrett, be included. McKee, knowing Barrett, agreed.

The brigadier then set himself to also selecting the brigade's best intelligence officers so as to form the nucleus of an intelligence section, which would be placed under Collins' command.[12] Patrick Caldwell, a twenty-three-year-old Dublin Corporation employee since his own return from post-Rising imprisonment, was top of McKee's intelligence list.

Soon afterwards Caldwell and McKee met at 10A Aungier Street, a regular haunt of McKee's (it was from here that *An t-Óglách* was now being printed). Caldwell was instructed to report to Liam Tobin, who was acting as Collins' deputy director of intelligence. Soon afterwards, George Fitzgerald was also recruited for intelligence by McKee, following a brief rendezvous between the two close associates at Peadar Clancy and Tom Hunter's 'Republican Outfitters' tailor and drapery shop in 94 Talbot Street. The business – its motivations anything but clandestine – had been established in 1917.

Then, on 19 September, the men shortlisted to form the proposed special duties 'squad' assembled at the Keating Branch of the Gaelic League. This branch – situated two doors away from GHQ, at 46 Rutland Square – had for many years been an IRB hotbed. They included: Daly, Leonard, Barrett, Seán Doyle – a Dubliner and veteran of the Rising and the Collinstown raid – and recently blooded James Slattery and Tom Keogh. Mulcahy, McKee and Collins met them there. Next to the GHQ triumvirate stood Peadar Clancy, the thirty-year-old Clare man acting as director of munitions, and Special Duties Unit commander and Quartermaster Mick McDonnell. It was apparent to all summoned that this would mark the beginning of something big.

Following initial formalities, Mulcahy, with typical sternness, addressed them. It was proposed to form a squad with which to take vigorous offensive action against the British executive and political detectives who were harassing Dáil Éireann and members of the HQ staff.[13] This squad would take orders directly from Collins. However, in the event of his absence, their orders would be given to them from Mulcahy or McKee. Mulcahy then emphasised that they were not to discuss their movements or actions with IRA officers or with anyone else.[14] He then added that they would be required to give their whole time and thought to the arduous tasks encompassing membership of this squad, but nonetheless, were to co-operate with the Dublin Brigade when required.[15]

Collins then addressed them with quintessential forcefulness. Pacing the room, the Cork man elucidated that he had been given their government's authority to deal with spies and informers. He gave a short speech on recent Irish history, asserting that they would know that no organisation such as their own in the past had an intelligence system through which spies and informers could be appropriately dealt with. This deficiency was to be rectified by the forming of an intelligence branch to which those chosen would be seconded as assassins.

Collins then called out three names: Leonard, Doyle and Barrett, informing them that they were to consider themselves squad members under Daly's command. He told them to quit their jobs, reassuring them that they would be compensated for their loss of earnings. Each member would be paid £4.10 as a weekly wage, which was the equivalent to a skilled worker's wage. Additionally, they would henceforth require a fixed point from where they could be contacted and mobilised. Daly then provided such an address: a small cottage at No. 10 Bessborough Avenue in North Strand, owned by Volunteer Michael Love. Collins concluded with a caution: they were not to shoot anyone off their own backs unless in self-defence, adding that certain police and G-Men were particularly good friends of the movement.

McDonnell, Slattery and Keogh then spoke, asking why neither they, nor Tom Ennis, had been selected. McKee interjected, reassuring the three that they had special work to do.[16] McKee then pulled McDonnell to one side and told him precisely what this was, as far as he was concerned. He was to travel to London with George Fitzgerald and Liam Tobin to assess another colossal possibility, albeit a repeated one – wiping out the British cabinet; this time with the addition of several other prominent adversaries such as the editors of hostile newspapers.[17] McDonnell would hear shortly from Mulcahy with his full instructions. Slattery, Keogh and Ennis were to remain in their occupations for the time being and await further orders.

The following day, the British authorities, making some of their own additional moves, launched a series of raids on printing presses they considered subversive and dismantled their machinery. Those visited in Dublin included *The Nationality* – edited by Arthur Griffith, *The Voice of Labour, New Ireland, The Republic, The Irish World*, the bi-lingual *Fáinne an Lae*, and *The Leader*. Circulation of each halted immediately. Similar raids took place nationally.

Newspapers carrying Dáil Loan advertisements also received censorious visits. Unfortunately for those behind the strategy, however, none of the more radical underground papers were affected; their presses rolled away at an even greater pace, including *An t-Óglách*, the mere possession of which could result in six-months imprisonment with hard labour.[18]

Five days later, on 25 September, Lord French submitted a memorandum to the Whitehall cabinet, calling for the enhancement of the secret service in Ireland in conjunction with the broader provision of prison accommodation in England for rebel deportees forecasted to be captured as a result of the enhanced service. England was considered a more secure overall location despite the embarrassing escapes at Usk and Lincoln. Additionally, Mountjoy was in the grips of another embarrassing hunger strike; French felt that less sympathy would presumably be felt for such public relations nuisances in English cities and towns. He also called for further financial advances to the RIC to assuage plummeting morale, now also impacting dreadfully on policemen's families, while stressing the urgent need to reinforce the DMP's G Division.[19] His proposals were largely approved. September also saw the arming of rank-and-file DMP with revolvers.

The next two weeks saw Michael Collins focusing on public relations in his ministerial capacity, as well as the less charismatic task of adding four provincial members to a sixteen-man finance committee he had set up in July to lay the groundwork for the administration of the funds anticipated to soon flow in for the Dáil loan, domestic and foreign.[20] As McDonnell, Tobin and Fitzgerald hooked up with Sam Maguire – Collins' chief intelligence officer in London – and began stalking politicians there, Collins, side-stepping his endless profusion of paperwork, took centre-stage in a short propaganda film designed to raise public awareness of the Dáil bond scheme and mitigate the setbacks caused by the recent press closures. The seven-minute feature co-produced by John MacDonagh – brother of late 1916 leader Thomas – featured an array of family members of other lost Easter Rising leaders and prominent separatists including Arthur Griffith, Erskine Childers, William Cosgrave, Robert Barton, Seán Milroy and Hanna Sheehy Skeffington. It was filmed during the making of the movie *Willy Reilly and his Colleen Bawn* at the Pearse family home in St Enda's in Rathfarnam. Collins is seen reading a letter from the bishop of Killaloe, Dr Michael Fogarty, pledging support and asserting 'We need to build up a new Ireland'. He is then joined by Diarmuid O'Hegarty, following which the sanguine-looking and impeccably dressed pair issue bonds to the featured participants, symbolically, on the wooden block used in the beheading of Robert Emmet in 1803.[21] The film cost £600 to make.[22] It was subsequently smuggled throughout Irish cinemas, receiving a rapturous reception, justifying its expense.

Its propaganda success stood out sharply against the Hunter Committee Report – commissioned by the Legislative Council of the government of India – released the same month, which provided a damning indictment of British colonial occupation there. It referred to the massacre of almost 400 non-violent protesters, and the wounding of thousands more at Amritsar in the Punjab province the previous 13 April, when crown forces opened fire upon a peaceful crowd in an enclosed arena – an ominous precursor for Dublin … The report was pounced upon by republican propagandists.

Collins, unsurprisingly, did not share Lord French's faith in the security of English prisons. He was simultaneously planning another breakout, this time from Strangeways in central Manchester, which was a prison many considered escape-proof. Austin Stack and Piaras Béaslaí were incarcerated there alongside numerous other republicans. Stack, following a series of hunger strikes and disturbances, had been transferred to Manchester from Belfast with several others in April; Béaslaí had recently arrived there from Leeds Prison, following a stint in Birmingham. Collins had since been presented with maps of the prison and its surrounds, and an escape plan, by former inmate Fionán Lynch – a Kerryman and close associate. Collins corresponded regularly with Béaslaí using coded messages. He eventually visited Stack in the prison under a false name, accompanied by Paddy O'Donoghue's wife. Plans were further discussed in cloaked language under the close watch of prison warders. Meanwhile, as Collins travelled back and forth from Dublin, several IRA men, including Rory O'Connor, Peadar Clancy and Owen Cullen, prepared to travel to Manchester under O'Connor's command to oversee their escape alongside the Manchester IRA. Arrangements were finalised. Again, a rope-ladder would be employed for the breakout.

Meanwhile, Mick McDonnell returned to Dublin from London after a fortnight with the unfavourable news that it would be impossible to make a simultaneous swoop on the entire cabinet, or anyone else earmarked for execution.[23] He explained this to Mulcahy, Brugha and Collins, emphasising that due to lack of adequate support from the London IRA it would take at least thirty of their own best men, few if any of whom could expect to return alive.

His discouraging analysis was accepted by Mulcahy and Collins but not Brugha, who still felt it should be done. McDonnell was dismissed but ordered to remain in Dublin while further investigations were carried out. Collins, familiar with London, would assess the situation in the city for himself.

***

On Monday 19 October Dublin's Mercer Hospital was again the setting for the tempestuous arrival of a blood-soaked gunned-down policeman. Const. Michael Downing, twenty-five years old, from Castletownbere in West Cork, with two years' policing experience was shot in the stomach at 2 a.m. when he approached three suspicious-looking men in High Street. They were Volunteers from the 4th Battalion, moving explosives from a dump in Winetavern Street to Marrowbone Lane.[24] One of them, after unsuccessfully warning the constable to back off, pulled a pistol from his trench-coat and fired. Despite frantic efforts to save him, including a blood transfusion from a fellow detective, he died during the morning.

By the time this latest shooting had taken place, four of the Soloheadbeg and Knocklong gunmen: Séamus Robinson, Seán Treacy, Dan Breen and Seán

Left to right: Seamus Robinson, Seán Hogan, Seán Treacy and Dan Breen: 'The 'Big Four'. Seated to Breen's right is Michael Brennan of the East Clare Brigade, a close associate of Peadar Clancy's. *(Courtesy of Mercier Archive)*

Hogan, had established themselves in the capital. Recent developments provided an auspicious setting in Dublin for the militaristic talents of the 'Big-Four' as they soon became known. Breen, recovered from his Knocklong wounds and with a £1,000 reward out for information leading to his capture, and the three others, first made their way to Kathleen Boland's house (Harry's mother) where they arrived 'soaked from the rain and starving'.[25]

Next stop was Phil Shanahan's pub in Montgomery Street. Shanahan, the forty-five-year-old proprietor and TD for Dublin Harbour, was a former Tipperary hurler and 2nd Battalion veteran of Jacob's biscuit factory and Frongoch. The pub was situated in Corporation Street, the heart of the 'Monto' red-light district, which sat between Gloucester Street, Amiens Street and Gardiner Street.[26] The four fugitives were fed and housed in the pub. Local newsboys kept watch for police and military – at least those not known to visit the pub, its surrounding establishments, and the area for less official reasons.

Their regular presence in the bustling and smoky establishment soon became an open secret. Richard Mulcahy, still exasperated over Soloheadbeg, had initially advocated sending them to the USA, but they refused. Collins – who on the other hand recognised their potential as fearless gunmen – was a frequent visitor, as were McKee and Clancy.

Soon alternative lodgings were arranged. They then found themselves moving between Shanahan's, the Boland home in Clontarf, and IRA comrade Mick Fleming's residence at 140 Drumcondra Road Lower, situated above the family's grocery shop. On one occasion they turned up at the ironically named Crown Hotel, a republican haunt next door to the Gresham in Sackville Street run by republican Annie Farrington. They looked like they had been sleeping rough for several nights. The offer of mattresses on a drawing room floor was greeted as though they had been offered a stay in a luxury resort.[27]

Back across the Irish Sea, on 25 October, Béaslaí, Stack and four others finally escaped from Strangeways. Following two initially unsuccessful attempts at securing the rope-ladder, the six men, having subdued and tied up the chief warder, climbed over the prison's twenty-foot wall into an adjacent street that had been sealed by two IRA teams disguised as passers-by and tradesmen. Stack lacerated his leg escaping. From there they and their rescuers dispersed by car and bicycle to safe houses within the bustling city. Collins, also in Manchester, called on them over the ensuing days.

Collins then took a train to London. Once there, he checked in with Tobin and Fitzgerald, who had stayed put while McDonnell returned to Dublin. The pair were residing in Clapham. Having briefed them with typical gusto on the Strangeways escape, the three took a long walk through Whitehall, roaming between principal government buildings and New Scotland Yard.[28] Tobin and Fitzgerald protested at their mission's monotony. The bleakness of the dusky city as winter loomed did little to assuage this. Tobin, twenty-four years old, was studiously persistent in his work. He was lanky, dark-haired and angular, and, unlike his fellow Cork man Collins, not known for exuberance. However, they would remain in place pending further orders. Soon afterwards Collins, having assessed the situation in London, returned to Manchester to oversee the safe return home of the recent escapees. Béaslaí and Stack, his now-septic leg still bandaged, eventually travelled to Liverpool with Paddy O'Donoghue and Liam McMahon by train, playing cards and acting as if on holiday to avert suspicion.[29] Soon the escaped pair were once again crossing the Irish Sea to Dublin and met at the quayside by Joe O'Reilly. Their rescuers had already returned. Stack recuperated at Batt O'Connor's house, which Collins visited daily for lunch. Stack soon assumed the ministry of home affairs from Arthur Griffith, eventually establishing offices in Wellington Quay in a premises cloaked as an electrical engineers. Béaslaí quickly resumed his work with *An t-Óglách*.

Lord French, meanwhile, was back in London. A cabinet committee convened there on 4 November with the purpose of projecting Britain's conformity with both pre-war pledges and post-war ideals to the international community – particularly the USA and the dominions – by creating two separate Irish Home Rule parliaments: one in Dublin, the other in Belfast. A parliamentary bill with which to instigate such a partition was considered necessary to alleviate growing moral pressure to fulfil the 1914 pledge to concede Home Rule once the war was over. A Council of Ireland, with members from both parliaments, was also to be set up to mediate both parliaments where necessary and facilitate the country's potential future re-unification.

This committee had all but agreed in principle to this by the time IRA GHQ had decided, once and for all, to remove Lord French from the picture.[30] On

Monday 10 November Mick McDonnell was informed by McKee of plans to assassinate the lord lieutenant the following day – Armistice Day. French, having returned from London, would be attending a banquet in Trinity College. Intelligence had been received that he would also review a military parade from the front of the Bank of Ireland in College Green. This provided an opportunity for a sniper to shoot him from an upstairs office window opposite.

McDonnell was stunned by the plan's audacity. This heightened when McKee alluded to the obvious; the man selected for this job would not come back.[31] He then asked McDonnell if he could recommend such a man. McDonnell, still absorbing the proposition's temerity, replied that he could not. McKee then asked: 'Will you do it?'[32] McDonnell, further dumbstruck, hesitated. If he agreed then this would, without doubt, be his last day on earth. Nevertheless, after a few additional moments, he accepted the mission.

That same early evening Paddy Daly and Joe Leonard had been looking for twenty-nine-year-old Det. Sgt Thomas Wharton with similarly dire intentions. This particular 'G Man', from Killarney in Co. Kerry, was at the top of their target list of political policemen. He had assisted the late Det. Smyth at Béaslaí's arrest and trial. Days had been spent exhaustively trawling Dublin's streets with fellow Special Duties Unit members seeking him out, but to no avail. Then word was received from Joe O'Reilly that the detective would be patrolling Harcourt Street accompanied by a colleague on the evening of 10 November. However, orders were that his colleague was not to be harmed as he was a double-agent. He would draw and fire his pistol when the attack took place, but his shots would merely be a decoy and not directed at the attackers.

Daly and Leonard, with no time to mobilise the rest of their unit, took the job on themselves and began their hunt as darkness descended. They strolled up the lengthy incline of Harcourt Street with their eyes scanning both sides of the cobbled and tram-lined roadway, stepping into the numerous side-streets while trams, cars and horse-drawn hackney cabs trundled in both directions among the early evening traffic. They paid particular attention to the train station at the street's southern end, as well as its handful of hotels and bars. When they eventually spotted two detectives, however, neither fitted the particular descriptions assiduously provided by intelligence that generally referred to age, build, clothing style, height, hair and eye colour, facial features, and gait. Joe O'Reilly, working in nearby No. 76, was quickly summoned. His further investigation revealed that neither man was the target. Frustrated, Daly and Leonard then made their way on foot to College Street, intending to replicate the tactic employed to kill Det. Hoey by lurking and ambushing their man as he returned to Brunswick Street barracks while trying not to draw unwanted attention. Several drawn-out hours passed until, with no sign of Wharton, they gave the mission up as a bad job.[33]

Joe Leonard left his pistol at fishmonger Michael O'Flanagan's arms dump in Wexford Street before taking a tram home to Mount Pleasant Avenue. Soon afterwards, however, Daly suddenly spotted Wharton from up close in the company of two other detectives strolling into Grafton Street from College Green. Fitting the precise descriptions provided, he was certain it was him. He pursued and shadowed the three as far as Harcourt Street, then made his way briskly the further half-mile to No. 3 Mount Pleasant Avenue – Leonard's address just yards from the Grand Canal near Portobello.

Ten minutes later both Daly and Leonard were quick-stepping back down Harcourt Street on their way back to Wexford Street to collect the pistol left earlier by Leonard, when they spotted Wharton, with three other detectives, approaching Cuffe Street to the left of the bottom of Harcourt Street. Still trying to avoid attention, Daly told Leonard it would be a pity to let such an opportunity pass.[34] Leonard, however, was hesitant, having no weapon, and the dump was only minutes away. Daly then reassured him, reminding him that one of the detectives would cover their retreat.

Daly's eyes became fixed on Wharton. They closed the distance. Then, just before the policemen reached Cuffe Street, and yards from the Sinn Féin headquarters, Daly stepped up behind Wharton. He then side-stepped into the roadway, pulling his Luger parabellum pistol from his coat-pocket. Quickly drawing back its toggle-bolt, he flicked off its safety, aimed and fired.

The crack that echoed out was quickly followed by a thud as Wharton collapsed to the pavement, shot through the back. The three detectives with him reacted instinctively, turning instantaneously to face the direction of the attack. Then, to his horror, as he pointed and pulled the trigger again to finish his prone victim, Daly's pistol jammed. He and Leonard were helpless. Desperately trying to unjam the gun, he saw one detective draw his pistol before stepping in front of the remaining two. This was the man they had been assured would cover them. His act covered the palpitating pair as they then sprinted into Cuffe Street to make their getaway. An ambulance was quickly summoned to the scene.

The following morning's newspapers expressed horror at the attack. Daly and Leonard were themselves shocked to learn from the same sources that a young female student, Gertrude O'Hanlon, had also been shot by the same nine-millimetre round that had felled Wharton when, having passed through the detective, it had badly grazed her scalp. To add to their consternation, Wharton, despite being critical, was still alive. The bullet had torn through his right shoulder blade before entering and exiting his right lung.[35] Nonetheless, his career as a detective was over.

Given that 11 November was Armistice Day, many of Dublin's streets were decked out again with Union flags and red, white and blue buntings, marking the first anniversary of the western front's guns falling silent. This occasion was also deemed opportune by the Dáil's publicity department, based in No. 22 Upper Mount Street, to release the first issue of *The Irish Bulletin*. This cyclo-styled gazette-type publication was to be typed up several times per week by twenty-one-year-old Kathleen McKenna under the oversight of twenty-six-year-old Frank Gallagher and thirty-eight-year-old Robert Brennan. It was under the overall authority of Desmond Fitzgerald. He had been given responsibility under his brief four days earlier by the Dáil with overcoming the 'paper wall' – spoken of derisively by Arthur Griffith – of press propaganda that had enveloped the assembly since the suppression of so many newspapers and journals on 20 September.

Fitzgerald's strategy was simple: portray the struggle as the defence of a lawfully elected government and supplant crown accounts of escalating events with candid, credible and unassailable reportage. Thirty copies of its first edition were to be circulated to journalists and others of influence both within and outside Ireland. Its reach did not remain so modest. Among its earliest allegations against the British government – that very day celebrating victory in a war to defend small nations – were some staggering statistics, claiming that between 1 May 1916 and 30 September 1919 it was responsible for: '58 murders, 2,076 deportations, 431 armed assaults on unarmed citizens, 5,859 raids on private houses etc., 1,998 sentences, 292 proclamations and suppressions, 51 newspapers suppressed, 524 courtmartials'.[36] However, Dublin Castle did not intend to take this lying down.

FORMATION OF THE 'SQUAD'

While the *Bulletin*'s authors celebrated its inaugural copy, Mick McDonnell was getting to grips with the prospect of the same Tuesday morning likely representing his last day alive. A sleepless night at the home he shared with Tom Keogh in Richmond Cottages, a quiet cul-de-sac near Summerhill, had seen him making his final arrangements and reflecting on his life, particularly its more recent years, while finding some consolation in the anticipation of his looming heroic status as a martyr.

Prepared for his imminent demise, and having prayed it might be mercifully quick, he reported to Dick McKee in 35 North Great George's Street, informing him of his readiness to carry out Lord French's assassination. McKee unburdened him; the mission had just been altered. Cathal Brugha had, similarly to the previous July, insisted the job was called off given the crowds expected. However, McKee then informed McDonnell that, according to more recent intelligence, the military parade was due to take place in Trinity College's Parliament Square, not College Green. McDonnell felt tremendous relief as McKee then added that, instead of his proposed one-man mission, French's cavalcade was to be attacked in greater numbers as it travelled through the streets towards the college. Plans were already in train. Soon afterwards McDonnell was fully briefed and dismissed in order to take his part. McKee then made his way to an appointment with Michael Collins in Harcourt Street.

Following the raid on No. 6 Harcourt Street in September the Dáil's Department of Finance had relocated to a new address roughly 200 yards further up the street on its opposite side: No. 76, a former dentist's. Batt O'Connor had purchased the four-storey building in July for £1,130.[37] O'Connor was a prosperous forty-nine-year-old builder with a particular skill in constructing secret compartments. A substantial one had just been built into No. 76 on its second floor. Another existed beneath the concrete floor of O'Connor's home, where significant amounts of National Loan funds, including some gold bullion, were concealed in boxes and in a baby's coffin.

Soon after McKee arrived at No. 76 and spoke with Collins in his ground floor drawing room, one of the department's secretaries, Dáithí O'Donoghue – a recently dismissed civil servant, owing to his refusal to take an oath of allegiance to the crown – stepped out of the building's front door, impeccably dressed and wearing a bowler hat, to make his way to the Sinn Féin bank with some papers. He observed a raid taking place on the Sinn Féin headquarters. Fearing an imminent similar assault on No. 76, he re-entered to warn the numerous others inside before rushing to the secret compartment upstairs to hide his documentation, as well as some ledgers he scrambled together in his first-floor office on the way. Others then rushed feverishly throughout the building with the same purpose. McKee, realising his own papers could see him hanged if captured, was among them. Lookouts hastened to the windows.

Soon afterwards, O'Donoghue ventured back outside and mingled with the curious crowd at No. 6 watching the raid. Their murmurings of the fracas being connected with the previous evening's shooting of Det. Wharton blended with the rattling of two truck engines. Such assumptions were incorrect, however; the police were simply desperate for whatever Dáil Loan documentation and intelligence they could get their hands on. Many papers were seized before the police and troops eventually withdrew from the building. Their lorries' four-cylinder engines whined as they whisked them and their passengers away in the direction of Stephen's Green where they turned right and out of sight.[38]

Then, pacing back towards No. 76 and conversing with other Sinn Féin and Dáil workers, O'Donoghue observed, to his sudden alarm, several more drab-green military trucks making towards him from the street's upper end, until they pulled up, screeching to a halt outside No. 76. His instincts had proven correct. O'Donoghue and his companions then had no choice but to keep walking as the building's front door was hammered on by detectives and soldiers, a full platoon of which stood on the street with bayonets fixed. He then turned around just before the train station and made his way back down the street's opposite side until he could mix discreetly with another recently gathered crowd of onlookers.

Meanwhile, inside No. 76, chaos had descended. Seán McCluskey, the caretaker of the Dáil offices and a member of the Dublin Brigade's 3rd Battalion, had rushed to the front door with Bob Conlon, the building's porter, to block access. This had bought precious moments for Michael Collins to rush up three floors to an open skylight and escape by ladder to the rooftop, jam-packed briefcase in hand. From there, pulling the ladder up after him, he quickly traversed the slippery peaks until he reached another permanently unlocked skylight above the Standard Hotel four doors away in No. 80.[39] It was precisely for such a purpose that it remained unsecured. Conlon and McCluskey had also bought time for many more sensitive documents in No. 76 to be safely stashed or burned.

FORMATION OF THE 'SQUAD'

After the front door had yielded to the torrent of rifle-butts and sledgehammer blows, one of the first to rush in was Insp. McFeely. However, when he came face to face with McCluskey, he quietly warned him to go downstairs to the basement, where he had living quarters, and remain there with his wife. McCluskey's wife was in bed lying with their newborn baby who, despite the commotion, was sleeping blissfully on top of a pile of paperwork concealed hurriedly by Eithne Lawless.[40] He moved downstairs to join them, pondering how the detective had known his wife was there. McFeely's allegiances appeared obscure.

His less conflicted colleagues then fanned out throughout the building, arresting and sifting through papers. Contrarily, however, Det. Const. David Neligan made his way to an upstairs room and, instead of apprehending victims, counted the roses on the wallpaper until the raid was over.[41] The twenty-year-old policeman from Limerick, a keen hurler with growing sympathies for those fighting for independence, had no interest in this business.

Meanwhile, Collins, panting, found himself in an unforeseen predicament; only now did he realise that the well of the Standard Hotel's staircase was situated directly beneath its skylight. He would need to hang precariously and swing his way onto a landing, avoiding a banister. If he miscalculated he faced a forty-foot drop to the ground floor and certain death. However, the startling sight of a khaki helmet emerging from the other skylight from which he had just escaped provided enough motivation to risk it. Hurling his briefcase successfully through to the landing, he quickly followed, hanging and swinging to gain momentum. Luckily, he slung himself successfully onto the landing, though he did sprain his ankle as he landed. Then, grabbing his briefcase, he dusted himself down while descending the staircase to the ground floor, whistling his way past the reception to the hotel's exit on Clonmel Street. Fortuitously for Collins, a tram arrived soon afterwards, which he managed to board, unseen.

Back across the road, Dáithí O'Donoghue noticed a large piece of paper being held up by Paddy Sheehan from a first-floor window in No. 76. In large ink it read: 'All hands arrested'. Soldiers then appeared on the rooftop. Minutes later, Joe O'Reilly, fusing with the growing crowd, tapped O'Donoghue on the shoulder and slipped a note between his fingers before he stole away. The note read: 'Follow them up, send in food, smokes, mattresses and blankets, M.C.'

O'Donoghue remained among the crowd as the prisoners were placed in the lorries. Shouts and taunts were hurled from the crowd at the military. Onlooking reporters who had been in the area drew comparisons with the German occupation of Belgium.[42] The prisoners included Dick McKee, Diarmuid O'Hegarty, Fintan Murphy – who had recently arrived from Manchester – and TDs Seán Hayes, Seán O'Mahony and Frank Lawless.

The secret compartment, concealed behind a mahogany wardrobe, was undetected. Notably, however, just as the raid was drawing to a close, a detective grabbed a handful of blank official Dáil paper, sensing that it could prove profitable in the future. It would, but in a most malevolent fashion.

Collins eventually made his way to Batt O'Connor's house. O'Reilly followed him soon afterwards.

Each of those arrested were subsequently sentenced to two months' imprisonment. O'Donoghue adhered to Collins' instruction: with the exception of bedding, the detainees were well supplied with food and cigarettes soon after their arrival in the bridewell police station's holding cells. O'Donoghue then returned to his home in Drumcondra. Collins returned to 76 Harcourt Street that evening and began transferring his office to nearby 5 Mespil Road, the home of one of his secretaries, Patricia Hoey, but not before his aide-de-camp O'Reilly had briefed him on something disconcerting that had struck him since the raid: the unexpected presence at the front door of No. 76 half-an-hour before it occurred of twenty-four-year-old Timothy Quinlisk – a man O'Reilly rightly looked upon with suspicion.[43] Collins also transferred some of his office to 22 Henry Street.

Quinlisk, from Wexford, had been a corporal in the Royal Irish Regiment. Captured by the Germans early in the Great War he had then joined Roger Casement's Irish Brigade. Returning to Ireland after the war, he had been denied his soldier's back pay from his time as a prisoner. Recognising that this was due to his joining the Irish Brigade, Collins had helped him out financially, frequently sharing the same address in 44 Mountjoy Street while he groomed him as a Volunteer training officer. However, Quinlisk – tall, cultivated, well built and with ashen features – was vain, arrogant, cavalier and outspoken. He did not fit the bill of a training officer. He was subsequently marginalised. Disgruntled and seeking revenge, he had written a letter to the under secretary offering to tell him everything he knew about Sinn Féin. The letter was presented on the same day as the raid.

FORMATION OF THE 'SQUAD'

Meanwhile, Sinn Féin's headquarters in 6 Harcourt Street suffered yet another attack from loyalists that night. Once again, the building was badly vandalised, but the attackers were eventually fended off.

While 6 Harcourt Street was assaulted, Trinity College, draped throughout in Union flags, was a hive of activity. Invited guests, both civilian and military, resplendent in their finest formal attire and full-dress uniforms, began arriving for the Armistice Day banquet. Under the eyes of rooftop snipers, soldiers paraded and patrolled the 300-year-old college to the barks of NCOs. Officers gathered in clusters, awaiting the arrival of Field Marshal French. However, the British military were not alone in preparing a reception for the lord lieutenant; IRA GHQ had received further intelligence of the hour he was expected to travel the two-mile length of the quays from the vice-regal lodge to the college, as well as the bridge his car would most likely cross *en route*. Nothing was left to chance. IRA sections were posted on the southern side of each of the Liffey's bridges where they hid in plain sight with lookouts on the opposite sides ready to signal them at the first sight of French's entourage.

Grattan Bridge, straddling the Liffey halfway between Sackville Street and the Four Courts, was anticipated as French's most likely crossing point. Awaiting their opportunity to strike between the bridge's ornate lanterns and balustrades were Dan Breen, Seán Treacy and Seán Hogan, the former two armed with pistols and Hogan carrying a hand-grenade in each hand. The night was frosty.

At the time French was expected, Hogan, pacing backwards and forwards, removed the pins from both grenades and clutched their striker levers tightly to prevent them exploding in his hands. He then stood ready to throw them while Breen and Treacy, both spread well apart, scanned the quays, imminently expecting French. They waited fruitlessly then as, time after time, the first sight of the headlamps of approaching east-bound vehicles grated on their nerves. This eventually dragged on for two hours until a runner arrived with the vexing news that their target had already reached Trinity College. The wily cavalryman had deviated from his planned route. It was a tactic he employed with increasing expertise to upset any potential plot.[44]

More vexing for Hogan, however, was the fact that he had long since discarded the pins for his grenades, having carelessly not foreseen the need to replace them. Raw with cold, he then paced through the crowded streets, thronged with revellers, cursing profusely and clutching the bombs tightly until he reached an arms dump. There, he secured replacement pins from exasperated IRA comrades to deactivate them.

French had outfoxed his pursuers, for now; nonetheless, they were closing in.

8

G-DIVISION UNDER PRESSURE

'One is enough to be gone'

As the November days shortened, the hunt for Lord French escalated. On one occasion when he attended a function in Trinity College, Paddy Daly's unit attempted again to kill him. An ambush was laid, this time with the assistance of several Dáil members – including Piaras Béaslaí, J.J. Walsh, Diarmuid O'Hegarty and the Cork Number 1 Brigade commandant, Tomás MacCurtain. The TDs, knowing Collins was short of men, had stepped in. They would attack his entourage with pistols and bombs as it departed the college, driving them in the west-bound direction of Parliament Street where Daly's men would lurk, similarly armed. French, however, again outfoxed them by unexpectedly driving out of the college through its Lincoln Place exit on its eastern side and taking an alternative route back to the vice-regal lodge.

Another ambush was laid in November on the quays close to the Four Courts. French, however, changed his plans yet again at the last minute and frustrated the plot. MacCurtain was involved in another attempted attack, planned for 5 a.m. one late November morning, along with, among others, Michael Collins and the 'Big-Four': Robinson, Treacy, Breen and Hogan. Yet again they suffered disappointment; they had planned to intercept him in the city centre on his way from Kingstown (Dún Laoghaire), having apparently disembarked there while returning from London. However, their intelligence was wrong. French was in Roscommon at the time.

Meanwhile, pressure mounted on the police. Six months into the boycott – since broadened to encompass the DMP – the effective application of their work had become all but impossible. With losses mounting – more than one in ten members had left since the boycott through resignations that, to aggravate, were most prevalent among younger, more spirited members – and rural and urban garrisons being either evacuated or fortified in increasing numbers countrywide, on 11 November an order was prepared from Insp. Gen. Byrne's office to recruit non-Irishmen into the force. This further paved the way for the recruitment of ex-military. Additionally, revolvers, semi-automatic pistols and hand grenades were also being stockpiled as they strove to re-set the balance. Meanwhile, Byrne's deputy, Thomas Smith, was superseding his own authority as deputy as Byrne continued to fall from French's favour. French considered him far too diffident for his position. He favoured Smith – an Ulster man – seeing him as far more offensive minded.

Three days later – not to be overlooked – Chief Commissioner Edgeworth-Johnstone, following French's September overtures, whipped up the issue of the looming crisis within DMP's political section of G-Division to the Westminster cabinet. He emphasised that, given its comparatively small size, it was being hit disproportionately hard.[1] Nevertheless, the DMP commissioner shared Byrne's grave misgivings with the idea of ex-military police reinforcements.

Counterbalancing these developments, Dick McKee's deputy, Michael Lynch, was also exerting his influence in the brigadier's prison absence. The Dublin IRA battalions and companies drilled and exercised rigorously, as did their younger counterparts in the Fianna and their female Cumann na mBan auxiliaries. Arms and ammunition procurement remained a priority, as did discipline; many IRA members, frustrated at the singular strategic targeting of the police, were itching to also attack the military. This problem was even worse outside the capital, where Volunteers sought to compensate for their lack of action in 1916. City and rural operatives were reassured that the time would come. Simultaneously, McKee was making typically profitable use of his detention in Mountjoy, despite continuing protests and strains. He lectured his fellow inmates daily during lengthy periods of free association on issues such as sniping tactics and leadership strategies.

The intelligence branch McKee had helped initiate had by now broadened. Each IRA company was ordered to employ its own intelligence officer. His orders would be to report to a battalion counterpart, generally a quartermaster, who, in turn, would report to his brigade intelligence officer. While perfecting this at brigade level took considerable time to accomplish effectively, intelligence officers at street level quickly became attuned to recognising the significance of the most seemingly trivial morsels of information.

At the same time, republican arbitration courts were springing up, bolstered by impeccably trustworthy courier and mail networks – the latter operating from an array of shops and clearing houses while employing ingenious concealment systems – that were beginning to grease the wheels of the entire revolutionary organisation, with a central communications centre known as 'the Dump' as their hub.[2] The courts' lack of pomp, grandeur and obscure legal terminology compared to those of the crown was an added positive to those before them, reluctantly or otherwise.

These profitable developments for the revolutionaries were, meanwhile, being slowly bolstered by the redoubtable labours of the local government ministry. Clearly, usurping the British-run municipal apparatus necessitated delivering an effective replacement. Recently married William Cosgrave – employing his ten-year pre-revolutionary experience as a member of Dublin Corporation – and his indefatigable twenty-seven-year-old assistant Kevin O'Higgins, were, together, despite very limited means, beginning to lay the foundations for an eventual series of contrivances that would stifle the influence of their crown counterparts.

These developments were set against the countrywide banning by Dublin Castle on 26 November of Sinn Féin, the Irish Volunteers, Cumann na mBan, and the Gaelic League.[3] Banning the Gaelic League in particular presented a bounty to the Dáil's publicity department, allowing it to capitalise on the conflict's portrayal as not just political, but a struggle for cultural survival.

***

Unfortunately for the DMP, it was about to suffer another calamitous blow. In late November Michael Collins received intelligence that Det. Sgt Johnny Barton had recently transferred from B to G-Division and was investigating his colleague Det. Wharton's shooting. Following the attempted assassination, Barton, a thirty-nine-year-old from Co. Kerry, had arrested a newspaper vendor and former soldier, James Hurley, who operated from a stand in Cuffe Street, on foot of a witness statement from British Army Capt. William Bachelor. The statement erroneously asserted that Hurley had fired the wounding shot.[4]

Barton, a policeman for sixteen years, was a formidable and recently decorated detective with an impressive track record in criminal investigations with the DMP. He also had a vast web of informers throughout the city. His recent reassignment sent out a marker that he was undaunted by republicans, and would employ his pervasive network of touts to undermine the IRA. This made him a serious problem as far as Brugha, Collins and Mulcahy were concerned. It was soon agreed that he would have to be shot.

Barton had previous form with the Volunteers: along with his late colleague Det. Hoey, he had unrelentingly goaded the surrendered 1916 prisoners in Richmond barracks. In addition to cruelly mocking Joseph Connolly over the death of his brother, he had singled out Seán MacDermott from a line-up and laughingly heralded that there would be 'six for him in the morning' – referring to bullets.[5] His prediction regarding MacDermott's fate transpired to be broadly accurate. These two episodes were part of a long list of transgressions that meant there would be little remorse felt among those responsible for executing the fate soon to befall him.

Orders were quickly dispatched from GHQ to Mick McDonnell: neutralise Barton. Wasting no time, McDonnell relayed his orders to Paddy Daly: gather his squad – Joe Leonard and Ben Barrett – find Barton and eliminate him. Orders were also sent out to Jim Slattery and Tom Keogh to report at once to McDonnell; two units would simultaneously hunt the detective.

Then, on the cold and damp evening of Friday 28 November, Vincent 'Vinny' Byrne, nineteen years old, was summoned to McDonnell's two-storey dwelling adjacent to the Royal Canal. Keogh and Slattery – the latter a work colleague of Byrne's – were already there. McDonnell wanted two separate pairs of assassins to work within his own unit. Tom Ennis was unavailable, and Byrne, whom he trusted, seemed the perfect fit to take up the fourth place. He had acted as a courier on numerous occasions for the quartermaster, carrying pistols, rifles, ammunition and various messages from time to time.

Byrne was only fifteen-years-old when he had taken part in the Rising as a member of the 2nd Battalion and had been positioned in Jacob's biscuit factory. The youngster had made himself sick gorging on a sack of chocolate biscuits on Easter Monday, to the amusement of McDonnell and others at the time. He had seen the effects of gunfire close up both at the factory and afterwards when, escaping, he had narrowly avoided capture when a rebel sniper shot a soldier attempting to apprehend him. Arrested soon afterwards, he had enjoyed the unexpected pleasure of a steak dinner provided by an army sergeant before his brief incarceration in Richmond barracks. The sergeant had been amused by Byrne's youthful commitment to his cause; Byrne had professed, when asked, to being willing to shoot him without hesitation if necessary. Three-and-a-half years later, McDonnell, sitting at his fireside, had a similar question, albeit with far more purpose. Testing the water, he asked him, 'Would you shoot a man, Byrne?' Byrne replied that it would depend on whom he had in mind. 'What about Johnnie [*sic*] Barton?' asked McDonnell. Slattery and Keogh looked on as he replied: 'Oh, I wouldn't mind,' as it turned out that he had raided his house.[6] McDonnell, satisfied, then asserted: 'That settles it. You may have a chance'. Byrne nodded. They then arranged to meet at College Green the following day at 5.30 p.m.

Slattery and Byrne were both employed as cabinet makers in the 'Irish Woodworkers' unit based at 3 Crow Street, situated just off Dame Street, a short stroll from Dublin Castle. Both carried out their duties as normal during the following morning until lunchtime when Slattery, having by now been fully briefed ahead of Byrne, muttered to him: 'You had better bring in your gun after dinner'.[7] Byrne's one-sided smile in response betrayed no apprehension.

That evening, Byrne and Slattery, their hands gripping .45 revolvers in their coat pockets, met with Keogh and McDonnell in College Green as planned. They exchanged forced pleasantries under the glowing street lamps, lit cigarettes and blended with the passing pedestrians. During their discourse McDonnell eventually ordered Slattery and Byrne to proceed to Grafton Street to see if they could pick up Barton, while he and Keogh would search him out on College Green's cobbled open expanse. Barton was known to patrol both areas.

Their wait was short. Within minutes of setting off, Byrne turned suddenly to Slattery, uttering sharply: 'There he is on the far side of the street'.[8] He was sure that he had just spotted Barton close to Grafton Street's Nassau Street junction. The detective stood out from the evening crowds at over six-foot-four but with a stoop. A closer look at the clean-shaven officer's distinctively styled attire, particularly his large heavy-looking boots and prominently sharp facial features confirmed that it was him. Barton then strolled up Grafton Street, keeping to the left, while his stalkers followed discreetly behind on the street's opposite side. Every so often Barton stopped and peered into a shop window that contained a mirror and used it to covertly scan the street.

At one-point Slattery and Byrne, nervously observing this, became convinced he was staring directly at them, mocking them.

They remained in pursuit until, fifteen tense minutes later, Barton paused at a bookshop at the very top of the street. Both men kept walking, doing their best to keep the detective in sight without drawing suspicion. They then resumed their shadowing as Barton turned back down Grafton Street on its opposite side, carrying out the same actions as he had done on the way up the street.[9]

Frustratingly, they lost sight of him as they approached Trinity College. Fearing they had lost him, they carried on towards College Green, hoping to catch sight of him there, when Byrne, glancing behind one last time, spotted him exiting a hallway on Nassau Street, then crossing the street, skirting the college railings and walking briskly in their direction. Anticipating that the detective was making his way to Brunswick Street, they quickly made contact with McDonnell and Keogh, who were conveniently nearby. The four men, seeing that Barton had passed them at this stage and entered College Street, rushed to intercept. Then, Byrne, to his surprise, spotted Paddy Daly, Joe Leonard and Ben Barrett on the northern side of College Street.

McDonnell, Keogh, Slattery and Byrne, with no time to act on their comrades' unanticipated arrival, moved in on Barton. Working in their pairs they quickly closed the distance, their hearts pounding. They dashed through the numerous pedestrians, trying desperately to move in for the kill only to find their target blocked time and time again by small groups or individuals blissfully oblivious to their intentions. Time was running out.

Paddy Daly and his men also began to close the distance on Barton, having spotted him. Then, as Barton reached the convergence of D'Olier, Poolbeg, College, Townsend and Brunswick streets at the Crampton Monument he stepped onto the road, yards from the police station. McDonnell's section, now much closer, sprung to action first, opening fire.

Several shots rang out. Daly, Leonard and Barrett stopped in their tracks, unaware who was shooting; they had not yet noticed the others. Barton collapsed to the cobblestones as terrified civilians gasped and screamed. Some froze while others fled. Motorists passing nearby either sped away or hit their brakes to maintain distance, their drivers and passengers gaping. Startled carriage horses tried to bolt.

Barton fell on his right-hand side, shot in the back at such close range that there were powder burns on his overcoat.[10] One shot had torn through his lung and exited his chest. He tried desperately to raise himself up, gurgling and crying out of his bloody mouth: 'Oh, God, what did I do to deserve this?'[11] He then, summoning his draining strength, drew his revolver and fired two shots towards Byrne and McDonnell who were sprinting towards Westmoreland Street, before crumpling helplessly.

More civilians screamed, stunned by the abrasive pistol cracks. Byrne and McDonnell jolted as they heard them. Then, just as they neared the corner with Westmoreland Street a uniformed policeman stepped out in front and went to grab them. Byrne drew his gun and roared 'Move!' The policeman, unsteady with sudden panic, side-stepped before summoning colleagues with his whistle. Keogh and Slattery, meanwhile, made their escape in a different direction, as too did Daly, Leonard and Barrett. Policemen rushing from the station quickly surrounded Barton; then, like Hoey and Downing before him, he was driven to Mercer hospital. There, having received the last rites, he died fifteen minutes after arriving.

***

The news of Barton's killing sent shockwaves throughout the DMP. He may have been unafraid of the IRA, but this did not save him from its ubiquitous tentacles, or its increasingly resolute gunmen. Once again the horrified press expressed contempt the following day for his assassins and those associated with them. Their incessant wrath towards the revolutionaries was not going unnoticed by rank and file Volunteers who grew more impatient with every headline protesting not just killings, but also the steady disintegration of day-to-day government as the ripple effects from the conflict of which they formed the vanguard seeped unrelentingly into the machinations of day-to-day life. Barton was buried in Kerry.

Lord French was all too aware of republican infiltration, as well as the increasing grip by Sinn Féin on Ireland's wider population. Worse: the citadel of crown rule – Dublin Castle – was correctly considered to be a nest of enemy sympathisers, and, no doubt, spies. As far as the viscount was concerned, it was high-time to unshackle his sphere of control from perceived handicaps, such as his wavering RIC inspector general. Byrne, on the other hand, remained at odds: convinced that the only truly realistic solution was to find accommodation with Sinn Féin. He persisted in his fierce opposition to martial law, extolling repetitively in the corridors of power as a means of coercing his compatriots. Thomas Smith, meanwhile, skulked in the wings, waiting for the opportunity he knew would soon come along with his colleague's further marginalisation.

The disarray threatening G-Division was exacerbated by the fact that the assassination of each detective not only cost the unit the man himself, his knowledge and experience, but it also meant the loss of his touts. Barton's extensive network was a striking example. Now his particular channel, like those preceding it, was permanently dammed. If the trend continued, the result would be a complete intelligence drought.

A select committee was swiftly formed in response to advise French on intelligence matters. It consisted of: Assistant Under Secretary Sir John Taylor, Dep. Insp. Smith, and Res. Magist. Alan Bell. Sixty-two-year-old Bell was the brother of James Bell, the Gloucester Prison doctor who had warned the government in March about the dangers of Spanish Flu to the German Plot internees. Alan worked in more shady areas, under the direct control of Sir Basil Thompson, also acting as the home office's intelligence director at New Scotland Yard, as well as maintaining his assistant commissioner rank. Thompson had already selected agents to infiltrate Sinn Féin and the IRA; these were put under Bell's control.

The committee's formation was quickly succeeded by the arrival in Dublin of the first of Bell's agents, John Charles 'Jack' Byrnes, an ex sergeant-major in the Royal Field Artillery who operated under the alias of 'John Jameson'. This thirty-four-year-old, stout and heavily tattooed Londoner had, in recent months, infiltrated the burgeoning socialist circles in Britain, gathering regularly at Speakers' Corner in Hyde Park alongside other agitators such as the Irish Self-Determination League (ISDL). He had also infiltrated the Gaelic League in London, formerly acting for army intelligence, posing as a Marxist sympathiser. He had even gone as far as having himself thrown out of his local ex-servicemen's association for revolutionary agitation.

He made contact with various Sinn Féin contacts that were moving within similar spheres, including recently dismissed RIC firebrand, Sgt Thomas (T.J) McElligott. Collins had also become intrigued by reports relating to him. Byrnes, whose grandparents came from Co. Wexford, was impressive enough to attain a letter of introduction to the IRA from Arthur (Art) O'Brien, the Dáil's forty-seven-year-old envoy to Britain. With the letter of introduction in hand, 'Jameson', operating under the remit of Civil Intelligence, set off for Dublin and surreptitiously established himself in the city as a jewellery salesman. He was well established by the time the select committee deemed, on 7 December, that an organised conspiracy of murder, outrage and intimidation existed and that Dublin city was the storm centre and the mainspring of it all.[12] Their solution was simple and ruthless: infiltrate the movement with spies and, when opportune, assassinate selected leaders.

One such spy, Quinlisk, had been interviewed at G-Division HQ on 12 November. This was the day after he had written to the under secretary before turning up suspiciously outside 76 Harcourt Street shortly before the massive raid. Luckily for Michael Collins, Ned Broy had been able to get word straight to him of Quinlisk's visit to G-Division. However, Quinlisk, aware of Collins' pervasiveness, had approached Collins immediately afterwards asserting to have been in the police station simply to secure a passport to travel to the USA.

Collins, dismissing this given that Broy had typed up Quinlisk's statement, but feigning otherwise, saw a rare opportunity to arrange a trap for a burgeoning nemesis – Super. Brien: knowing that Brien would have been informed about Quinlisk, he arranged for twenty-eight-year-old Tom Cullen to telephone Dublin Castle, pretending to be him, and asking for a meeting with Brien at a premises in Eccles Street, promising to have valuable information on Collins.

Super. Brien, falling for the ruse, expressed a preference for Parliament Street instead given its closer proximity to Dublin Castle, and accordingly, arranged a meeting outside the *Mail* and *Express* building. Then, on the day itself, both special duties units stood ready to pounce on their target – a thorn in the side of the IRB and Volunteers for several years. A decoy was sent to Parliament Street posing as Quinlisk to draw Brien into the street, trapping him.[13] The superintendent, however, sensing something was not right on the day – the street was uncharacteristically deserted – had trusted his instincts and retreated to the Castle from where he rarely ventured out. Meanwhile, Quinlisk, caught in a mire of duplicity and misinformation, and sensing the walls were closing in, quickly provided Dublin Castle with Collins' address at the Munster Hotel. Officers, under the command of Det. Insp. John Bruton, raided it the same night. Collins, however, again a step ahead, had watched the raid from across the street in No.

30, the residence of his twenty-three-year-old sweetheart, Madeleine ('Dilly') Dicker.[14] Quinlisk was right to be afraid; fate was indeed circling.

***

Three days after the convening of the intelligence select committee, on 10 December, French played his final card against Insp. Byrne, dispatching him on a month's leave for 'health reasons'. He then copper-fastened his antagonism towards him by asserting to Ian Macpherson that Byrne's discharge – by whatever means – was a resignation issue for himself if not realised. Byrne, however, would not go quietly. Before taking up the role of inspector general, he had insisted on being made a permanent civil servant. This eventually saw him off on the first of a series of comfortable colonial governorships.[15] French wasted no time officially appointing Smith as acting inspector general of the RIC. Accordingly, the recruitment of police from outside Ireland could soon begin.

The select committee's decision to assassinate certain preferred IRA leaders was not an unrequited sentiment. GHQ simultaneously decided to step up the hunt for the lord lieutenant. He was to be dealt with at all costs. His shooting would not only remove a formidable and dangerous adversary; it would also make the entire civilised world sit up and take notice of Ireland's situation. Collins passed the order to McDonnell, who promptly took to the task.

On Wednesday 10 December McDonnell received pressing intelligence from Tom Ennis: 2nd Battalion Volunteer Paddy Sharkey had been told by his father, a guard on specially designated trains, that such a train would take Lord French to Roscommon that very night. It would depart Broadstone at 11 p.m. and collect French and his party soon afterwards at Ashtown station, the closest to the vice-regal lodge.

McDonnell quickly mustered thirty men. Their number encompassed most of the Special Duties Units, the 'Big Four', as well as Peadar Clancy. Fortunately for them the cold night was dry as they had to cycle from their initial gathering point in 46 Rutland Square. No taxis were available due to a strike over driver permits, a measure instigated by the authorities to curtail the availability of motorised transport to the revolutionaries.

When they eventually arrived, they took up positions in silence among the cluster of buildings surrounding Kelly's public house at Ashtown crossroads. They then spread out and trained their sights on the Phoenix Park's Ashtown gate. Lit up by gas lamps and only wide enough for a single car to pass, their target would be a sitting duck as he passed through. Even if his transport made it through, it would have to run a further gauntlet of fire.

However, frustratingly, French yet again slipped through their fingers. Following hours of waiting in the biting cold, the job was abandoned. With no sign of him at this point something had obviously gone wrong. The dejected, weary and hungry Volunteers cycled back to the city, which was to their relief mostly downhill. Most contemplated a tough day's work ahead following their sleepless night. McDonnell discovered later the following evening from an informant that French had hosted a party, but had then become too drunk to travel. His train had waited under steam at Broadstone all night when word had failed to reach the station of the unforeseen change of circumstances.

Soon afterwards, Joe Leonard carried out a reconnaissance, accompanied by twenty-two-year-old 1916 veteran Robert Holland, within the Phoenix Park itself. The objective was to assess the feasibility of training a Lewis gun on the vice-regal lodge, then to lie in wait for French to appear as he left for his next scheduled engagement. However, the lack of any cover from which to launch such an attack scuppered the proposition.

Mick McDonnell, meanwhile, did not have to wait long for the next attempt on the charmed viceroy's life. At 9 p.m. on 18 December Vinny Byrne was chatting with Sharkey by the fireside of the Seán Connolly Sinn Féin club in North Summer Street, when Sharkey stood up abruptly and said he had to leave.[16] When Byrne asked what his sudden hurry was, joking that he must have a nice date, Sharkey explained that he had to prepare his father's luncheon basket; his rail guard father was scheduled to leave early the following morning for Roscommon in order to: 'bring ould French back to Dublin'.[17] Pouncing on such valuable intelligence, Byrne asked him what time the train would be back in the city the next day: the answer was around lunchtime.

McDonnell's house was just minutes away on the opposite side of the North Circular Road. Byrne made his way straight there. McDonnell smiled at Byrne's word of French's imminent arrival, saying: 'That's the best bit of news I've heard for a long time'.[18] Confident that Sharkey's information was reliable – it was merely French's uncanny luck that had scuppered their most recent plan – he ordered Byrne to return the next morning at 10 a.m. when they would, again, 'have a go' at him.

McDonnell then set about planning the attack. With the short notice, his first priority was getting the necessary men, particularly as French was due to arrive during working hours. Paddy Daly's squad were available full-time, and his own unit were a sure bet, but this would not be enough. He then remembered that Seán Treacy had recently assured him that he could call on himself, Robinson, Breen and Hogan at any time. A dozen men, he felt, should tip the balance in their favour.

He then made a series of phone calls, the first of which was to Tom Ennis. He was to find out from Sharkey as early as possible the following morning if French's train had left Broadstone on schedule and inform him immediately. A subsequent call was made to Mick Fleming's house in Drumcondra where Dan Breen received the message: they would be needed again in the morning. Breen immediately informed Treacy and, an hour later, Robinson. He was staying at a safe house, 71 Heytesbury Street on the city's south-side. Robinson was frustrated at the series of farcical failures thus far. When told of the pending action he protested to Breen that he was 'not taking part in any more of these Dublin exploits'.[19] Nonetheless, the pair eventually convinced him to see sense. Hogan was also informed.

The next morning those selected for the job – nine in all, excluding Byrne, McDonnell and Keogh – gathered at initial muster points, then cycled to McDonnell's house. Their bicycles were discreetly placed against the kerbs for the length of the street to avoid drawing attention. When Joe Leonard arrived unexpectedly with Martin Savage – not a unit member – Paddy Daly, momentarily aghast, asked why he was there. Savage interjected, insisting that he was coming on the job. Daly cut him off: 'You should not have known where we are going'.[20] Savage, assistant quartermaster for the 2nd Battalion, was a trusted and respected comrade; nevertheless, it drove home the point that their unit's security was porous. Savage insisted. Daly relented. They needed men. He was in. It was a fateful decision that would, inadvertently, within hours, bring the entire Dublin Brigade to the brink of catastrophe.

Vinny Byrne, on foot, was the last to arrive at the house at the prearranged time of 10 a.m. He had barely stepped inside when McDonnell ordered him to go to their arms dump – a converted stable within which he kept his motorcycle sidecar combination in nearby North Great Charles Street – to fetch some grenades.[21] He set off, returning soon afterwards to see McDonnell issuing pistols and ammunition where needed, while detailing specific orders to the men assembled. Once given the word to go, they were to make their way in twos and threes, cycling to their rendezvous at the scene of their most recent failed attempt – Ashtown Cross. Kelly's public house, the small thatch-roofed establishment also known also as 'the Half-Way House' would be their initial marshalling point. It sat on the junction of the Navan road, which ran north-west of it, and two others: Ashtown Gate Road which lay to its south-west, and Ashtown Road, a byroad running to its north. Here they would have an unobstructed view to the Phoenix Park's Ashtown Gate, 250 yards south-west, and the station itself, 300 yards north on the byroad.

When the telephone suddenly rang, McDonnell answered. Through the brass earpiece he heard Tom Ennis relay the news of French's train's departure from Broadstone to collect him in Roscommon: 'That left this morning alright'.[22] Byrne distributed the grenades – some home-made and some British Army Mills bombs – from a satchel. Having not taken part in the most recent attempt, he was then briefly introduced to Hogan, Breen, Robinson and Treacy, before being handed back a grenade, some ammunition, and told to get a bicycle from out the back and get a move on. It was approaching 11 a.m.

In their small groupings, the thirteen men cycled as fast as they could without drawing attention along the North Circular, Cabra and Navan roads. Forty-five minutes later, McDonnell, Treacy and Daly took stock of Ashtown's surrounding topography. Ben Barrett was ordered ahead to the station. His job was to discreetly signal which car French was in once he arrived. The rest ambled into the pub, its entrance facing the Navan road on its eastern side, and ordered drinks. Some ordered minerals while others ordered beer, sherry or port. They passed the time smoking, discussing agriculture, handball – the pub had a handball alley out the back. They discussed anything banal that came to mind, such as horse-racing, to draw off suspicion, while also exchanging casual pleasantries with a few local labourers and farmers. They struggled to suppress their nerves while McDonnell stepped stealthily out the back to get a better view of the station.

Once outside McDonnell's eyes fell upon a large farm-cart standing on its heels.[23] He thought fast: this could be improvised to block the road. Re-entering, he adapted and quietly issued the final orders: Daly, Treacy, Robinson, Hogan and Leonard, would take up dispersed positions towards the train station, concealed along the hedgerow's length just above the Ashtown Road on its eastern side. From this vantage point they were to concentrate their flanking fire on the second car, as it was standard procedure for the lord lieutenant to travel in the second car of a convoy. Breen, Tom Keogh, and Savage would push the farm cart by its shafts out from the yard onto the road at the last minute and block off the crossroads between the first and second cars, trapping the second one under the withering hail of fire they would subsequently unleash. McDonnell, Byrne, Jim Slattery and Seán Doyle would take up positions around the crossroads itself and open fire with the others.

Soon afterwards, Byrne finished his drink, then set off pedalling towards the station to monitor developments. Suddenly, he heard vehicles approaching from behind. A horn sounded, so he stopped to let them pass. A motorcycle and four cars containing military personnel sped past him down the hill towards the station. Byrne, palpitating, turned around and rushed back to alert McDonnell.

When he did the special force quietened. Seán Treacy kept checking his watch. Waiting anxiously in the pub for the signal to go they then heard the whistle of the approaching train's engine as it steamed into Ashtown.[24] This was followed by tense silence; the tick of the pub's clock indicating the approach of lunch-hour was the only sound. Then, McDonnell quietly gave the word to go.

Daly, followed by his own section, stepped calmly out the back into the field and took up defilade positions. They hugged the hedgerow as they made their way along it, Daly was nearest the station so he could see Barrett's signal from there when the time came.

The signal was soon given: Barrett rubbed his nose with a handkerchief in his right hand, indicating by his choice of hand that French was, as expected, in the second car. Breen, Savage and Keogh made for the cart once signalled in turn by McDonnell, while the remaining men stepped briskly to their positions in a ditch near the crossroads.

Things then started to go wrong. Breen, Savage and Keogh found the cart difficult to move due to its weight. They were pulling it by its shafts instead of pushing it. Seeing this, McDonnell cursed them for disregarding his earlier instructions to do otherwise. When they eventually got it out onto the road they were then confronted unexpectedly by a recently arrived policeman, Const. McLoughlin of the DMP, standing conspicuously tall and polished on point duty in the centre of the crossroads, awaiting French's arrival. Assuming they were farm-hands, he shouted at them, approaching their position while pointing north towards the station: 'You cannot go down there for a while. His Excellency is to pass along here in a few seconds!'[25] The cart then got trapped in a dip next to the road while Breen started arguing with the policeman, playing dumb to avoid triggering his suspicions.

The sudden whinings and throbbings of approaching vehicles from the station coincided with the unfortunate policeman getting struck in the head by a grenade, hurled from nearby, momentarily stunning him. Disorientated, he then staggered away through the crossroads towards Phoenix Park while Breen and his two comrades, cursing the thrower's apparent recklessness, flung themselves to the ground unaware that the pin had purposely been left in the bomb to prevent detonation. Just then a police motorcycle outrider thudded by. Seconds later the first of the four-car convoy reached the ambush point.

Daly and his unit behind the hedge to the east of the byroad sprung to action. Daly noticed the flash of uniforms in the dark blue first car as it passed, then, he and Hogan let fly with their grenades at the khaki coloured second car. Simultaneously Robinson, nearby, flung a bomb at the rear of the first car. Its driver reacted instantly to the ambush and pressed down his accelerator. The air suddenly crackled with small arms fire, shattering glass and resonating thuds of exploding grenades, one from inside the second car, whose windows blew out with the blast.

Vinny Byrne, on the crossroads, primed himself as the first car sped towards him. Det. Sgt Halley – who had driven off the raid on his home the previous April – shot his pistol from the same car's front passenger window, but his aim was inaccurate; his right hand had just been badly wounded. Breen and his two comrades, using the cart as cover, returned fire. Byrne then saw his opportunity as the same car slowed to navigate around the partially protruding cart. He threw his grenade with all the force he could muster as it accelerated away again. It hit the car's rear, bounced off, and exploded, causing no damage. Const. McLoughlin, returning to the scene from the same direction, having since gathered himself, was blown across the road by the blast. The car raced on and made the Phoenix Park, passing the motorcycle outrider who had just turned around to investigate the grenade blasts and shot reports. The outrider then turned again and followed the car through the park gates.

The second car, believed to contain French, had come to a complete standstill on the ambush side of the crossroads, forcing the next one, which had a canvas roof, to swerve around it with guns blazing from its terrified occupants. There hardly seemed to be room for two vehicles to pass on the roadway but its driver made it. Breen, Savage and Keogh, reloading when necessary, poured fire mercilessly at the stranded car. Rounds pinged as they struck its metalwork.

Back behind the hedgerow on the byroad Daly, pistol in hand, heard Hogan roar suddenly 'Look out!' Hogan had accidentally dropped a grenade between the two of them having pulled its pin to throw it. Both men hurled themselves to the clay, which soon covered them from the ensuing explosion. Both were unharmed. Hogan grinned at Daly, shouting: 'That was a near miss!'[26] Daly, half-deafened from the blast, was momentarily furious, until the comic aspect also struck him in the surrounding bedlam.

Their attentions were quickly drawn back to the task at hand just as the last car, a large open-top Sunbeam, sped up the hill from the station, passing them towards the crossroads and desperately manoeuvring around the stalled second car. They sprinted after it from behind the hedgerow, their three comrades joining them. Its driver dodged this way and that, at one point ramming the second car from its way. Sgt George Rumble, a seasoned British Army sharpshooter, his sergeant chevrons visible, was positioned prone across the back of the car, firing from a rifle.[27] His legs were wedged in a supporting position. His right hand worked feverishly, almost gracefully, on the bolt and trigger, his .303 calibre Lee Enfield making distinctive repeating cracks among the still resounding pistol shots as the sergeant zeroed in every couple of seconds.

Moments later, Dan Breen felt a sudden sharp pinch in his left leg as the Sunbeam's driver took his turn to manoeuvre around the stalled car, then the farm-cart, and accelerate again through and beyond the crossroads. Vinny Byrne heard the whisps of flying rounds and the ricochets from Sgt Rumble's rapid fire smashing into the nearby pub wall. Then, just before it too slowed to approach the park gate, another brief fusillade sent several more three-ounce bullets at twice the speed of sound in Breen's direction, one of which shot the hat off his head and grazed his scalp. As the car disappeared from sight he then heard Savage behind him sputtering: 'Oh, lads, I am hit!'[28]

Breen turned instinctively. Savage collapsed into his arms. Breen, quickly becoming covered in his blood, lay him down on the roadside. Savage had been shot in the jaw and neck but his lips still moved and quivered. Blood streamed, spurted and gushed profusely from his gaping wound. Breen put his ear close to his lacerated, broken, and greying face, and heard him straining to say: 'I am done, Dan. Carry on'.²⁹ Within moments, the twenty-two-year-old bled to death.

By now the firing had stopped. Daly and his section arrived at the crossroads and saw what had just happened. Breen sat on a crate, dazed and holding his own head. Daly noticed blood oozing from Breen's wounded leg. Breen had been shot, but luckily, the bullet had passed clean through. Breen, pumping with adrenalin like the others, had barely noticed it other than the brief but nonetheless now-familiar sting he had initially felt. The

Martin Savage, assistant quartermaster of the 2nd Battalion, IRA, killed at Ashtown on 19 December 1919. (*Courtesy of Mercier Archive*)

rest of the ambush party, including Barrett, stood at the crossroads, panting, their eyes scanning for further danger. An act of contrition was whispered in Savage's ear.

Then, suddenly, Byrne saw a white handkerchief being waved from the driver's window of the now-smouldering stationery second car. Pistols were trained towards it again. 'Come out!' was barked by the attackers heatedly, wide-eyed at the possibility of French still breathing inside it and straining to control the urge to pull their triggers and avenge their comrade. A corporal staggered out, miraculously unharmed but stunned and dishevelled, his ears ringing, pleading loudly in an English accent as he saw hatred in the eyes fixed firmly upon him: 'I did not fire!' with his hands in the air.

Daly addressed him: 'Whether you did or not makes no difference. We don't shoot our prisoners!' Then, the corporal, seeing Savage's body, but reassured that he was not about to accompany the dead man to the hereafter,

Lord French's car being examined following the Ashtown ambush.
(*Courtesy of the National Library of Ireland*)

expressed: 'One is enough to be gone.'³⁰ Daly's mistaken impression, however, was that he was referring to French, still in the car. To confirm this he asked him: 'Is he dead?' The NCO responded 'He is', but was referring instead to Savage, clearly dead.

The corporal – named Appleby – was soon joined by Const. McLoughlin, still in shock from the grenade blast and under pistol guard. They were both placed seated off the road and told if they remained quietly there for one hour they would be in no further danger. They were then warned that they would be tracked down and shot if they provided any descriptions or evidence against them.

The ambush was over, but it would be only minutes before the area crawled with military. Savage's body was searched for weapons and documents, then carried from the huge pool of blood that had quickly formed around it to the front door of the pub; they had no way themselves of transporting the body. The landlord's brother, Bartholomew Kelly, however, slammed and bolted the door.³¹ Inside the pub its few shocked patrons sat and stood, perplexed at what had just happened as the body was placed on the ground outside.

With no time to spare, Daly mounted his bicycle, carrying Breen – too wounded to cycle himself – as a passenger and set off for the city. Byrne pedalled just behind. The others soon followed. McDonnell, mopping up before he too departed, glanced into the destroyed car only to discover that it was full of luggage that appeared to have inadvertently saved the corporal, blasted to pieces by the grenade. Furthermore, to his utter dismay, there was no sign of French. He had escaped them once more. Astonishingly, the lead car had stalled as it left the station and French's car had overtaken it. It had contained four passengers, Det. Halley, Capt. de Pret – French's aide-de-camp, and driver – and a woman named Seymour, as well as the viceroy himself.[32]

Within minutes, the attack area was again silent. All the attackers had cycled away. The corporal and policeman remained as ordered, motionless and wordless until military lorries arrived. The area was then secured with patrols. Witnesses from the pub were questioned. None, however, could describe the attackers. Savage's blood-soaked clothing was searched by an officer, revealing a piece of paperwork from a shop where he worked, and whose premises he resided above – Kirk's of 137 North Strand Road. This was a critical piece of intelligence that his comrades had accidentally left behind. His finger still had a grenade ring around it. The body was eventually taken to a stable within the vice-regal grounds, then to a disused DMP outpost, and from there to King George V Hospital, the military hospital that sat between the Royal and Marlborough barracks. None of French's protection detail could provide descriptions other than vague ones. The policeman and corporal claimed the ambushers had worn scarves over their faces.

Marlborough barracks lay between the escaping IRA men and the city, 300 yards west of the Navan Road at its south-eastern end. Vinny Byrne feared as he cycled his 'High Nelly' bicycle that they had no chance of making it past the barracks. To make matters worse, Séamus Robinson's pedal snapped off, forcing him to abandon his bike and ride as Treacy's pillion, not an easy task with the handlebars shaped in such a way as to leave little space for two. McDonnell remained behind them in support. This arrangement slowed them for a time until they saw an elderly man pushing his bicycle just ahead. They commandeered the bicycle at gunpoint, unaware that he was a retired RIC man. They did, however, reassure him where the bicycle would be made available the following day – in Sackville Street close to the Gresham Hotel. When they caught up with the remainder, as they pedalled downhill towards Cabra and Phibsboro, they were astonished to find no roadblocks. They eventually caught up with Paddy Daly – experiencing similar difficulty with his pillion –

to warn him that Breen was leaving a trail of blood from his still-dripping leg. Stopping momentarily, Breen, severely weakened, took the lace from his boot and tied it around his leg as an improvised tourniquet. It worked.

Soon afterwards, the dozen returning ambushers reached a safe house at 88 Phibsboro Road, Jack Toomey's residence at the junction of Connaught Street. When his wife answered the door, she was shocked at the sight before her, particularly having had no prior word of their pending arrival. Breen was near collapse.

McDonnell dismissed most of the unit. Vinny Byrne sped to his home for lunch, after which he would then report for work. As Breen was rushed inside and tended to by his comrades, Mrs Toomey quietly walked out with a cloth and wiped the blood from Daly's bicycle and from the ground next to it. A message was quickly dispatched to her doctor – Dr Ryan – but unable to attend, he in turn relayed the message to Dr Geraghty from the nearby Mater Hospital, who soon arrived. Treacy, Hogan and Robinson remained there after the rest of the unit had departed, until reassured by the doctor, having cleaned, disinfected and dressed Breen's wounds, that he was not in serious danger.

A mile away, soon afterwards, Vice-Brigadier Lynch noticed Joe Leonard speeding towards him on his bicycle as he cycled from the city centre towards his home on Richmond Road. Leonard looked agitated. He stopped and went to say something to Lynch, but curiously, stopped and pedalled away again. Lynch wondered what his comrade had been up to, but knew better than to press the issue on the streets. He would find out soon enough.

Soon afterwards, now at home and having just eaten lunch, Lynch heard his house's side-gate squeaking open on its hinges. Seán Treacy and Séamus Robinson entered to be greeted with a gasp at their appearances: both looked tired out and splashed with mud up to their knees.[33] Lynch at this point knew something had happened, but first told them to go upstairs to the bathroom and get the mud off their clothes. Then, following them, he asked: 'What is it, Seán?' to be told in reply: 'We were out after Lord French.' Lynch asked: 'Did you get him?'[34] Treacy answered: 'We are not sure.' Then Séamus said in a broken voice, 'We lost one man, killed.' 'Who?' Lynch asked. 'Martin Savage,' he was informed.

Lynch felt as if his mind was suddenly imploding. He had great regard for Savage, and had been using him as his personal assistant while Brigadier

McKee was locked up. But much worse: he had only recently handed him all of McKee's paperwork, as well as various other brigade papers to hide at his workplace. He had explicitly warned him not to appear at any parades, drills or anything that would draw attention upon himself while these papers were in his custody. He was unaware that Savage had carried documentation to the ambush linking him to the address, but could not take any chances. Fearing – correctly – his dead comrade's imminent identification and subsequent association with the shop, he immediately ordered Treacy and Robinson home. Treacy made his way the short distance to Fleming's house in Drumcondra. Robinson dumped his commandeered bicycle at a safe house *en route* back to Heytesbury Street, with instructions to relay it to Sackville Street the following day for its owner. Lynch, meanwhile, with no time to spare, sped to Mick McDonnell's house.

Confronting Lynch as soon as he entered the house ten-minutes later was Tom Keogh, his head resting on a table and his body shaking as he sobbed. Tom Ennis consoled him. Keogh lifted his head towards Lynch and asked him: 'Have you heard about Martin?' Lynch affirmed that he had but retorted that they had no time for grief. Grabbing him firmly by the shoulders he asked Keogh, referring to their late comrade: 'Do you know where he worked?' Ennis interjected: 'Yes, I know, in Kirk's of the North Strand.' Lynch then hit Ennis with the shocking revelation regarding the papers, ordering him to: 'Get over there, quick, and clear out Martin's room. All the Dublin Brigade papers are in his room and, if the British get them, we are destroyed.'[35]

Lynch was just in time with the order. Half-an-hour hour later Ennis was back with everything he had been sent for. He detailed how he had barely got back out of Kirk's; when he was leaving a lorry-load of soldiers had sped to the premises and opened fire on him as he fled the area. Nonetheless, he had made it. For now at least the Dublin Brigade had been saved from an ignominious disaster.

***

Later that evening, as word circulated frenziedly throughout the city of the daring attack on Lord French, Frank Thornton, twenty-eight years old, arrived by train in Amiens Street station. He had just been in Longford, organising Volunteers while masquerading as a director of New Ireland

Assurance, a company he had helped incorporate and which operated from 56 Bachelors Walk. New Ireland's name was a clear marker of its principal objective – redirecting the huge sums of Irish money spent overseas annually on insurance policies so that it remained instead in Ireland. Michael Collins had summoned Thornton, a hugely respected and pivotal 1916 veteran, to Dublin. He originally came from Drogheda where his family, of which two of his brothers were also Volunteers, ran a decorating and hardware business.

Thornton's first stop that night was Vaughan's Hotel. Meeting him there were Joe O'Reilly and Tom Cullen. Thornton was briefed on the day's momentous events and told he would be helping to move Dan Breen the next day.

Breen had, by the following day, been placed under the charge of Dr Ryan in Phibsboro. Vice-Brigadier Lynch, in the meantime, had formulated a similar idea of moving him to a safer venue to recuperate. Deciding it was worth the risk, he procured a car and driver from Joseph Lawless and instructed him to drive to the Toomey house where, to his surprise, he saw Breen being placed carefully into another car by Thornton, O'Reilly and Cullen. Seeing no reason to stop and delay matters, he ordered the driver on. It was shrewd: both his and Breen's car left just before police and soldiers in huge numbers swept through Phibsboro, blocking roads, tempestuously combing through houses and streets, trawling for French's attackers. Breen's blood-trail had led them all the way to St Peter's church, just minutes away from the Toomey residence. Luckily for Breen, the trail had then run dry.

Having ensured that Breen was safely in the custody of the Malone household a couple of miles away at No. 13 Grantham Street, Thornton reported to Michael Collins. Collins' typically cheerful but foul-mouthed effusiveness was noticeably absent that day as Thornton briefed him about the tumultuous general situation in Longford, where he expected to be soon returning. However, he would not be; Thornton was informed that he was being transferred to IRA intelligence under Liam Tobin – since returned from London – a man Thornton knew. Tobin was, among his other roles also a New Ireland director.

Collins' intelligence department was now operating out of the second floor of No. 3 Crow Street, above Irish Woodworkers and Fowler Printers, masking itself as the Irish Products Company. The department was still recruiting from within the Dublin Brigade and was set to see continued expansion. It would therefore require an operational base. When it had been brought to Collins' attention that the endless shadowing, tracking and patrolling required before even getting to the point of consummating the grievous act of close-up killing would leave his men exhausted, or worse: 'picked up by the G-Division men and hanged by the neck', he had prioritised the office's procurement.[36]

Behind the inconspicuous east facing façade of the four-storey terraced building midway along Crow Street's narrow cobbled roadway, Tobin, a gifted administrator, was constructing a prodigious intelligence gathering operation with Assistant Director Tom Cullen and Thornton as deputy assistant director. They soon became known as the 'Crow Street Three'.[37] With a small complement of full-time salaried staff, dossiers would be built up on persons of interest such as spies and prominent enemy personnel, including staff officers, crown administrators, detectives and suspected informers. Messages were being deciphered, intercepted letters monitored and further contacts established. Publications such as the *London Gazette*, and the *Who's Who* also provided information on British Army transfers and promotions. Of particular interest to IRA intelligence in Crow Street would be those listed with 'Special Employment' indicated next to their names.

Intelligence staff casually entered and exited the building, looking like polite businessmen, carrying briefcases and sporting tailored suits, hiding in plain sight. Joe O'Reilly visited twice daily delivering and receiving dispatches on behalf of Collins, the Finance Minister himself spending his days carrying himself with similar apparent abandon, flitting between a host of other clandestine offices on his high-framed black Lucania bicycle.[38]

No. 3 Crow Street, the shortest of strolls from Dublin Castle, soon became the pivot of an intelligence service that in the coming year proved deadly to those operating from behind the Castle's parapets and walls. It also became the nerve centre that saved scores of IRA operatives from capture. Couriers stood by primed to deliver warnings of impending raids and round-ups in Dublin and throughout the country.

9

WAR DECLARED, ELECTIONS AND RAIDS

'A crooked English bastard'

Dan Breen was tended to by Brigid and Áine Malone in 13 Grantham Street. Both Cumann nan mBan members, they were sisters of Lt Michael Malone, who had been killed in 1916 fighting desperately for the Volunteers at Mount Street Bridge, and William Malone, killed in action in 1915 fighting for the British Army in Belgium. When Breen heard confirmation that Lord French had escaped the ambush, he was disconsolate. Seán Treacy's philosophical words: 'You can't have a Knocklong every day, Dan', provided solace.

The viceroy's attempted assassination not only sent shockwaves throughout the establishment, it had marked personal effects on both French and Chief Secretary Macpherson, who would himself, within months, be under the surveillance of IRA assassins. For French, the attack's trauma set the scene for him fading from public life. Lloyd George's response was more insouciant. He merely reflected on the assassins' aims, saying: 'They are bad shots'.[1] It was, however, obvious that police intelligence was completely ineffective. Consequently, as far as Dublin Castle was concerned, it was time to increase the powers of the military and intelligence services. Matters in this regard accelerated. Dozens of letters congratulating the lord-lieutenant on his escape reached the vice-regal lodge over the ensuing days.[2]

19 December 1919 was also the day for momentous events in Downing Street; Lloyd George reported to his cabinet that the issue of dividing Ireland into two separate parliaments as proposed on 4 November would not be straightforward. Its perception up to now regarding the planned initial segregation was that a simple division would be made along traditional provincial lines, separating the geographical province of Ulster from Ireland's remaining three.

It became clear, however, that unionist leaders, assisted by Walter Long, had something radically different in mind: a six-county area excluding the three predominantly nationalist counties of Monaghan, Cavan and Donegal. This would ensure an unassailable loyalist majority for the six, under the premiership of James Craig, a founder of the UVF. This did not sit well with the cabinet as a whole; nine counties was considered a more economically and politically viable proposition for Ulster's future which, given time and stability on both sides of the divide, could eventually lead to a united Ireland, devolved and peaceful, with the crown remaining at its head deciding on matters such as defence and foreign policy, leaving more practical issues such as judiciary, postal service, taxation, transport, agriculture and health in the hands of a devolved parliament.[3]

This overview, however, failed to take into account that this would be unsatisfactory to the most influential separatists. George Creel's prediction the previous spring regarding the need for expediency to offset a hard-line being adopted was proving accurate. This actually sat well with the more contriving unionists and Conservative Party members who had anticipated this. They assumed that by throwing ostensibly reasonable propositions back in their faces, the separatists would lose their bedrock of international support, perhaps even facilitating the maintenance of direct rule. Notably, this was at odds with the more naïve perceptions of their Liberal counterparts, who assumed Sinn Féin would grasp at such outwardly prudent proposals. It was also seen as an opportunity to isolate Ulster from the ceaselessly impassable Irish question and would therefore be a step towards a permanent solution.

Meanwhile, when news of the Ashtown ambush reached London, an old friend of Lord French's, General Sir Cecil Frederick Nevil Macready, serving as Metropolitan police commissioner, wrote forebodingly in his diary about Ireland – a country he had significant experience in, and whose tribulations he felt utter contempt for: 'Will Lloyd George want me to go there?'[4]

December had also seen the Dáil involved in a game-changing enterprise; the creation of the National Land Bank. This bank facilitated land redistribution through already established co-operative farming societies, and strove to lend money to enable tenant farmers to purchase land from landlords willing to sell.[5] It was placed under Robert Barton's chairmanship, owing to his expertise in both agriculture and co-operative banks, one of which he had chaired in 1908.[6]

Barton was still a fugitive since his March prison escape. Oxford University graduate Lionel Smith Gordon and Barton's cousin, Erskine Childers, a Cambridge graduate, directed the Land Bank. Paid up capital of £203,000 was invested by the Dáil. The bank was camouflaged with the fictitious name: 'Natland Limited', and operated from 68 Lower Leeson Street, where Barton maintained an office but employed a secretary, John Callaghan, to administer it.[7] Barton resided at 44 Oakley Road in Ranelagh, the home of Áine Ceannt, widow of Éamonn – executed in 1916. He also maintained an office there and rarely ventured out as three policemen who knew him from Wicklow had been dispatched to Dublin to track him down and he feared recognition by them. The bank quickly gained traction. When it came to the attention of its directors that its cheques were not being accepted by other banks, owing to a decision by the Bankers' Committee, several committee members were paid a visit by Dáithí O'Donoghue, who, typically well-dressed, and on instructions from Michael Collins, persuaded them that the consequences of such an antagonistic posture would have imminently negative consequences for them. The matter was resolved without hesitation in favour of the Land Bank.

Meanwhile, serious consequences were also set to befall the editor of the *Irish Independent* newspaper, Timothy Harrington. On 20 December the newspaper, along with most others, ran with Ashtown as its headline. The majority of other newspapers were, notwithstanding their escalating animosity towards them, viewed by Volunteers as an organ of the British government. The *Irish Independent*, conversely, was seen as the paper whose existence depended on the support of the very people who had voted for the establishment of the Irish Republic.[8] Since the annihilation of the IPP in December 1918, it had been generally supportive of Sinn Féin, recognising the wind-change and adapting more energetically to its target audience than its broadly comparable *Freeman's Journal*. That day's edition had, nonetheless, as far as they were concerned, flown in the face of this; it had portrayed the ambush as a criminal outrage. It also featured repetitions of the words assassins and murder. The Volunteers were incensed. Directing such antagonism towards their backbone of support was considered a blatant act of treachery.

The following evening, Sunday 21 December at 6 p.m., Vice-Commandant Lynch, passing through Rutland Square on GHQ business, ran into a large gathering of Volunteers. Realising something was afoot, he asked them what they were up to. The answer shocked him; they were going over to the *Independent* to 'bump-off' the editor, knowing he would be there working on shift.⁹ Lynch, aghast, insisted they were to do no such thing. Sympathetic to their fury over the labelling of their fallen comrade as a murderer, he nonetheless insisted that if Harrington was killed without direct orders they would be guilty themselves of such a crime. He then emphatically insisted: 'We have no place for murderers in our army'.¹⁰ He suggested instead they follow him to GHQ to broach their grievances with Richard Mulcahy.

When Mulcahy was brought up to speed soon afterwards he concluded that something did need to be done straight away to teach the newspaper a lesson. Killing its editor was, however, out of the question. They would, instead, destroy the printing press and take the paper out of circulation – at least for a time. This measure, Mulcahy felt, would also send a clear signal to the British administration that further suppression of publications favourable to republicans could see similar measures employed against publications aligned with Dublin Castle. Messages were dispatched for men to oversee the job.

Capt. Garry Holohan, older brother of Patrick, was spending the same evening in the company of his sweetheart Bríd O'Hegarty in a house in Cabra Park, when one of Mulcahy's messages arrived. He was instructed to report to GHQ immediately. Holohan was O/C 2nd Company of the IRA's recently constituted 5th Engineer Battalion of sappers.

When he arrived twenty minutes later, Holohan was informed that he was to take immediate charge of the destruction of the *Independent*'s printing presses. Volunteer Paddy McGrath, twenty-six years old and also of the 5th Battalion, who worked at the paper's printing offices, had also just arrived. He detailed to Holohan where the various rotary and typesetting machines were situated and how best to destroy them. Holohan then sent word out to his unit members who worked in the docks to report for action with sledgehammers and similar tools.

Peadar Clancy, detailed to lead the assault, briefed Holohan on the operation: Clancy and an armed team would hold up staff and initially secure the offices. Holohan and his sappers would follow. When signalled, they would then enter and destroy the machinery.

Ninety-minutes later, when the requisite several dozen men had assembled, they set off in groups, cutting through Moore Lane and Henry Place, and then other deserted backstreets to get to their objective. When Clancy and his men, now masked, arrived at the printing offices' entrance, close to Middle Abbey Street's junction with Liffey Street, they quickly subdued the shift-workers at gunpoint. Then, moving from room to room, floor to floor and office to office Clancy eventually came face to face with Harrington. He informed the shocked editor that his paper was being suppressed for having endeavoured to misrepresent the sympathies and opinions of the Irish people through its coverage of the ambush.[11] This was met with stunned silence.

Holohan waited outside on Middle Abbey Street with his unit. Stragglers filtered into the group from nearby William's Lane. Looking up at the building's lit windows Holohan spotted the shadows of staff members standing against the blinds with their hands held over their heads.[12] He felt uneasy about this, knowing some of them were probably IRA sympathisers and friends of Paddy McGrath. Nevertheless, he had a job to do. When the signal came he ordered his men in.

Holohan and his sappers quickly set to work, and soon the entire building echoed to the clanks of lump and sledgehammers smashing against iron and steel machinery. Soon the destruction was complete. Smashed parts of printers and typesetters were strewn across the various floors. Huge reels of paper were scattered. Ink was spilled throughout. The Volunteers then withdrew. The workers' reactions varied. Some were horrified, others, more sympathetic to the cause, were impressed by the audacity of what they had just witnessed but dismayed at the prospect of what the attack might mean for their jobs.

Most of the Volunteers went afterwards to 25 Rutland Square, another Gaelic League building, where they ditched their tools and weapons, then cleaned and dusted themselves off. Afterwards they joined in with the usual Sunday night revelry, which was particularly merry that night given the festive season. They quietly congratulated themselves for avenging the dishonouring of their fallen comrade, raising glasses to him as they spoke together, smoked cigarettes and pipes. Others made their way home, similarly satisfied with their night's work. Holohan returned to Cabra.

The *Irish Independent*, not to be outdone, managed to get an abridged version of the paper out the following day by using the nearby *Irish Times*' printing press in D'Olier Street. Nonetheless, the *Independent* heeded the warning. No further such headlines appeared. Notably, the editor's son soon joined the IRA.

Martin Savage's body was released to his relatives following an inquest two days after this episode, on 23 December. His employer had identified the remains three days earlier. They were then taken quietly in the night to Broadstone railway station to wait overnight in a box car until being brought by train to his home early on Christmas Eve for burial in Ballisodare, Co. Sligo. Two churches, Dublin's pro cathedral and St Laurence O'Toole's in Seville Place, had refused to allow his remains repose there before their final journey; the latter was Savage's parish church.

Risking further indignation, IRA GHQ opted not to honour him with a military procession in Dublin, much to the chagrin of some of Savage's prominent 2nd Battalion officer comrades such as Oscar Traynor and Seán Russell; since the Easter Rising every Volunteer killed in the line of duty had been afforded such a ceremony. Richard Mulcahy, knowing that the game was well and truly on and fearing identifications and arrests in such a procession, instead issued a morale-boosting pledge to all Dublin Brigade units, affirming that the IRA would carry on the fight for which Lt Savage had given his life.

Volunteers were, nonetheless, given sanction to form up in the station on the morning of the train's departure, but the need to avoid detection or arrest was pressed. Frank Henderson, as the 2nd Battalion commandant, addressed its men that night to pay tribute to Savage, and to reaffirm that his death would not be in vain. The following morning, forty Volunteers, mostly from Savage's D Company, stood to attention on the platform in Broadstone and saluted as the train carrying his remains pulled slowly away. Savage's funeral in Ballisodare was, contrarily, a huge affair. His Tricolour-draped coffin was carried two miles on the shoulders of Volunteers to his burial place, attended by thousands of mourners and onlookers and ringed by RIC cordons.

***

Back in Dublin's tram-lined streets Christmas arrived with characteristic sentiments of peace and goodwill. Despite a coal shortage, it was still a less grim affair than the previous year, given the comparative absence of the Great War's immediate ramifications and the abeyance of the Spanish Flu, both of which had shredded families and communities. Nonetheless, the festivities were tempered by the sense of uncertainty facing nationalist and unionist alike, whether penniless and cold slum dwellers, or those indulging the festivities in the warmer comfort of the city's leafy suburbs.

The year closed with more shootings. Decorated Lt Frederick Boast, twenty-years old, and civilian Laurence Kennedy, were killed on Sunday 28 December. Boast had been on guard duty at the vice-regal lodge. Hearing shots from within the Phoenix Park, he and several soldiers rushed to investigate, fearing another assassination attempt on Lord French. They challenged Kennedy, a forty-seven-year-old farm labourer from Lucan, to stop. An ensuing struggle saw both Kennedy and Boast open fire, killing each other.

Meanwhile, Volunteer GHQ reflected positively on the modest but evolving success thus far of the strategy of isolating and dismantling the RIC, and the more strikingly successful near-eradication of the DMP's intelligence service while also cementing the foundations of their own. Eleven RIC officers had been killed by Volunteers during the year and twenty more wounded, plus four G-Division detectives neutralised. Handsome rewards of £5,000 for information to track the killers of Smyth, Hoey, Downing and Barton had proved fruitless. Furthermore, ostracisation had decimated police morale. The policy's less favourable effects on family members, particularly their children, was dispiriting, but considered a necessary evil. It had got to the point where church congregations conspicuously avoided pews occupied by policemen and their families. Tradesmen and shopkeepers dealt with them with apprehension. Romantic liaisons were becoming impossible for single officers; their female companions risked having their hair cropped. At one point, a donkey was even killed for carrying turf to an RIC barracks.[13] Cab drivers carrying policemen risked having their cars burned. Barrack servants were warned they would be banished from their communities if they did not cease work.[14] Volunteer morale, by and large, conversely, continued to improve, notwithstanding the 'lack of spirit on the part of the men, lack of knowledge on the part of the officers' that still prevailed in parts.[15]

However, the crown's servants were also making plans to address their problems. The RIC was seeing whisperings of improved recruitment due to better pay. Furthermore, following Insp. Byrne's side-lining in favour of Insp. Smith, the order initially prepared on 11 November was finally issued on 27 December, permitting recruitment from Britain into the RIC. Advertisements for recruits quickly began to appear in prominent British newspapers, seeking men to 'face a rough and dangerous task' and bolster the forces' ranks.

However, the most pressing issue was G-Division, as the detective branch was a shambles. Without sourcing even a forewarning whisper of the Ashtown attack, it was clear to the authorities that their intelligence had dried up. Moreover, a political intelligence police unit was futile if each of its detectives needed a bodyguard to simply keep them alive when they walked Dublin's streets. G-Division needed resuscitating. To see to this, assistance was sought from Belfast in the form of forty-five-year-old RIC Dist. Insp. William Forbes-Redmond. A no-nonsense veteran detective with an indefatigable reputation, he had grown up in Co. Down and served in the Great War with the rank of major. Edgeworth-Johnstone would remain in place as the DMP's head while Forbes-Redmond, as assistant commissioner, would whip G-Division back into shape. Meanwhile, Alan Bell was charged with investigating the Ashtown ambush. He also began chasing down the Dáil Loan with fervour.

Sinn Féin's evaluation of the year was equally buoyant to that of its military wing. No less than fourteen productive Dáil meetings had been convened since the assembly's widely publicised inauguration, some taking place secretly in 3 Mountjoy Square – home of former Sinn Féin alderman Walter Cole – others in Fleming's Hotel on Gardiner Place after the Mansion House was no longer available.[16] Diarmuid O'Hegarty took responsibility for organising such clandestine conclaves. Despite the setback of the peace conference's refusal to recognise it, significant groundwork had been laid to underpin the strategy of supplanting the British government with a functioning domestic counterpart, albeit with considerable room for improvement. The all-important propaganda strategy was also germinating. The Bond Scheme was a success; money was starting to flow in from both foreseen and less anticipated sources, including unionists – some hedging their bets to forestall a potential backlash should the revolution succeed, others feeling coerced to contribute. The loan was also about to be launched to great fanfare in the USA. The Land Bank had also been established.

Nevertheless, Westminster was not taking these political developments lying down. The introduction of the Better Government of Ireland Bill – formulated to advance Ireland's partition – to the House of Commons on 22 December followed in the wake of its Dáil adversary having been driven underground. Far fewer Dáil meetings would henceforth be possible given the former development, and those that were convened would have far fewer attendees than the since unequalled fifty-two members present the previous

1 April. It was hoped that the bill, magnanimous in the British government's eyes, would draw support from Sinn Féin by convincing large numbers of the less militant Irish electorate that their support for full independence, which would inevitably involve increased bloodshed, was unwarranted.

Essentially, as the new year church bells chimed for 1920, Dublin Castle was still in control. Determined to maintain its grip on the levers of power – and backed by a government that, despite obvious concerns, saw the recent troubles as, by and large, far less pressing than other recent global convulsions rippling throughout the empire. However, the coming year would see a multi-pronged and unrelenting assault from the IRA and Sinn Féin that would propel Ireland to the forefront of the empire's agenda. The three-legged guerrilla war strategy of making Ireland ungovernable, of urban and rural ambush, and irrefutable propaganda was about to commence in earnest, spearheaded in Dublin, and casualties on both sides would not remain so light in the coming year.

***

New Year's Day saw an instantaneous escalation of hostilities, at least on an executive level, with the official authorisation from IRA GHQ for attacks on the police.[17] The previous September's outlawing of Dáil Éireann, seen as a declaration of war from Dublin Castle, had provided justification to GHQ for the successful and attempted assassinations that followed it, but until now, GHQ's strategy regarding such attacks on individuals – and barracks' – had been unspoken. This position was clear.

Dublin District was that same day established by the crown as a divisional military command under forty-two-year-old Major-General Gerard Farrell Boyd – a decorated veteran of both the Boer and Great Wars. Under Boyd's command were nine understrength infantry battalions plus one cavalry regiment and one machine gun battalion. The responsibility for restoring order in the capital – at least as far as Westminster was concerned – was, largely, to fall upon the shoulders of these troops.[18] In the minds of GHQ, this was further evidence that a *de facto* state of war existed.

In London meanwhile, fifty-eight-year-old Sir Basil Thompson, now in command of the secret service in Ireland – with the exception of army intelligence – began organising and recruiting more agents. These would be drawn from the Irish diaspora and would be directed towards deep undercover work. Following deployment, for security reasons, they would report directly to Thompson's offices at Scotland Yard.

Back in Dublin, the British Army's two chief intelligence officers in Ireland, Brigadier General Sir John Brind and his subordinate, Lt Col Stephen Hill-Dillon, were busily trying to reorganise Army Intelligence, located at Irish Command HQ on Parkgate Street. Twenty agents were currently on their books, some still serving soldiers, others de-mobbed veterans who had since volunteered. However, classed as novices to the treacherous sphere, it was proposed that these would initially be sent in small batches to London for training.

Col Hill-Dillon looked optimistically to the future, believing he had an airtight department. Aware that a significant drawback existed – most of his men would already be known to the enemy; familiarity pervaded Dublin's population – he was nonetheless confident that he could periodically feed an unknown agent into the mix. He was blissfully unaware that the very core of his growing intelligence redoubt would soon be under the vigilant and utterly reliable eyes of Lily Mernin. From the garrison adjutant's office in Dublin Castle's Lower Yard, the shorthand typist's duties, crucially, included typing weekly updates of the names and addresses of British personnel residing at private addresses in the city; in other words those who would be operating directly under Hill-Dillon. Mernin, thirty-two years old and living at 113 Middle Abbey Street, would soon be known to IRA intelligence under the deflective code name: 'Lt G', an abbreviation of 'Little Gentleman'. Her duplication of such lists became an inestimable intelligence source to the IRA and prove fatal to its enemies.

One such unknown agent, albeit under Alan Bell and therefore Basil Thompson: 'Jameson' – still masking as a jewellery salesman and residing in Sackville Street's Granville Hotel – had been making significant progress in recent weeks, and had already penetrated IRA GHQ. When word emerged regarding his credentials and his ability to source arms, Collins, further intrigued, had agreed to a meeting, albeit against the advice of Joe O'Reilly who had developed an instant mistrust of Jameson. O'Reilly's misgivings were cast aside. Collins subsequently set up the meeting between Jameson and some GHQ members, including Richard Mulcahy, at O'Keefe's restaurant in 1 Lower Camden Street. GHQ people were impressed enough with his bluff to arrange a subsequent meeting. Collins, ever cautious, stayed away from both meetings, but following the second, agreed to meet with him at a later date at Batt O'Connor's house.

Joe O'Reilly was not alone in his doubts about Jameson. The sentiment had rubbed off on Frank Thornton, Liam Tobin and Tom Cullen. When Jameson approached Tobin on New Year's Day, showcasing his arms procurement abilities by way of a promise of a portmanteau case full of Webley revolvers, Tobin and Cullen formulated a plan to smoke him out. Tobin met with Jameson first thing the following morning and escorted him to the New Ireland offices.[19] Kapp & Peterson tobacco occupied the same building's ground floor and basement. Jameson, as pledged, brought along the portmanteau full of Webleys. Thornton, waiting inside, then took it from Jameson and made sure the Englishman saw him descend the staircase to the building's basement. Ten minutes later, when Tobin and Jameson had left, Thornton snuck the portmanteau to 32 Bachelors Walk. There, Tom Cullen placed its contents under the charge of IRA quartermaster staff.

However, before this meeting, Tobin had made contact with Det. Jim McNamara: a young protégé of Det. Joseph Cavanagh who came from a unionist family, and was considered beyond scrutiny by Dublin Castle. Cavanagh had, nonetheless, carefully sounded him out and discovered the opposite: McNamara was prepared to assist the separatists. Now, along with Broy, he was working for Collins. Tobin had asked McNamara to keep his ears tuned for any raids planned that day and to try to forward such information.[20] The result was McNamara's forewarning of a raid due to take place at 3 p.m. at Kapp & Peterson. Jameson, following the arms exchange, had contacted a handler. Then, Thornton, Tobin and Cullen, having ensured no intelligence or Dáil Loan paperwork had been left inadvertently in the New Ireland office, watched the raid – right on the stroke of three – from McBirney's department store across the river on Aston Quay. Their instincts had been correct.[21]

When the raid revealed nothing the detectives were exasperated. However, they returned that night, armed with more precise information from Jameson regarding the whereabouts of the pistols, and when frustrated again, even dug up the basement's floorboards with pickaxes and shovels to find, to their further consternation, nothing but a dusty Volunteer hat left there during the Rising when the building's hurried evacuation was forced under artillery fire.

As far as Tobin, Cullen and Thornton were concerned, Jameson was a marked man.

The new year also saw Assistant Commissioner Forbes-Redmond arrive in Dublin, accompanied by a small team of equally industrious and loyal detectives from Belfast. Eager to get to grips with the situation, he made his way straight to Dublin Castle – its gates closed to the public. When he addressed his men and their new G-Division colleagues, New Year wishes were distinctly lacking. To the disgust of G-Division's beleaguered veterans Forbes-Redmond's determined, weathered eyes focused on them. Standing rigid, lean, straight-lipped, square-jawed and sporting a thin moustache typical of his rank, he castigated them pitilessly, contending that they were neglecting their duty. He gave them a month to catch Michael Collins and those responsible for the recent shootings; failing that, he would demand resignations.²² This horrified his audience.

Among the assembly were Ned Broy, Jim McNamara and David Neligan. Neligan's thinking was veering daily in a similar direction to McNamara's. When Redmond concluded that he would need a guide to see him about the unfamiliar city, and an administrative assistant, he selected McNamara. It was his first mistake.

As soon as his shift was over, McNamara set out to inform Collins of developments. Collins' conclusion was immediate: Forbes-Redmond had to go. Seeking out Cathal Brugha straight away to sanction the measure, Collins emphasised the dangers of a reinvigorated G-Division; all the work thus far in undermining and demoralising it would be wasted if they did not act immediately. A resurgent G-Division, he argued, would also act as a morale booster for the country's entire police force. Brugha needed no further persuasion. He approved the assistant commissioner's killing.

Cathal Brugha, who, as the Dáil's minister for defence, sanctioned assassinations by the IRA special duties units. (*Courtesy of Kilmainham Gaol Museum OPW, KMGLM 2018.0189*)

Back at London's New Scotland Yard on 2 January, one soon-to-become-infamous aspect of the forces being assembled against the Dáil – the Royal Irish Constabulary Special Reserve (RICSR) – recruited its first member: Henry Batters, an ex-soldier from Nottingham.²³ Forty-four-year-old RIC Major Cyril Francis Fleming, a Corkman, was in overall charge of recruitment to the reserve force. Others quickly followed Batters. Recruiting offices would soon spring up, particularly in Liverpool and Glasgow.

Meanwhile, Assistant Commissioner Forbes-Redmond took a room in the Standard Hotel on Harcourt Street following his Dublin arrival, no rooms being yet available in Dublin Castle. Jim McNamara reported this to Collins, plus the fact that while awaiting his Castle accommodation, Forbes-Redmond wore a bulletproof waistcoat under his jacket.

Lord French, at the same time, was preparing to swoop. Capitalising on Macpherson's post-Ashtown consternation, he had pressed him in recent days on the need to issue as many internment warrants under DORA as he could. Walter Long had further underscored French's reactionary outlook by affirming that Dublin Castle could go even further if warranted, and impose martial law without referring to the cabinet. French, emboldened, had then scoffed to Macpherson: 'So long as we refrain from arresting people like Arthur Griffith and others simply for making seditious speeches there will be no comeback from Westminster'.²⁴

On Wednesday 7 January, the British military was empowered under DORA regulation 14B to round up, deport and intern 'the perpetrators of outrage' and to 'search individuals and buildings for arms, explosives, and seditious literature', randomly if necessary.²⁵ Royal Navy destroyers began dropping anchor at Kingstown and elsewhere along the east coast to ship the anticipated haul of prisoners across the Irish Sea. Lists of wanted men were soon fed to military commanders who, in turn, were given latitude to, effectively, arrest those they saw fit.²⁶

Two days later Frank Thornton was dispatched by IRA intelligence to Belfast to obtain a photograph of Assistant Commissioner Forbes-Redmond. He was instructed to make contact with RIC Sgt McCarthy there, a Kerry man who was working for Collins in the city. McCarthy subsequently facilitated Thornton's procurement of a photograph from Chichester Street station. The Police Amateur Boxing Championship was taking place in the Ulster Hall that night. Consequently, there were few policemen on duty and so McCarthy was able to slip Thornton into his office to get the photograph. Forbes-Redmond had barely taken up his post in Dublin by the time Thornton had returned the next day, his picture in his pocket.

Several days later Jim McNamara had more invaluable information: the content of Forbes-Redmond's latest brow-beating of G-Division during which he had ridiculed the fact that none of them had caught Collins while asserting that, in the meantime, an agent just brought over from England had already met him several times.[27] Collins suspected this man was 'Jameson'. By now Collins had met Jameson twice at Batt O'Connor's. Incredibly, despite the repeated warnings from Cullen, Tobin and Thornton, Collins had at least partially fallen for the guise of the man whom Cullen referred to as 'a crooked English Bastard', and had met him in the company of O'Connor, Tobin, Joe O'Reilly and Austin Stack.[28] He had even confessed to liking him. On the second occasion, Jameson and Forbes-Redmond laid a trap: a detective had been watching O'Connor's house; his orders were to alert Forbes-Redmond – standing by with a small convoy of police and soldiers on nearby Waterloo Road – as soon as Jameson left the residence. They would then pounce upon the house, arresting all, chiefly Collins. However, when Tobin had unexpectedly left the house with Jameson to catch a tram back to the city from Morehampton Road, the detective had mistaken Tobin for Collins, and rushed by bicycle to advise Forbes-Redmond to cancel the raid. Tobin's tram had been passing Waterloo Road when he saw the convoy speeding towards Morehampton Road.[29] If it had turned left – the Brendan Road direction – Collins, to all appearances, would have been done for. However, following the detective's faulty information there had been no reason to, so the convoy had unexpectedly turned right, instead making for the city. While Tobin had breathed a quiet sigh of relief, Jameson suppressed his perplexity. Jim McNamara had been among the raiding party. He later informed Collins about it.

Collins then activated his own traps: it had been slipped to Jameson that Collins ate lunch daily at O'Connor's. Collins then sent word to Mrs O'Connor that neither he nor anyone else would be there the following day, but still made his way there by bicycle with O'Reilly, expecting to see another detective waiting in the area – which he did. Once the detective had seen him and sped away, however, Collins and O'Reilly detoured to a concealed vantage point from which to watch the anticipated raid. The police and troop convoy soon stormed into the house, as expected, only to find, to their disgruntlement, no one of interest there. Collins smirked some distance away. Forbes-Redmond, confounded, eventually came across a photograph of Dáil delegates which he went to seize, but left it when asked to by Mrs O'Connor.

173

He then apologised for the inconvenience and, hoping to lull her into a false sense of security, reassured her that he would not trouble her again. Given what Collins had in mind for him, however, it was a prophetic remark.[30]

Another earlier trap had seen Collins deliberately allow Jameson to overlook a fictitious document with the address 9 Iona Drive – the address of a loyalist former lord mayor of Dublin – written on it. This resulted in a raid soon afterwards during which the fashionable residence was ransacked to the former mayor's vociferous protestations that he had once received the British king at the house.[31]

During the first two weeks in January throughout Ireland, riding on the back of the official all-clear from IRA GHQ, both sporadic and well organised arms raids took place in Cork, Galway, Kerry, Limerick, Longford, Clare, Tipperary, Waterford and Wicklow. Weapons kept as keepsakes from family members killed in the Great War were taken reluctantly. In many cases, arms commandeered from civilians were accounted for with receipts and the promise of their return once hostilities were over. Raids and arrests followed.

Otherwise activity remained comparatively subdued in the run up to the local elections for urban councils that took place throughout the country on 15 January. Since the Dáil's inauguration separatist political planners, working equally feverishly as Collins' intelligence services, had begun to turn their attentions to local government. It was an important objective to gain more local representation. Control of issues such as roads, water, lighting, sewage disposal, poor relief, dispensaries, hospitals, housing and other public services would greatly enhance the republican counter-state and represent a colossal strategic victory.[32]

The Westminster government, to hamstring Sinn Féin, employed Proportional Representation (PR) rather than the 'first past the post' voting system that had seen Sinn Féin gaining proportionately more seats than their overall share of the votes in the 1918 general election. By way of the Local Government (Ireland) Act 1919 this was, notably, only introduced in Ireland. Sinn Féin, however, unexpectedly embraced the idea, having actually advocated PR as far back as 1907.[33] The prospect of engagement with the wider populace, as Sinn Féin sought to educate voters about the new system's intricacies, was grasped. Candidates came out of hiding. Voters were energetically canvassed and often driven in relays through wintry weather to polling booths. Another swoop on Sinn Féin headquarters and bank on 7 January – still operating there despite the ban – combined with a campaign of arrests, intercepted mail and telegrams, the tearing down of posters, and a newspaper campaign which painted a grim picture of reinforced military repression in the event of a Sinn Féin majority, failed to derail the party. It ultimately gained control of nine of eleven corporations and sixty-two of ninety-nine urban councils, as well as forty-two seats out of eighty in Dublin Corporation.[34] The *Irish Bulletin* made hay of this, while pointing out how soldiers in battle-dress had paraded intimidatingly close to polling stations.[35]

Ulster remained the bulwark that once again bucked Sinn Féin's trend, with Belfast remaining unionist dominated. Elsewhere, the overall picture was of a populace that had provided further endorsement for the Irish Republic, even if the results themselves, when rigorously analysed, did not fully reflect this. Politically, the next course was set for Sinn Féin to steer these councils towards Dáil Éireann's growing local government ministry.

The election results highlighted the crown's need to track down and curtail the Dáil Loan's expansion; Sinn Féin's strategic victory had depended on these finances to back its campaign. The importance of this was not wasted on Alan Bell. The 7 January raid had seen cheques and receipts seized. Bell found these mouth-watering as he began to zero in on the related accounts. However, Bell was not the only one honing in on his quarry; IRA intelligence was gearing up to hit back.

10

G-DIVISION DECIMATED AND BRITISH INTELLIGENCE PUMMELLED

'Walk warily, listen keenly, and halt promptly'

Within days of Frank Thornton's return from Belfast, Joe Dolan, twenty-one years old, of A Company 1st Battalion Dublin Brigade, was summoned to meet the 'Crow Street Three'. Dolan, having recently been recruited to intelligence, noticed the *Who's Who* and *London Gazette* spread across a table when he reached the top floor, but was not there to peruse newspapers. Thornton then showed him Forbes-Redmond's picture, and provided additional details of his description. Dolan was told to track his movements.

Dolan, a Collinstown raid veteran, was quick to catch sight of a man fitting the assistant commissioner's description, having quickly secured a vantage point from which to observe the comings and goings at the castle. He then followed him to the Standard Hotel, further convincing him that he had the right man. Continued observation during subsequent days in the Dame Street/Parliament Street area showcased his target's idiosyncrasies: he wore a bowler hat and a black or grey coat with a velvet collar, resembling a stockbroker more than a detective.[1]

Dolan began timing Forbes-Redmond's journeys between the castle and hotel, noticing he rarely deviated from his route: Dame Street, Grafton Street, Stephen's Green and Harcourt Street his preference, taking a leisurely twenty minutes. Dolan quickly became familiar with his characteristics and how he reacted to others, studying him obsessively, even picturing him in his dreams. Meanwhile, Tom Cullen was booked into the Standard Hotel to perform similar surveillance during evenings.

Forbes-Redmond was blissfully oblivious, convinced he was unknown in the city, and walked to the castle unguarded. Opportunities arose for his

G-DIVISION DECIMATED AND BRITISH INTELLIGENCE PUMMELLED

enemies to kill him. However, orders were that assassinations were, for now, to be avoided during daylight.

Such sensitivities regarding daytime killings were forced aside, however, following a raid led by Forbes-Redmond on Cullenswood House on the night of Tuesday 20 January during which Collins and Mulcahy had come within minutes of capture. 'Jameson' had since acquired and provided the address to Forbes-Redmond, who relished the prospect of capturing Collins and Mulcahy there and shattering IRA morale. Collins had long since been singled out by Jameson as the IRA's lynchpin. However, once again IRA intelligence had been a step ahead – Jim McNamara informing Cullen of the imminent raid. Cullen had already suspected something was afoot, as had Joe Dolan; Forbes-Redmond had not left Dublin Castle at his usual evening departure time, nor had he returned to the hotel. Cullen quickly rallied Thornton. Both men then sped by bicycle to Oakley Road, alerting Collins, still labouring with paperwork in the basement. Collins quickly fled. Thornton and Cullen then roused Mulcahy and the three escaped the building minutes before the arrival of police and military, who, again, left empty-handed and frustrated.

The following day, Wednesday 21 January, marked the first anniversary of the Dáil's inauguration, but there was no time to celebrate. With Forbes-Redmond at large, the entire assembly's future was in peril. An IRA meeting was called during the early afternoon in 6 Gardiner Row – soon to be established by Countess Markievicz as a Trade Union Hall. Among the attendees were Collins, Mulcahy, Oscar Traynor, and both Special Duties Units. Collins got straight to business: Forbes-Redmond would be leaving the Castle around 6 p.m. that evening. It was imperative that they got him as his rooms in Dublin Castle were ready. Once residing within its walls, he would become untouchable. He warned forcefully: 'If we don't get him he'll get us.'[2]

Mick McDonnell detailed the units into groups. Tom Keogh and Vinny Byrne would proceed to the castle gates, rendezvous with Dolan, and shoot Forbes-Redmond at the first opportunity. As back-up: Paddy Daly, Joe Leonard and Seán Doyle would patrol the area between the Standard Hotel and the corner of Harcourt Street/Cuffe Street, Tom Cullen would maintain watch from the hotel, while the remaining unit members would be spread out along Grafton Street and, additionally, South Great George's Street in case Forbes-Redmond changed route. He was not to escape.

Hearing this, Daly protested sarcastically that his own unit would be more likely to read about his shooting in the next day's newspaper than to take part in it. Collins retorted, referring to his beloved Gaelic games: 'The goalman often gets as much of the ball as any of the team'.[3] Daly appreciated the metaphor.

As darkness drew in that evening, the unit members took up positions. Forbes-Redmond left the castle at 5.30 p.m. Dolan, seeing this, muttered to Byrne and Keogh: 'Here he comes'. Then, Forbes-Redmond stopped unexpectedly, turned around, and walked back into the Castle. The three stalkers feared he was on to them until he came back out and began strolling up Dame Street towards Trinity College. The three initially ensured that he was not being followed by a guard detail. Minutes later, satisfied he was not, Keogh turned to Dolan and Byrne and told them to cover him as he pressed ahead, shadowing the target.

Soon Forbes-Redmond walked up Grafton Street, his followers increasing in number. His steady pace then took him alongside Stephen's Green, its railings to his left, the Royal College of Surgeons to his right. Just ahead stood Harcourt Street. Seán Doyle stood by on adjacent Clonmel Street, next to the Standard Hotel's distinctive portico. Daly and Leonard strode up and down nervously to the front of the Children's Hospital on the same side of Harcourt Street as the hotel but towards the foot of the street, opposite Montague Street; they stayed within sight of Doyle, gripped with fear. Every passing face seemed to glare at them, as if each knew what they were up to, so eye contact was avoided.

It was almost 6 p.m. when Daly suddenly spotted the faces of his comrades approaching on Harcourt Street from Stephen's Green. Their quickening pace initially marked them out from other pedestrians as they strode past Sinn Féin headquarters, Keogh in front. Daly turned sharply to Leonard: 'Look out, Joe, here is Keogh and the gang'.[4] His increasingly honed killer instinct began to kick in at the prospect of the target's imminent proximity. He quickly signalled Doyle. Suddenly, Forbes-Redmond caught his eyes next to Montague Street ten yards away. Tom Keogh also zeroed in, bursting into a run, drawing his revolver.[5]

Daly's reaction was instant. He drew his pistol and stepped onto the road towards Forbes-Redmond, pulsating and drawing breath as he hurriedly

G-DIVISION DECIMATED AND BRITISH INTELLIGENCE PUMMELLED

cocked the weapon. Forbes-Redmond saw him and instinctively grabbed his revolver while simultaneously turning to flee, but with Daly having the element of surprise the policeman had no chance. Daly fired from two yards. The shot reverberated. Forbes-Redmond was blown off his feet with the force of the round that struck the back of his head under the ear and exited, taking with it a lump of spinal cord and brain as well as shattering his jaw.[6] He slumped to the road, his bowler hat falling and rolling nearby, along with Daly's ejected cartridge.

Keogh rushed up and fired another bullet into the back of the body that jerked grotesquely under the additional impact. His bullet penetrated the back of his body armour, pulverising the liver, stomach and lung. Another spent cartridge tinkled. Blood and grey matter seeped and streamed into the street's cobbled recesses. The gunmen's eyes quickly darted around, pistols cocked to shoot at anyone attempting to intervene. This was anticipated; there were military personnel in the area, but no such threat manifested. The assassins, pumping with adrenalin, made their escape into Montague Street surrounded by shocked onlookers, rooted in terror.

After the gunmen had dispersed, Forbes-Redmond's limp body was carried by horrified passers-by, including a local doctor, into a nearby chemist shop where the father of two was pronounced dead. The message was clear: three weeks since his arrival in the city to inject fervour into G-Division had been enough for the IRA to track and ruthlessly gun him down in the busy streets. It carried the required weight; soon afterwards, the detectives who had accompanied him from Belfast returned there.

Forbes-Redmond's death marked the end of G-Division as a competent counter-insurgency unit. In the main they would only investigate ordinary crime and endeavour to steer clear of political work. The few remaining G-men willing to continue with political work fled to the sanctuary of Dublin Castle, only venturing out on raids with military protection. The Castle authorities, reacting, decreed that troops be called on to assist the police in all their duties.[7] Soldiers soon began patrolling Dublin's streets alongside armed constables.

Meanwhile, a £10,000 reward was put in place on 25 January for any civilian providing information leading to the capture of Michael Collins or any of those responsible for Forbes-Redmond's killing, as well as those killed previously in similar circumstances. No one took up the offer.

***

One hundred miles away, the day before Forbes-Redmond's killing had seen the first unofficial police reprisals of the conflict. Const. Luke Finnegan had been shot while walking in Thurles. His incandescent colleagues, backed up by soldiers from the Sherwood Foresters Regiment, attacked property belonging to local Sinn Féin members, as well as public property and shops. Shots were fired along the town's Mall and into nearby side-streets. Windows in the local Sinn Féin hall were also smashed. No one was injured. Republican propagandists quickly seized upon what they referred to as the 'sacking of Thurles'. It set an ominous precedent.

In Dublin Castle, meanwhile, Under Secretary MacMahon joined Insp. Byrne in suffering Lord French's wrath. The viceroy was far happier with Sir John Taylor's credentials as far as commitment to the cause, and more importantly, security, were concerned. MacMahon, a moderate with nationalist sympathies, was seen as a security risk and side-lined. Given that MacMahon had unwittingly recruited Michael Collins' second cousin as a decoder, French's fears were not unfounded. Sir Henry Wilson's virulently unionist influence was also growing as the field marshal became more watchful from London. Wilson was abhorred at the increase in military activity in Ireland given wider pressures within the army, and favoured doubling the size of the police instead to deal with what he termed as: 'Spies and murderers everywhere'.[8] He had also become concerned about the pitiful lack of motor transport along with other logistical and communications equipment available to the army in Ireland, which risked hamstringing, and ultimately prolonging its deployment in such numbers.[9]

Despite such logistical constraints mass raids took place in Dublin on 30 January, the same day fifty-two-year-old Thomas Kelly was elected as Dublin's new lord mayor. A Tricolour flag flew above City Hall, next door to Dublin Castle marking the occasion. Kelly had recently been interned in Wormwood Scrubs Prison, a measure that immediately impacted his health, as well as rendering him incapable of occupying the mayoral position, meaning Laurence O'Neill remained in his place. The propaganda value of this was employed with customary proficiency by Sinn Féin. Meanwhile, that night, sixty-four arrests were made in the Dublin District and 5th (Curragh) Divisional area. Robert Barton was the bounty of one such raid. He was recaptured in Oakley Road at 4 a.m. on 31 January, to be subsequently court-martialled and sentenced to three years' penal servitude.

G-DIVISION DECIMATED AND BRITISH INTELLIGENCE PUMMELLED

By the end of January, 220 political arrests had been made in Ireland since the year's beginning. Hundreds more homes had been raided in the bitterly cold dead of night. Vehicles carrying raiding parties typically halted several blocks from the houses of those they sought in urban areas, avoiding the possibility of noisy or misfiring engines alerting their occupants.[10] The banging of rifle-butts on front doors recognised no loyalties; separatists and unionists, as well as neutrals, experienced the intrusions of fully kitted soldiers rummaging through personal and intimate belongings for weapons and evidence. Strident questioning was directed at men and women in night-clothes, often holding crying children closely while trying to reassure bewildered and frightened siblings. Many cursed the IRA, as well as the British military, for causing such intrusions. The scene set in Phibsboro following the attack on Lord French was replicated daily throughout cities and towns as streets and areas were cordoned off with checkpoints, roadblocks and military vehicles. Bayonets glinted under street lamps.

As in all military units, dispositions among soldiers varied. Some acted with restraint, others availed of opportunities for theft, violence and insult. The same pattern grew throughout the country, providing ample sustenance for Desmond Fitzgerald's burgeoning propaganda machine and driving further voluminous numbers of indignant civilians into the arms of Sinn Féin. Nonetheless, the recipients of such swoops were not the only ones suffering sleepless nights. The night of 4 February saw a grenade lobbed into Kevin Street DMP station's sleeping quarters from the nearby tenement houses. The explosion caused significant damage but no casualties.

8 February saw McDonnell, Byrne, Keogh and Slattery back in action again, bolstering an operation deemed a brigade affair, which was under Vice-Brigadier Clancy's command. Clancy had recently assumed the rank following Michael Lynch's reassignment to his own former role as director of munitions. A party of two-dozen 3rd Battalion Volunteers raided the Navy and Army Canteen Board garage in Bow Lane near Mercer Street. Several vehicles were taken having been filled first with fuel, tools and motor parts.[11] GHQ soon ensured these were put to good use during a particularly lucrative mail raid yielding a bounty of blank postal orders as well as a wealth of valuable intelligence. The proceeds from the postal orders were shared equally among the delighted raiders.

On the same night as the Bow Lane assault Arthur Griffith was in London, delivering a speech at a mass protest in London's Royal Albert Hall organised by the ISDL. His reception was rapturous, as was that for Charlotte D'Espard, who spoke equally vociferously of injustices in Ireland perpetrated under the watch of her own increasingly disillusioned younger brother – Lord French. By the same date, sixty-one recent round-up victims were languishing in British prisons, having been deported since arrest. The remainder in Ireland – growing daily – were expected to eventually be tried by the civil authorities.

During the ensuing days, Clancy and recently released Dick McKee found time to pay visits to Dan Breen, still recuperating in the Malone household while falling in love with one of his carers, Brigid. Their visits were greatly appreciated.

Clancy was in charge again four days later when an attempt was made to rescue Robert Barton in transit from Ship Street barracks to Mountjoy Prison from where he was scheduled to be transported to Portland Prison in England. McKee oversaw the operation from GHQ. Barton's strategic importance to the counter-state gave this job top priority.

During early afternoon a large party of 2nd Battalion Volunteers under Capt. Pat Sweeney and several Special Duties Unit members were detailed to the junction of Berkeley Road and Nelson Street, within minutes' drive of Mountjoy. Mick McDonnell and Vinny Byrne lay in wait two miles away, close to Ship Street, in McDonnell's side-car combination. Observing a military truck leaving Ship Street in that direction, they sped to warn their awaiting comrades who included Leonard and Daly. Construction was taking place on a house in Nelson Street. The builders, known to the IRA men, happily provided a hand-cart upon which sat a forty-foot ladder which could be used to block the road just as the truck approached from Mountjoy Street.

Ten minutes later, the truck seen by McDonnell and Byrne rumbled towards them. The cart was pushed across. The Volunteers then pounced from several directions with pistols drawn. They quickly subdued the driver and two officers. A shot rang out. Passing civilians rushed for cover, terrified. Then, the assailants found, to their astonishment, that the vehicle was carrying medical equipment, but not Barton. He had been transported in a different vehicle. To add to the farce Volunteer Henry Kelly writhed in agony nearby. The recent shot had been Kelly shooting himself in the foot while drawing his parabellum

G-DIVISION DECIMATED AND BRITISH INTELLIGENCE PUMMELLED

pistol. He was rushed to the nearby Mater hospital in McDonnell's side-car. Paddy Daly ordered the truck's terrified driver to turn back to the city with his passengers, hoping that this would at least cloak the mission's objective and avoid the propaganda repercussions from such an embarrassing blunder. He then sped on foot to GHQ to inform McKee what had transpired.

McKee, taking the failure on board, made his way immediately to the Mater to check on Kelly's condition. The latter's appreciation echoed Breen's growing admiration for the young brigadier. McKee then inspected the scene of the botched ambush on his return to GHQ. The following day the incident, its objective obvious, was ridiculed in the unionist press.

Fortunately for the republicans, this discomfiture was overshadowed two days later with the first successful capture of an RIC barracks from the enemy. This took place at Ballytrain in Co. Monaghan. Ernie O'Malley, a twenty-two-year-old former medical student, had been dispatched by GHQ to Monaghan the previous month as an organiser. He, along with the Monaghan Brigade commander, thirty-year-old Eoin O'Duffy, oversaw the operation. That night ninety Volunteers set up roadblocks throughout the surrounding area, as another thirty attacked the barracks itself. Its gable wall was blown in with gelignite after its half-dozen RIC complement defended the building for several hours. Much of the structure was destroyed and a small amount of arms and ammunition were seized. The policemen, wounded and terrified, were treated charitably; IRA medical officers tended them. O'Duffy's message was simple: he implored them to leave the force, emphasising that the RIC were acting against the proclaimed will of the people. GHQ was jubilant with the raid's success. Loyalist Ulster looked on fearfully at the significance of such prominent IRA activity having penetrated the province.

Four days later, 18 February, Timothy Quinlisk was shown no such mercy. Fate had finally closed in on the hapless wayfarer. His pursuit of Collins had brought him to Cork, lured there by false information that Collins would meet him in the city. He was monitored for a time, until eventually taken a mile south of the city and shot in the head and body nine times by three members of the Cork Number 1 Brigade.[12] He was the first spy to face a lonely roadside execution by the IRA in Cork. Many would follow.

Collins was, thanks to the diligent work of agent 'Jameson', Dublin Castle's most wanted man. To lighten some of his load, his responsibilities as adjutant general were delegated henceforth to his twenty-nine-year-old cousin, Gearóid O'Sullivan. Both men were residing at 16 Airfield Road in Rathgar, home of O'Sullivan's aunt, forty-eight-year-old Julia O'Donovan. Jameson had departed Ireland to report directly to Sir Basil Thompson soon after Forbes-Redmond's killing, informing Liam Tobin that he had urgent work undermining the British Army in England on behalf of communist associates; he hoped to maintain his perceived allure of importance and, accordingly, maintain an open line of communication, despite fears of his cover having by now been blown. Tobin had been happy to see the back of him, presuming this would represent a far less repugnant means of removing such a stone from his shoe than assisting in his killing. He was wrong; Jameson returned to Dublin, as ordered by another handler, Lt-Col Ralph Isham, a distinguished intelligence operative, who was, unknowingly, sending him to his death.[13]

Meanwhile, the Dublin Brigade was back in action on the night of 19 February on both sides of Dublin's docks. Under orders from Dick McKee and led by Peadar Clancy, Vinny Byrne and thirty comrades from the 2nd and 3rd Battalions, backed up by engineers, raided the B & I Steam Packet sheds on Sir John Rogerson's Quay at 11 p.m. These were situated at Lime Street's junction, three-quarters of a mile east of Butt Bridge, which many participating Volunteers had crossed earlier en route. Intelligence had been received of a large consignment of military stores and ammunition having recently arrived at the red-bricked sheds. The plan was to plunder what they could and destroy everything else. Two police vehicles had been commandeered under Joe O'Connor's watch as transports. A first-aid station, recently opened in 5 South Frederick Street, the family home of the 3rd Battalion Volunteer Gus Connolly, stood by in case of casualties. Annie Cooney and her sister Eileen waited in nervous anticipation. It was one of many such stations being set up within the city, with Rose McNamara – like Cooney – a veteran of the Rising and former Kilmainham Gaol inmate, taking charge of allocating Cumann na mBan members to them throughout the city.

Unfortunately for the Volunteers their intelligence was, again, inaccurate, and the raid yielded nothing but a large quantity of liquorice, which Byrne gorged himself on, and some packs of coffee that were stuffed into everyone's pockets. Afterwards, Byrne made his way home towards South Anne Street, but hearing shooting on the way, he decided to investigate. Paddy McGrath

G-DIVISION DECIMATED AND BRITISH INTELLIGENCE PUMMELLED

and his twenty-year-old brother Gabriel, making their way home to Rathmines from another unsuccessful raid – this time undertaken by the 5th Engineer Battalion to destroy a large consignment of tyres for British Army vehicles on North Wall Quay – had become involved in a fire-fight with DMP members next to the Bank of Ireland on College Green. The police and army had been out in force that night in an attempt to reclaim the streets. Const. Patrick Dennis shot Paddy in the shoulder when the policemen, spooked, opened fire on them. Both men had then zig-zagged before returning fire until Paddy, badly wounded, collapsed. Gabriel then retreated under further fire after his brother shouted at him to run, only for him to then encounter another patrol at the junction of Grafton Street and Nassau Street. Acting on instinct, Gabriel shot Const. John Walsh through the heart and wounded Sgt James Dunleavy. Walsh died instantly. Police reinforcements sped to the bloody scene but the IRA man escaped. Paddy McGrath was eventually taken to King George V Hospital and kept under armed guard while treated. By the time Vinny Byrne passed through the area, he was too late to intervene.

The Dublin streets were certainly turning ever more dangerous. Another gun battle had taken place a short time earlier that night, just minutes away, in Marlborough Street; Peadar Clancy, George Plunkett and Michael Brennan had eventually escaped from the brief skirmish in a taxi-cab, while in nearby Waterford Street three men also returning home from the North Wall raid – Mick Kelly, Phil Leddy and Jack Shaw – were arrested with loaded revolvers by a large police and army patrol.

The following night, raids and searches took place throughout nearby Aungier Street, seeking Const. Walsh's killer. Military back up included a Mark A Whippet medium tank, crewed by members of the 17th Battalion Royal Tank Corps. The tank was armed with four Hotchkiss .303 Mark 1 machine guns. Its huge metal tracks clashed noisily against the cobblestones and could be heard streets away. Buildings adjacent its path shuddered as if shook by an earthquake as heightened tension gripped the area. The presence of the metal monster grinding its gears through populated city centre streets at night was further fuel for the industrious writers of the *Irish Bulletin*. Erskine Childers, his prowess as a writer made evident many years earlier in his best-selling spy thriller *The Riddle of the Sands*, was contributing and delivering propaganda blows with surgical precision.

The hunt for McGrath was fruitless. Nevertheless, the resulting disappointment was short-lived. Cullenswood House was raided again the following night, after an initial botched raid on Áine Ceannt's nearby home, when both addresses were confused for one another. Richard Mulcahy, employing an array of addresses to avoid detection, was staying at Cullenswood House again. Once again his luck held – at least partially; he escaped into the darkness in his pyjamas at the last moment and sped away. Crucially, however, this time he left behind a massive amount of seditious literature, including the complete rolls and addresses of the now 3,000-strong IRA Dublin Brigade.[14] Their discovery following a thorough search represented an unmitigated disaster for the IRA, one they had narrowly avoided the previous December following Ashtown. This was also a much needed intelligence boost to the exultant police and military. Crown confidence skyrocketed.

Two nights later, on 23 February, a proclamation was issued by the general officer commanding (GOC) Dublin District, on instructions received directly from the lord lieutenant, of a military curfew between midnight and 5 a.m.[15] The Kingstown area, covered by DMP F-Division, was exempt. That and subsequent nights saw twenty separate military patrols deployed in the affected metropolitan areas, each consisting of one officer and twelve other ranks in lorries, with various forms of improvised protection riveted and bolted on, along with searchlights. Bicycle patrols were also deployed. Permits became available for night workers but most refused to apply.

In protest at this measure Dublin Corporation began extinguishing all street lamps at 11.30 p.m., refusing to light them for the benefit of an 'alien people'.[16] Municipal officials and employees were forbidden to apply for permits and overtime payments were quickly stopped to workers during curfew hours. The street lamps policy was criticised as providing opportunities for reprobates. Official curfew notices posted throughout the city warned the public to: 'Walk warily, listen keenly, and halt promptly'.[17] The curfew quickly proved advantageous to the authorities in singling out insurgents, particularly as there was no one else on the streets to blend in with on night operations. It did, however, eventually prove a double-edged sword by facilitating the identification of crown agents in civilian clothes carelessly assuming they could move around, particularly when drunk, without suffering the consequences.

***

G-DIVISION DECIMATED AND BRITISH INTELLIGENCE PUMMELLED

Several days later Paddy McGrath was struck by the unexpected arrival of a visitor to the hospital where he was still being held and treated for wounds received on the 19 February: a priest who tried to persuade him to allow him to take his confession. Something appeared amiss to McGrath, however, and he refused, suspecting an enemy agent was actually soliciting him.

Notably, two such agents, Bell and 'Jameson' had been engaged relentlessly in their pursuits of Michael Collins during February's final days, Bell preparing to launch an inquiry into banks suspected of facilitating the Dáil Loan, Jameson in pursuit of the man himself by means of harassing known associates. The recent seizure at Cullenswood House emboldened Jameson. Joe O'Reilly was followed and accosted at one point by the tenacious Londoner, declaring he had urgent information for Collins. O'Reilly humoured him and subsequently took appropriate measures to shake him off. Orders were, at this point, merely to avoid Jameson at all costs. O'Reilly then suffered Collins' wrath at having allowed himself to be tracked down in the first place. Collins regularly vented at his aide-de-camp, O'Reilly exercising superhuman patience by appreciating it was never personal; it was a side-effect of the continuous mind-boggling strain Collins was under. Nevertheless, colleagues and comrades marvelled at O'Reilly's composure under such repeated assaults. Another more forceful means of venting was employed by the finance minister – wrestling. Associates were often, to their complete surprise, pounced upon by Collins and grappled to the floor. Collins' favourite means of achieving victory was to bite his opponent's ear. Some saw this as a jovial means of ventilating and gave as good as they got, others were appalled at its savage absurdity.

Eventually, given Jameson's refusal to give up, a final trap was set. Jameson was to meet with Volunteers who would, as customary, escort him to Collins – but this time it would be to a fictitious meeting with the IRA intelligence chief. Salivating, Jameson was drawn from the Granville Hotel, providing time for Tom Cullen to, facilitated by a hotel employee, gain access to his room and discover what Collins needed: definitive damning evidence of his real identity in order to get GHQ sanction for his killing. GHQ's benchmark for ordering executions was set frustratingly high at times for those operating at the coalface of counter-intelligence. In the meantime Jameson, *en route* to the fictitious meeting, was told at the last moment that it was postponed. Meanwhile Cullen found what he wanted and relayed the information to

Cathal Brugha, who granted approval. Time was running out for Jameson.

On 28 February in Crow Street, Liam Tobin told Joe Dolan that he would be meeting a man on D'Olier Street at a specific time that day, and that he was to follow him, watch out for this man and take particular stock of him.[18] Dolan then turned up and spotted Tobin in conversation with the man. He was five-foot-eight-inches tall and wearing a dark coat with a fur collar. Dolan ensured he would recognise him again.

The following day, Tobin revealed to Dolan that the individual he had been talking to was an enemy spy and was to be shot. Dolan was then instructed to meet Paddy Daly outside Brennan & Walsh Drapers on Sackville Street and, from there, cycle to the Glasnevin area and select a spot to shoot him. An hour later Dolan and Daly arrived in Glasnevin and chose a location – an avenue running alongside Albert Agricultural College known locally as 'Lovers' Lane'.[19]

The next day, Tuesday 2 March, Jameson received an instruction to be outside Brennan & Walsh's at 4 p.m. From there he would be met and taken to Collins. He snapped at the bait. Leaving his hotel, he walked to where Paddy Daly was awaiting him. The pair then took the No. 19 tram the three-mile journey to their destination. Jameson was unaware that Joe Leonard had also boarded and had his eyes fixed firmly upon him. The tram's departure was also watched by IRA men, ensuring that their comrades were themselves in turn not followed. Daly and Jameson sat silently among their fellow passengers as the tram jolted along its rails. By this time, Joe Dolan had met up with Tom Kilcoyne – a twenty-two-year-old Volunteer captain from Wicklow – who had been recruited from those initially mustered the previous July but told to lie low, and Ben Barrett, at Upper Gardiner Street church. From there the three cycled out to Lovers' Lane.

Twenty minutes later Daly and the man he was escorting to his death alighted the tram. Daly was offered a cigarette as they walked uphill along the Naul Road (Ballymun Road) towards the college. Daly refused, remaining silent. Jameson then requested to stop at a public house a short distance ahead to their left. Daly said they had no time, suspecting his fellow traveller wished to use the telephone there to contact a handler. Leonard tailed them. Then, Daly instructed Jameson to turn right into the narrow country laneway adjacent to the college. His three comrades were waiting fifty yards into the lane.

They turned right and walked on. When Jameson's eyes fell on Dolan,

G-DIVISION DECIMATED AND BRITISH INTELLIGENCE PUMMELLED

Kilcoyne and Barrett he suddenly sensed the game was up. Daly quickly confirmed this, telling him: 'We are satisfied you are a spy, and you are going to die'.[20] Jameson's face dropped. Agitated and seeing no escape, he declared that they were making a huge mistake and that Tobin and Collins would punish them severely for it. He then looked at Joe Dolan, who had recognised him instantly from D'Olier Street, protesting: 'If you shoot me you shoot one of your best boys'. Dolan cocked his revolver, which ended the protestations – it was over. Daly stood back. Then, Kilcoyne and Barrett quickly closed in and searched him, pistols trained on his head and torso. Papers and belongings were taken from his trench-coat, jacket, waistcoat and trouser pockets as Leonard maintained watch some distance away. He was asked if he wished to pray. At this point John Charles Byrnes collected himself, drew breath and stood at attention. His executioners were suddenly struck with subdued admiration. He was then told, half-apologetically, that they were only doing their duty.[21] He replied unwaveringly: 'And I have done mine', finally adding, 'God save the King', and saluting.

Daly fired first into his back, the bullet tearing through his right lung and exiting through his chest. The shot shattered the evening stillness, sending birds scattering and squawking. Byrnes collapsed, slumping to the ground gasping and twitching spasmodically in agony. Barrett quickly stood forward and shot him in the head, just in front of the right ear, the *coup-de-grace* ending his torment. His executioners quickly escaped, making their way back to the city, Leonard among them.

At 5.30 p.m. James Scott McNaughton, a local man, found the still-warm corpse lying on its right side across the laneway, its feet sticking out from nearby bushes. The head and face were heavily blood-stained. Others soon arrived. Police and an ambulance were summoned and the body was taken to the Mater Hospital for post-mortem.

Meanwhile, Tom Cullen had undertaken another search of Byrnes' room at the Granville Hotel, accompanied by Tobin. Some fake jewellery was discovered, as well as some caged birds purchased earlier that day – a passion of the late spy. The incriminating documentation discovered previously by Cullen was removed to Crow Street and quickly analysed, revealing a disconcerting revelation: 'Jameson' had been in charge of a small network of spies in Dublin. The group fled the city within days, fearing a similar fate.[22]

The following Saturday, following identification by a porter in the Granville Hotel, and an inquest returning a verdict of murder, Byrnes' remains were shipped back to England for burial close to his home in Romford, Essex. Locals there were intrigued. He had told family and friends that he was working in Scotland. It was noted that his financial means appeared to have improved considerably in recent months. Walter Long – acting as first lord of the admiralty but, nonetheless, with his finger firmly on Ireland's pulse – later paid tribute to Byrnes as the best Secret Service man they had.

On the day Byrnes met his bloody demise, Alan Bell issued summonses to several bank managers to appear before a private sitting of Dublin's police courts to investigate the locations of the Dáil funds. The summonses stipulated that they were to provide a host of documents such as securities, telegrams, letters, books of account, ledgers, cheques, orders, and drafts that in any way related to the Dáil or Sinn Féin.[23] Failure to comply would result in arrest warrants pending approval by the attorney general, Denis Henry.

Then, on Monday 8 March, the inquiry opened, receiving a mixed reaction. Bell was accused by *The Freeman's Journal* and *Irish Independent* of attempting to eradicate long-standing commercial precepts of client confidentiality. The fact that the inquiry was held behind closed doors provoked further indignation. Bell's legal prowess was questioned. Ridicule accompanied the point that the six days' notice provided to bank managers had provided ample time for Sinn Féin to take measures to further secrete their funds. The *Irish Bulletin* alluded to Bell's investigations into Land League funding during the 1880s, accusing him of having acted then as an *agent provocateur* and forger, and suggested he was a spy employed by Westminster to crush the fledgling Irish economy. Unionist newspapers, conversely, reported little on the enquiry.[24]

Almost a dozen bank managers were questioned rigorously by Bell. Names such as Barton, Collins, Griffith and Duggan abounded, to name but a few. The managers deflected as many questions as they could. Responses were fragmented and uncooperative. Details provided were, largely, insignificant. Bell had been assiduous in his work, however, and had procured numerous cheques that forced the managers onto the back foot. Cheques applicable to transactions involving Michael Collins, Richard Mulcahy and Art O'Brien were produced. However, despite warnings of warrants for non-compliance with the enquiry none of the bankers produced their books, allowing them to deflect initial attempts at such scrutiny and buy time, appearing to prefer testing the resolve of the attorney general to the prospect of falling foul of IRA intelligence. The manager of College Green's Hibernian Bank, Henry Joseph Campbell, provided a telling articulation when asked if he was familiar with an account concerning Michael Collins. He replied: 'I would not like to say that from memory, I would have to go and look it up. It would be too dangerous for me to speak from memory'.[25] The implication of the word 'dangerous' was not wasted on those conducting the enquiry, or his fellow managers.

Collins was indeed paying close attention. Michael Noyk had attempted to access the inquiry on his behalf but was refused entry. Collins, ever the prankster even at the most trying of times, had then goaded Noyk the following Sunday night in Vaughan's about his failure to fulfil such a simple duty. Noyk was momentarily taken in before 'the Big Fella', as Collins was known affectionately to close associates, grasped his hand, shook it, and smiled jokingly.[26] Nonetheless, Collins had Bell under observation, recognising him at this point as the unofficial chief of Dublin Castle intelligence. He also had thirty-year-old Michael Knightly, a reporter who worked for the Dáil, chasing down a photograph of him from the *Irish Independent*. The photograph, clearly revealing Bell's genial looking and rotund facial features, meticulously maintained moustache and neatly combed thinning and parted hair, was soon on its way to Liam Tobin in Crow Street. Time was running out for Alan Bell.

Three days after the 'Big Fella' goaded Michael Noyk, Éamon de Valera – jokingly referred to similarly by some as 'the Long Fella' – delivered an impassioned St Patrick's Day speech in the USA. The speech was recorded at the Nation's Forum. De Valera was counted among distinguished speakers such as US Army General John J. Pershing, and politicians Calvin Coolidge and Franklin D. Roosevelt. De Valera employed the occasion to implore the 'sons and daughters of the Gael' to combine their strength 'to break the chains that bind our sweet, sad mother' at what he described as an unprecedented opportunity to display to war-weary Europe, and the world, the best that Ireland could give. He compared Irish people to the tip of a spear heralding a new dawn for 'the despairing and wretched everywhere'.[27]

GHQ was well aware that breaking such chains would require a lot more weapons and explosives. An opportunity to replenish supplies of the latter was successfully exploited during mid-March in a daring raid on the Great

Northern Railway Yard at the rear of Amiens Street station. Tom Keogh, having spent some time working there, had received word of the precise location of two railway wagons with boxes of gelignite. He had then shared this information with Mick McDonnell. McDonnell was buoyant at the prospect of such a haul. When Vinny Byrne and Jim Slattery called at the house on a social visit soon afterwards he declared: 'Just the right men in the right place'.[28] He then ordered them to gather as many men of E Company 2nd Battalion as they could and report to Oriel Hall, a building situated in a small cul-de-sac off Upper Oriel Street, conveniently located just yards from the rail yard, but separated by an eighteen-foot granite wall, at 11 p.m.

That night two-dozen Volunteers, most armed with pistols, mustered at Oriel Hall. Byrne and Slattery were then ordered to mount their bicycles and patrol the surrounding streets, particularly Sheriff Street and Seville Place, both going in opposing directions in the curfew-deserted streets. Tom Keogh was first to scale the granite wall, he and his comrades having employed ladders and an array of loose blocks and wooden boxes to create steps, and was followed by a dozen men whom he then directed to the nearby wagons after they had pulled another ladder over the wall once the coast was clear. They navigated the debris and machinery-strewn yard as silently as possible in the moonlit darkness. Keogh, familiar with the yard, then opened the wagons. McDonnell, characteristically stern, directed the remaining ten men at Oriel Hall to remove their shoes and boots and take positions at the wall. Minutes later, Keogh's men, using the ladder, passed the gelignite to the shoeless men on the far side, who, in relays, transported them silently on foot 200 yards away to the home of Patrick Ennis, a thirty-two-year-old Volunteer and cousin of Tom Ennis, in 3 Oriel Place. Prayers flashed through their minds as they did. The prospect of imminent vaporisation by the gelignite ensured their steps were light and their prayers sincere, the cold pavement underfoot occupying a very distant second place in their anxious minds. Ninety minutes later, the entire haul was secured.

The following day saw no mention of the raid in the newspapers. However, the entire area was quickly cordoned off by the military for several days and nights. Houses and vehicles were searched. There was no way to safely move the gelignite without encountering a patrol. Luckily for Ennis, his home was one of the last searched. By the time the troops arrived, the explosives were secured beneath his floorboards and went undetected. Dick McKee, entering his third year as Dublin Brigadier, applauded McDonnell and E Company on their initiative. McKee then oversaw the haul's removal from Oriel Place at the earliest opportunity. Soon the gelignite was distributed throughout the city's bomb factories and used to fabricate grenades. It was a much needed morale boost to the Dublin Brigade, suffering from incessant round-ups and arrests.

IRA morale on a national level was badly buffeted on Saturday 20 March with news of the shooting dead during the previous night in Cork of Tomás MacCurtain. As well as being Cork Number 1 Brigade commandant, he was the city's recently elected mayor. Thirty-six years old that day, he was gunned down at his home above the clothing factory he co-owned at 40 Thomas Davis Street in Blackpool, in which slept his wife Elizabeth, their five children and his wife's brother.

MacCurtain had retired to bed following his observation of a scheduled signal from his front window that all was clear outside, provided by the local lamplighter. However, unknown to the lamplighter, the whole Blackpool area was being isolated at the time by plain clothed and uniformed police who had begun to stop people entering the vicinity of Thomas Davis Street.[29]

Two men with blackened faces barged into his house and past his wife

Tomás MacCurtain, commandant of Cork Number 1 Brigade, who was shot dead by members of the RIC at his home in Cork on the night of 19-20 March 1920.
(*Courtesy of Mercier Archive*)

after nearly knocking the front door from its hinges at 1 a.m. They shouted: 'Come out MacCurtain we want you'. The men ran upstairs, confronted MacCurtain and shot the lord mayor twice.[30] One of the rounds went through his chest, glancing his heart. Several more shots were aimed at his brother-in-law but missed. Accomplices held his wife at the front door while the shooting was carried out upstairs. After the gunmen departed, further shots were fired at the building.

The night had then echoed with screams of terror and disbelief. A doctor and priest were summoned to the dying lord mayor's side, his nightshirt and the carpet beneath drenched in blood. Crowds quickly gathered outside. He remained alive long enough for the priest to quietly perform last rites while his traumatised children sobbed close by. His wife, composing herself as best she could, leaned in and spoke softly: 'Remember darling, it's all for Ireland'.[31] Moments later, he passed away from shock and blood loss.

MacCurtain's death was met with sadness, shock and anger. He was a founding member of the Irish Volunteers and a senior IRB member. He had been fundamental to the reorganisation of the Cork Volunteers after the 1916 Rising. Fingers pointed immediately at the RIC for his killing. The public were outraged. It was suspected as an act of retaliation to the shooting dead of policemen in Cork, including that of forty-six-year-old Const. Joseph Murtagh the same night in Pope's Quay in the city; ironically, MacCurtain – appalled by the shooting – had spent several hours making enquiries into the dying policeman's condition. This was despite a written warning on Dáil notepaper which read: 'Thomas MacCurtain, prepare for death. You are doomed', having been delivered to his address four days earlier in an attempt by the authorities at black propaganda. MacCurtain's killing set the scene for events that catapulted Ireland's independence struggle to the forefront of the world. His death would not go unanswered.

11

THE BLACK AND TANS ARRIVE

'All cells open, all awake but silent'

By now, one of Col Hill-Dillon's most enthusiastic recently recruited agents had been making his presence felt in Dublin. He was twenty-four-year-old Frederick McNulty, a former army deserter who had successfully re-enlisted, posing as Brian Fergus Molloy. 'Molloy' hung around haunts soon to be frequented with increasing regularity by intelligence operatives from both sides, such as the Cairo Café in 59 Grafton Street and Kidd's Back pub on adjacent Nassau Street, as well as other haunts visited by the full assortment of Dublin's intellectuals, revellers, businessmen, civil-servants and revolutionary separatists. He had initially gained an introduction to Batt O'Connor via Dr Robert Farnan who had sheltered De Valera upon his return from Lincoln a year earlier. Farnan was following the recommendation of an associate from Mayo, where Molloy cited strong historic connections: his father, James, had come from Foxford.

Molloy had told O'Connor he was employed as a pay-clerk in Army HQ Parkgate Street and had recently been solicited by anxious superiors to join the Secret Service.[1] This, he claimed, afforded him the opportunity to act as a double-agent for the IRA. Speaking with a Manchester accent, Molloy claimed his father had been forced to emigrate many years previously, and therefore, he could not in all good conscience act against his own people. In reality he was, like Jameson, eager to garner the attentions of Michael Collins by promising to procure arms as well as intelligence. Under Hill-Dillon's instructions, however, he could settle for Tobin or Cullen, also known to British intelligence since agent Byrnes, masked as 'Jameson', had briefed his police handlers on the existence of both.

Molloy was, unfortunately for himself, under the attentions of Lily Mernin. Mernin's handler was nineteen-year-old Dubliner Frank Saurin, recently recruited to IRA intelligence from the 2nd Battalion. Mernin sent word to him soon after Molloy's deployment and Saurin had been quick to relay the message on. It eventually got to Collins who, notwithstanding the recent scare with 'Jameson', was unsure, and detailed Tobin, Cullen and Thornton to meet him under pseudonyms to sound him out. Several meetings followed at his favoured venues, where he was played in a nerve-racking game of duplicity. Police and off-duty military also frequented such establishments. On the evening of 15 March he was followed to Dublin Castle's gates by Patrick Caldwell. When Caldwell reported this to Tobin he was told to keep tracking him. Then, at a subsequent meeting, Molloy offered to get Tobin and Thornton inside the Castle to pore over secret files. The proposition's temerity heightened both men's awareness of the potential threat posed by their plucky adversary, envisaging what could really happen to them inside the Castle's walls. Nevertheless, they persevered with the game, hoping to learn what they could from him while biding their own time and awaiting conclusive proof. At one point, to further test him, they suggested enlisting his help to assassinate Hill-Dillon who was residing at a known private address in the city. The colonel quickly moved; a fact soon relayed to Collins.

Finally, at a later meeting in the Cairo Café, Molloy pressed both Tobin and Thornton for snippets of information to show to his superiors that would prove he was achieving something.[2] This, he claimed, would ingratiate him further, thus leaving army intelligence more susceptible to letting him in on their own operational secrets, which he would in turn divulge to the IRA. Arms dumps or less significant leaders of their movement, the losses of which or whom could be compensated for, were his suggested choice, preferably the latter.

What then followed shocked Thornton and Tobin, and sealed Molloy's fate: Molloy produced a sheet of Dáil notepaper – the same paper that had been removed from 76 Harcourt Street during the Armistice Day raid the previous November – and suggested they write the names and addresses of such low importance figures. Hot on the heels of MacCurtain's demise at the hands of a police death squad, Molloy's requests for the addresses of Countess Markievicz or Count Plunkett, as two notable examples, triggered alarm bells in the minds of the IRA intelligence pair that they struggled to mask. This was clearly a trap: a plot to assassinate anyone whose address was written there. The notes would then be left behind at the scenes to cynically suggest that such killings were the handiwork of the IRA – the result of in-fighting; worse: the handwriting would identify which IRA member had written each address. The potential consequences were horrifying. Tobin went straight to Vaughan's to brief Collins. His response was rapid: 'We have to shoot that fellow'.[3] Meanwhile, when Molloy returned to his lodging in the Wicklow Hotel, he was observed speaking with the hotel's porter, William Doran. The porter would himself be watched.

On Tuesday 23 March Thornton met Molloy at the Cairo Café, promising him a subsequent introduction to the enigmatic Tobin. Molloy still remained unaware of having met Tobin already. Vinny Byrne, a full-time paid-up member of what was now officially referred to as 'The Squad', had been detailed to follow them to the café in order to identify Molloy afterwards for his execution.

'The Squad' in its current form had recently come into being after Crow Street intelligence noticed army intelligence operatives were only venturing out during business hours. They quickly deduced that this was because their units' killings had all been done outside business hours, leading the enemy to conclude that the assassins held down daytime occupations. Tobin had informed Collins that measures were needed to overcome both this, and the additional complication of the curfew. GHQ ultimately decided to alter their strategy to daytime assassinations. The increased risk of unit and civilian casualties was deemed a necessary evil. However, they needed the men to facilitate this. Meanwhile, the 'Big Four' were no longer available; Robinson, Treacy and Hogan were back stirring up trouble in Tipperary, while Dan Breen was convalescing in Fingal. GHQ had noted that the intelligence department was working exceptionally well with the Special Duties Units so it was decided to expand both whilst allowing for overlap. More importantly, both Special Duties Units were combined into one, with full-time paid-up members. Dick McKee, at this point, had already been feeding the intelligence department with men like George Fitzgerald, and more recently, twenty-two-year-old 3rd Battalion veteran Joe Guilfoyle, as well as seventeen-year-old Charlie Dalton of the 2nd Battalion. He also had a list of additional recruits for the unit: Eddie Byrne and Mick Kennedy among others – built up since the previous July – but he first needed to test them, notwithstanding Kennedy's successful involvement in Det. Smyth's shooting. Vinny Byrne had left his employment on 9 March, so had Jim Slattery and Tom Keogh; the three counted among the other full-time members of the IRA Special Duties Unit known as The Squad.

Byrne stepped inside the bustling, smoky Cairo Café, taking the next table to Thornton and Molloy and ordering tea. He took stock of the man to be eliminated. Thornton turned, greeted Byrne under a false name, and introduced him to Molloy.

Then Thornton said to Byrne: 'Our friend is very anxious to meet Liam Tobin and I am sure you could arrange it'.[4] Byrne feigned unease but then relented and agreed. Molloy, taken by the ruse, also agreed and the proposed rendezvous was scheduled to take place outside Noblett's sweet shop at the junction of South King Street and Grafton Street at 4.45 p.m. the next day. Both men would wear a flower on their coat lapels to help recognise each other among the early evening crowds.

Molloy turned up as appointed, Byrne did not. Instead he remained some distance away, accompanied by Mick McDonnell, Jim Slattery, Tom Keogh and Joe Dolan, the five concealing themselves in doorways and under shop canopies between South King Street and Grafton Street, primed to attack. Byrne pointed out Molloy to the others. They would work in pairs, McDonnell with Slattery, Keogh with Byrne, and Dolan as lookout. Nearby, within signalling distance stood Joe Guilfoyle and Patrick Caldwell, briefed only moments earlier by Tom Cullen, also nearby, of the job at hand and deployed as a covering party. Tactically, given the crowded streets and likelihood of obstruction, it was decided that one pair, when the opportunity presented itself, would move in on the target while the other would also cover.

They waited and watched their target until 5.30 p.m. when he gave up and began walking down Grafton Street, quickening his pace between the huge stores and fashionable cafés, as if he sensed something was up. Both units, plus Guilfoyle and Caldwell, followed from both sides of the road, matching his stride, closing distance until within pistol range. Frustrated by the crowds, however, it proved impossible to get a shot.[5]

Molloy maintained his brisk pace. He turned left onto Wicklow Street at Switzer's department store, 300 yards down the street from South King Street, knowing Dublin Castle was just minutes away. His intended executioners followed, gaining relentlessly, passing the Wicklow Hotel on their right and, among the numerous retail units, the concealed office of the Dáil's Department of Local Government to their left in No. 29.

Then Molloy slowed down momentarily. The four caught up at the junction of St Andrew Street. The Central Hotel, full of British military, was just 100 yards in front; therefore McDonnell and Slattery, leading, had no option but to get him there and then. They rushed up just as a local woman, Annie Hughes, seeing their pistols being drawn, screamed, causing Molloy to suddenly turn his head. McDonnell opened fire from Molloy's left just as he passed in front of the International Bar, sat on the road junction to his right. Civilians screamed in terror as the shot suddenly pierced the early evening air and echoed through the streets. Molloy was propelled sideways at speed by the bullet smashing through his skull, then collapsed into a crumpled heap. Byrne and Keogh played their part in finishing him off while he lay prostrate, face down on the cobbled street. The head shot shattered his lower skull, two followed to the leg and chest. The scene became a grisly mess.

Shouts erupted: 'Stop them! Stop them!' 'Don't kill him!' 'Help!' The killers walked casually to the corner of St Andrew Street, then sprinted away. Seeing this, Guilfoyle, Cullen and Caldwell turned and walked back to Grafton Street and eventually College Green. Byrne had to threaten a man with his pistol after he pushed his bicycle in front of him to try and stop him on the narrow pavement outside St Andrew Street church. Civilians sped to the victim's aid. Annie Hughes had been pushed aside by McDonnell and Slattery as they went to shoot him. She desperately tended the dying man, turning him over and wiping blood from his forehead and trying to get him to speak. Others then helped load him into a hand-cart. He was rushed to Mercer hospital 250 yards away. Despite their best efforts, Frederick McNulty was pronounced dead soon afterwards. By then, the assassins had already merged with the city-centre crowds and dumped their weapons.

As McNulty's body lay in the Mercer Hospital mortuary, the raids and arrests throughout Dublin continued. The previous evening had already seen both Nos 6 and 76 Harcourt Street badly damaged once again in searches for seditious literature and persons on arrest lists. It was the second night running that No. 6 had suffered an onslaught. The night before that, 22 March, had seen large numbers of infantrymen from the Royal Berkshire Regiment pelting the building with missiles following a night of drinking in Grafton Street after which several civilians in the area had been assaulted. Running battles through the streets followed, culminating in a brief gun battle in Lennox Street in Portobello during which a soldier was shot in the chest. When reinforcements arrived from Portobello barracks the crowds fell back into Camden Street, but not before further rifle volleys had seen two civilians killed and many more injured.

Then, on Thursday 25 March 1920, North Wall Quay was witness to the arrival of the first detachment of the RICSR, soon to become known as the 'Black and Tans' almost a year after they had first been mooted. Onlookers stared curiously and warily as the 'tough looking crowd' disembarked.[6] Drawn primarily from their London, Liverpool and Glasgow recruiting stations, they had been offered ten shillings per day for the task to hand, a tempting payment for a great many former soldiers stagnating in poverty and unemployment since their demobilisation following the war that had brutalised most of them. They were described by Winston Churchill as: 'selected from a great press of applicants on account of their intelligence, their characters and their records in the War'.[7] They were soon transported to the Curragh Camp in Co. Kildare for training and issued with their curious-looking khaki service dress supplemented with constabulary uniform.[8]

Additionally, the same day saw the enlistment of several military ex-officers to supervise the defence of vulnerable RIC barracks'.[9] It also saw the creation, under the watch of Sir John Taylor, of an extra divisional HQ in Dublin for the hard-pressed police force, aligning with the recent establishment of Dublin District Military Command under General Boyd. This paved the way for proposed closer cooperation between police and military.

Military and police raids continued the following morning. During the previous night, fifty raids had yielded a bounty of forty arrests.[10] Among the premises raided was Liam Tobin's home at 24 Munster Avenue in Phibsboro, and another of Richard Mulcahy's hideouts. Neither were home at the time, nor was Frank Henderson, whose home was also raided. Phil Shanahan was arrested, as was Laurence Ginnell at the home of Dr Kathleen Lynn in Rathmines. Ginnell was recovering there from health problems due to his most recent incarceration. This was not wasted on the *Irish Bulletin*'s authors. Also raided were Liberty Hall and the headquarters of the IWWU, as well as several other establishments that had been deemed seditious.

However, the authorities were not alone in deploying tactical units on 26

March 1920. Alan Bell was at this point directly in the crosshairs of the IRA Squad and three attempts had already been made to kill him, all of which had failed. The first involved blowing his car up with a specially designed grenade – manufactured in 198 Great Britain Street – near the Four Courts. The second was a planned shooting by a small team outside Dublin Castle, to which he travelled following each court session. This was seen off by a cunning counter attack by plain clothed armed agents in a tense game of cat and mouse which only ended when the IRA men retired across Ha'penny Bridge to more favourable ground, leaving the agents on the brow of the bridge, fearing, wisely, to proceed further. The third involved the truck seized in Bow Street the previous month; its cargo area was filled with Squad members and driven close to Bell's luxurious Victorian residence at 19 Belgrave Square in Monkstown where they planned to shoot him. The address had recently been discovered by Joe Dolan and Joe Guilfoyle. The job was called off, however, when large numbers of police were observed guarding the house.

That Friday morning, an elaborate ambush was set in motion, having been planned the previous evening in Crow Street. Four men – McDonnell, Byrne, Slattery and Guilfoyle – rendezvoused with Tobin and Dolan at Ailesbury Road's junction with Merrion Road, four miles south of the city centre. The plan was to shoot Bell as he took his morning tram to Dublin Castle.[11] This was their only option; Bell had refused the offer of a guard to accompany him daily on his tram ride to and from the city, content instead with a two-man escort from his house to the tram, and another meeting him opposite Trinity College for the short walk from there to the Castle once he alighted. The veteran policeman, magistrate, and spy, carried a revolver as an additional protective measure.

The problem of detecting which particular tram he would be on was delegated to Keogh and Daly. Both would cycle to Monkstown and monitor Bell as he and his escort walked from his front door to the tram, then keep up with the tram for the three-mile journey to Ailesbury Road, and there signal their comrades.

Bell left Monkstown that morning at 9.30 a.m. on the tram from Dalkey, Keogh and Daly in hot pursuit, having noted where he sat in the tram's lower saloon. They struggled to keep up at times as the tram sped along Monkstown Road, whining and chiming, powered by its overhead cables. Its passenger cargo increased as it trundled slowly through Blackrock village, then sped up again along Booterstown, and eventually towards Ailesbury Road where the assassins waited, some chain-smoking nervously among commuters boarding different passing trams, each of which had set the assassins' pulses racing in anticipation as they approached.

Then, suddenly, Keogh was spotted ahead of Daly in the distance, cycling at speed. Moments later, pedalling for all he worth, he reached his comrades. Hyperventilating, Keogh pointed at the No. 83 tram just behind. The six waiting men got the message and climbed aboard as soon as it stopped. It contained over forty passengers, mostly businessmen and clerks. Byrne, Slattery and Guilfoyle went upstairs, the remaining three stayed below. Daly caught up just as the tram pulled away, too late to relay where Bell was sitting. He and Keogh then cycled again, just behind.

Bell was quickly spotted nonetheless, sitting close to the door downstairs on the tram's left, absorbed in reading a newspaper. McDonnell and Tobin sat down facing him, Dolan close by, each recognising him from Knightly's photograph. McDonnell and Tobin observed Bell momentarily before conferring in code to ensure beyond doubt that he was their man. Horse racing provided the perfect cypher for their sinister discourse; a tip for a race in that day's English Grand National – a horse named *Poethlyn* – followed by responses suggesting the horse was a particular favourite, followed then by the confirmation: 'Oh he is a dead cert', prompting the last action that sealed Bell's fate.[12] McDonnell suddenly leaned across, asking: 'Are you Mister Bell?' The answer was a reflex 'Yes', McDonnell swooped, declaring: 'Come on Mr Bell, your time has come'.

The momentarily stupefied target was then wrested by the pair as McDonnell, proclaiming forcefully: 'We want you!' summoned Dolan to rapid action. Passengers were shoved from his way as he rushed to join the sudden assault. Byrne, Slattery and Guilfoyle heard the commotion from upstairs and sprung to action. Byrne and Guilfoyle combined their efforts to bring the tram to a halt, cutting the rope mechanism that secured its bow collector in place, disconnecting its power supply from the overhead cables. Slattery, his pistol primed, ensured no one interfered. The tram jolted and screeched to a halt at Simmonscourt Road adjacent to the Royal Dublin Showgrounds.[13]

Bell desperately employed all the vigour his body could muster to resist but was overwhelmed by his three assailants and pulled off the tram. Horrified passengers looked on as his hand was beaten and wrenched from the vice-like grip it had momentarily held the tram's exit handle with. As he let go, he collapsed to the platform, his strength quickly sapped from his petrifying grapple. Byrne, Guilfoyle and Slattery rushed downstairs just as the tram conductor, Patrick Kearns, brushed past in the opposite direction, shouting in alarm: 'There's going to be a man shot!'[14]

Passengers, both upstairs and downstairs, gasped and screamed in fright. Bell was quickly surrounded. Byrne, Slattery, Guilfoyle and Dolan took up covering positions. Tobin then drew a pistol from his right-hand coat pocket and pointed it down at the back of Bell's head and fired. Bell fell flat. McDonnell then fired, his shot striking the foundered body in the groin, then ricocheting and shattering his left wrist.[15]

Bell's head was pulverised by Tobin's bullet, which had entered just behind the left ear. The newspaper he still clasped as he died was quickly removed from his hand and placed over his head to conceal the gruesome mess before the six men ran away along Simmonscourt Road, observed by stunned upstairs

Squad members who took part in Alan Bell's assassination on 26 March 1920. From left to right: Mick McDonnell, Tom Keogh, Vincent Byrne, Paddy Daly and James Slattery. (*Courtesy of Mercier Archive*)

passengers until the trees lining the road concealed them from view. Passengers alighted and fled from the scene. An ambulance was called from a nearby house.

As the killers sped on foot towards Donnybrook, they met Patrick Caldwell, late for the ambush. Keogh told him the job was already done so he joined them in escaping. A motorcycle with a sidecar combination thudded past them, its driver's gaze fixed on them as he sped by. Otherwise the street was deserted, an alarming situation for those fleeing given the lack of crowds to camouflage them; if the military arrived in force they would be sitting ducks. They ran the mile distance to Donnybrook and leapt on a tram for the city, its conductor joking as they then stood panting: 'Here come the Harriers', referring to a local running club.[16] They spotted the motorcycle sidecar outside Donnybrook police station as they eventually passed it to their left. Vinny Byrne strained his eyes to get its registration number, but was unsuccessful.

Daly and Keogh had maintained their route towards the city after witnessing the unfolding horror they had helped orchestrate in Merrion Road. Soon afterwards, cycling leisurely to avoid attention, they were stopped by a policeman asking: 'Was there an accident up there?' while he pointed south. When Daly turned he saw a crowd of people running in different directions.[17] Daly replied: 'Yeah, it looks like it'. The policeman's subsequent response was telling: 'I heard a shot, but if there is any shooting business there I am not going near it.'[18]

Bell's body was taken by ambulance to Baggot Street's Royal City of Dublin Hospital and pronounced dead. The esteem with which he was held by Dublin Castle was made evident by the breaking of the news of his death to his wife by Lady Taylor, wife of the under secretary.[19] His demise marked the effective end of the inquiry into the Dáil funds and the end of the investigation into the Ashtown ambush. Despite having lost over £71,000 at the hands of this formidable nemesis, the funding for the continued revolution was, henceforth, comparatively secure.

Unionist newspaper reports in stop-press editions later that day were scathing of his killers. Bell was portrayed as a respectable long-standing civil servant, gunned down by cold-blooded killers intent on dragging Ireland into anarchy. Other newspapers such as the *Irish Independent* and *Freeman's Journal*, which had held his enquiry up to ridicule, were also targeted for vitriol. As far as IRA intelligence was concerned, however, Bell had played the puppeteer to others dabbling in such malignant crafts. He knew the risks, carried a loaded revolver, and ultimately fell at the hands of those whose assassinations he had advocated for during his involvement in the previous December's select committee with Lord French, Insp. Smith, and the under secretary. His death was the talk of the country that night. It was celebrated with champagne at an IRA arms dump in 22 Upper Baggot Street – right next door to the hospital in which his body was laid out.[20] McDonnell and Tobin took note of the irony that *Poethlyn* – the Grand National favourite – had fallen at the first fence.

Bell's demise was a monumental benchmark illustrating the incompetence of the Dublin Castle administration, particularly when set against the unprecedented prowess of the composite forces marshalled against it. Since Ashtown in December the IRA had seen off numerous assaults from the Castle's most formidable operatives and allies, and confounded counter-insurgency strategies perfected throughout the British empire for two centuries. G-Division, the inheritor of a lineage that, in a different form, had derailed the United Irishmen in 1798 and their multitude of radical successors since, was all but a spent force. The money to finance the revolution's further escalation was safe and public opinion continued to veer towards the separatists. Since the Dáil's inauguration fourteen months earlier over 20,000 raids had taken place throughout Ireland by crown forces, a staggering recent increase. This added to more than 400 arrests and deportations, and 429 proclamations to suppress meetings and newspapers.[21] Yet, the situation continued to deteriorate. It was time for change.

Bell's burial in Dublin's Deansgrange Cemetery was subdued, unlike the military's display of homage to the remains of Frederick McNulty, whose Union Jack draped-coffin was transported through the city the same week under a heavy military escort on its way to burial in England. The same week also saw a significant move by the British government to reverse the deterioration in Ireland. General Macready was approached in London by his prime minister with the proposition that he would replace General Shaw as C-in-C Ireland. The fifty-eight-year-old's foreboding the previous late December had been accurate – much to his chagrin. His proven competencies as both a police and military commander marked him out for the job in Ireland, particularly given the strategic direction towards closer cooperation that existed between both arms. Macready, six-foot-tall and with a markedly unruffled but steely expression, had also served as adjutant general for the British Army for the last two years of the Great War. He detested Ireland without prejudice to affiliations or ideologies, having felt acute exasperation at the machinations he had witnessed in 1914 during the Home Rule crisis, which had struck him as derisory. Nonetheless, his experience in overseeing military deployment to support civil power in Ulster, as well as at Tonypandy in South Wales during riots related to coal-mining disputes there made him Lloyd George's ideal man.[22] He was also an admirer and old friend of Lord French and his sense of duty towards the viceroy convinced him to accept the posting, despite having additional misgivings over the recent deployment of the RICSR.

The IRA's initial response to the same deployment of the 'Black and Tans' came in the form of a proclamation on 30 March from IRA GHQ, which read:

1. Whereas the spies and traitors known as the Royal Irish Constabulary are holding this country for the enemy, and whereas said spies and bloodhounds are conspiring with the enemy to bomb and bayonet and otherwise outrage a peaceful, law-abiding, and liberty loving people.

2. Wherefore we do hereby proclaim and suppress said spies and traitors, and do hereby solemnly warn prospective recruits that they join the R.I.C. at their own peril. All nations are agreed as to the fate of traitors. It has the sanction of God and man.[23]

Also making way for new blood was Ian Macpherson. On Thursday 1 April he resigned as chief secretary, blissfully unaware how close he had come to his own assassination at the hands of George Fitzgerald.[24] He had recently lurked again in England's capital, this time accompanied by Joe Leonard, watching Macpherson's every move, primed to pounce with local IRA back-up upon receipt of orders to kill him.

The outgoing chief secretary was replaced three days later by fifty-year-old Sir Thomas Hamar Greenwood, a barrister and Liberal MP with an inflexible temperament and limited vision. He was soon also to find himself under

George Fitzgerald's surveillance. Like Bonar Law, he was Canadian born. Despite having little knowledge of Ireland, Greenwood felt eager to get to grips with the challenge ahead, which was fortunate for him, as he would need every ounce of enthusiasm he could muster.

The day before Greenwood took office, 3 April, was Easter Saturday, and Dublin – particularly Dublin Castle – was once again on lockdown, the authorities fearing another Easter Rising. A nationwide insurrection was anticipated by the entire IRA, estimated erroneously by Macpherson recently to be at 200,000 men.

The fact that the city would be sealed was lost on Dan Breen. Having fully recuperated from his Ashtown wounds, he had been staying with Vincent Purfield in Balbriggan. Séamus Robinson had recently visited him there to brief him on the situation in Tipperary, where he would soon return. On Easter Saturday the three drove to Dublin to celebrate Easter, only to run into a heavily manned military checkpoint at Whitehall. Luckily, the three dapperly attired men were able to bluff their way through the checkpoint, feigning an important social function to attend alongside his majesty's most respectable and loyal subjects. Elsewhere Dublin District military command maintained checkpoints at main roads, river and canal bridges. This was replicated throughout the country. Beaches and ports were also watched in case of arms landings.

And the authorities, it turned out, were right to be concerned. IRA GHQ were about to surpass anything previously considered within their capabilities: a daring nationwide campaign of arson and bomb attacks on abandoned RIC barracks'. Between 3 and 4 April, despite the crackdown, approximately 300 'tombstones of British prestige in Ireland' were destroyed, rendering their future reoccupation impossible – a strategic imperative given the recent arrival of the RICSR.[25] In one night this accounted for the destruction of twenty per cent of the entire country's number of barracks.

A year since Det. Broy had suggested such a sweeping strategy, it had come to fruition. Vast tracts of the countryside and their myriad of localities and hamlets were ungovernable by the crown. Coastguard stations were also pillaged for explosives and signalling equipment. The concerted actions were seen as an impressive display of coordination by the underground army and another strategic disaster for the British government. Attorney General Henry estimated that 25,000 IRA men had participated in the attacks.²⁶ However, GHQ was not done yet.

Dick McKee, celebrating his twenty-seventh birthday that same Easter Saturday, had once again recently raised the prospect of attacking the Custom House. The destruction of its local government and revenue offices would greatly hamstring the British government. GHQ decided, however, to go a step further, and – mirroring the attack in 32 Nassau Street the previous Easter but on a much larger scale – mobilised all Dublin battalions, as well as their country counterparts, to by-pass the Custom House for now and instead attack revenue offices city and countrywide that night.

At 7.30 p.m. income tax offices all over Dublin city were set alight. It was another demonstration of the IRA's ability to orchestrate harmonised destruction of enemy property right under the military's noses despite their high-alert status. Gaining access to a multitude of tax offices, using crowbars to force their doors, Volunteers stacked their papers in piles, doused them in petrol or paraffin, and set them alight. First-aid stations stood ready to receive casualties, their edgy Cumann na mBan members checking their kits and practising drills for burn injuries.

Alongside vital local government documents, large amounts of cash were also confiscated. George Fitzgerald and Joe Dolan led one such attack on the tax office directly opposite the Custom House in Beresford Place, the former back in Dublin between his missions to England stalking politicians. McKee and Patrick Holohan had been pivotal in its planning. Volunteers from A Company 1st Battalion, nicknamed 'the Forty Thieves' due to their recently honed proficiencies in breaking and entering, were dispatched to the building's four floors, papers were piled, doused, and burned, starting from the top floor and working downwards.²⁷

Smoke from burning buildings added to that from Dublin's multitude of chimney-tops and hung throughout the early spring air on both sides of the River Liffey as darkness fell. IRA men working with Dublin's Fire Brigade added their part to the destruction by ruining with water anything undamaged by fire. In total, more than 100 tax offices were burned throughout the country, some located within private residences, in which cases measures were taken to ensure minimal property damage. Breen, Robinson, Purfield and McKee had much to celebrate that night, as had the father of one 3rd Battalion Volunteer, when his son, from K Company, told him later that he had watched his tax liability papers go up in smoke in a building in Dawson Street.

The new chief secretary then had to contend with hunger strikes. On Easter Monday – an occasion that still resonated strongly four years after the clock of rebellion had struck in Dublin on the same public holiday – sixty-six IRA prisoners in Mountjoy, led by Peadar Clancy, following his arrest a month earlier, began a hunger strike.[28] This followed an ultimatum delivered to the governor eight days earlier, declaring that the prisoners would adopt such a measure unless granted prisoner-of-war (POW) status. Following breakfast on 5 April, a pledge was taken, which read:

> I pledge myself, to the honour of Ireland and the lives of my comrades not to eat food or drink anything except water until all here have been given prisoner-of-war treatment or are released.[29]

Among them was eighteen-year-old 4th Battalion Volunteer Todd Andrews. He had only been incarcerated in a one-man cell the previous day, following a brief detention at the bridewell after his arrest at home. The bridewell had provided little food. Then, having barely eaten in over twenty-four hours, he had considered requesting a second helping of breakfast – sweetened porridge, a hunk of bread and margarine – at Mountjoy, but had then decided to hold his tongue. Hearing of the hunger strike, he wished he had asked. When an older Volunteer was later told of Andrews' age, he told the young Volunteer that he was not expected to take part in the hunger strike. Nonetheless, Andrews told him he had been a Volunteer for three years and saw it as his duty.

Also imprisoned was twenty-one-year-old Andrew McDonnell. He had been arrested after a meeting at the 3rd Battalion HQ in 144 Great Brunswick Street during which Brigadier McKee had provided a tactical lecture and pep-talk. Like other internees he had initially been lined up in the prison's passage leading to its wings, and overseen by the monacled governor, Major Munro, and head-warder, who took names. He was then searched. All his possessions were laid out on a table and listed before he was escorted to the bath house. There he was stripped. Any marks on his body were recorded in a ledger before he was bathed and taken up to a wing and placed alone in a cell.[30]

News of the hunger strike quickly reached the press. The mood among the prisoners was initially buoyant. One hunger-striking prisoner, nicknamed 'Giggler', shouted to his fellow hunger strikers through his locked cell door the first day that a comrade had recently been sentenced to five years for possessing ten rounds of rifle ammunition; he then wondered aloud if any budding mathematicians among them could calculate what he would get for the pistol and thirty rounds with which he had been caught. The answer: 'Giggler, you are a lifer!' was met with laughter all along his echoing corridor.[31] However, the mood soon plummeted. Four days into the hunger strike, their number increased to ninety, the vast majority of which were untried in court.[32] Hunger strikes were, at this stage, a well practiced tool that was used effectively by republicans to showcase their conviction in the justice of their cause. It was a demonstration of their preparedness to suffer a slow and painful death rather than accept the existing situation of being classed as criminals.[33] Effective as they were, they nonetheless represented an excruciating challenge individually and collectively.

Many hunger strikers took to their beds after a few days. Clancy encouraged them to keep up their waning spirits in the face of the enemy. Extra warders flooded in, becoming anxious as the strike progressed, some out of sympathy, others fearful of a backlash if prisoners started dying. Dispositions varied similarly among medical staff. One quick-witted doctor named McCormick, affectionately nicknamed 'Brown Bowler' due to his choice of hat, provided a tonic with his sharp sense of humour, unlike some of his stony-faced colleagues.[34]

McDonnell found the hunger strike terrifying, aggravated not just by constant gnawing hunger, but also by tortuous sleepless nights with his mind playing tricks, focusing involuntarily on the ever-looming prospect of death. He questioned his own ability to maintain his protest in particularly desperate moments. Uncertainty also enveloped his comrades as the days passed. Breakfast, dinner and tea were brought as usual to cells and left on tables, an overwhelming temptation to the weakening men. As days passed some cell doors were left open, illustrating that prisoners inside had become too feeble to alight to the wings. Then spontaneous bursts of joviality alternated with stretchers being rushed past cell doors to the shouts of alarmed warders when it appeared a less robust prisoner, moments earlier lively and spirited, had taken a sudden turn, or his heart had given out. Telegrams were dispatched to relatives indicating the approach of death – a trick to summon them and hopefully prompt them to

British soldiers and a policeman outside Mountjoy Prison.
(*Courtesy of Mercier Archive*)

The British Army holding back crowds outside Mountjoy Prison.
(*Courtesy of Mercier Archive*)

KILLING AT ITS VERY EXTREME

A British tank deployed outside Mountjoy Prison during the hunger strikes, April 1920.
(*Courtesy of the National Library of Ireland*)

persuade their loved ones to reconsider their actions under emotional duress. Hymns could soon be heard from outside the prison.[35] Word came in from supportive warders that crowds in such vast numbers had assembled outside that the military with armoured cars were needed to control them.

The warders were correct. In the spring sunshine, bayonets glinted outside the prison's recently reinforced barbed-wire entanglements, as fully-kitted soldiers stood alongside a Mark IV heavy tank deployed unsuccessfully to disperse the crowds. They were desperate to keep the gathered masses back from the prison gates. The *Irish Bulletin* and *An t-Óglách* had field days describing thousands of women who were kneeling in prayer while being menaced by the mechanical mammoth. For days the air hummed with repeated rosaries that tested the patience of British Tommies more than the most monotonous barrack drills. As the crowds grew in size, daily tensions escalated; surges took place every time a hunger-striking prisoner was taken across the road to the Mater Hospital for treatment. The North Circular Road and its approaches were blocked. Cumann na mBan members stewarded the crowds. Annie Cooney was foremost among them, leading her unit in a chorus of nationalist songs. Rose McNamara led another unit close by. Her efforts were rewarded with a hosing down with water mixed with carbide from angry policemen.

When reports hit GHQ that troops and police were acting with increasing menace towards the crowds, Volunteers from the 2nd Battalion were sent in as protective parties. Frank Henderson oversaw this. They were given strict orders to act with restraint among the crowds, while tactfully signalling to the military that aggressive acts towards the massed protesters would be met with force. It was feared that jittery enemy troops would open fire at the merest provocation. Instructions were to shoot without hesitation at any troops who raised their rifles.

The government came under unrelenting pressure to release the prisoners. The decision was in the hands of Lord French, who stood fast. Then, on Monday 12 April, events last seen during the conscription crisis two years earlier were repeated. A general strike was called by the Labour Party and the Trade Union Congress (TUC) in support of the strikers with the full support of the Catholic Church. By the following day, once again, with the exception of Belfast and isolated parts of Ulster, the entire country was brought to a standstill. Picketers rapidly set upon any business establishments that chose to ignore the strike.

General Macready took office in the Royal Hospital Kilmainham on 14 April, two days into the general strike, when even army pay clerks came out in support of the strikers. With shops closed, workers committees endeavoured to distribute food directly from suppliers. Food and tobacco prices shot up following panicked buying. Ireland's railways and ports had come to a standstill. The poor suffered most, sudden scarcities aggravated by the now-chronic coal shortage in the city. This was all set against the backdrop of another killing of a policeman on Dublin's Streets on the same day.

Det. Const. Henry Kells, a six-foot-three, forty-one-year-old from Cavan with twenty-one years' service with Brunswick Street's B-Division, was gunned down within yards of his home in 7 Pleasants Street shortly before 10 a.m. The area, quieter than usual owing to the strike, still abounded with pedestrians, cyclists, carriages and motorists. Kells had been promoted since Alan Bell's death, which he was then investigating for G-Division, meaning he was unprotected by Dublin Castle's walls, behind which the majority of the political 'G-Men' remained.

Kell's fate had been sealed when, two weeks earlier, twenty Mountjoy prisoners led by Peadar Clancy had been taken from cells and brought to the exercise yard. There they had been lined up before a double file of soldiers with fixed bayonets. The prisoners had believed they were being deported in order to stifle their looming hunger strike. To show defiance they had shouted their intentions to carry the strike wherever they went.[36]

They were then marched out of the prison's main entrance, singing their anthem 'The Soldier's Song' as they went, and into the wood yard. It was there that Clancy and Tom Hunter quickly discovered what was really happening. Clancy then cried out in alarm: 'Keep your heads down lads. The windows! Identification parade.'[37] The men instantly lowered their heads. Frank Gallagher, of the *Irish Bulletin*, did so too, but not before glancing at the windows above to see G-men moving from window to window seeking out the faces of wanted men.

Clancy then ordered the men to move to the wall under the windows where they could not be seen, prompting their observers to make for the doorway of a balcony which offered another view. The soldiers guarding them looked on in mocking amusement as heads then popped out of the doorway to snatch a quick glance at the prisoners while straining to avoid their own recognition. Gallagher had noticed that it was both men and woman stealing such glances. The watchers then, apparently unsatisfied with their efforts, had changed tactics. Clancy noticed the G-men and quickly ordered anyone who recognised any of them to call out their names.[38]

The G-men then came into view, their backs to the prisoners. Each stole a backwards glance, until, suddenly, one turned and walked down a set of steps, his hat worn jauntily on the side of his head, his overcoat over his arm. Then, as he walked down the line of men, peering at each face as he passed, a cry came from the line that stunned him: 'Aha! Kells, is this the work you are on? Look out.'[39] Kells, having assumed he was unknown, was stopped dead in his tracks. A collective jeer followed from the line of prisoners. The blood had drained from his face. He then retreated back up the steps. The men were then taken back to their cells. Clancy had then ensured to get word to the outside about Det. Kells.

On 13 April George Fitzgerald smuggled a coded note into the prison for Clancy, which read: 'I am going to Kells tomorrow. M.', referring to the town in Meath as a code. Michael Collins wrote the letter. Clancy, Hunter and Gallagher knew what this could mean for them; a favourable settlement to the hunger strike would be far less likely if Kells was shot. However, they resigned themselves to the fact that the matter was out of their hands.

Paddy Daly and the Squad were mobilised on the morning of 14 April. Kells missed out on his usual customary tram ride to work due to the strike and made his way on foot. The plan was to intercept him en route. On the way, Daly was met unexpectedly by Capt. Hugo MacNeill – nephew of Eoin MacNeill, and Fianna Director of Organisation – who, upon hearing of the planned attack, volunteered to assist.[40] When this was agreed, he then set off with Joe Leonard.

Minutes later, with Squad members deployed in groups of two throughout Camden and Wexford Streets, Leonard and MacNeill caught sight of their target – Kells – his hat still worn jauntily on his head. Two shots rang out. Kells fell close to the junction of Camden Street and Pleasants Street, shot through the windpipe and chest.

His assassins then strolled away from the gruesome scene into Camden Street, where they soon met Daly again. Leonard spoke up: 'Kells is up there if you want him'. 'Where?' replied Daly. MacNeill answered: 'On the foot-path'. Daly understood. Kells was transported to the nearby Meath Hospital by a passing motorist but pronounced dead on arrival. Despite the crowds in the area no witnesses came forward.[41]

Back on the city's north side on the same blustery day the RAF became involved in events at Mountjoy. Military aeroplanes buzzed threateningly over the heads of the crowds – now 20,000 strong – outside the prison, causing momentary panic and testing the discipline of soldier and Volunteer alike, and yet again, providing fuel for stories which horrified a growing number of newspaper readers across the Irish Sea. The ability of the aeroplanes to fly effectively at such low altitude in a city in spite of inclement weather was noted by the British military, pondering their suitability for future deployment for crowd control or strafing sorties. Kevin O'Higgins retorted dismissively to such measures in a speech, declaring: 'The whole history of the world is the triumph of mind over matter. We are backing our idea against aeroplanes and armoured cars'.[42] Armoured cars filled the streets around Portobello that night as troops from the Berkshire Regiment, their memories fresh from the recent rioting, ransacked hundreds of houses, claiming to be searching for Det. Kells' killers.

***

Andrew McDonnell was one whose relatives had been summoned to Mountjoy by telegram warning cynically of his imminent demise. They had arrived in Mountjoy on 13 April to find him on a mattress on his cell floor, covered with an army blanket, weak but emboldened by the recent visit of a warder who had slipped him a piece of paper with news of the general strike. Nevertheless, that night was the longest one for McDonnell; it went on and on; 'all cells open, all awake but silent'.[43]

14 April saw Frank Gallagher entering his tenth day of hunger strike, barely able to sustain his mental torment. Half his mind appeared bent on self-preservation by eating, the other on holding out. Ultimately, it was the fear of the dishonour of letting his comrades down that convinced him to maintain his fast. He was struck by the irony of being too afraid not to die to give up his hunger strike.[44] The previous day had seen him refused absolution by the prison chaplain on the grounds that what he and his comrades were doing was tantamount to suicide, further fuelling his anguish, until an Australian priest reassured him that this was not the case. Thoughts of the sacrifices of Kilmainham Gaol in 1916 also convinced Gallagher and many others to stay the course.

Then things stirred. The lord mayor was summoned from a prison visit to the vice-regal lodge to meet French and Macready. French made an about-turn, concluding along with Macready that the government would eventually begin releasing prisoners as soon as they started dying, and that therefore, it was more pragmatic instead to begin releasing them straight away under conditions that might mitigate their own loss of face while simultaneously denying martyrdom to enemy propagandists.

Soon afterwards hope arrived in the prison amid rumours of unexpected deliverance. Capitulation by the enemy was anticipated. Then, the prison governor made the hunger-striking prisoners an offer of parole – French's proposed remedy for loss of face. However, Peadar Clancy, standing fast, immediately rejected the idea as a tacit admission by the internees of criminality. The prisoners stood by his refusal, but it was a crushing emotional blow in the wake of earlier hopes. Nonetheless, further rapid consultations followed, leading to the mayor proposing a verbal undertaking from each prisoner not to participate in sedition, which Macready then persuaded French to accept.

Tensions mounted in the prison with a resolution so tantalisingly close. Clancy again rejected this. Unconditional release was insisted upon. Finally, word came through that the authorities had submitted to this, albeit with the face-saving attempt of suggesting the releases were purely on medical grounds.

On the evening of 14 April, cheers resounded throughout the prison from the emaciated hunger strikers, other inmates, and particularly from the warders.

Towards evening, Andrew McDonnell heard a succession of names being called out. Each man was to await his call, then descend a spiral staircase to the main concourse to be met by the mayor, the prison governor and several of the Capuchin monks from the Bow Street friary. These were the same monks who had ministered to the executed 1916 leaders four years earlier, their distinctive brown cassocks marking them out. Eventually, after what seemed like an eternity, his own name was called. He was then helped by warders to the concourse where the governor, not to be bettered, insisted on at least reading the undertaking not to participate in further sedition to each prisoner – the reason for the tortuous delay.

It was now the early hours of 15 April. Fr Albert, a Capuchin monk, then accompanied McDonnell by ambulance to Richmond Hospital on North Brunswick Street, where, to McDonnell's surprise, he found himself examined by Dr Myles Keogh. The irony of this struck him; the last time their paths had crossed was on Lower Mount Street on 30 April 1916 following his garrison's surrender. At that time, when a British officer had told McDonnell that he and his comrades were to be shot, McDonnell's cavalier smile in retort had seen the same officer address Dr Keogh, accompanying him, in a resigned tone, saying: 'There you are, there you see – from the oldest to the youngest they don't care a damn'.[45] The doctor had not been amused. This time around he was far more sympathetic towards the young, exhausted and gaunt-looking IRA man.

By the time the Mountjoy prisoners were released, hunger strikes were breaking out in Belfast's Crumlin Road Prison. Soon the hunger strikers were taken from the city, suffering a barrage of abuse on the way out from loyalist mobs, and eventually found themselves, after an arduous journey by sea and rail, in Wormwood Scrubs. Once there, another hunger strike commenced. 174 prisoners refused food in the prison. Soon afterwards, amid growing street demonstrations in London involving thousands of protesters, and the realisation that tens of thousands of workers on Liverpool's docks were threatening to down tools in further support, the government caved. The prisoners were eventually released in batches under the Prisoners (Temporary Release for Ill Health) Act 1913. Also referred to as the 'Cat and Mouse

Act', its purpose was to release badly emaciated prisoners until they could be reincarcerated once their health recovered. However, none were rearrested; instead they dissolved into Irish communities before returning to Ireland.

William Cosgrave had also recently been interned at Wormwood Scrubs, but was released in late April on parole due to his wife having become very ill following the birth of their first child, Liam. He later returned to the prison to turn himself in on the grounds that he was not prepared to stand over an undertaking he had initially been forced to make not to re-enter revolutionary politics. Nevertheless, he was not be re-interned.[46] Meanwhile, his deputy, Kevin O'Higgins, had stepped into his shoes.

While such events were unfolding in London, the opposite end of England saw Sir Hamar Greenwood contesting the Sunderland by-election, under the watchful eye of George Fitzgerald, having again crossed the Irish Sea.

Fitzgerald had been born and spent a good part of his youth in the eastern USA, and struck up a rapport with one of the chief secretary's election agents, an army captain named Snow, who claimed to have worked there during elections. The upshot of their burgeoning friendship was, astonishingly, an introduction for Fitzgerald by Capt. Snow to Greenwood in the company of his wife. Following this, Fitzgerald was given passes to numerous events attended by Greenwood during which he successfully monitored his security staff, recognising them from their previous assignments protecting the chief secretary's predecessor. Details of his cars, and numbers and descriptions of bodyguards were soon making their way back to Liam Tobin and Michael Collins.

Back in Dublin, the DMP were aghast at the Mountjoy prisoner releases, as were their RIC counterparts both in the capital and throughout the country. The army felt similarly. All their work since late January had amounted to nothing. Worse, detectives who had identified prisoners under the expectation that the internees were securely locked away for the conflict's duration, risked a similar fate to Const. Kells, now that those they had identified were back on the streets.

Suggestions abounded throughout the police that matters would have to be dealt with by their own hands, an ominous sentiment in the aftermath of Lord Mayor MacCurtain's killing in Cork – since heralded by his inquest as an act of murder by a host of guilty parties acting under and including the British government. The way was being paved for acts of extreme brutality. To further aggravate police ire: not only political prisoners had been freed, there were numerous common criminals among them. Morale also buckled in Dublin Castle. Assistant Under Secretary Taylor took a month's leave, exasperated at French's capitulation. Amid the tumult, however, new players stood by, soon to take centre-stage.

12

NEW PLAYERS AT DUBLIN CASTLE

'We are sitting on a volcano'

General Macready did not lament Sir John Taylor's month-long departure. He was horrified at the bureaucratic disarray that had festered under his watch and manifested in widespread police inefficiency and demoralisation; a situation aggravated by Insp. Gen. Smith's politically tainted approach. This demoralisation had struck Macready as soon as he set foot in Dublin Castle, prompting him to comment forebodingly to Walter Long that: 'as regards the RIC we are sitting on a volcano'.[1] Macready's disconcerting message was conveyed subsequently to the prime minister as police casualties in Ireland mounted. This coincided with Lord French's protestations to Conservative Party leader Bonar Law that the Dublin Castle administration needed to be completely re-jigged.[2] Consequently, action was taken in the form of an investigating committee soon placed under the imposing chairmanship of the permanent secretary to the treasury and head of the civil service, forty-one-year-old Sir Warren Fisher. After the committee's investigations, Fisher would write up a report of their findings.

Macready's influence was not just felt in Downing Street. He had the ear of the British king, to whom he also conveyed his frustrations. Astutely, he spared Lord French his allocation of blame and instead funnelled any such castigations towards since-departed Ian Macpherson. Macready also spoke of amending the Government of Ireland Bill with greater concessions to moderate nationalists, aiming to offset the need for martial law throughout the country.[3] However, he also protested that, failing such concessions, the government needed to act decisively in favour of strong military measures which, he felt, would at least restore order, notwithstanding his clear preference for concessions. Meanwhile, in Westminster, former Prime Minister Asquith was soon arguing for the immediate offer of dominion status to Ireland, albeit with options for Ulster, broadly echoing Lord Haldane's recommendations to French, and, again, George Creel's conclusions to President Wilson the previous year.

Another whose growing influence was felt here was thirty-nine-year-old Dublin Castle law adviser William Wylie, who was also calling for changes to the bill in favour of dominion status. Wylie considered himself a moderate unionist, though his record as prosecutor during the 1916 courts martial had apparently marked him out as otherwise. Wylie was, however, simply a strict adherent to the law. He had, following the Rising, been appalled by the shortcuts employed by the military to circumvent due process and at times had persevered to assist the unrepresented defendants. Now, four years on, he found himself in unison with Macready. He baulked at martial law, but advocated for it if he deemed it absolutely necessary to maintain order. Nonetheless, he pleaded with political leaders not to confuse crime with politics; in other words, he was again echoing Haldane in asserting that Sinn Féin was an entity that could, and should, be taken seriously.[4]

Macready also recognised Sinn Féin as containing 'men of substance and deep feeling', that 'could not be dismissed as a party of murderers'.[5] However, the growing acceptance of the Government of Ireland Bill's propositions amongst the unionist followers of Edward Carson and James Craig soon rendered it unassailable.[6] There would be no worthwhile concessions to nationalists. Martial law was, nonetheless, politically unacceptable to Lloyd George, as he felt it was an unwitting acknowledgement that a military occupation or state of war existed. He favoured the portrayal of the revolutionary nationalists as criminals and murderers, to be dealt with under the ostensible authority of the police, later proclaiming dismissively to Lord French when pressed about such a policy: 'You do not declare war against rebels'.[7]

***

On Wednesday 20 April at 12.30 p.m., two policemen, Det. Consts Laurence Dalton and Robert Spencer, made their way in driving rain towards Dorset Street from Broadstone railway terminus. Dalton, a twenty-six-year-old bachelor from Limerick had seven years' service, and had transferred weeks earlier from B to G-Division. He had recently arrested Mountjoy escapee J.J. Walsh close to the latter's shop unit on Berkeley Road and was subsequently warned to back off. He ignored the warning. Dalton had been detailed to identify and keep tabs on IRA and IRB members travelling to Dublin from the west of Ireland who alighted at the station. Spencer, from Queen's County, was not a political detective and was detailed as Dalton's protective escort. Dalton was unaware that Liam Tobin had lately shadowed him; the oversight was about to cost him his life.

The Squad assembled at St Mary's Place. Paddy Daly was dispatched to nearby Dominick Street to keep watch, while Mick McDonnell, Tom Keogh and Jim Slattery took positions on Dalton's known route. They stood on either side of the bleak-looking Black Church, their collars turned up, nodding and smiling at passing pedestrians who were sheltering under umbrellas.

It was nine months since Slattery's shooting of Det. Smyth. The anxiety and remorse were still present, but far less arresting at this point given what had passed since. Liam Tobin had earlier pointed Det. Dalton out to Slattery as the former lurked in the station. Tobin had then departed on foot to Crow Street. Slattery had also been warned that the target wore a steel waistcoat.[8] Spencer was unknown to the pursuers and was not a target. The three waiting men were to undertake the killing while Joe Dolan and Vinny Byrne acted as their covering party.

The tyres of passing motorists sloshed through the puddled cobblestones as both policemen, in blissful ignorance of their stalkers, crossed Mountjoy Street towards the Black Church. The street's red-bricked terraces looked particularly grim in the rain. Just then, the three gunmen closed in from both sides. Shots were fired. Det. Dalton suddenly bolted in terror back across the road while Spencer, slightly wounded, sprinted in the opposite direction towards Dorset Street. The three assassins then opened fire on Dalton again, his pace hindered by his steel waistcoat, hitting him initially in the leg to drop him. He collapsed, protesting: 'Let me alone!'[9]

Keogh and Slattery closed for the kill. Two additional shots then rang out before the gunmen made their escape on foot. Dalton lay barely alive, the shots having pierced his steel waistcoat at such close range and fragmented as they tore into his body, ripping at its organs.

A nearby woman shrieked in terror and pain, accidentally hit in the leg by one of the first pistol rounds. Horrified passers-by then rushed to her aid as she lay screaming in a growing pool of blood. An ambulance soon tended to the dying policeman, who was also bleeding profusely, his bodily fluids flowing with the rain into the street's gutters. Two hours later, despite a blood transfusion, Dalton was pronounced dead in the Mater Hospital. The wounded woman was also treated there.

When David Neligan heard of Dalton's killing he was deeply unsettled. Neligan had resigned as a detective the previous month and returned to his native Limerick, but not before offering his services formally to Sinn Féin. He had not been aware of his former colleague's involvement in political work. Dalton had been popular, known for his geniality and sense of humour, not unlike many of his colleagues. Before resigning, Neligan had begun to notice some of his less diligent fellow detectives drinking heavily while on duty. This was considered a far less dangerous means of passing the time than carrying out orders. Frequently they wandered aimlessly from pub to pub, engaging in harmless chit-chat with punters and barmen, returning eventually to Dublin Castle nursing hangovers, to invent fictitious reports for their impatient and unforgiving taskmasters.

Two days after Dalton's killing another G-Division colleague, twenty-seven-year-old Const. Michael McCarthy, was shot six times while on leave at his family home in Cork. He died the following day in hospital.

Meanwhile, General Macready was busily observing the escalating killings and maimings that were affecting both sides throughout the country. Notably, word was coming in of military reprisals against civilians which, despite being unwelcome, were noticed to have a marked 'soothing' effect on the locality in question, further underscoring his belief in the efficacy of martial law, if called for.[10] However, he entertained no such accord with the RICSR when they carried out the first of many reprisals in Limerick city on the night of 28 April following an earlier affray, smashing windows and assaulting civilians, though these were crimes which would soon be eclipsed by their unabated capacity for drunken brutality. Macready's disgust was shared by Frank Thornton and Joe Dolan, both of whom witnessed the rampage first hand while in the city investigating the shooting of a Volunteer by comrades who had erroneously suspected him of spying for the enemy. *An t-Óglách*, three days later, referred to the Black and Tans as physically and morally degenerate Englishmen with no understanding of Ireland, and boasted that the IRA would make 'short work of them'.[11]

Macready had been asked to combine his command to both the police and military, a request he declined. He recoiled at the strategy of unleashing former soldiers, hardened by trench warfare, with minimal training, to bolster the policing by an already demoralised force on a resentful population. These were, after all, men who had never before been asked to behave like law enforcers, nor had they experienced hit and run insurgents. Their careers among the army's lower ranks had taught many of them the merits of theft as an enterprise, and honed their abilities to lie effectively in the face of accusations concerning theft or worse. The military discipline that had kept them steadfastly in line while faced with unimaginable horrors had no hold over them and they were free to drink, steal and inflict a myriad of atrocities with nothing but the sanction of dismissal as a deterrent.

Exasperation among the police and military heightened even further on 3 May – two days after *The Irish Times* had claimed that 'the crown forces were being driven back by an advancing enemy' – when the special powers granted in January under Regulation 14B of DORA were revoked, making it apparent to them that all their work so far during the year had been for nothing, and that, effectively, the recent hunger strike had represented a decisive victory for the republicans.[12]

Macready used this to again call urgently for increased political concessions to Sinn Féin moderates to avoid the necessity for a period of martial law to subdue the rise of their radical counterparts. He knew that, despite its stabilising effect, martial law would nevertheless jeopardise precious political support among liberals at home and Irish sympathisers abroad. He knew he was walking a fine line in this respect, what with less pragmatic unionist hardliners both at home and in Ireland to contend with. Greenwood soon expressed his full agreement with Macready, however, perceiving that the latter's strategy was to restore order one way or another and, accordingly, facilitate the enactment of the Government of Ireland Bill. Training was stepped up in the military as a contingency.

Macready also oversaw a redoubling of efforts to salvage the hard-pressed RIC's footprint in the country. With so many barracks' now destroyed and many others dangerously isolated, a strategy was implemented whereby military detachments would be deployed in central positions within affected regions. They would then be provided with vehicles in sufficient strength to form small tactical columns, using RIC members as guides.¹³ Rocket alert signals would be employed until effective wireless systems could be put in place. 'Dropping circles' - marked out circles on the ground - would be employed as targets for air-drops of communications and small-scale resupply. What they failed to factor in at this point was that the IRA could, and would, eventually fool the pilots by creating their own bogus dropping circles, not to mention digging up unpaved roads – accounting for more than half the country's roads – and felling trees to hinder their proposed tactical columns.¹⁴ Greater coordination methods with the DMP were also studied.

Notwithstanding Macready's organisational dynamism, the revoking of the DORA powers – albeit with the curfew remaining in place – was a forerunner of a marked change in Britain's overall strategy.

On the opposing side, Kevin O'Higgins had been putting his endeavouring spirit into his role as, effectively, the Dáil's acting local government minister. On 3 May Dublin Corporation declared allegiance to the Dáil. Turbulent waters lay ahead for the local government ministry in the form of serious financial concerns. This did not deter councillors from recommending that, following the upcoming rural elections, local bodies with Sinn Féin majorities should break from Dublin Castle, a move that could cut off much needed funding. There were mixed feelings among councillors about cutting the umbilical cord of Castle finance. Vacillation took hold.¹⁵

***

No such hesitancy affected the Squad. Their next target presented as forty-six-year-old Det. Sgt Richard Revell, a six-foot-tall policeman originally from Carlow with twenty-five years' experience, nineteen of which were within G-Division. He was a father of five who lived in 10 Connaught Street in Phibsboro. Like Det. Dalton, he wore a steel vest travelling to and from Dublin Castle, as despite the danger, he chose to live with his family instead of at the Castle.

On Friday 7 May, Vinny Byrne, having been briefed by Liam Tobin that Revell represented a 'danger to the movement', was ordered to track him and report his movements to the Squad. Byrne, unarmed, took position on the eastern side of Phibsboro Road at 9 a.m. fifty yards south of the Connaught Street junction, towards Doyle's Corner, and waited.¹⁶

Soon afterwards, the detective, acting chiefly as a clerk but with a long history of antagonising republicans, strolled from his red-bricked terraced bungalow – situated less than 100 yards from the Toomey residence, which had sheltered Dan Breen after Ashtown – onto Phibsboro Road. He then stepped towards Doyle's Corner on the opposite side of the road to Byrne, but glancing over, caught his eyes. He walked on. Byrne crossed the street and tailed him for 150 yards, but by then the game was up. Revell was experienced enough to sense he was being followed, and began walking briskly towards a uniformed policeman on point duty at Phibsboro crossroads. Seeing this, Byrne quickly stepped onto a passing tram. He alighted just minutes later at Lindsay Road/Botanic Road junction and made for Mick McDonnell's house on foot. There, twenty minutes later, he reported to McDonnell and Tobin what had just happened.

Tobin was satisfied enough to deploy the Squad the following morning to kill Revell, determined to get him in case he chose to move inside the Castle – far more likely now, given that he appeared alerted to the fact that they knew his address. Accordingly, Paddy Daly, Joe Leonard and Tom Keogh made their way to the area at 9 a.m. However, recent protests from other Squad members over the fact that they were effectively acting as passers-by while their more seasoned comrades took the credit for their work, saw four others standing by in their place in the same area as Byrne had the previous morning, awaiting their chance to prove themselves. Two had been detailed for killing, the other two for cover. Much had changed since the first shooting the previous July – scruples were certainly far less prominent. Daly, Leonard and Keogh instead provided back up, the former two from the direction of Cross Guns Bridge, Keogh from towards Doyle's Corner. Vinny Byrne did not take part for fear of being recognised and jeopardising the mission.

Revell left his home at 9.30 a.m. and this time cycled to the junction of Phibsboro Road. He turned right, again towards Doyle's Corner, and almost immediately, the two detailed to shoot rushed at him from the pavement next to Phibsboro picture house, firing their pistols. Revell went down, panicking and struggling to free himself from his bicycle as he did. More shots followed. He was beaten across the road by gunfire. Screams and shouts sounded out from civilians.

The policeman back on point duty at the nearby crossroads drew a revolver and ran to the scene, hampered by his cumbersome overcoat. Revell was then dragged free of the bicycle by the shooters who fired several more shots until he was motionless, flat on his back. The attackers turned away and ran, quickly catching up with Daly and Leonard who began running alongside them, pistols drawn. Tom Keogh soon caught up, laughingly heralding: 'Those fellows will do a bit of crowing now', referring to their blooded comrades.[17] They passed a nearby policeman who did nothing to intervene, explaining afterwards that he knew better than to get in the way of the gunmen. The seven-man unit made their escape into Drumcondra.

However, they were unaware that Revell, miraculously, had survived; his steel vest had saved him. He had received four bullet wounds: one in his neck, two in his left arm and one in his leg, but remained more or less alert. Luckily for him a momentary loss of consciousness under the attack had convinced his less-experienced assailants that he was dead.

His wife had heard the shots from their nearby house and sped to the scene, horrified but relieved that he had survived. Passers-by also rushed to his aid, the wounded policeman was given water. An elderly man insisted on giving him a small drop of whiskey from a hip-flask. When an ambulance arrived soon afterwards Revell, despite his growing agony, refused to be taken to the Mater hospital – just minutes away. He suspected it was a nest of IRA sympathisers and feared them finishing him off there. Instead he was taken with his wife to the Adelaide Hospital in Peter Street. Surgery was performed immediately and the plucky policeman survived. However, his career as a useful member of G-Division was over. Nonetheless, when Vinny Byrne read of Revell's miraculous escape, he realised that he could never be taken alive afterwards – for fear of recognition by him.

***

The recent hunger strike may have been a resounding victory for the republicans, but it was not without casualties. The day after Revell's shooting, 9 May, members of F Company 2nd Battalion mourned the death of their twenty-five-year-old comrade, Frank Gleeson. He had picked up a liver infection while on hunger strike. The lingering infection killed him while he underwent surgery for appendicitis. His subsequent funeral was a typically huge affair with high-ranking Volunteers from throughout the country attending, including the man who had stepped into the shoes of

Tomás MacCurtain as both Cork Number 1 Brigade Commandant and the city's Lord Mayor: forty-one-year-old Terence MacSwiney.[18] MacSwiney soon embarked upon his own hunger strike, the repercussions of which reverberated around the globe.

While republicans gathered in mourning, their political enemies sat in ministerial conclave on 11 May in Downing Street in a conference chaired by Bonar Law. Among the attendees were Greenwood, Macready, Churchill and Field Marshal Wilson. Speaking from beneath his thick hanging moustache and looking from face to face, Bonar Law declared that: 'All the requirements of the Irish Executive should be promptly met'.[19] Given Macready's initial accounts of the escalating situation, army battalions already in Ireland would be brought up to full strength while eight additional battalions would prepare immediately for deployment. Transport was to be doubled and communications would be urgently improved.[20]

Field Marshal Wilson, hearing this, pressed Macready for clarity and justification on the necessity for such measures; reserves, he argued, were needed for deployment elsewhere. He advocated for far cruder methods, like 'shooting by roster'; that is, if the IRA carried out killings in an area then hostages taken from lists of known sympathisers would be shot.[21] He accused Macready of being naive in the assumption that mobile military columns were the key to regaining control, given IRA sophistication, recently proven beyond doubt at Easter.

Wilson was, additionally, far more partial to an idea articulated by Churchill: a 'Special Emergency Gendarmerie' comprising former

Field Marshal Sir Henry Wilson, the bellicose chief of the Imperial General Staff. (*Courtesy of Kilmainham Gaol Museum OPW, 19PC-1B14-18*)

military officers to reinforce the RIC. A committee, chaired by Macready, was set up to examine this. It reported soon afterwards about the perceived pitfalls of such an enterprise, owing to RIC indiscipline. To add a gendarmerie with – similarly to the Black and Tans – little experience in law enforcement and only a short-term interest in its mandate was seen as foolhardy. Macready proposed instead the formation of eight special garrison battalions, solely for use within the United Kingdom 'with a high establishment of officers and NCOs' placed under exclusively military control.[22] This was initially looked upon favourably, until negative public relations ramifications were highlighted: it could be seen as the military 'reconquest of Ireland'.[23]

Macready's patience simmered at the indecision. Simultaneously, other measures were discussed that would see the secret service radically bolstered in Ireland, and placed under the control of a single officer of appropriate rank.

12 May saw Sir Warren Fisher's committee report delivered to the British cabinet. It was a damning indictment of Dublin Castle, whose governance was deemed obsolete, its advisory capacity being effectively non-existent.[24] The report recommended maintaining Under Secretary MacMahon, despite his recent marginalisation. Fisher was being judicious in terms of striving to maintain some relationship with the Catholic church – given that MacMahon was a Roman Catholic – but he was also being pragmatic, given MacMahon's less archaic outlook in comparison to hardliners such as his usurper Sir John Taylor, whose recent month's leave Fisher recommended making permanent. Fisher advocated placing thirty-eight-year-old Scotsman Sir John Anderson, chairman of the board of inland revenue, in the position of joint under secretary alongside MacMahon, while replacing Taylor as assistant under secretary with forty-three-year-old Alfred (Andy) Cope, a buccaneering ex-customs & excise detective, working in the ministry of pensions. Cope had assisted Fisher in compiling the report. Cope would be accompanied in the position by thirty-five-year-old Mark Sturgis, a popular former Etonian with a passion for good living, but who nonetheless shared Anderson and Cope's comparative prudence set against their more hawkish cabinet members.

The Irish revolutionary movement was faced with a two-pronged adversary; one bent on crushing it, or at least forcing it relentlessly into a position of near-subjugation. Also proposed in the report was the replacement of RIC Insp. Gen. Smith. He had contrived to attain the position the previous year; now, he could not wait to return to the comparative sanctuary of Belfast and draw his pension. A supplementary report delivered three days later saw discretion thrown to the wind, when Fisher accused practically all Castle government officials of being 'woodenly stupid', with notable exceptions, including Macready.[25] He went on to reinforce Macready, Wylie and Asquith, as well as echoing their 1919 predecessors, in calling for dominion status, arguing that the vast majority of Sinn Féin supporters had 'no desire to murder or be murdered' and whose apathy in this impossible situation could be won over by a less hard-line stance by the government.[26]

Back in Dublin, more barracks burned. With the influx of the Black and Tans, IRA GHQ considered it imperative to deprive them of quarters countrywide. Dick McKee set the Dublin Brigade to such actions, more challenging in the capital owing to the increased prevalence of the enemy. Crumlin police barracks was attacked by Volunteers from D and F Companies 4th Battalion. The evacuated barracks was mined by engineers to complete its destruction.[27] However, in a portentous display of the hazards of poor training, some Volunteers entered the building holding candles which were then lit in disregard of the fact that the building had been doused with petrol only moments earlier. The building quickly caught fire with the Volunteers still inside. Casualties included Joe Larkin, an engineer tasked with setting the fuses. Dr Kathleen Lynn treated him afterwards. Fortunately for them, their injuries were not life threatening.

This was not the case on the night of 12 May: at 10 p.m. Volunteers descended in force on the south of the city to destroy Ballybrack and Kill o' the Grange RIC barracks, both evacuated by their garrisons. IRA cordons were deployed throughout Loughlinstown, Cabinteely, Killiney and towards Kingstown as the task was undertaken. Commuters getting trains in Killiney were detained in the area to prevent them interfering. Elsewhere, roadblocks were set up and telephone lines cut.

Ballybrack barracks was still inhabited by Mrs Hurst, the barrack sergeant's wife.[28] She, and her children, were given ten minutes to vacate. As she did, the IRA entered and spread hay and straw soaked in petrol throughout the building. However, when it was presumed through ineffective coordination that the building had been fully evacuated, a Volunteer struck a match, causing a vapour explosion. Within seconds the entire building was engulfed in flames.

When Capt. Peadar O'Mara, suddenly hearing screaming, realised Lt Thomas Dunne and Quartermaster Patrick Meaney were trapped inside, he ordered the rest of the men to break the steel shutters on the barrack windows to extricate them. Several dozen men, cursing and racing against time, broke the shutters and eventually wrenched them out. They were in a dreadful state, their head, faces and hands badly burned, their clothing smouldering and fused with their skin. Realising they needed urgent medical attention a passing motorcyclist with a large sidecar represented their only option. He was held up at gunpoint and ordered to take the two badly disfigured men to the Mater hospital, which made for a harrowing twelve-mile journey. They would both be dead within days.

During the same incident, forty-two-year-old William McCabe, the head gardener on the estate of Privy Counsellor Lawrence Ambrose Waldron, was shot dead in nearby Strathmore Road, less than half-a-mile from Waldron's Killiney estate. He was shot four times, once in the head and three times in the chest.[29] An IRA cordon had been deployed nearby. McCabe had refused to halt at it when called to.

Despite the tragedy, the night was another strategic success for the IRA, with seventy barracks in total destroyed countrywide. Dick McKee issued a directive subsequently instructing Volunteers to use paraffin henceforth rather than petrol to avoid further such injuries.

***

On 15 May Major General Sir Henry Hugh Tudor, a distinguished former artillery officer and close friend of Churchill, was appointed as police adviser to the Irish government. Thomas Smith, whom he was supposed to be advising, was side-lined as Tudor became the *de facto* chief of both the RIC and the DMP. Macready had called for the appointment of a military officer to inject discipline into the police. However, his knowledge of Tudor was limited. Tudor was not a strict disciplinarian when it came to those under his command, a fact that would soon backfire, although his close relationship with Churchill insulated him from repercussions. Nonetheless, his overall strategy broadly mirrored that articulated by Macready: from concentrated centres mobile forces would be deployed in sufficient numbers to restore order.[30] Tudor soon set about rearming the RIC with Lee-Enfield rifles and Lewis guns. He was

Major General Sir Henry Hugh Tudor, police adviser to the Irish government, and *de facto* chief of police in Ireland. Tudor failed to instil discipline in the forces under his command, a fact which aggravated the suffering of Irish civilians resulting from their reprisals.
(Courtesy of Mercier Archive)

a colourful figure, and imported his own female clerical staff, soon known as 'Tudor's typists', whose glamour raised eyebrows, as well as morale, in Dublin Castle.[31] Tudor himself also raised eyebrows when he advocated flogging as a counter-measure against republican insurgents.

Anderson, Cope, Sturgis and Tudor's arrivals on the scene mirrored Greenwood's baptism of fire the previous month. They occurred against significant backdrops. On 17 May in Ballinrobe, Co. Mayo the first public sitting of the Dáil Land courts were convened. These courts soon spread like wildfire and were hailed for their impartiality. Even unionist property owners soon spoke of their success as equitable courts. Solicitors throughout Ireland would soon be drawing most of their revenue from them as they rapidly supplanted the British legal system. It was a devastating propaganda blow to British rule exploited in full by republican propagandists.

Then, events of 20 May dwarfed Ballinrobe when Dublin's dockers upped the ante by refusing to unload military supplies and equipment. This was inspired by dockers in London having earlier refused to load a freighter with armaments to be used by Poland against Soviet Russia. The Labour Party's William O'Brien – acting as general secretary of the Irish Transport and General Workers'

Union (ITGWU) – had recently returned from London's Wormwood Scrubs hunger strikes. O'Brien, thirty-nine years old, had been a close associate of the late James Connolly and had been arrested and interned following the Rising. Before departing London, he had penned a newspaper article praising the actions of London's dockers. A small handful of the same ICA veterans who had successfully raided the USS *Defiance* the previous year, still working in Dublin's docks, had since read it. One of them called to O'Brien's office, informing him of two arms shipments that had just docked in Dublin, and advocated similar actions to those taken by their London counterparts. O'Brien then contacted his union president Tom Foran, and they both subsequently instructed their members not to unload the ships. This marked the genesis of a munitions strike that quickly expanded throughout the country. When the authorities discovered what was happening, a second ship, *Polberg*, was diverted to Kingstown where the military unloaded it. However, when its huge cargo was then taken by train to Westland Row station the railway workers there refused to handle it. All workers in the station came out on strike in support. The consignment – thirty box-car loads – remained there for three days, heavily guarded to prevent the IRA's Dublin Brigade from seizing it.[32]

On 24 May rail workers in Inchicore refused to transport military supplies to Thurles. Then, North Wall's London and North-Western Railway (LNWR) yard was heavily picketed for storing arms before their transport. A lock-out of employees ensued. Soon the huge red-bricked building was under military guard. A rail embargo on arms quickly ensued and spread. Unions, despite considerable hurdles, worked to ensure strike pay for railway and dock workers refusing to operate trains and unload ships. From here the strike fanned out countrywide, and eventually broadened to include the refusal by drivers to operate locomotives carrying soldiers bearing even their own weapons. In some cases, IRA intimidation was employed against less supportive railwaymen.

Macready endeavoured to compensate for this by broadening the use of the country's many ports and employing his slowly burgeoning fleet of vehicles. However, as transports, these vehicles were then unable to be deployed in tactical pursuit of IRA units as Macready had intended; a situation further aggravated when the same IRA units began trenching the country's roads to impede their use even as transports. This situation was made even worse by the state of the roads themselves; most narrow, windy, muddy and suitable therefore for ambushers whose proficiency in counter-mobility tactics grew by the day. Added to this was the increased strain on the vehicles themselves, many already half-worn out from use in the Great War.[33] Macready's strategy of mobile units, similar to that of Tudor but derided by Field Marshal Wilson, had been throttled – at least for now – by the actions of unionised labour in conjunction with the insurgent forces that Macready had been warned by Wilson not to underestimate. Half-a-mile east of the LNWR, along the same quayside, the large fuel tanks of the Shell Trading Company – fundamental to Macready's strategy – were heavily guarded. This safeguarding of military fuel supplies from sabotage or theft tied up hundreds of troops.

Meanwhile, Anderson, Cope and Sturgis took up residence for a time in the luxurious Royal Marine Hotel in Kingstown. From there they commuted under the protection of bodyguards to Dublin Castle. Sturgis ensured to savour his surroundings, enjoying the best of food and the finest wines, taking the pleasant early summer coastal air and revelling in the view of Howth Head across Dublin Bay. Beneath his hotel windows infantrymen and naval personnel worked like ants along the mile length of Carlisle Pier, unloading military supply ships. Six miles to his north, Dublin's smoggy city centre grappled with the daily grind of life in a capital whose appalling slums remained among the worst in Europe. Babies and infants continued to die at horrific levels from infectious illnesses, many cases aggravated by chronic malnutrition, cold and poor sanitation. Merchants, businessmen, tradespeople and labourers alike struggled with interruptions to the supplies of food, goods and materials for work.

***

May 1920 marked a year since Harry Boland had departed for the USA. The last week of the month saw his brief return to inform the Dáil cabinet of De Valera's overall progress in raising support and finance. Following a typically boisterous reunion with Collins, he also quietly filled his IRB colleagues in on arms and ammunition supply issues. His official reports, typed up by Eithne Lawless, met with overall approval. Seeing his old comrades again, as well as Kitty Kiernan – an old flame – was a tonic for Boland, whose labours over the previous year had been both physically and mentally draining. Prolonged infighting between seemingly irreconcilable Irish-American factions had been particularly taxing to witness.

Boland, staying in 44 Mountjoy Street for safety rather than his Clontarf family home, noticed a marked change in his comrades. It was clearly evidence of the constant strain that they were under. Collins, also harbouring strong affections for the same Kitty Kiernan, had changed considerably, but understandably. Collins expressed his unabating anxiety as to: 'which would last longer, the body or the lash'. He also pointed out to his good friend that his recent repeated expressions of esteem for the tireless efforts of the 'Chief' – De Valera – were one thing, but Collins asserted: 'As always, the battleground is here at home, and, to my mind, it is now a question of our own nerves'.[34]

Collins also filled Boland in about the contents of a letter he had come across from the sister of the late enemy agent Frederick McNulty, alias Brian Fergus Molloy. It had referred to a letter she had received at her home in the western USA from her brother. Boland would eventually visit her home, posing as a life assurance agent, and ask to see the letter. Its contents were revealing: McNulty bequeathed her his few worldly possessions, adding that he had expected to die soon, but expressed no regret at having led an adventurous life. He also wrote of Sinn Féin, the IRA's prowess, and the dangers of underestimating its intelligence forces.

Before returning clandestinely to the USA, Boland also took note of the RIC's unrelenting demise. De Valera had declared at the first anniversary of his ground-breaking ostracisation speech that policemen should be approached individually, or, if necessary, through their increasingly tormented families, and persuaded to leave. This depended on circumstances, of course: those with over thirty years' should retire on their pensions, while younger members should simply resign. All who resigned would be offered membership of a 'Free Men's Association'.[35] Funds were in place to assist in repositioning such members' careers either in Ireland or the USA.

In essence, the entire revolutionary strategy had been founded upon the ability to create a credible alternative to British rule. The successful usurpation of the police needed to be similar – alternative employment was needed for them. After all, this was the only job most policemen had ever had. It was natural that most would seek to weather the current storm, barring a realistic substitute. T.J. McElligott, following a conference with Collins, proposed a novel idea: drafting a circular suggesting that all policemen with less then fifteen years' service should resign. Collins sent him to Erskine Childers, his influence on such affairs growing enormously, whereupon the former RIC man paid the Englishman's home at 12 Bushy Park Road in Terenure a visit. Childers, however, to McElligott's surprise, adopted a harder stance. He derided the police as the enemy who maintained British rule, a force 'organised on national lines, to resist freedom' and simply reaffirmed that all members should be called upon to resign regardless of the number of years served, notwithstanding his agreement in principle with pragmatically facilitating alternative livelihoods.[36]

An amended circular calling for outright resignations was subsequently dispatched to every Sinn Féin club in the country. Gearóid O'Sullivan was equally uncompromising. Agreeing with Childers' blanket approach for existing members but, nonetheless, referring back to the 30 March proclamation, he expressed that new recruits to the force should simply be rendered unfit for carrying out such duties, by whatever means.[37]

McElligott, using the *nom-de-plume* 'Pro-Patria', then proposed organising a conference in Dublin at which police representatives from every county could work together to organise mass resignations, then report on progress at further monthly conferences. Boland, hearing of McElligott's efforts, had congratulated him on doing work worthy of battalions. Boland's conviviality was reinforced by the DMP disarming at its own request in late May, rendering it an impotent organisation. He had much positive news to report back to De Valera.

Nonetheless, continuing events, aggravated by the arrival of the Black and Tans, resulted in the RIC becoming much too disjointed to adopt McElligott's proposed measures. Insp. Gen. Smith summed up this overall state of affairs by cautioning Under Secretary Anderson that he was faced with two likelihoods: wholesale resignations, or the men running amok.[38] Many members, like Smith, coveted transfers to the country's north. Additionally, the representative body of the RIC had recently called for the abandonment of Ireland's most violent counties and their replacement by the army.[39]

Pressure was set to mount on both sides, however. May also saw the appointment by Winston Churchill of forty-five-year-old Col Ormonde de L'Épée Winter as the suggested single officer in overall charge of intelligence. Winter, a dapper, slightly built chain-smoker who had spent time in Ireland during the pre-war years, looked every inch the spy-master: round-faced with a receding well-oiled hairline beneath which sat studious, self-assured but malevolent eyes, over one of which he wore a monocle. In 1904 he had been acquitted of a manslaughter charge against a teenage boy who died after Winter had struck him in the head for throwing stones at his boat. He had confessed to, as a Royal Artillery officer, having enjoyed some of the Great War's more notorious battles such as Gallipoli, whilst being understandably horrified by other experiences on the western front at Passchendaele. He was a genius at cards, an expert horseman and spoke several languages. Mark Sturgis marvelled at his looks, persona, lack of morals and bawdy sense of humour, comparing him to a 'wicked little white snake'.[40] When an army officer in Dublin Castle who had known Winter when both had served in India heard he was on the way he was overheard saying: 'God help Sinn Féin, they don't know what they are up against'. He would operate under the codename 'O' but eventually become known as 'the Holy Terror'.

13

INTELLIGENCE WAR INTENSIFIES

'A straw that showed how the wind blew'

Col Winter's appointment coincided with a complete overhaul of British Intelligence. At Basil Thompson's behest, Sir Mansfield Smith-Cumming, a one-legged Royal Navy captain, veteran spymaster and director of Special Intelligence Services (SIS), set up a spy school in Cavalry barracks, Hounslow in West London. Smith-Cumming placed the school under the command of two intelligence operatives formerly based in India: Charles Tegart and G. C. Denham. These men would train operatives for the recently established Dublin District Special Branch of Military Intelligence. Suitable former or still-serving military intelligence personnel were transferred to the 10th Royal Fusiliers Service Battalion. This battalion was, however, merely a cover for the spy school.

Colonel Ormonde de L'Epée Winter, the British intelligence chief soon to become known as 'the Holy Terror' among his IRA enemies.
(Courtesy of Mercier Archive)

Then, as soon as training commenced, sixty-one-year-old Smith-Cumming began deploying to Dublin his own veteran intelligence agents from India, Egypt and Palestine. These moves coincided with the appointment of Lt Col Walter Wilson, a former England rugby international and accomplished soldier, as head of the Dublin District Special Branch. Some of Col Hill-Dillon's men already operating formed the nucleus of the new branch. Col Wilson got straight on the job. Within months he had ninety-seven staff, seventy-five of whom were operatives sent from Hounslow.

Meanwhile, sixty of Basil Thompson's own deep undercover agents drawn from the ethnic Irish in Britain had been planted in Dublin and were immersing themselves in city life. Each had been highly trained by an espionage officer on Thompson's staff, and had an individual job to fulfil, as well as a suitable cover story and identity. Completely independent of military intelligence, they reported directly to Basil Thompson. Each man was given an address where his correspondence was to be sent, using invisible ink, a frequent ingredient of which was human semen.

Col Winter found the police intelligence in Ireland shattered and concluded that he would have to rebuild it from the ground up. Winter was officially under police intelligence, and ultimately answerable to Basil Thompson. He would for now work alongside Cols Hill-Dillon and Wilson. Intelligence sharing between services had been and would remain a problem; processing would remain fragmented, and coordination between police and military would remain hamstrung by petty frictions. However, it was clear that unprecedented measures were about to be taken to penetrate, undermine and destroy the IRA.

Nevertheless, events on Tuesday 1 June 1920 got the month off to an embarrassing start for the military in an action that, whilst appearing relatively insignificant at the time, would, within a year, have a colossal indirect impact. At 4 p.m., despite facing a guard complement of more than a dozen infantrymen, the IRA executed a successful arms raid at the King's Inns building, which operated as a legal records office for the British government. Intelligence had been obtained of rifles, Lewis guns and ammunition stored there.

This particular afternoon had been chosen by Dick McKee and Peadar Clancy – the latter since recovered from his hunger strike – because it was warm, bright and sunny. Therefore the building's guards were expected to be lounging around, seeking the attentions of local women on the spacious lawn that sat between the building itself and Constitution Hill, where stood gated entrances between nine-foot-high walls and railings.[1] The main entrance was at the top of Henrietta Street. All three entrances were accessible to the public. Recent reconnaissance by Joe Dolan suggested this slovenliness was typical of the guards. A legal clerks' strike was also under way, thus reducing the numbers of staff available to hinder the operation. Squad members: Jim Slattery, Tom Keogh, Joe Guilfoyle, George Fitzgerald and Dolan himself were to be assisted by thirty 1st and 3rd Battalion members to execute the raid, which would be launched from 46 Rutland Square. The mission had been initially planned for the previous day but the inclement weather did not present such advantage. Some Volunteers with day-time employment that clashed with the proposed enterprise's timing took leave by whatever means they could; none wanted to miss this opportunity.

Dolan was to be the 'first man in and the last man out'.[2] At two minutes to four, he casually strolled up the 200-yards of Henrietta Street with three six-man sections shuffling behind, inconspicuously kicking footballs with youths. Tenement dwellers basked in the sunshine. Children played and darted between the houses while their older siblings and parents congregated around their open front doors, checking and chastising the youngsters in thick Dublin accents. Skinny dogs barked at the unfamiliar men strolling up the cul-de-sac. Locals looked on, sensing something was up. Another IRA section formed a roadblock at the bottom of Henrietta Street. Dolan readied himself when he saw the sentry, a private, on duty at the cast-iron gateway beneath the pedestrian arch to the left of the main carriage entrance, above which was a much larger arch. On the far side of this arch was another set of iron gates, behind which sat the lawn. The primary target building – the guardroom – was positioned to the left of the second set of gates.

At precisely 4 p.m., Dolan, having initially approached the sentry bearing file-papers to present a business-like impression, pounced on the sentry with his pistol, rough-handling him while driving the revolver barrel firmly into his neck. The sentry froze. Dolan then quietly reassured him that he would be fine if he remained compliant and silent. He did.

Surprise and speed were essential; McKee and Clancy had pressed the need to accomplish the mission within seven minutes, as well as the desire 'not to shoot unless in extreme circumstances'.[3] Within moments, the first section stepped briskly past the gate and entered the building, spreading out inside to disconnect its telephone lines. They were followed by the second section, led by Keogh, Slattery and George Fitzgerald. Once inside, they assaulted the guardroom, their ferocity and speed stunning the guards into instantaneous submission. The last section spread out between the huge grey three-storey building itself and its Constitution Hill exits. Seán Prendergast, of C Company 1st Battalion, was among them and he kept watch outside, nervously scanning every detail in the area, counting the khaki-coloured uniforms and watching their every move.

Inside the guardroom, Keogh and Slattery stood with their pistols pointed at the handful of motionless and terrified guards lined up against a wall. Keogh demanded the keys to the rifle-racks. One soldier attempted to say they were elsewhere but became flustered. Keogh conveyed to the young soldier that he was not messing around. The keys were promptly produced.

By now three cars – including a captured RIC Hudson – driven by Billy Fitzgerald, James Fitzgerald and Davy Golden, had taken position at the top of Henrietta Street, their backs to the building's entrance and their engines ticking over quietly. Civilians were warned to keep clear. Suddenly, Prendergast, to his disbelief, spotted eighteen-year-old Section Commander Kevin Barry, of H Company 1st Battalion, running from the building, laughing and carrying a Lewis Gun across both arms and wearing a British infantry helmet. He was taken aback by his young comrade's audacity. Soon the rest of the raiding party, including Prendergast, were following in Barry's footsteps, passing Dolan – still at this point holding up the sentry – and exiting the building laden with weapons and ammunition. By the time the languishing soldiers on the lawn knew what was happening, the raiders were gone, some – including Slattery, Keogh, Fitzgerald, and lastly, Dolan – by car, others on foot down Henrietta Street having placed the haul, including Barry's helmet, into the cars.

The total captured arms included two Lewis Guns, two-dozen rifles, several thousand rounds of ammunition, which had been placed in haversacks, as well as a field telephone. Prendergast ran with the remainder of the men down Henrietta Street, its inhabitants relishing the entertaining spectacle and cheering them on. Despite the street's downhill gradient, the brief journey felt like an eternity to the anxious raiders. Nevertheless, they laughed as they ran; particularly at one Volunteer who, in the tense excitement, still had his hand clasped tightly around a useless telephone receiver attached to its torn cable. One Volunteer articulated his hankering for a bottle of stout – to more laughter.

The raid's success was a huge morale boost to the Dublin Brigade. McKee's and Clancy's reputations as aggressive, fearless leaders soared. King's Inns' guard complement were court-martialled afterwards with the exception of one, a Victoria Cross holder. He was subsequently deployed in mufti to patrol the city, seeking out attackers he might recognise. Notably, the authorities subsequently withdrew small-sized military guard units from a number of prominent city buildings to prevent a repetition of the raid. Crucially, one such building was the Custom House.

The weapons and ammunition were transported to various dumps. One of the Lewis guns and 1,000 captured rounds were placed in the care of IRA engineer John Plunkett, son of Count Plunkett. His job was to prepare the gun for a later planned action against the Black and Tans. He was also ordered to arm it with captured ammunition. Plunkett was alert to the fact that there were different types of ammunition in his haul; the erroneous loading of the weapon with a wrong round could cause it to jam in action, with catastrophic consequences. What troubled him, however, was the discovery of doctored bullets. He had, by now, got wind of 'funny' rounds turning up in bars and other establishments where weapons were traded. These were filled with TNT and would explode in the gun barrels. It was apparent where they originated – from the British Army. Meanwhile, the two-dozen rifles were taken to a dump in Fitzwilliam Place and examined by George Fitzgerald. When he saw that each was fully loaded, including their breeches, and worse – that their safety catches were off – he gasped at the miracle that no one had been killed handling them.[4]

Plunkett quickly saw that his information was relayed to IRA intelligence. It reached Crow Street alongside word of another even more sinister recent discovery: typed letters on Dáil notepaper being sent to prominent Sinn Féin leaders warning them of their imminent deaths, similar to that sent to Tomás MacCurtain before his assassination in March. Dublin Castle was upping its game.

Meanwhile, more good news of a successful arms raid was on the way to the republicans. Both militarily and politically, 5 June saw the disarming of a large police and military patrol at Milebush in East Cork. Their transport was also commandeered. The police and soldiers were then sent on their way. The military's response was to open fire blindly along Midleton's main street that night with a machine gun.[5]

A week later saw Sinn Féin win a crushing victory in the country's rural council elections. It was the last such election before the partition scheduled for the following December under the pending enactment of the Government of Ireland Bill. Sinn Féin, 'standing on a platform of expanded public housing, health services and education', gained majorities in twenty-nine of thirty-three county councils.⁶ Two prominent victories were wrestled from unionists in counties Tyrone and Fermanagh. Republican propaganda went into overdrive on such favourable news, which was also featured in prominent English newspapers such as *The Nation* and *The London Daily News*. These carried pronouncements that the election results represented an extensive broadening of the Republic's fighting front, and that the British Army and Navy were all but useless set against such public support for Irish independence.⁷

Frank Thornton had spent late May and early June travelling between Dublin and Wexford, laying the ground for an assassination that would – as a side-effect – see the fruition of a pledge made quietly by Liam Tobin during the early hours of 30 April 1916, immediately after the Rising. Tobin, along with Collins and several hundred surrendered Volunteers, had watched helplessly in horror as British Army Capt. Percival Lea Wilson had humiliated and degraded the late republican leaders Edward Daly and Tom Clarke as they sat together under guard in the Rotunda grounds. Tobin had quietly vowed that he would avenge their mistreatment one day.

Four years on, IRA intelligence strongly suspected that thirty-three-year-old Lea Wilson – now RIC district inspector for Gorey – was involved in reprisal shootings. Liam O'Leary, Wexford IRA brigade adjutant, had recently been detailed to arrange the interrogation of suspected enemy collaborators by Thornton in Wexford.⁸ Information had reached IRA intelligence before this that Tomás MacCurtain's killers had been harboured in a large country house close to New Ross. Ominously, another reprisal killing had taken place nine days after MacCurtain's that bore striking similarity: shortly after midnight, a number of disguised men had hammered at the front door of twenty-one-year-old Thomas Dwyer's home near Thurles Co. Tipperary before barging in and shooting him several times.⁹ The Wexford IRA subsequently raided the country house in New Ross. Several prisoners were taken to a safe house in Ballycarney, where their interrogation by Thornton led to blame being assigned for both reprisal shootings to Lea Wilson and several others. They were then released under warning – such leniency soon became uncharacteristic in Ireland.

On 8 June Thornton returned to Wexford, this time to 'Antwerp' – local Volunteer HQ in 4 Main Street Enniscorthy – with Tobin. There, Thornton revealed to Adjutant O'Leary and several other Wexford Brigade officers that they planned to shoot Lea Wilson, but needed an initial reconnaissance carried out in Gorey. Tobin was the only one who could recognise Lea Wilson out of uniform – he had ensured to remember every detail he could about him four years earlier – so they requested local assistance. Volunteers Joseph McMahon and Seán Whelan later stepped up. Michael Synott was then also selected as a driver. Other scouts from Gorey itself were detailed to help locate him.

Seven frustrating days passed with sightings of Lea Wilson but no opportunities to shoot, until just after 9.35 a.m. on Tuesday 15 June, he was spotted walking leisurely in the morning sunshine in the direction of Ballycanew Road towards his home. Ironically, Thornton had, just moments earlier, warned the Wexford men that if they did not get Lea Wilson that day they would be ordered by GHQ to carry out the job themselves. Lea Wilson stopped in the train station to buy *The Irish Times*. He then parted company with an RIC sergeant who had strolled for a time with him, and made his way towards his awaiting assassins, who stood around their Ford Hackney car as if trying to fix its engine.

Moments later Thornton, Tobin, McMahon and Whelan pounced, their guns suddenly blazing. Lea Wilson was initially hit twice. He collapsed under the impacts of the shots, but raised himself and struggled away for fifteen yards before falling again. The killers, with Synott also firing, pumped another dozen shots at him, blasting him to pieces; then, finally, there was a shot to the head.

The car took off southbound towards Ballycanew. Eventually, Tobin and Thornton were transported to Borris in Co. Carlow, and from there to Dublin, where news of Lea Wilson's demise was greeted with glee by 1916 GPO and Four Courts veterans working with IRA intelligence.

***

Meanwhile, 190 miles away, in Tralee, Tadhg Kennedy, Kerry County Council's accountant, had become friends with David Neligan, the former detective whiling away his recent days in the town. Kennedy was also the intelligence officer for the Kerry Number 1 Brigade. In mid June he informed Neligan that Austin Stack had just relayed word that Michael Collins wished to see him. It appeared that Collins wanted Neligan to return to the DMP. Neligan and Kennedy then arranged, as a cover for such an enterprise, for threatening letters to be sent by post to Neligan as a result of his previous stint with the force.[10]

Det. Chief Insp. John Bruton had recently taken over a special wing of G-Division inside Dublin Castle. Dets Broy and Cavanagh were still detailed to Brunswick Street surreptitiously working for Collins. Jim McNamara was still assigned to the assistant commissioner – the late Forbes-Redmond's successor, Denis Barrett – who was keeping his head down. Therefore, Collins had, effectively, no one working directly for him within G-Division in the Castle. Neligan appeared to fit the bill.

Neligan initially met Stack in Wellington Quay's Clarence Hotel. Liam Tobin – back from Wexford – and Joe O'Reilly met Neligan again there the next day to sound him out. Tobin's instincts at this point were well honed. Neligan passed the test. The following day Neligan sat opposite Collins upstairs in Bannon's pub, 41 Upper Abbey Street, having been escorted there by O'Reilly.[11] Collins wore a tweed suit and an old coat was slung on the next chair. The room smelled of stale beer. Smoke hung in the air. Collins expressed how he had become aware that Neligan and his brother were friendly to the movement. He apologised that Neligan's earlier offer of help in March was not acted upon, then said: 'We need you at the Castle. You will have to go back. You are a man they trust. We also trust you'.[12]

Collins was typically persuasive. Soon afterwards, Neligan applied to Col Edgeworth Johnstone to be reinstated, citing the threatening letters as his motivation. A meeting soon afterwards with the chief commissioner, whom Neligan liked personally, resulted in Edgeworth Johnstone's confession that he wanted Neligan back; set against so many recent resignations he felt it optimistically suggested he was 'a straw that showed how the wind blew'.[13] He could not have been more wrong. Neligan then briefed him on conditions in the country's south, painting a bleak picture for the police. Once reinstated officially back at G-Division, he reported to Bruton, who was surprised that he had come back, and warned him to lie low for a while.

Neligan's bleak picture was an accurate one. His departure from Kerry coincided with signs in the county that General Macready's fears of sitting on a volcano were well founded. Listowel barracks saw a mutiny among its officers following an incident on 17 June. The barracks' nineteen-strong detachment, had, the previous evening, been informed of their pending redeployment from Listowel to more isolated outposts. Their own barracks was to be turned over to the military, with three sergeants to remain as guides. This reflected a countrywide trend of a lack of billeting quarters for the military reinforcements arriving in the country.

When the news broke, Const. Jeremiah Mee, thirty-one years old and recently transferred from Sligo, in the absence of anyone else to take charge of the issue, addressed his colleagues. He heralded that the occupation of the barracks by the military represented a declaration of war against the Irish people. The consequences for them as policemen were dismal; if they succeeded in helping the British authorities subdue their own countrymen they would have to live with the shame; if they failed, matters would become far worse for them personally. Mee persuaded his colleagues to defend the barracks by force if necessary from the military.

The following day saw repeated arguments between Mee, acting as representative, and County Insp. Power O'Shea.[14] The outcome was O'Shea's instructions for the policemen to line up on parade on the morning of 17 June, insisting that the barracks must be handed over to the military in line with recent policy for all such headquarters stations in Munster. The province was, since 3 June, under the command of Col Bryce Ferguson Smyth, a thirty-four-year-old highly decorated war veteran, acting as divisional police commissioner for Munster. Insp. Power was exasperated by Mee's typed list of demands which had stated simply that they were capable of maintaining order in their own community without soldiers, many of whom were suspected by the police of being low in character, as evidenced by their insatiable appetite for prostitutes. Mee and his colleagues insisted that they would resign if they were overruled and forced to accommodate the soldiers.

The barracks was due to be handed over at noon. When noon arrived with no sign of movement the police savoured their apparent victory. But when the hours passed into the following day the tension mounted. Then, at 10 p.m. on the 18 June, a telephone message was received for the men to be on parade for the commissioner the following morning at 10 a.m.

At 10.30 a.m. on 19 June, a large heavily armed police and military convoy arrived at the barracks. Insp. Power then introduced General Tudor, Col Smyth and a captain named Chadwick to an increasingly fearful Const. Mee in the barrack day room. Mee, with no experience of oratory or leadership, was apprehensive; nevertheless, when Smyth spoke up he interrupted him, demanding to speak only with the police authorities. He took stock of Smyth. The colonel had lost his left arm and was clearly a formidable soldier. Mee's respectful recognition of this was, however, dashed when Smyth spoke again, addressing the gathered policemen as he would a ruthless military unit going into combat with a speech that stunned and appalled them.

Smyth, completely misjudging their frame of mind, told them he had words they would not want their wives to hear; the police had done splendid work but were not strong enough. It was time to turn the tables on Sinn Féin and this would require working offensively with the army. Police and army were to be coordinated by 21 June to initiate martial law, and 7,000 police reinforcements were currently on the way from England. The military would act in force, assisted by large numbers of RIC. Henceforth, if a barracks was burned, the nearest 'best house' was to be commandeered, the occupants thrown in the gutter – 'the more the merrier'. Operations were to be launched six nights per week and police were to leave stations unseen by their back doors with smaller patrols acting normally as decoys. They were to lie in ambush, to shout 'hands up!' at civilians and shoot with effect if disobeyed. Civilians looking suspicious with hands in pockets were to be shot on sight. The more shot the more favourable would be the colonel's reaction. Mistakes were permissible, and no man would be punished over the findings of inquests. Policemen would no longer be compelled to even attend inquests, which, in any event, would themselves soon be set aside.

Hunger strikers were to die in jail. Smyth emphasised that it was a pity that so few had been allowed to die thus far. He then hinted ominously at some being dealt with in a manner no one would ever hear about, then alluded to a ship soon to be filled with 'Sinn Féiners' that would sail but never dock. He finished by declaring that anyone not up to the job should resign.

Col Smyth then turned to the nearest policeman and asked if he would cooperate. The policeman replied dismissively: 'Constable Mee speaks for me'.[15] Mee, his confidence bolstered, then spoke up, pointing out initially that Smyth's accent was that of an Englishman, only to be abruptly interrupted by Smyth's contention that he was from Banbridge in Co. Down. Mee continued regardless; losing his temper, he removed his police cap, belt and sword, placing them on an adjacent table, and declared that he and his comrades were proud Irishmen and that Smyth was a murderer. Mee's colleagues at this point were terrified of being shot. Nevertheless, Smyth appeared rattled and left the room.

General Tudor appeared after a time. To diffuse the tension he shook hands with each gathered policeman. He then told them that Dominion Home Rule would soon be implemented in Ireland; all they had to do to facilitate this was obey orders, for which he promised them twelve years' extra service to their pensions. The response was unexpected: they professed to having heard it all before and were simply not prepared to go out and get shot like rats.

Eventually, the entire military party left the barracks. Dist. Insp. Thomas Flanagan congratulated the suddenly elated men. Mee then went to a back room and wrote the contents of Smyth's speech while his memory was fresh. He then had it signed by several police witnesses. Telephone calls were quickly made to Tralee, Castleisland, Killarney, Kenmare and Dingle – all headquarters barracks' – with the news. When similar measures were subsequently attempted there the barrack garrisons responded by shouting: 'Up Listowel!'

When, two weeks later, the RIC in Munster received a pay-rise to improve their morale, the measure backfired. As soon as police throughout the rest of the country were informed they expressed disgust at such favouritism. Mee set himself to getting Smyth's speech contents to Sinn Féin in Dublin, and kept it closely guarded until the opportunity arose.

Ironically, two days after Mee and his colleagues had successfully stood their ground, the IRA increased its pressure on the RIC. The boycott was officially widened to include persons having any dealings whatsoever with them. Business and trades people inclined to maintain such enterprises were warned that this was not in their long-term interests. The message was, in the main, interpreted correctly. The boycott's devastating nature was illustrated to Michael Collins when he was informed of the RIC 'taking goods at the point of a revolver' in Co. Leitrim. He replied: 'When we have driven them to this position our boycott is a success'.[16] This was repeated elsewhere; bizarrely, goods and provisions were taken at gunpoint, but then paid for. General Tudor noted that his men were: 'living behind sandbags and wire entanglements; they were boycotted and life was altogether intolerable'.[17] The rail embargo also applied to armed police.

By late June RIC resignations were endemic, with their ranks being rapidly replaced by Black and Tans as well as standard replacements who, despite being welcome by some, were without the knowledge and experience of their forerunners and less likely to be effective and earn the trust of their veteran colleagues. Simultaneously the IRA police – acting as official units following a 19 June directive from Richard Mulcahy to activate such a force – stepped into the breach in greater numbers.

Such units, established in Dublin a year earlier in far smaller numbers, were bolstered throughout the city and country, albeit with similar challenges in expertise. Police Volunteers began to wear green armbands with the letters I.V. (Irish Volunteers) embroidered onto them to identify themselves when present at Dáil courts, the official setting up of which took place on 29 June. IRA members wearing the same armbands soon policed public events like horse-racing meetings. Ironically, they frequently rubbed shoulders with British service personnel at such events – an unofficial truce of sorts largely applied to race meetings and similar sporting gatherings, though on 9 July the military broke up such a meeting policed by Volunteers in Bellewstown just outside Co. Dublin. Notwithstanding this embarrassing episode, policing became hugely popular among Volunteers, so much so that soon afterwards, *An t-Óglách* had to issue a reminder that there was a war on and their primary duty was to fight. Meanwhile, this unofficial truce at race meetings was exploited by IRA intelligence. It funnelled British officers, desperate for distraction, into the crosshairs of IRA intelligence. Members such as Tom Cullen attended meetings, linking arms with Lily Mernin, who, among other women performing such perilous work, would then introduce Cullen, or perhaps another male 'suitor', to her Dublin Castle 'colleagues', thereby identifying them.

The Dáil courts were empowered by Dáil Éireann to compel people to appear before them on both criminal and civil charges and, despite teething problems, were set up throughout Dublin and the country. In one particularly problematic case, Dick McKee, overseeing with others a rape case in Rutland Square, sought the advice of a clergyman; the case was settled as a civil issue.[18] In other cases, persons found guilty of less grievous charges were ordered to be paraded after Sunday mass in their localities. A variety of criminal charges resulted in fines, or orders to leave the country. Civil cases were adjudicated with similar success to the land courts and were viewed as being equally impartial. Within weeks the British court system ceased to function effectively.

All in all the British authorities in Ireland were reeling during the summer of 1920. Two days after Mulcahy had given the green light for the republican police, no less than eighty-five public bodies declared their allegiance to Dáil Éireann. An effective system of local government was being implemented, notwithstanding chronic financial constraints that radically worsened as soon as Dublin Castle withdrew funding from such bodies on 29 June. Local councils quickly reacted and were soon levying rates on business and property holders to support the Dáil government, providing some relief. A friend warned Walter Long at the time that: 'Everybody is going over to Sinn Féin, not because they believe in it, but because it is the only authority in the country'.[19] Jurors could not be found for the periodic courts known as the summer assizes; they were under warning that to attend would constitute 'an act of treason'. A clear marker also came in the form of the Dublin Chamber of Commerce – traditionally unionist – calling for an immediate measure of self-government for Ireland.

Meanwhile, the arms transportation embargo continued to frustrate the British military. It was not, however, without its drawbacks for those participating. Wages were drastically affected. Railway operators were unsympathetic to their striking employees, as were the authorities to the operators themselves. Funds were raised for striking railwaymen, but were meagre nonetheless. British unions drew the line in supporting the measure with strike action, and instead made arbitrary calls for the military to withdraw from Ireland.

Dublin's hospitals also suffered considerably under the constrained and uncertain conditions. Private philanthropy was successfully employed to buffer pending financial ruin in more than one state-funded institution, while associated fund-raising also increased. Additionally, local authorities contributed funds. Strikingly, IRA GHQ introduced a directive in June that its battalions would need to cover their own medical expenses. This was in conjunction with a decree compelling wounded Volunteers to have measures put in place on their behalf before their transfers to Dublin for treatment. They included: a doctor's referral under false identity, advance notification of injury type and treatment requirements, travel dates and provisions for accommodation.[20] Meanwhile, to help cope with the growing number of wounded Volunteers from Dublin and the country, units such as that which operated in 62 Eccles Street during early summer 1920 stepped into the breach.

INTELLIGENCE WAR INTENSIFIES

Run by Geraldine O'Donel, this was a private nursing home where Volunteers could be treated, often in adjacent rooms or floors to sick or wounded British servicemen. Twomey's Chemist in Great Denmark Street operated as a liaison office between the nursing home and GHQ.

***

Apart from the King's Inns raid, June was a comparatively quiet month in Dublin as both sides regrouped and took stock of the enemy. The same could not be said for Derry city, which saw an outbreak of vicious sectarian violence on Sunday 20 June, and was succeeded by street fighting the likes of which had not been seen since Dublin's Easter Rising. It was also a sinister harbinger of what lay ahead for Ulster.

At 8 p.m., loyalist gunmen, displaying proficiency in military coordination, opened fire on civilians in Catholic and nationalist areas of the city. The indiscriminate onslaught coincided with the departure of armed police from affected areas. Over three hours five civilians were shot dead and another twenty-four were wounded. A battalion of the Dorset Regiment and several hundred police were already deployed in the area but did not become involved. From dawn the following day, silence hung on the traumatised city. IRA leaders then marshalled what meagre resources they could and set about organising counter-measures to ward off further attacks.

Then, early on Monday 21 June, nationalist dock workers came under well directed fire from the opposite banks of the River Foyle. Loyalist snipers repositioned themselves in dominant vantage points throughout the city and communicated with one another using Morse code signals. Six civilians died and many more were wounded under their fire before the IRA were effectively deployed to counter-attack, with roving patrols clearing individual areas at a time and driving enemy snipers away under heavy fire. RIC officers who had also joined the fighting alongside loyalists were driven to the city's courthouse, some wounded and had their weapons taken. St Columba's College on Bishop Street was eventually occupied as IRA HQ. As fighting intensified, Catholics were driven from their homes in large numbers. Vicious fighting took place in the Waterside area, with rioting, small arms fire and burning houses causing further terror and panic. Streets were then barricaded while reinforcements for both sides filtered into the city.

When the college was secured, Cumann na mBan members were summoned. Despite the incessant gunfire, a dozen of them set up first aid posts and cooking facilities. When republican reinforcements had arrived in sufficient numbers, further assaults were made to reclaim areas of the city that had been cleared of Catholics. However, this coincided with the deployment of the Queen's Royal Regiment to subdue IRA resurgence. Repeated assaults were then made by the military to drive the IRA from their gained ground. Civilians huddled in their homes, frozen in fear as food began to run out. Both stray and well-aimed bullets shattered windows. Several bodies lay in Bishop Street, including that of a young girl.

The city had come to a complete standstill by the time Dick McKee and Peadar Clancy arrived, having rushed from Dublin as soon as news arrived at GHQ of the fighting's intensity. Once they had managed to sidestep the city's enclosing cordon they were guided successfully into the college where they both helped to coordinate its defence. Ammunition was re-supplied, and eventually a Lewis gun was deployed to bolster the building's defence. McKee took stock of the topography and layout of buildings, referring to his experiences during the Rising and his detailing of defence in depth positions to the Dublin Brigade during the conscription crisis. His eventual conclusion, however, given the strength of enemy forces and escalating civilian casualties, was to arrange for the college's evacuation at the end of the week, but this could not be attempted until attack after attack had been fended off in a series of actions that reminded one British infantryman of the fighting for 'Hill 60' three years earlier in Ypres in Belgium, such was its intermittent ferocity.

The civilian death toll for the week was eighteen, but scores more were badly wounded and hundreds rendered homeless by the time the fighting had ceased. McKee and Clancy were spirited back to Dublin. Ulster simmered, but soon boiled over again.

Clancy was not idle upon his return, nor was McKee. Soon afterwards, an opportunity presented itself to finish the month as it had started – with another arms raid. Nicholas Laffan, of G Company 1st Battalion, informed Clancy of a tantalising haul of weapons and ammunition being kept at the home of an army officer at 15 North Circular Road. The address was subsequently raided, yielding a haul of several rifles, bayonets, pistols, bombs, and even a sword.[21] These were expedited to an arms dump in Rutland Place.

Meanwhile, on the city's south side, McKee was busily liaising with James O'Donovan, GHQ's director of chemicals. O'Donovan was making significant progress in his workings of fulminate, chlorate mixtures and gelignite to create significant improvements in grenade manufacture, with additional emphasis on fragmentation – the process that caused the enemy most injury. Grenades were tested close to the Bottle Tower in Churchtown, a regular haunt of game-shooters. When deemed satisfactory, consignments were then dispatched to Michael Flanagan's arms dump in Wexford Street.

Fermoy in Co. Cork, having remained comparatively peaceful since the events there the previous September, suffered under its military garrison again on the night of 27 June. This was in retaliation for the kidnapping of forty-one-year-old Brigadier General Cuthbert Lucas of the 17th Infantry Brigade by the IRA under Liam Lynch while the general fished five miles east of the town. Lucas, having erroneously assumed the tacit truce applicable to equestrian events applied to all sports, was held at gunpoint and spirited away from a fishing cottage along with his batman and several other officers. Their own military car was commandeered as extra transport. The kidnapping was in retaliation for the arrest and imprisonment of Michael Fitzgerald, thirty-eight-year-old commandant of the 4th Battalion Cork Number 2 Brigade.[22] During the getaway Lucas' officers made a spirited escape attempt. When one of them was shot in the face during the struggle, he was subsequently

Brigadier General Cuthbert Lucas among several of his captors.
Lucas developed a surprising relationship with his kidnappers and spoke very highly of them.
(*Courtesy of Mercier Archive*)

left in the care of his fellow officers while the general was driven to Limerick.

The following night 400 troops ransacked Fermoy in revenge, killing one man and causing tens of thousands of pounds in damage. The picturesque town of Lismore, a dozen miles away in Co. Waterford, was also subjected to bombs and burnings. General Macready immediately proposed taking six known IRA members hostage in the Fermoy area but was overruled by John Anderson and Hamar Greenwood, fearing further hunger strikes. Winston Churchill was furious at Lucas' lack of diligence, and, similarly to *An t-Óglách*, called upon British officers to 'recognise that the country was in a state of war'; the expression was of course at odds with Lloyd George's articulated policy of Ireland's conflict representing a mere law and order issue.

Ironically, General Lucas enjoyed his captivity. His captors included Joe Good, since transferred to Munster from Co. Mayo following his return from stalking politicians in London two years earlier. Good and the general struck up a rapport. Lucas was even permitted to send letters to his wife; her responses were simply addressed to 'General Lucas, The IRA' but reached her husband nonetheless. He was provided with whiskey and cigarettes, good food and allowed to play tennis; he even went fishing and on one such occasion saved Good from almost drowning. He spoke very highly of his captors, complimenting them on their decency and bravery and agreeing that Ireland, with its staggering fertile beauty, was a country worth fighting for.[23] While being transferred between safe houses during clear summer nights in Limerick and Clare his captors noticed him navigating by stars, employing the River Shannon as a landmark. Lucas reassured them, however, that he knew he was among gentlemen, and insisted that accordingly, he would never divulge their locations, knowing that the kindness shown by those whose homes and villages provided his good treatment would suffer horrific reprisals. The general stuck to his guns in professing his loyalties and sense of duty to the crown, despite contentions articulated by Good and others that sentiments such as the country being worth fighting for had also been felt by the likes of Oliver Cromwell. Nevertheless his wit and charm grew on his captors, and his sincerity impressed them.

Two days after Lucas' abduction, Ireland's struggle received a boost from an unlikely quarter: in Jullundur in India's Punjab, only fifty miles from the scene of the horrific Amritsar massacre, a company of Connaught Rangers refused to carry out duties because of the news of growing crown atrocities at home. The mutiny then spread to other Rangers units, who began waving Tricolour flags and pledging allegiance to Sinn Féin. The mutiny was suppressed when a large number, fearing they were about to be attacked, tried to access their weapons but were fired on by guards. Two Rangers – Privates Smythe and Sears – were killed, while one more was wounded. Afterwards sixty-one men were convicted for their parts in the mutiny, fourteen of whom were sentenced to death.

When news reached Dublin it caused consternation among unionists who considered the British Army a bastion of discipline and loyalty – this sentiment was particularly applicable to regiments such as the Rangers whose recent war record was exemplary. Despite occurring thousands of miles away, the mutiny created its own murmurings among Irish unionists that time was ripe for self-government.

Meanwhile, Dublin, barring isolated incidents, remained inauspiciously calm as summer 1920 approached its height. Nonetheless, warnings were issued to troops to stick to the city's main thoroughfares, semi-automatic pistols were issued to officers. IRA units maintained constant readiness.

In charge of one such IRA unit was Lt William Stapleton, twenty-three years old, he was just one among many Volunteer officers in early summer 1920 overseeing street patrols and small scale ambushes in his company area of Drumcondra, Fairview and North Strand. Stapleton organised his men from B Company 2nd Battalion into eight sections of three to four, armed with pistols and grenades, and set them to various jobs. Drumcondra was the main thoroughfare for military traffic to and from the city to Collinstown aerodrome and beyond. Several attacks were made on vehicles from the high ground behind the castle-like wall surrounding the archbishop's palace. While these had a negligible effect on the enemy, they nonetheless had a positive effect on his men's morale. DMP officers were held up and questioned, the majority gave no trouble, but on one occasion two policemen drew weapons. One was shot in the mouth but survived. Arms raids were an additional feature of such unit actions. These actions were replicated throughout the city. Nevertheless, the comparative calm in the capital was merely the lull before a gathering storm.

14

SHOOTINGS, REPRISALS AND AUXILIARIES DEPLOYED

'Digging the grave of her own democracy'

In early July Jeremiah Mee and four of his RIC colleagues took leave from Listowel without informing their more senior officers. They eventually made their way to Dublin, hailed as heroes in some of the communities they passed through, experiencing hair-raising interactions with British officers in others. When they eventually arrived in the capital a meeting was discreetly arranged with Michael Collins, Erskine Childers, Countess Markievicz, Thomas Johnson and William O'Brien.[1]

The day preceding their arrival, 10 July, had seen Col Smyth's speech as recounted by Mee published in *The Freeman's Journal*, copied word for word from the most recent edition of the *Irish Bulletin*. The *Journal*'s reward was a visit from the British Army that proved similar to the one carried out by the IRA the previous December upon the *Irish Independent*: the premises were vandalised and machinery destroyed. Smyth himself also sued the paper subsequently for libel; a suit which would, however, be short-lived. Nevertheless, the reaction to the speech, both nationally and internationally, was of horror.

During the meeting, Collins expressed disbelief that a highly decorated senior ranking British officer could so freely articulate such a criminal strategy, and claim, albeit indirectly, that it was endorsed by the British government. Collins understood it was one thing dispatching secret service agents to participate in the deadly intelligence game he and his staff excelled in, but it was another to reveal such explicit malevolent disdain for an entire population. He was, therefore, perplexed at the idea of Smyth speaking as anything other than a renegade. Childers, however, thought otherwise, and having worked in Westminster as a senior clerk, as well as a stint with British intelligence, understood the sentiment as a tacit acknowledgement that the government was reeling under the escalating conflict.

That pressure increased soon afterwards when Johnson and O'Brien travelled to London's International Labour Conference. There, they distributed hundreds of copies of *The Freeman's Journal*, detailing the incident, causing uproar. A delegation was formed to travel to Ireland to investigate the growing list of atrocities reported by the increasingly ubiquitous *Irish Bulletin*. An official investigation was demanded into Listowel. Then on 14 July, Hamar Greenwood admitted in the Commons that Col Smyth had reported to him personally of such sinister sentiments having been expressed by the attorney general the previous May. Amid further uproar, particularly in the USA, Col Smyth was summoned by Lloyd George to London to present his account of the episode. Smyth eventually arrived and lashed out at the government, accusing them of assigning him a task, the backlash from which they wished to cynically distance themselves.

Robert Erskine Childers, fifty years old, was employing his formidable literary talents to the detriment of British colonial rule. Since 1918 he had been sickened by what he saw as the hypocrisy of Westminster's claims to act as the guardian of small independent nations while conspiring to undermine such claims to independence in Ireland. He had once hailed Great Britain as a liberal beacon in a dark world, but recoiled and saw Britain instead as an aggressor that viewed its holding of Ireland as, simply, a strategic asset on its Atlantic seaboard. Once a proponent of Home Rule, he threw in his lot with the quest for full independence, and devoted his considerable energies to Sinn Féin propaganda.

On 9 July he published his booklet *Military Rule in Ireland* – a series of vociferous indictments – with Dublin's Talbot Press. He wrote of the numerous raids earlier in the year, pleading with English women to show solidarity with Irish women whose homes were ransacked, their hus-

Robert Erskine Childers, the enigmatic writer and propagandist, former British intelligence officer and zealous convert to the cause of Irish independence. (*Courtesy of Kilmainham Gaol Museum OPW, 20PC-1A57-18*)

bands spirited away. He portrayed policemen hiding their heads in shame as soldiers pilfered belongings, and of elected officials held in custody without trial, their only means of escape to starve themselves almost to death. He attacked the military for the previous September's looting of Fermoy, claiming the guilty regiment should have been withdrawn to England, not transferred to nearby Cork to create further outrage. He wrote of the more recent reprisals against Fermoy and Lismore, as well as other smaller towns throughout the country the same night, including Swords. He expressed exasperation at hard-pressed local councils forced to levy rates to repair such damage, and accused the government of orchestrating reprisals as a strategy to bankrupt defecting councils.

Childers then attacked a tactic recently employed by Dublin Castle where they issued daily 'Summaries of Official Reports of Outrages' to the press. He dismissed its credibility, castigating the fact that no government outrages were listed. He validated this dismissal with statistics: claiming that between May 1916 and March 1920 Sinn Féin attributed 26,721 outrages to the British government, whereas Dublin Castle had publicly admitted to committing a mere 2,000 actions against republicans. He accused Britain of destroying law and order while striving to be seen to be maintaining it, and in so doing: 'Digging the grave of her own democracy'.[2]

After another appeal, this time to the people of England, he lauded the republican local government, particularly the courts. While ridiculing Lord French's assertion that the 'troubles' were a fundamental result of over 100,000 idle young Irishmen not being able to emigrate as a result of the recent war, he attested to the success of the republican courts in assuaging the chronic 'land hunger' that plagued Ireland because of so many disenfranchised young men. He then painted a picture of magistrate courts lying empty by comparison, while alluding to the injustice of republican judges and police suffering arrest and imprisonment. He also claimed that the RIC was a defunct, detested force.

Regarding recent killings in Derry, he claimed such targeting of civilians was a culmination of British policy dating back to 1914: that of allowing one segment of population to arm whilst striving to disarm the other. He then highlighted the dangers of such disregard for justice, envisioning the ominous increase in such atrocities. His predictions soon proved accurate.

Meanwhile, mediation talks had almost commenced between Sinn Féin and the British government. Basil Thompson, under cabinet instruction, employed American journalist and former war correspondent Carl Ackerman to present peace feelers and act as a clandestine liaison between both camps. Ackerman was instructed to 'disregard bellicose and hard-line statements by the British cabinet' as simple posturing. However, the proposed talks fell apart after Desmond Fitzgerald travelled to London with a list of demands for Thompson to forward to Hamar Greenwood, but the latter declined to meet him. Fitzgerald was under instructions to engage only with elected ministers, not police officials.[3] He, nevertheless, later met with Assistant Cabinet Secretary Thomas Jones.[4] While in Ireland, Ackerman was also surreptitiously seeking out Michael Collins. Thompson had told him that Collins, not Arthur Griffith, was the rebellion's real leader, and urged him to discover what would be required to bring Collins to the negotiating table at some stage in the future.

***

By mid-July it was clear to IRA intelligence that not only peace feelers were in play. More threatening moves were also being made by Dublin Castle; the recent lull had simply been a signal of its intelligence services regrouping. A tried and tested means of assessing such developments was to intercept Castle mail deliveries. Dublin's telephone network was considered unreliable by the authorities, therefore, mail was the preferred choice for informers, government agencies, non-sensitive state communications and prospective agents. However, since the most recent successful raid, security had tightened. Nonetheless, a flaw was soon detected and exploited. Again, Dick McKee was pivotal to this.

McKee and Frank Henderson planned a raid on the Rotunda Rink sorting office for the morning of Thursday 15 July. Oscar Traynor, thirty-four-years-old, would lead it. It had been observed that a military party arrived at the Rink's western side each morning shortly before 8 a.m., but there was a two-minute lapse between the Castle mail bags being sealed and their subsequent collection. Patrick Moynihan, a post office director working for Michael Collins, had briefed him on both the location and the distinctive green colour markings on the Castle bags. Collins had then instructed Squad members to form a cordon around the Rotunda at the appropriate date and time.

Speed and precision would be paramount. Traynor organised two parties from the 2nd Battalion to synchronise watches and then attack the building –

a temporary structure – at 7. 27 a.m. from both its eastern and western sides. They included Seán Russell, Charlie Dalton, Harry Colley, Traynor himself and several others. Joe Dolan also took part, alongside William Stapleton.

The attack was launched initially by taking two policemen stationed outside the building hostage. Dolan and Stapleton then entered from Cavendish Row, seeking to isolate the emergency telephone. Traynor and his men simultaneously rushed the building. Unexpectedly, he and his section then spotted a shortcut – a chute leading to the sorting room. Improvising, Traynor and the others slid through the chute and emerged, pistols ready. Mail sorters looked on in stunned submission as the second section quietly then rushed in. Dolan disabled the telephone as Stapleton stood guard, while their comrades directed themselves to the green-coloured Castle bags. Minutes later, Traynor blew a whistle and the raiders departed. The mail sacks were then collected at the western entrance by car and driven to Crow Street. The raid was so effective that when its participants had departed, many of the staff had not even realised it had happened.

The Squad dispersed when they saw Traynor and the others depart by bicycle and on foot just after the car had pulled away. Then, Traynor, laughing, instructed Russell that they were both going for a morning swim. He had, to Russell's confusion, instructed him to bring towels to the raid. They then cycled away. The two policemen, meanwhile, returned to duty.

The raid was reported in newspaper stop-press editions. It was said that the raiders had descended through the chute 'like bolts from the blue'.[5] Meanwhile, 3 Crow Street bustled as each letter was scrutinised, revealing a great deal to IRA intelligence. Unimportant envelopes were simply re-sealed and posted again. The raid's subsequent publicity also acted as an effective deterrent to informers sending messages by mail. When Traynor was informed later that a postal worker had mentioned recognising him from his previous career as a footballer, IRA intelligence responded by finding the individual and cautioning him that if he opened his mouth again the words he spoke would be his last.

Then, two days after the raid, Lord French received a letter with a notice stamped on the envelope. It read: 'Opened and censored by the Irish Republic'.[6] He was incandescent with rage. However, worse revelations were on the way. That Saturday evening, 17 July, as Col Smyth sat smoking with RIC County Insp. George Craig at the County Club in Cork's South Mall – considered safe

SHOOTINGS, REPRISALS AND AUXILIARIES DEPLOYED

– he was shot dead by a unit from IRA Cork Number 1 Brigade. Intelligence Officer Seán Culhane, having had Smyth under surveillance, entered the club's smoking room with his unit. As soon as Smyth was identified, nineteen-year-old Culhane and his comrades opened fire. The commissioner fell reaching for his pistol under a deluge of bullets.[7] Insp. Craig was then shot by Culhane – a market trader by day who had recently sold him a pair of socks – and feared recognition. Nevertheless, he survived.

Cork was placed under a similar curfew to Dublin following Smyth's killing, a measure that only served to fuel surging unrest in the city and county. Tremors were also felt in Westminster where the House of Commons echoed once again to calls for the restoration of order. Jeremiah Mee expressed a more cynical view of the political posturing following Smyth's killing. He suspected it came as a reprieve to Lloyd George, as Smyth could no longer tarnish the government with recriminations over his alleged pre-deployment instructions.

Smyth was buried with full military honours in Banbridge on 20 July. Sectarian violence broke out in the town afterwards, as well as in nearby Dromore. Catholic homes and businesses were attacked and burned. Tens of thousands of pounds worth of damage was done during the rampage, which lasted several days. Scores of civilians were beaten and driven from the towns. This was, however, only a taste of what was to come twenty-five miles away in Belfast.

On 12 July Sir Edward Carson had delivered a fiery speech to a 120,000-strong crowd at Finaghy outside the city. His words stirred up the hatred consuming large sections of loyalist Ulster. Carson spoke of an insidious plot by Sinn Féin and the Catholic church to undermine unionist cohesion in Ulster by infiltrating the trade union movement. Industrialists who had baulked at the unity displayed by all denominations during the previous year's strike for the forty-four-hour week savoured his divisive tones. Carson warned that loyalists were in imminent danger, and that the government could not be trusted to defend them, adding that they would therefore have to rely upon themselves. He spoke of being 'sick of words without action'.[8] Subsequent days saw similarly volatile protestations from Belfast's unionist press.

On 21 July this boiled over into unprecedented – predominantly sectarian attacks on Catholics, nationalists, and suspected Protestant sympathisers. In the city's Harland and Wolff shipyards over 5,000 workers were driven from their workplaces by 25,000 of their unionist colleagues. Ironically, over 3,000 of the victims had fought shoulder to shoulder with their assailants during the Great War. This counted for nothing as they were driven relentlessly from the yards and pelted with industrial bolts and rivets. Many were driven into flooded dry docks and channels twenty-five-foot-deep where a rain of similar missiles followed causing lacerations and near drownings. Others were attacked with lump and sledgehammers and beaten along the dockside, suffering blow upon blow and horrific injuries. But this violence was not confined to the shipyards. An additional 3,000 were driven from their occupations in engineering and coal transport throughout the city.

The nationalist Falls Road area was then stormed by mobs of unionist attackers from the nearby Shankill Road. When the military and police – backed up by Black and Tans – arrived to restore order they eventually opened fire on Catholic areas. Three civilians were killed and a dozen wounded. This worsened the following day when a dozen civilians died under police and military fire, the latter using Lewis guns. A further forty-six were badly wounded. Burnings, lootings and evictions of entire streets followed and continued for days. Dublin prepared for a refugee influx. Unfortunately for Belfast's Catholics and nationalists, hundreds soon-to-become destitute, more was to come.

When Carson was challenged subsequently by the IPP's Joe Devlin in parliament he rebuked responsibility for such outrages, claiming to deplore retaliations. Deflecting, he castigated railworkers for refusing to transport Col Smyth's body from Cork to Banbridge, and asked pleadingly if loyal Protestants were the only branch of society not to be allowed have feelings about such matters. General Macready, horrified, had his own feelings about Carson; referring to his 1914 subterfuge – the perilous military consequences of which he was fully aware of – and more recent speech, he blamed him for 'a large measure of responsibility for the blood spilt throughout the length and breath of the island'.[9]

Macready was becoming inundated with reports by now of RIC killings and reprisals on top of the Belfast barbarity. Most disquieting was the news that Tuam in Co. Galway had seen the latest scourge of Black and Tan fury. Many of the town's buildings were damaged and burned on the night of 19 July in retaliation for further police killings. The general called for the Black and

Tans to be fully uniformed in police attire, lest they brought further dishonour to the forces under his own command.

Macready was in London attending the first cabinet session convened with the Irish Executive since its recent establishment.[10] The general, along with Executive members including John Anderson, Mark Sturgis, Andy Cope and William Wylie, broadsided the government with overtures supporting Dominion Home Rule. Deputy Secretary Jones agreed in principle, but recognised the impossible position regarding Ulster. Greenwood enunciated the inevitability of compromise with Sinn Féin, but stressed the importance of gaining the upper hand through martial measures beforehand. Anderson warned that they simply did not have the manpower to achieve this, and underscored the disaster that would succeed such a forceful strategy if it failed. Walter Long and Winston Churchill were aghast at the seemingly impossible situation.

Then, amid further recriminations of the prospect of dealing with murderers, Wylie interjected: emphasising that they would not be; on the contrary, they were up against people who saw no other choice, and could envision no other means of gaining the attentions of the wider world than adopting such measures. General Tudor hit back when Wylie alluded to the RIC's continuing disintegration and the rampant indiscipline of its Special Reserve: calling instead for the force's full militarisation, then adding that he was presently recruiting 'a fine body of men' consisting of ex-officers to further bolster them.[11] Tudor then proposed martial law as a solution among a host of other restrictions in tandem with the issuing of compulsory identification cards and – notably given the recent Rotunda raid – a purging of the post office of Sinn Féin sympathisers. Anderson scoffed at this, further insisting that there was simply not enough time to win the upper hand in the country by coercion given the time frame they had in mind for enacting the Government of Ireland Bill. Cope reinforced the prediction that coercive measures would, in any case, backfire. When Lord French subsequently articulated his agreement with Tudor, Churchill quietly mused about such divisions. Long remained inflexible.

Lloyd George found himself walking a political tightrope. A liberal at the helm of a Conservative and unionist cabinet, he agreed in principle with his less-hawkish executive, but could not be seen willing to compromise. Additionally, he appeared unable to free himself from the delusion that the British had the upper hand in 'out-murdering' the enemy, a sentiment that exasperated Field Marshal Wilson. Ultimately, the task fell upon Greenwood to navigate a solution. This would soon follow in the form of the 1920 Restoration of Order in Ireland Act.

***

Two weeks after the Rotunda raid, Dublin Brigade members succeeded in further daring assaults that left the authorities blushing. On 29 July British military police, nicknamed 'Redcaps', were disarmed in College Green.[12] The police had deployed these personnel in two three-man patrols with an additional five on guard duty outside the Bank of Ireland. Emerging suddenly from crowds of civilians, the IRA held up both patrols, one at Trinity College and the other at Westmoreland Street, and seized their weapons. They then came under fire from the soldiers outside the bank. A brief but intense firefight ensued, during which the crowds dispersed to the sounds of terrified screams, shots and ricochets. Three soldiers were wounded as they took aim from the bank's Palladian pillars while the IRA men made their hasty escape. Soon afterwards, military guards at Harcourt Street train station suffered a similar weapons seizure.

Then, on the following day, a Friday, the Squad was back in action. GHQ policy on legitimate targets had recently changed to include civilian or political opponents who were actively supporting or assisting the British regime in Ireland. Frank Brooke, sixty-eight years old, had come to the attention of IRA intelligence for precisely this – being a member of Lord French's advisory committee, as well as an advisor to the military on moving troops by rail. He regularly stayed at the vice-regal lodge. Classed as the richest man in Ireland, he was also the virtual head of the British establishment in the event of French's absence. A former adventurer who had travelled the world, funded by his family's massive estate based at 'Coolatin House' in Shillelagh, Co. Wicklow, he was also a naval lieutenant, justice of the peace for Fermanagh, a privy council member, and a prominent member of the Commissioner for Irish Lights and the Turf Club. Brooke had been previously warned to desist from his anti-Irish activities. He ignored the warning and was issued with police protection. Now the Squad was closing in. Vinny Byrne and Tom Keogh had shadowed him close to his rural estate, but without success.

SHOOTINGS, REPRISALS AND AUXILIARIES DEPLOYED

On 30 July Brooke sat at his boardroom table in Westland Row station, meticulously dressed and sporting a well-groomed beard; in addition to his numerous other roles, he was chairman of the Dublin and South Eastern Railway. Aware that his activities closely assisting Lord French rendered him vulnerable to assassination, he carried a loaded revolver in his coat pocket. He had, however, recently dismissed his police protection. At 12.15 p.m., Vinny Byrne, Paddy Daly, Tom Keogh and Jim Slattery made their way surreptitiously up the station's staircase. Daly then stood guard while the other three suddenly made for the boardroom.

As soon as the door opened Brooke saw what was happening and reached for his pistol, but it was too late. Three shots reverberated to the background cacophony of a train's arrival. Brooke collapsed in a heap, killed instantly by two rounds that smashed through his chest and exited the far side, spattering his blood on the surrounding walls and windows. Then, as they made their escape, Daly hurriedly questioned Slattery: 'Are you sure we got him?' prompting Keogh and Slattery to return to make sure.

As they then stepped back into the boardroom they saw another man named Cotton rushing in from another door. Slattery fired a shot in his direction. Cotton fled. Slattery then pumped two more shots into Brooke's distorted body. They then made their escape. Brooke's corpse was soon rushed by ambulance to nearby Sir Patrick Dun's hospital where he was pronounced dead on arrival. Later, when the police sought witnesses, they found none. Afterwards, Ormonde Winter grumbled to Mark Sturgis, cursing the fact that their enemies were able to act with such impunity in a city thronged with soldiers.

The same 30 July saw a frenetic skirmish take place involving Dan Breen, Seán Treacy and others from the previous year's Soloheadbeg ambush. They had lain in wait close to Oola in Tipperary to intercept an army truck carrying mail, unaware that its cargo also included General Lucas who had escaped from his IRA captors early that morning by climbing out a window. Lucas had made his way cross country from Herbertstown, Co. Limerick, eventually arriving at Pallas RIC station in Tipperary, from where he was eventually placed in the passing vehicle. The truck came under fire from Breen, Treacy and the others who had felled a tree to block the road. Military and police reinforcements arrived and during a thirty-minute engagement two soldiers from the Ox and Bucks light infantry were shot dead and several more injured. Eventually, Breen, Treacy and the others retreated when ammunition ran low. The authorities incorrectly interpreted the ambush as an attempt to recapture the general. Lucas was back in England within the week.

Despite this news for the British government, 1 August 1920 was met with an unwelcome manifesto from the Connaught RIC calling for the force to be wound up. This was aggravated by the Representative of the Leinster RIC issuing pamphlets calling for the same measure. Mark Sturgis commented sardonically that for all the recent Westminster talk of coercion, they might now need to coerce the RIC.[13]

On the other hand, General Tudor had been making progress with the 'fine body of men' he had recently characterised to buttress the beleaguered force. Having sought official sanction from Dublin Castle to create the force on 6 July, its first members arrived in Ireland three weeks later.[14] Then, on 3 August, the 'Temporary Cadets', as they had been referred to, were inaugurated under the command of highly decorated forty-one-year-old Brigadier General Frank Percy Crozier, a former Ulster Volunteer of similarly diminutive physical stature to Tudor. Two days later, Britain's lord chancellor, Lord Birkenhead, expressed his approval for the scheme and enthusiastically pledged that no limits to recruitment numbers would be applied. Thus appeared the ADRIC (Auxiliary Division Royal Irish Constabulary) to Ireland.

Brigadier General Frank Percy Crozier, the Auxiliary commander who quickly became horrified by their behaviour and indiscipline. *(Courtesy of Mercier Archive)*

July had seen prominent newspaper advertisements broadly similar to those aimed at recruiting the Black and Tans months earlier. The 'Auxiliaries' or 'Auxies', as they were quickly to become known, were referred to as a 'corps d'elite' for ex-army, air force and navy officers, who would require 'courage, discretion, tact and judgement'. Pay of £1 per day was offered, as well as generous leave and full uniform. Applications came in hundreds. Recruits were directed to Scotland Yard where Major Fleming once again took charge. Service contracts were for six-months duration with a provision for an additional six. Successful candidates were given a 'first class one-way ticket to Ireland', where initial training would take place in the Curragh.[15] Basic law enforcement and power of arrest were taught alongside refresher courses in musketry, bombing and general weapons training under instructors they themselves selected.[16]

They got off to a bad start upon their arrival in Ireland. Frictions quickly developed with regular army units in the Curragh. When General Crozier arrived to take charge he was horrified by their drunken indiscipline. Like the Black and Tans, whose nickname they also inadvertently assumed, their uniforms were a composite distinguished by bonnet type 'tam-o-shanter' caps with golden harp badges. They were to be equipped with the best of weapons and vehicles that would enable them to take the fight directly to the IRA throughout Ireland.

6 August saw the Dáil reacting to Belfast's recent convulsions by ordering a boycott of goods and services from the city. The boycott was decreed mandatory until the employments of those expelled were restored. Banks with Belfast branches were also targeted; deposits to such banks were to cease and funds transferred at the earliest opportunity to alternative banks. It was added that until those firms not persecuting Catholic employees could be identified, all Belfast companies would be boycotted. Critics condemned it as a counter-productive measure further dividing the country. The campaign's chairman, Joseph MacDonagh – brother of executed 1916 leader Thomas – echoing General Macready, parried such criticism back to Edward Carson.

IRA companies, particularly from the 2nd Battalion, whose area encompassed that through which Belfast trains passed en route to Dublin, were quickly ordered to enter shops and business units in the city, particularly around Talbot Street. Goods that breached the boycott such as cigarettes, snuff, tobacco and linen were confiscated, redistributed among the poor, or destroyed. Local business owners quickly complied with the boycott as a result.[17] Another blunt instrument heralded during late summer was an emigration ban. Alluding to Childers' recent publication referring to an excess of young men in Ireland, the Dáil claimed it suited the crown for these men to emigrate, and that cunning measures were being employed to encourage it. In retaliation, it was stated that: 'Ireland wants all her young men. Their presence in the country is more necessary in the country now than ever'.[18]

The next few days saw many such young men taking to Dublin's streets, lighting bonfires and rioting. This came in the wake of another public relations fiasco by the British authorities in refusing Archbishop Daniel Mannix of Melbourne permission to land in Ireland from the USA. The archbishop had made several speeches castigating Britain's hold over Ireland and had recently pledged to kneel on the graves of the executed 1916 leaders. Three years earlier he had spearheaded Australia's anti-conscription campaign. His ship, SS *Baltic*, *en route* to Queenstown (Cobh) was intercepted and Mannix taken from it to a destroyer and landed instead in Penzance in Cornwall. Newspapers then had a field day nicknaming the Royal Navy the 'Pirates of Penzance' after the famous play. Uproar ensued throughout liberal Britain and Ireland at the flagrant attack on free speech. When bonfires were lit in protest in Dublin after curfew, British troops opened fire at one point and killed twenty-three-year-old Thomas Farrell in Church Street, causing days of vicious fighting during which soldiers were, at times, overwhelmed, disarmed, and thrown into the Liffey.[19] Military lorries were fitted with further armour while drivers began wearing body armour.[20] Elsewhere Black and Tan reprisals saw buildings burned in Roscommon, Galway, Cork, Tipperary, Kerry and Limerick.[21]

It was to this savage backdrop that the Restoration of Order in Ireland Act (ROIA) was passed on 9 August and given royal assent four days later, superseding DORA. Now, in Ireland's troubled areas, trials by jury – despite being non-existent at this stage – were to be replaced by courts martial held in camera. In cases of capital offences at least one court officer was to be certified by the lord chancellor of either England or Ireland as legally trained. It was hoped that convictions could be finally obtained for political slayings for which, thus far, not a single one had materialised. Coroners' inquests were done away with and replaced by military courts of inquiry.

However, as had been the case with each successive measure employed by the British authorities, there was soon to be an effective counter-measure; in the case of ROIA the result was the advent of flying columns, as extolled by Seán McLoughlin over two years earlier. As arrests inevitably increased under ROIA, so would the number of those 'on the run'. The logical conclusion for this as far as IRA GHQ was concerned was to form them into such bands and, supported by local populations, take the fight to the enemy on a full-time basis.

***

Four days after John Anderson, Mark Sturgis and Andy Cope were ordered to move inside Dublin Castle for their own protection, additional moves were made by the authorities. On 13 August, its public information department, under the remit of recently arrived Basil Clarke – a one-eyed forty-one-year-old veteran war correspondent and propagandist – issued its inaugural copy of *The Weekly Summary*. This was a four-page news-sheet directed at the police, the Black and Tans and Auxiliaries. It aimed to provide them with a more supportive version of their exploits compared with the *Irish Bulletin* and its associated enemy publications. Its release formed part of an overall strategy of 'propaganda by news', whereby twice-daily press briefings contained disinformation cloaked alongside genuine journalism, fostering an air of plausibility.

The strategy soon resulted in the Castle's answer to the *Irish Bulletin* in the form of its 'Survey of the Week's Activities'. Clarke soon enlisted the services of three Auxiliaries named Menzies, Dowdall and Vignoles, the first of whom he would work directly with in painting a less unpalatable picture of intensifying reprisals.[22] The IRA retaliated by dispatching units to long-suffering retailers with warnings not to stock these publications. Meanwhile, *An t-Óglách*'s editors ridiculed the 'Weekly Summary' with regular chastisements, and, to further antagonise the police, editions of *An t-Óglách* soon began turning up at barracks' bundled alongside it.

August was, meanwhile, providing plenty of further news. Limerick was, again, the victim of Black and Tan marauders on the fifteenth with widespread burning, looting and shooting in the city during which they shot dead one of their own men. The following day, Cork's forty-one-year-old lord mayor, Terence MacSwiney, announced to a packed military courtroom that he had begun a hunger strike against his unlawful detention alongside eleven fellow recent hunger strikers, including Comdt Michael Fitzgerald.

MacSwiney was arrested at Cork's City Hall four nights earlier and charged with possessing RIC cyphers and other incriminating documents 'likely to cause disaffection to His Majesty'.[23] The authorities then made the mistake of – having sentenced him to two years' imprisonment – transferring him to London's Brixton Prison, and, accordingly, close proximity with the world's media in England's capital, who pounced sympathetically on his – and Ireland's – plight.

Then, events took a turn towards the supernatural when it was reported that religious statues, including those in the town's RIC barracks, were crying tears of blood in Templemore. The Tipperary town had just suffered horrendous reprisals from the Northamptonshire Regiment along with the Black and Tans following the shooting dead of an RIC district inspector. Two soldiers had also been burned to death while setting fire to the town's buildings. When word subsequently circulated of the bleeding statues, tens of thousands of pilgrims descended upon the town.

Back in Dublin, Raheny RIC barracks was soon to go up in flames in a conflagration visible for miles. Joseph Lawless was returning towards the city in a 1916 Maxwell touring car accompanied by Monica Fleming, having spent the early evening touring in Howth, when he was suddenly flagged down by a man he could barely see in the darkness. It had just started raining and his car had no wipers. Then, the stranger jumped onto the running board on the vehicle's passenger side, and shouted repeatedly to stop. Lawless had been doing the car up and its brakes were all but useless, therefore it took several seconds to halt. This was misinterpreted by the assailant as non-compliance. He fired a shot. Lawless then stopped the car and saw several more men suddenly approach. He discovered they were D Company 2nd Battalion members charged with intercepting traffic approaching Raheny village. He then introduced himself as a Volunteer and was subsequently told all approach roads to the village had been blocked. The barracks was about to go up.

Lawless and his date waited, chatting with his comrades. Nearby the barracks' four-man detachment surrendered the building. Soon afterwards, Lawless saw paraffin flames soaring skyward, providing enough light for him to see a large bullet-hole in the car's side panel. He resisted the temptation to tell the gunman what a 'high powered ass he was'.[24] The bullet had narrowly missed Miss Fleming. Nonetheless, soon afterwards, Lawless packed as many Volunteers into the car as he could and drove them home to Fairview.

August also saw the burnings of Rockbrook, Stepaside, and Skerries RIC barracks' in Dublin.[25] It also saw the world's first ever successful use of an electrically detonated mine against an enemy vehicle outside Dingle in Kerry. Its victims were members of the East Lancashire Regiment.

The month saw further arson on a massive scale to the country's north. On Sunday 22 August, Lisburn erupted into an orgy of burnings following the shooting dead of RIC Dist. Insp. Oswald Swanzy. The thirty-eight-year-old inspector had been among those accused of murdering Tomás MacCurtain. As a result, he had since been reassigned from Cork 250 miles away to Lisburn for his own safety. However, despite struggling to obtain information on his whereabouts and routine owing to the atmosphere of terrific fear pervading

SHOOTINGS, REPRISALS AND AUXILIARIES DEPLOYED

north-eastern Ulster since July's pogroms, a five-man IRA unit from Cork, aided by the 1st Brigade 3rd Northern Division, and with sanction from Cathal Brugha, shot him dead in Lisburn's Market Square. The first shot was fired by Seán Culhane with a bullet from the late MacCurtain's own pistol.

The assassins were lucky to escape with their lives when an angry mob almost caught hold of them immediately afterwards. Not so lucky were the Catholic inhabitants of Lisburn. Vicious sectarian violence broke out in response. Hundreds of Catholics were forced from their homes to seek refuge in Belfast where many were attacked as they desperately made their way to supposed safety, only for Belfast to explode three nights later into further burnings, killings and maimings. At one point a six-year-old girl had petrol poured over her; luckily, her mother managed to drag her from the enraged mob attempting to set her on fire.[26] At times the attacks prompted horrified Protestants to step in to shield their Catholic neighbours, only to suffer the wrath of the murderous mobs who labelled them 'Rotten Prods'. Over the course of the following week seventeen civilians in Belfast were killed, 170 seriously injured and over 1,000 less seriously wounded. One million pounds' worth of damage was caused, and 180 Catholic houses completely destroyed.

It was to this backdrop that the Irish Peace Conference commenced on 24 August in 47–49 Great Brunswick Street's majestic Antient Concert Rooms. The event was attended by over 600 delegates, including clergymen from all Ireland's denominations, landowners, businessmen and men of education, 'moderation and influence', including Sir Horace Plunkett.[27] He was the Anglo-Irish agricultural reformer whose vision had pioneered cooperative creameries in Ireland, a hugely successful concept. Since July, however, many of these creameries – simply due to the dependence so many communities had upon them – were being targeted and burned in crown reprisals.

First on the conference's agenda was a request to the British prime minister, followed later by another to King George V, for Terence MacSwiney's immediate release. Concerns were growing rapidly over the Cork lord mayor's deterioration. Rioting took place outside Brixton Prison on the conference's first day in protest at his treatment. More peaceful daily protests and prayer meetings were also being organised there by the ISDL. Accompanying these requests were a series of conspicuous broadsides from unlikely quarters: a prominent Ulster unionist protested that if Lloyd George did not reign in the Black and Tans he would inadvertently turn all the conference's attendees into republicans.[28] An equally unlikely expression followed from a fellow well-known Ulsterman and barrister who suggested that a united Ireland could have significant economic benefits.

The conference ultimately proposed full nationalist self-government for Ireland and labelled the idea of dividing the country repugnant, notwithstanding the need to negotiate a peaceful settlement with Ulster unionists to bring them in to a united Ireland under dominion status as a 'free contracting party'.[29] While such formulations were discussed, killings continued: three shop assistants were burned to death in a Dundalk drapery store after it was set alight on 27 August by local ex-military who were angry at the Belfast burnings. Warnings by the local IRA not to retaliate in such a way against the shop owner, Mr Craig – because he was a Protestant and therefore labelled 'unionist' – were ignored.[30]

Just days later IRA GHQ began the successful coordination of over 1,000 arms raids throughout Dublin and Ireland. These were typically aimed at military and police barracks', but even more prominently at homes and businesses. The authorities had recently compelled firearms holders to be issued with licences. Now these traceable weapons were called in nationally to prevent the IRA getting their hands on them. However, the IRA sought to get them first. Thousands of weapons were captured in the raids and well as large quantities of ammunition. Nevertheless, huge amounts of small arms began arriving at various barracks. This necessitated mountains of paperwork and subsequent storage, guarding and maintenance.

The military also had its hands full with setting up its own nationwide postal service in the wake of the recent IRA mail penetration. Bi-planes began taking off from wind-swept Baldonnell aerodrome in west-Dublin delivering mail to its forces nationwide. It was at this point that the IRA began creating their own 'dropping circles' to fool the enemy; the first in Bantry where five Volunteers dressed as British soldiers received a large bundle of mail dropped from the sky. When, soon afterwards, rumours began circulating that the IRA was training its own pilots Scotland Yard baulked at the bewildering prospect of a 'Sinn Féin air force'.[31]

Meanwhile, to add to the military's burden, troops were being called upon to occupy trains. This was a measure of brinkmanship to call the bluff of those orchestrating the rail embargo by bringing the entire country's rail system to a halt unless the embargo was lifted and the trains moved, but tied up

SHOOTINGS, REPRISALS AND AUXILIARIES DEPLOYED

many battalions and their much needed transports at a time when, due to widespread violent labour disputes in England, Field Marshal Wilson was calling for troops to be brought home from Ireland. The mundane measure also decimated unit morale. Meanwhile, military officers living in Dublin's private residences were ordered to wear civilian clothes outside work, as were chauffeurs and military intelligence personnel.[32]

As August came to an end Terence MacSwiney spoke to his sister Mary on the nineteenth day of his hunger strike. His words echoed those of Seán MacDermott four years earlier. MacDermott had spoken prophetically – awaiting his fate in Kilmainham Gaol – with words to the effect that it would be a good thing for the republican cause if he and his fellow leaders were executed. On 30 August MacSwiney declared similarly: 'I am convinced I will not be released, and it will be better for my country if I am not released'.[33]

Terence MacSwiney, Lord Mayor of Cork, whose seventy-five-day hunger strike greatly increased worldwide awareness of Ireland's independence struggle.
(Courtesy of Mercier Archive)

Richard Mulcahy looked on from Dublin, having had notable ties to both men: he had married MacDermott's former sweetheart in June 1919, and been MacSwiney's best man when the Corkman married his wife Muriel two years earlier. MacSwiney was paving the way for his own martyrdom, fully aware of the sympathy it would bring to his cause. As the world looked on with increased interest at the growing drama in Brixton – and the *Irish Bulletin*'s reach grew alongside it – eyes also fell upon Dublin to provide its own spectacle. The city, and county, would not disappoint.

15

AUXILIARIES TAKE ON IRA AND PROPAGANDA DISASTERS FOR BRITAIN

'If these men ought to be murdered'

By early autumn 1920 a publican, Liam Devlin, had started to allow his public house, Devlin's at 68 Great Britain Street, to be used as a republican clearing house. Recently travelled from Scotland, Devlin had been an IRB member there before moving to Ireland. The building sat adjacent the street's Moore Lane junction. Its bar was at ground level. Three floors above provided rented accommodation. Devlin had been approached and introduced to Michael Collins when nearby Vaughan's came under intense enemy surveillance.

Now, Collins held nightly councils there with Gearóid O'Sullivan, Liam Tobin, Diarmuid O'Hegarty, Piaras Béaslaí, Frank Thornton, Tom Cullen and Joe O'Reilly. IRA leaders from within and outside Dublin reported there, the latter fed and sheltered afterwards. They merged with the establishment's footfall and aroused little suspicion entering and leaving. Collins would depart most evenings just before curfew and cycle to wherever he was residing at the time, unarmed and unescorted, as would Tobin, Cullen and Thornton as they made their way home to their shared lodgings on Grosvenor Road, Rathmines. Munster Street was no longer safe for Tobin.

Collins had once been aide-de-camp to the late 1916 leader Joseph Plunkett, who had introduced him to the novel *The Man Who Was Thursday* by G. K. Chesterton. The thriller's theme was based around revolutionary anarchists, featuring one who extolled the art of 'hiding in plain sight' to avoid police detection. Collins and the others had adapted this practice to their movements around Dublin, rationalising that if they did not appear to

AUXILIARIES TAKE ON IRA AND PROPAGANDA DISASTERS FOR BRITAIN

be hiding they would avoid attention. Collins took this to extremes; at times purposely approaching checkpoints in a cavalier manner while looking around for new faces among enemy officers he would then engage in casual conversation to glean intelligence.

Thornton and the others liked and admired Collins. He astounded them with his memory and ability to manage a bewildering array of tasks. From dawn to dusk, he sifted through dispatches and dictated responses, signed correspondences, liaised with intelligence officers, GHQ members and brigade commanders – all before he even took to his finance portfolio. Afternoons and evenings would be spent bluffing his way through city checkpoints, meeting couriers carrying Dáil funds, officers seeking arms and politicians. He met bishops, arms dealers, forgers, fanatics, lunatics, spies and adventurers, always within a hair's breath of capture and death on cobbled streets filled with touts. His ability to engage with characters from all walks was astounding. He grasped what made people tick, remembering subtle but important details that kept them onside. He was a tough and ruthless taskmaster – one did not want to be late for an appointment or engagement – but was equally sensitive to individual hankerings. An IRA casualty or prisoner, considering him or herself insignificant, might receive their favourite brand of cigarettes or tobacco from Collins with an encouraging note. Simple acts of consideration made a huge difference to men and women in desperate and frightening circumstances and fostered intense loyalty.

This was not without its cost upon Collins and the others who grappled daily with pressure and self-doubt. Collins gave up smoking, drinking and took up Pelmanism, a memory exercising game, to help concentrate under such terrific pressure.[1] Close calls earlier that year had proven Collins was, nevertheless, not infallible. More recently, Carl Ackerman had succeeded in gaining access by seeking interviews for the American press. Collins' subsequent accounts of Sinn Féin's aims for Ireland allowed for much interpretation by Ackerman. His conclusions – that Collins was much more politically flexible than his hard-line persona suggested – were then sent directly to Sir Basil Thompson in Scotland Yard.[2] Nonetheless, both Ackerman and Thompson were wary of Collins actually playing them in his own game.

Devlin's saw plenty of close calls during early autumn. On one occasion, while enemy night raids – once again an incessant part of Dublin life in the wake of ROIA – were mounted throughout Rutland Square, the IRA leaders hid upstairs, only to hear hobnailed boots on the roof slates. Expecting enemy troops to pounce from above and below, they were much relieved to discover instead that the troops had merely been using the roof as a vantage point to cover the nearby raids. On another occasion, the pub's ground floor was searched but the IRA leadership, hiding upstairs, were left miraculously alone. Then, one day the entire street outside to the west was sealed behind barbed wire as a huge military cordon was put in place, followed by house-to-house searches throughout the street. Thornton and several others waited to escape over the surrounding rooftops. Astonishingly, however, Devlin's – just outside the cordon – was untouched.

Luckily for Collins and the others the landlord and his wife were tolerant of the damage that was repeatedly done to upstairs rooms during numerous overnight stays as Collins provoked wrestling matches and pillow fights to relieve the endless tension and suspense. Crude language abounded in the pub itself and upstairs, as did play acting with hapless punters. Less riotous associates attending meetings there frequently found themselves the butt of unexpected jokes and wisecracks, and were often perplexed by Collins' capacity for histrionics and disregard for his hosts' property.

Collins still had his work cut out as finance minister. September 1920 saw the timeline for the Dáil Loan drawing to a close, with over £380,000 collected.[3] He commenced a scheme to lay the groundwork for a more permanent enterprise: income tax collection – his eyes fixed firmly on the fifteen million pounds of Irish money annually filling the coffers of the British exchequer.[4]

By now IRA Intelligence was operating two branches. The first was assigned to British armed forces and dealt primarily with troop deployments and numbers, as well as arrivals and departures of units and noteworthy commanders. The second dealt specifically with enemy agents such as secret service personnel, military intelligence officers, and police/Auxiliary/Black and Tan intelligence. Tobin, Cullen and Thornton strove to infiltrate each enemy section with two agents; one to inadvertently keep an eye on the other – not knowing he or she was also working for the IRA. Agents were also operating within Scotland Yard and throughout the British civil service.

With the post office well infiltrated by republican spies copies of coded letters sent by the authorities to those on the IRA 'suspect list' quickly found their way to Crow Street where they were decoded.[5] Agents within the telegraph office regularly tapped telephones and intercepted coded telegrams. IRA Intelligence had long since been in possession of enemy codes; slowly pieced together from snippets obtained from their castle agents. Dublin Castle's monthly code changes were sent out using live codes, and were therefore in the hands of IRA intelligence immediately.

IRA agents within the post office were known only by number for their own protection, and were also charged with intercepting mail sent by habitually indiscreet enemy soldiers. Huge quantities of information from such sources were pieced together in Crow Street like a jigsaw providing a live picture of enemy plans. Such was the extent of IRA postal infiltration and code-breaking, and its synergy with the Dáil's propaganda department, that British units occasionally discovered details of their own future missions from copies of the *Irish Bulletin* they obtained through their own activities, before they themselves were briefed about them by their own senior officers.

Meanwhile, agents within the DMP were rapidly multiplying in number. Ned Broy's recommendation in April 1919 to view the force – aside from G-Division – as a potentially valuable resource was reaping rewards. A recent lengthy meeting at Julia O'Donovan's house in Rathgar between Thornton, Sgts Matt Byrne and Jerry Mannix, the former of Rathmines barracks and the latter Donnybrook, had seen a successful plan adopted to recruit officers to help compile intelligence reports for the IRA.[6] Among those recruited were: Constables Ahern, McEvoy and O'Dea from Donnybrook, Neary from Kevin Street, Feely from Kingstown – recently renamed Dún Laoghaire – and Sgt O'Sullivan from Fitzgibbon Street.[7] As raids continued incessantly and increased in number these men, and others, became invaluable and regularly contacted IRA intelligence about future planned raids, giving Volunteers precious time to escape. On occasions without such warnings policemen travelling with raiding parties covered for Volunteers they knew.

Det. Neligan was also providing Thornton and his comrades with much to keep them busy. On one occasion, he introduced Thornton and Tom Cullen to several secret service agents at Rabiatti's Saloon on Marlborough Street, a regular hangout for agents.[8] Thornton became unimpressed with their prowess when he and Cullen were asked by the Englishmen as to how they had both managed to adopt such authentic Irish accents in such a short time, and who then took them at their word when they responded that it was simply an art they had perfected. Neligan and Jim McNamara spent most evenings in Dublin Castle perusing journals and notebooks used by detectives. Any useful information soon found its way to Liam Tobin.

By now Dan Breen had also found his way to the IRA deputy intelligence director, along with Seán Treacy. Breen had been wounded again during a recent attack on Rearcross RIC barracks in Tipperary and brought back to Dublin for treatment. Treacy had followed. Treacy's fiancé, music teacher May Quigley, was from Dublin. Once Breen was recovered, Tobin and Tom Cullen made the most of the ructious pair's talents. Breen found Tobin impressively courageous and 'ice-cool in a crisis'.[9] He found Cullen to be impetuous but 'a very bad shot'.

Tobin had a mission for Cullen and Breen on a particularly wet September night involving a troublesome G-Man. They were to shoot him in Exchange Street after the detective had ventured there on a fool's errant fabricated by Tobin. The pair lurked, taking shelter from the rain in an archway adjacent the *Evening Mail* entrance, and were soon joined by a tall stranger who grumbled about the weather and engaged them in small talk for several minutes before saying: 'I'll be off'.

Members of F Company Auxiliaries pictured outside Dublin's Mansion House. They were excellent fighters and tacticians, but atrocious policemen. (*Courtesy of Mercier Archive*)

Auxiliaries at a sports meeting at King George V Hospital, Dublin. (*Courtesy of Kilmainham Gaol/Museum OPW, 19PO-1A25-22 3*)

AUXILIARIES TAKE ON IRA AND PROPAGANDA DISASTERS FOR BRITAIN

Members of the Auxiliary Division. (*Courtesy of Kilmainham Gaol Museum OPW, 19PC-1A58-06*)

Auxiliaries at their headquarters in Beggar's Bush barracks in October 1920. (*Courtesy of Kilmainham Gaol Museum OPW, 19PO-1A32-14*)

Tobin approached soon afterwards, berating the pair – the men they had just spoken with had been their target. Cullen and Breen, however, had expected Tobin to lead him to them. It was an uncharacteristic communications breakdown that nonetheless bore fruit; later in the Castle when the detective reflected on the puzzling presence of both men, combined with the appointment with a mysterious source – Tobin, who had suspiciously not shown up – he immediately realised he was in the IRA's cross hairs. He took the next available boat to England and stayed there.

Dublin Castle remained locked down. Identification cards, as advocated by General Tudor in July, were required to access the citadel. Each night its squares were lit up by the headlights of conspicuous three-ton Crossley Tender trucks.

These comparatively short wheel-based vehicles were quick and agile and could carry more than a dozen well-armed men – three in the driver's cab and a dozen-or-so in the rear. When they left the castle gates, reinforced with barbed-wire blockades, their cargo of men from F Company Auxiliaries, 100-strong, bristled like porcupines with rifles, pistols and Lewis guns. The company's composite of army, air force and navy officers were billeted there. Some of their public school accents were distinctive, as was their ruthlessness and taste for action. Also carrying grenades, they made excellent fighters and tacticians, but, in General Macready's opinion, atrocious policemen.

Each Auxiliary company was placed under the command of a captain or major of military rank, but with the official police rank of 1st district inspector. This gave them significant power; the equivalent rank to RIC district inspector, subordinate only to county inspector and more senior ranks. Three section leaders operated within each company under its commander. Auxiliary HQ was based in Beggar's Bush barracks on the city's south-eastern side, having moved from the Curragh in early September due to escalating frictions with the army. This move had done nothing to improve their discipline. On one occasion Ned Broy recounted to Michael Collins how a group of F Company Auxiliaries, having drunk all their money, simply raided City Hall and stole a huge amount of cash.[10] F Company acted independently of Beggar's Bush.

General Macready had issued a decree in August warning of severe disciplinary measures for soldiers caught looting, but had no official control over the Auxiliaries or 'Tans'. He did, however, warn that troops would be pulled back from supporting police carrying out reprisals and looting. General Tudor had been supposed to issue his own simultaneous order against police reprisals, but could not bring himself to do it because of growing casualties.[11] Meanwhile, Hamar Greenwood considered both RIC paramilitary units to be doing an effective job of taking on those he considered murderers. His stance had become more hawkish over the summer, and he favoured more coercive means over seeking dialogue with Sinn Féin.

Macready remained frustrated at the lack of strategic coherence, a sentiment echoed by Mark Sturgis who advocated a single 'war council' with overall authority to dictate and implement strategy.[12] Some progress was made nonetheless. Tudor persuaded Macready to postpone winter quartering of troops away from the country's more remote regions until December instead of early

AUXILIARIES TAKE ON IRA AND PROPAGANDA DISASTERS FOR BRITAIN

October. Victory was seen as close. General Brind wrote on 23 September that 'things were getting better'.[13] Therefore it was time to increase the pressure on the IRA, not back off.

However, victory was, at this point, an illusion. By now IRA GHQ had issued an official order for the formation of flying columns as an effective counter measure to ROIA. The adaptability of the republican military wing to strategic shifts, despite looming disasters, would see the containment of British military aims. Now, in early autumn, the IRA was about to be gifted a series of monumental propaganda bounties.

The first of these came courtesy of IRA counter-intelligence. John Henry Gooding, alias Frank Digby Hardy, was a lifelong fraudster. The fifty-two-year-old had first been imprisoned in 1886. More recently, he had been incarcerated for three years. He had subsequently written to Lord French offering his services as an intelligence agent in return for his early release, which was eventually granted. 'Hardy' was soon among the numerous agents filtering into Dublin in early autumn 1920. However, Hardy's letter to French had been intercepted by IRA intelligence. Michael Collins, having then read its contents and subsequently had its author tailed for a time by Frank Thornton, arranged a trap. He also compiled a comprehensive dossier of Hardy's previous convictions.

On 16 September, a meeting was convened in a building close to Great Brunswick Street's Queen's Theatre. Arthur Griffith and Desmond Fitzgerald attended along with several prominent journalists from both Britain and the USA who would play their own parts in a drama befitting the location. Michael Knightly, the journalist who had procured the late Alan Bell's photograph for IRA intelligence, and a colleague, Seán Lyster, played the parts of IRA inner circle figures.[14] The foreign journalists acted as more junior ranks, and would sit silently.

Hardy entered, having been frisked on the way in, and was greeted by an initial silence before he sat down. When prompted, he spoke up and initially offered to procure arms and, addressing Knightly and Lyster, said he accepted he might be expected to carry out a shooting to prove his loyalties; he did not appear averse to this. Knightly feigned interest, replying that he need not worry in this regard; they themselves 'would look after any shooting that had to be done'.[15]

Hardy then upped his game; he presented an opportunity to draw his commander, Basil Thompson – described by Hardy as 'the man responsible for all the dirty work in Ireland' – into a trap.[16] Thompson would be lured to Carlisle Pier in Dún Laoghaire with the promise of an opportunity to neutralise Michael Collins and other senior IRA men. This would then provide the IRA with a rare opportunity to kill Thompson. He then boasted of having knowledge of UVF arms dumps and then offered to help lure a force of Auxiliaries into an IRA trap. Finally, he suggested his listeners divulged Michael Collins' location, at which point time could be provided for Collins to relocate, before he would share the knowledge with his superiors. The ensuing 'close call' would further his own influence with Basil Thompson and make him a valuable IRA asset.

At this point Griffith, having heard enough, stood up to play his leading role. He unmasked the charade, addressing Hardy, exclaiming: 'Now listen to this!'[17] He revealed Hardy's true identity and berated him as a 'scoundrel'. He then quickly read out his list of former convictions and declared contemptuously that this was the calibre of man employed by the British government to supress Ireland's legitimate claim to independence.

Hardy, taken by complete surprise, sat up. His right hand reached for his coat pocket, Knightly momentarily fearing he was reaching for a weapon that had eluded his searchers on the way in. Griffith, however, offered Hardy an unexpected escape, proclaiming: 'Now, Hardy, there is a boat leaving Dún Laoghaire this evening and my advice to you is to take it'.[18] Hardy's hand relaxed. Flabbergasted, he took his leave. IRA intelligence ensured that he made the boat. The press had a field day. The result was international ridicule for the British secret service, and embarrassment for Lloyd George's government. But this was only the beginning.

**

For all Hardy's talk of trapping the Auxiliaries, it was, however, the cadets themselves who drew first blood in Dublin on the morning of Sunday 19 September. The previous evening had seen their Depot Company in Beggar's Bush receive intelligence of an IRA unit active in the Kilmashogue area at the foot of the Dublin Mountains. Thirty Auxiliaries dressed in mufti and under thirty-five-year-old Major George Vernon Dudley, had then occupied nearby St Columba's College the previous night, holding the groundskeeper at gunpoint, while preparing an ambush.

The following morning, the weather warm and bright, two companies of

AUXILIARIES TAKE ON IRA AND PROPAGANDA DISASTERS FOR BRITAIN

the IRA 5th Battalion engineers assembled nearby at a regularly used camp area while several high ranking officers – including Richard Mulcahy, Rory O'Connor, Jack Plunkett, and others accompanied by a six-man guard detail – oversaw the testing of explosives at a nearby quarry. They were testing a highly explosive but unstable substance nicknamed 'War Flour' owing to its resemblance to corn flour, as well as standard gelignite and ammonite. The explosives were detonated by electric detonators placed with the explosives in jam-jars. Thomas Bryan, a twenty-three-year-old electrician, was on hand to help ensure everything ran smoothly.[19] The officers planned on inspecting the rest of the men some distance below them following the testing. This was despite a warning from local Volunteers of enemy activity in the area.

After half-a-dozen explosions yielding impressive results and the near deafening of those in the quarry, further testing saw jars placed beneath large rocks. Two or three explosions later the officers were covered in dust from falling debris. Finally, a thirty-pound rock was placed on top of an explosive charge.[20] It was launched into the air following a gigantic blast and a huge broken clump landed just inches from a Volunteer lying prone to seek cover – almost killing him. Then, distant gunshots were heard. A runner was dispatched to investigate. He did not return. Another was sent, and returned soon afterwards with news that the nearby camp had been raided, one man killed and the rest arrested. Plunkett, Liam Archer and several others sped to investigate while Mulcahy, O'Connor and the others escaped using alternative routes. When Plunkett arrived, he found the blood-soaked body of nineteen-year-old Seán Doyle, son of veteran Volunteer and Alderman Peadar Doyle. The area was strewn with camping equipment and bicycles.

Major Dudley had dispatched a ten-man flanking party under Sgt William Duffy around the IRA camp while attacking head-on himself from the college with his remaining twenty cadets. Shots were fired over enemy heads alongside shouted commands of 'Hands up!' while kicks and rifle butts were employed to subdue those who looked like they might resist despite the rifle barrels pointing suddenly at them. Meanwhile, Sgt Duffy's men had been surprised themselves at the sight of Doyle and several others breaking cover to engage them. Doyle had drawn his revolver before being shot through the chest with a rifle round that shattered his ribcage and lungs, leaving a huge exit wound and killing him instantly. His comrades surrendered.

Meanwhile, the first missing runner, having gone to ground to evade the Auxiliaries, had managed to stalk them briefly. He overheard them referring to the explosions as indicating a large heavily armed IRA party there that they had opted not to engage, instead withdrawing to the college with their prisoner haul and setting up a perimeter.

Forty crestfallen IRA men were captured and detained for several hours before lorries transported them eventually to Mountjoy Prison. The runner then ran into Volunteer Patrick McGrath, arriving by bicycle late for the drill, and briefed him as to what had happened. Both men soon set off to the city to warn their comrades' families of likely raids.

That night Volunteers made their way to a battalion arms dump in 12 Parliament Street – less then 100 yards from Dublin Castle – in case of a raid there. They removed several rifles, one Lewis Gun and some detonators to another dump in Adelaide Road. Accusations abounded among Volunteer officers over who was to blame for the debacle – the loss of forty trained and skilled men – by disregarding local intelligence. The importance of such intelligence would not be ignored again. Doyle's funeral in Lucan several days later was a typically huge affair. His killing drew murder accusations against the Auxiliaries. Protesting crowds gathered at King George V Hospital while his military inquest took place. Armoured cars brandishing machine guns were deployed to keep them back.

***

The day after the Kilmashogue ambush, 20 September 1920, Kevin Barry was entering his second year of medical studies in UCD. He was due to take a test that afternoon. Barry was a resolute IRA section commander. As well as his membership of H Company 1st Battalion, he also supported local units while holidaying near Hacketstown in Carlow with his family. He lived in 58 South Circular Road.

Following the embarrassment suffered by the military after the King's Inn's raid, General Macready had instructed military personnel in Ireland not to surrender their weapons without a fight. One such unit from the 2nd Battalion Duke of Wellington's (West Riding) Regiment was dispatched by lorry from Collinstown Aerodrome that morning to collect bread rations from Monk's Bakery at Upper Church Street's junction with the eastern section of North

King Street. Barry's company was mobilised to intercept them and seize arms. They were confident following the King's Inn's success and sought to replicate it. Dick McKee and Peadar Clancy had sanctioned the attack, the former congratulating the men on their initiative in suggesting it. Their commander, Capt. Séamus Kavanagh, then saw to the details. McKee warned them of one important tactical detail: the men in the lorry would be six feet above them when they attacked.[21]

Typically, the troop lorry carried seven-to-eight troops and called to the bakery between 8 and 9 a.m. An officer and NCO normally entered its yard on Church Street while the guard detail took turns to enter the shop to purchase cakes and minerals.[22] Two dozen Volunteers would take part in the raid; four would cover the lorry's rear initially and then, with the guard detail subdued, take their weapons. Three, including Barry, would cover the lorry's right hand side, with five covering its left, and an additional three covering its front as it faced north towards Constitution Hill. Two outpost positions would be taken at North Brunswick Street and the western end of North King Street with Tom Kissane and Maurice Higgins detailed there carrying grenades. Additionally, Davy Golden and Jimmy Carrigan would take position in a Ford van at the nearby Spinning Wheel pub, covering eastern North King Street while waiting to transport the expected haul of weapons.

Five Volunteers from G Company were detailed to follow the officer and NCO into the bakery yard and hold them up while also dismantling the bakery's telephone to prevent the authorities being contacted. Every position had been covered at a mission briefing at the O'Flanagan Sinn Féin Club on Ryder's Row the previous night, with precise positions drawn with chalk on a blackboard. Afterwards, with all weapons dumped, they were to rendezvous at the Parnell Monument in Sackville Street.

Barry was ten minutes' late for the unit's initial 9 a.m. rendezvous in O'Flanagan's the next morning, having been held up at a college appointment. When he arrived Séamus Kavanagh handed him a parabellum pistol. Barry requested the Webley he normally used but was told it had already been assigned. Barry's boyish enthusiasm gave way to a momentary scowl that saw his comrades tease and goad him jokingly. Parabellums were prone to jamming. This soon proved catastrophic for Barry. Kavanagh had the previous evening offered to excuse Barry from duty owing to his pending test. Barry had replied that not taking part would be more detrimental to his academic performance than participating. He had also laughingly suggested that the raid might yield him another Lewis gun.[23]

Following last-minute checks to ensure no man was carrying any documents or identification, the attackers strode to Church Street in small groups and took positions, each armed with a pistol and six rounds, aside from those with grenades. Apart from the transport and outposts the remainder dispersed themselves between ten and twenty yards from where the lorry was expected to park. Then, unexpectedly, nothing happened. They had to avoid arousing suspicion for ninety minutes, reading newspapers in the autumn sunshine, savouring the aroma of freshly baked bread, nervously puffing cigarettes and nodding at passers-by until the truck eventually arrived. Capt. Kavanagh had taken position in Reilly's pub across the road from the bakery with three others, ordering minerals.

As soon as the truck had come to a halt and its tailboard dropped, Seán O'Neill, next to Barry, was perturbed to see that instead of the expected handful of soldiers it contained eighteen in the cargo area and three in the driver's cab. An NCO, Sgt Arthur Banks, and a private then alighted and stepped briskly into the bakery yard. The officer uncharacteristically remained in the cab. Capt. Kavanagh quickly assessed the situation while an agitated Volunteer next to him quietly cursed Frank Flood, seen poking his head suspiciously from around the Church Street/North King Street corner. Kavanagh and the others left the pub. He then blew his nose loudly with a handkerchief – the signal to attack.

The ambushers converged on the lorry while the five G Company men followed the NCO and private to the bakery. O'Neill, Barry and Lt O'Flanagan stepped towards the truck from its right, O'Flanagan concealing a pistol under a newspaper, Barry with his parabellum under his trench coat. O'Neill suddenly shouted: 'Hands up!' The others then repeated the command. The startled troops complied momentarily, before some raised their weapons to shoot, prompting Kavanagh to roar: 'Open fire!'

The crossroads suddenly witnessed frenetic gunfire the intensity of which it had not seen since the horrific battle of North King Street over four years earlier. Civilians scattered in fright, screaming and shouting to the echoing cacophony of gunshots. The smell of baked bread was replaced with cordite from falling spent bullet cartridges. Shots flew from the surrounding IRA men, accompanied by angry shouts. Some troops still held their hands up. Others fired repeatedly. Soldiers collapsed in the truck, one killed instantly by a head shot as he swung his rifle to club a nearby attacker, two more suffering horrific stomach wounds.

As their comrades fell among them gushing blood and screaming in agony and terror, the firing increased. Lee Enfield rounds narrowly missed Volunteers and ricocheted from the streets and buildings. Windows shattered as they were hit. Bob O'Flanagan was grazed in the head by a ricochet. In the bakery yard firing also broke out. Its staff rushed for cover. Back outside Capt. Kavanagh saw the enemy officer slump in the lorry cab with his arm dangling from its window, clearly wounded.

Amid the chaos, Kevin Barry's parabellum pistol jammed, forcing him to dash for cover beneath the lorry to fix it. Just then a retreat was ordered by Kavanagh, having not seen Barry and knowing his men had little ammunition. The IRA men retired quickly and in good order, with some providing cover. Those in the bakery made for its North King Street exit as planned. Kavanagh quickly looked around for casualties among his men but saw none except Lt O'Flanagan holding his badly lacerated head as he escaped and Seán O'Neill bleeding from his face – struck by debris from a ricochet. Mick Robinson tripped over a bicycle as he retreated along Church Street and cursed profusely. His comrade, Tom Kissane, laughed loudly at this as they passed Section Commander Maurice Higgins covering them, before he too followed.

Capt. Kavanagh escaped with several others into the nearby Capuchin church in Lower Church Street, and from there to an adjacent shop. From its windows they then watched two Crossley Tenders speed to the scene filled with Auxiliaries who quickly sealed the nearby road junction and bakery. The lorry moved off carrying the dead British soldier, fifteen-year-old Private Henry Washington – the first to die in action in Dublin since Easter 1916 – and wounded who were treated *en route* to the nearby North Dublin Union. Kavanagh stashed his weapon in the shop then made his way back to the ambush scene minutes later as large crowds gathered. Then, standing among them, he heard the disconcerting news that one attacker had been taken from under the troop lorry and brought inside the bakery. Later, Kavanagh met with the rest of the ambush participants on Sackville Street. Two were missing, Lt O'Flanagan and Section Commander Barry.[24] O'Flanagan was accounted for, but not Barry.

Kavanagh went to Barry's home to inform his parents. Any weapons were then removed from the house in anticipation of a later raid. Dick McKee was subsequently informed of the raid's failure and Barry's loss.

Barry, having eventually cleared his pistol's action under the lorry, had waited, hoping to escape once the vehicle moved off again, but was instead detected, before being dragged into the bakery. From there he was eventually rough handled to the North Dublin Union barracks by Sgt Banks and several others. Arriving there just minutes later the agonising shrieks of two infantrymen, twenty-year-old Private Matthew Whitehead and nineteen-year-old Thomas Humphries, as they slowly perished in a nearby infirmary, could be clearly heard. This led to a series of kicks, punches and shoves being administered to Barry before he was taken into the union's detention room under the care of two officers and three NCOs from the 1st Battalion Lancashire Fusiliers.

Interrogation quickly followed, some of it brutal. Barry revealed that twenty men had participated in the ambush and that a Ford car had been used with no number plate, but divulged nothing more despite being threatened with a bayonet and having his right arm twisted forcefully while he was repeatedly held face down on the floor, a fact that was later corroborated by a Royal Army Medical Corps (RAMC) officer. Barry was also told by a man in civilian clothes that he would be pardoned if he provided his comrades' names.[25] He refused.

Barry's arrest, rough treatment and subsequent trial set the scene for an outpouring of anti-British sentiment that, alongside that fomented by Terence MacSwiney's hunger strike, would match that which followed the 1916 executions. The Cork lord mayor's hunger strike in Brixton was drawing protests from as far afield as Australia, Argentina, Canada, as well as unrelenting pressure from the USA, within Britain itself and continental Europe. In Italy, thirty-seven-year-old Benito Mussolini had described MacSwiney's struggle as *una stoicismo superbo* (superb stoicism).[26] But as far as the propaganda war went, things were about to get much worse for the British.

***

That night, the port town of Balbriggan in Co. Dublin, situated twenty miles north of the city itself and with a population of 2,200, suffered an assault by the Black and Tans, the ferocity of which prompted former Prime Minister Asquith to compare it with German atrocities in occupied Belgium in 1914.

AUXILIARIES TAKE ON IRA AND PROPAGANDA DISASTERS FOR BRITAIN

The previous day had seen the town, childhood home of Sinéad de Valera, stage a sports day with the official purpose of raising funds for the church, as cover to raise funds for local IRA men on the run. The total raised was £98, a good deal from Black and Tans who had attended in their hundreds.[27] Ironically, the event was stewarded by the IRA who struggled to maintain composure as the day progressed and 'Tans' became drunk, boorish and abusive. Gormanston Aerodrome, also surveyed by the Royal Flying Corps in May 1917 along with Collinstown, Baldonnell and Tallaght, served as a training depot and deployment hub for the RICSR, and was just three miles away. The flat surrounding countryside's unsuitability for significant guerrilla operations made the aerodrome an ideal location for such purposes, as was its proximity with the capital. It also acted as RIC District HQ.[28]

Then, at 7 p.m. on 20 September, RIC Head Const. Peter Burke arrived in Balbriggan by taxi in Mary Smyth's public house at the junction of Vauxhall Street and George's Square with his brother Michael, an RIC sergeant. Both were from Kerry but *en route* to Gormanston.[29] Peter Burke had been informed earlier of his pending promotion to district inspector at the RIC depot in the Phoenix Park, and so stopped at the pub at the town's centre to celebrate. They left a taxi driver awaiting payment while they ordered drink inside with some accompanying Black and Tans. Initially refused service – publicans, like other business proprietors, fully understood the ramifications for ignoring the police boycott – they would not take no for an answer.

Then, as the time passed the policemen and their companions became rowdy and offensive towards fellow punters. The local RIC were summoned but had no success getting them to leave. The disgruntled taxi driver – wishing he too had complied with the police boycott – had also reported their refusal to pay him, and still waited as Michael Rock, William Corcoran and John Gaynor then made their way to the pub at 9 p.m., pistols in pockets. Rock, now O/C of Naul IRA Battalion, had recently developed a particular contempt for the Black and Tans, and an equal disdain for the RIC who acted as their guides and provided intelligence. Rock had been at nearby James Derham's pub at Clonard Street's junction with Drogheda Street a quarter-mile away, where he and Derham had been adding up the previous day's sports day takings.

Rock, Corcoran and Gaynor entered Smyth's to sudden silence. Rock immediately berated Head Const. Burke about his conduct. Within seconds

Burke and Rock were reaching for their weapons. Rock fired first, killing the policeman instantly as he rushed towards a doorway for cover. Rock fired again, shooting and wounding Burke's brother as he too drew his weapon. Others started shooting. In the chaos, and with bullets striking brick, timber and plaster around them the three IRA men escaped out the pub's back door.

The unfortunate taxi driver then had his car commandeered to transport the dead and wounded policemen and several enraged Black and Tans to Gormanston. Rock and his two comrades, meanwhile, expecting reprisals, sent warnings to Volunteers in the town not to sleep at their homes that night. Rock knew there were not enough arms and men in the town to fend off any large enemy numbers that might arrive.

Then, at 11 p.m., scores of Black and Tans descended on the town, transported in Crossley Tenders and Lancia armoured cars. For over an hour their transports acted in relays ferrying additional numbers and dropping them off outside the town's RIC barracks at Bridge Street's junction with Quay Street. The atmosphere intensified, with members arriving in the backs of their open backed trucks firing into the air with rifles and pistols along Drogheda Street on their way in, some carrying bottles of whiskey in one hand, weapons in the other, singing: 'We are the boys of the Bulldog Brigade'. Then, at 11.45 p.m., despite repeated pleas from local RIC to restrain themselves, they ran amok.

Over 150 Black and Tans began shooting and kicking in doors, ejecting terrified civilians. Whole families fled to surrounding fields seeking refuge in the darkness soon lit up by the fires of their homes being set alight with cans of petrol. Two dozen homes, mostly along a half-mile length of Clonard Street, were quickly burning. This street was nicknamed 'Sinn Féin Alley' by locals owing to its contingent of Volunteers and party members who included James Derham. His pub was soon set alight, as was McGowan's in nearby George's Hill, both having been looted first. Reinforcements arrived from the Dublin direction, shooting at houses and at livestock visible in fields as the fires, spreading throughout the town, further lit up the darkness. Connolly's pub, situated at the junction of Mill Street and Bridge Street was also soon ablaze, its content of liquors adding to scores of bottles being guzzled by the paramilitary policemen acting in a frenzy, screaming, shouting and laughing hysterically as they continued discharging weapons, smashing windows and burning buildings. The entire town stank of smoke and petrol, the pitiful cries of terrified and confused children mingling with the crackling of thatched roofs burning above their ruined dwellings, and the howls and yells of terrified animals.

William Straw, a mysterious thirty-year-old Englishman and former British Army captain, accompanied a large group of marauding Black and Tans. Straw, nicknamed 'Jack Straw' by locals, had moved to Balbriggan the previous April and resided with a family of fishmongers in Quay Street. His lack of any means of income had made him suspicious to the local IRA. Their conjecture was well-founded; Straw, also drunk, had been acting as a paid spy. He pointed out the homes of suspected 'Sinn Féiners' which were then attacked and burned. Two local IRA men, James Lawless and Joseph Gibbons, had not received Comdt Rock's earlier warning not to stay at their homes. Both were wrenched away from their front doors, Gibbons in Hampton Street and Lawless in Bridge Street. They were known Volunteers and patrons of the town's republican courts. Gibbons, twenty-nine-years-old, was a dairy owner; Lawless, forty-years-old, a barber.

As bullets whizzed like hailstones through the town and into the fields sheltering hundreds of its petrified residents both men were taken to the RIC barracks. Arriving there at 1 a.m. they were badly beaten, before being put up against an outside wall. Shots were then fired into the wall around them, the drunken gunmen disregarding the danger from ricochets. They then set about both men once again with punches and kicks. Then, a doctor and priest were fetched by horrified RIC officers to tend to them before they were dragged back out of the barracks.

Then, near the corner of Bridge Street and Quay Street they were suddenly set upon again and beaten severely about the head. The blows continued, soon added to with pistol and rifle butts. Both men died under the onslaught during which they were also shot and bayoneted, their blood and brains splattering an adjacent wall. A chunk of Gibbons' throat was then cut away. Their bodies were hacked again before being concealed in an outhouse close to the police barracks.[30] Pools of blood had formed where they had been killed. The rampage continued with scores of townsfolk brutally assaulted.

Balbriggan was home to two widely acclaimed hosiery companies. Deedes, Templar & Company, situated in Convent Lane and with strong English connections, was set alight with petrol. The conflagration from the huge factory soon lit up the sky for miles. Nearby Messrs Smyth & Company Hosiers in Railway Street, established in 1780, Irish owned and whose customers included European royalty and had been a favourite of Queen Victoria, had its windows broken but was not set alight or bombed. A prominent local civilian and doctor, as well as two police constables intervened successfully to prevent its destruction while struggling to cope with the intense heat from the adjacent factory. Deedes, Templar employed hundreds of the town and surrounding area's inhabitants. Now their livelihoods as well as their homes were going up in flames. The fires emboldened the town's attackers who then threw hand grenades into the burning factory, ensuring its complete destruction.

In total, forty-nine dwellings and businesses and four pubs were badly damaged or destroyed during the onslaught, which lasted until 5 a.m. on 21 September. Scores of others had their windows broken or were shot up. The damage stretched all the way from Dublin Street to Drogheda Street, a mile in length, as well as into the adjacent streets and alleys. By the time the last of the Black and Tans had returned to Gormanston, hundreds of thousands of pounds worth of damage had been done.

Throughout the following day a cloud of smoke hung over the smouldering town. Its inhabitants who had fled were too traumatised to return and remained in the surrounding fields, some for days. William Straw was seen in the town early in the day, still drunk, laughing at a burning building. He was covered in grime and his clothes were burnt. He would soon make his way to nearby Skerries, only to be run out of the town and later court-martialled by the IRA and shot. His body was discovered in a shallow grave outside Ballyboughal. Those who ran him from Skerries would soon themselves be killed in the seaside town by the Black and Tans in revenge for Straw's death.

Meanwhile, Comdt Rock made his way to IRA GHQ in Rutland Square to recount the previous night's horrors to Richard Mulcahy. IRA reprisals in England were later considered, one of which was briefly planned against the similarly sized town of Upton in Cheshire, before being abandoned.[31] When Rock eventually returned to Balbriggan, a wanted man, he found himself ostracised. People were too afraid to even acknowledge him.

Journalists and reporters flocked to the town over the ensuing days. Balbriggan received more publicity than other reprisals due to its close proximity to the

Charlotte D'Espard, sister of the viceroy, Lord French, but with very different sympathies to her brother, visits the ruins of Balbriggan, accompanied by Cumann na mBan member Dorothy Macardle. (*Courtesy of Kilmainham Gaol Museum OPW, 19PO-1A32-21*)

capital. Commentators and correspondents stared wide-eyed and gaped at the destruction. The accounts of a Canadian man visiting family in the town were pounced upon, being seen as impartial. He corroborated most of the horrific local accounts of the previous night. *The* (London) *Times* later asserted that the British were 'no longer acting in accordance with the standards of a civilised government'. *The Observer*'s Irish correspondent, Stephen Gwynn, suggested that martial law would be less extreme than 'the present anarchic and futile campaign of revenge'.[32]

An internal inquiry – not to be published – was soon ordered by the authorities; to ridicule from both the press and the *Irish Bulletin*. Hamar Greenwood later fanned the flames of scorn, transforming his image into a parody of ineptitude with assertions that Black and Tans and Auxiliaries were undeserving of the backlash from Balbriggan and elsewhere, and that such criminal acts in any case could not be proven to have been carried out by the RIC. Privately, he mused that the issue was delicate – the police were at breaking point. Andy Cope and Mark Sturgis visited Gormanston and suggested that a regime of radically increased discipline was urgently required.[33] Cope had by now spent several weeks travelling throughout

KILLING AT ITS VERY EXTREME

Dublin speaking liberally of his desire to make contact with republican leaders. He had even divulged to his Irish girlfriend that the entire British intention in Ireland was 'a great spoof'.[34] He looked on in bewilderment at the 'spoof's' effects. However, Balbriggan was soon to be eclipsed by even more savage reprisals.

***

In Rineen, Co. Clare, on 22 September, six policemen including one Black and Tan were killed in a hail of IRA gunfire and hand-grenades during an ambush led by a former Irish Guards member whose men also included a former US Army soldier.[35] It was later claimed that the IRA had used soft-nosed 'Dum-Dum' bullets, illegal under the Hague Convention, subsequently scoffed at by the IRA citing that most of their ammunition was captured from the British and regardless – they themselves were not afforded the protections offered by the convention by the crown; therefore its own forces could not have it both ways. The vehicle carrying the dead policemen was then set alight. With smoke seen for miles around truckloads of British infantry sped to the scene. A prolonged skirmish ensued during which two Volunteers were wounded but all escaped. That night the towns of Lahinch, Ennistymon, Liscannor and Miltown Malbay were attacked by Black and Tans with RIC members as guides. Six civilians, including a fifteen-year-old boy were killed and dozens of buildings burned. One man was dragged from his house in front of his wife and two children, tied up and killed, then their house was set ablaze and his body thrown into the flames.[36] A participant in the day's IRA ambush was himself burned to death in a shop.

Cork city was lucky to be spared similar vengeance two days later following an assassination attempt on Lt General Sir Peter Strickland, commander of 6th Division – headquartered in the city's Victoria barracks – as he was driven along the city's quays. General Macready commented: 'Had Strickland been killed, no power on earth would have restrained the troops from taking their toll of vengeance on the town'.[37] Nevertheless, Cork's turn came soon enough.

Then on Sunday 26 September Trim in Meath suffered serious damage throughout the ancient and picturesque town. Earlier that day South Meath Brigade IRA units had combined forces to capture and burn the town's imposing RIC barracks – the Meath Divisional HQ. A large quantity of arms and ammunition were captured. The barracks' head constable was badly wounded but was brought to a local doctor by Volunteers. Later, four lorries of Black and Tans swooped into the town centre. They shot and wounded two young boys playing hurling on their way. Locals were badly beaten. Children were terrified by Black and Tans dangling hand grenades in front of their windows. Homes and business were ransacked until the arrival of the military saw them disappear with the assurance they would not return. Nonetheless, many of the town's civilians, fearing another Balbriggan, evacuated to the surrounding countryside. It was a wise move; the Black and Tans, along with some Auxiliaries – again under Major Dudley; recently transferred from Depot to E Company Auxiliaries, and *en route* to Sligo – returned that night machine gunning buildings and setting fire to others, one of which contained several sealed wooden boxes of 500-year-old manuscripts, subsequently incinerated. Businesses and factories were also burned. A Volunteer who had participated in the earlier barrack burning had to hide in a freshly dug grave for fear of a similar fate to Volunteers Lawless and Gibbons in Balbriggan.

On the night Trim burned, three civilians were shot dead in Belfast by the RIC in retaliation for the killing of a policeman and the wounding of another earlier in the night.

Press coverage of such reprisals was scathing of British authorities. The government was accused of, among a long list of transgressions, promoting barbarism against women and children. The British general, Sir Hubert Gough, wrote in the *Manchester Guardian* decrying the deliberate policy of murder by the crown forces and demanding the immediate disbandment of the Black and Tans. The French newspaper *Le Matin* compared such reprisals with brutality not seen since the Middle Ages.[38]

Sir Henry Wilson, horrified at the loss of control of the forces he himself had advocated for, and their adverse impact on the wider civilian population, urged his political masters to reign them in urgently. Speaking of the IRA, he advocated a more focused approach, protesting: 'If these men ought to be murdered, then the government ought to murder them'.[39]

16

PEACE OFFERINGS AND TRAGEDY FOR THE DUBLIN BRIGADE

'If the ground opened up and swallowed him'

Sinn Féin councillor John Lynch of Kilmallock, Co. Limerick, was killed in Dublin by agents of Field Marshal Wilson's government during the early hours of 23 September. Lynch, forty years old, also a solicitor and republican judge, had arrived in Dublin eleven days earlier with a long list of assignments. The first was to outline to a Sinn Féin commission the effects of the levies enforced upon county councils for injury or death claims by the victims of crown forces. The last was the handing over of £23,000 in cash raised in the Limerick area for the national loan to Michael Collins.

Lynch accomplished the latter on 22 September, then enjoyed a show at the Abbey Theatre in Lower Abbey Street with Gearóid O'Sullivan and republican judge Kevin O'Shiel. Following this he returned to his hotel, the Royal Exchange on Parliament Street, and settled for the night in Room 6 on the third floor.

At 1.35 a.m., Capt. Geoffrey Baggallay, a one-legged British court-martial officer, was on duty at Ship Street barracks when he received a telephone call from the adjutant's office at Phoenix Park RIC depot. The caller claimed that a 'Sinn Féiner' named Lynch was staying at the Exchange Hotel. A car was needed to take one RIC officer and two constables to make the arrest. Baggallay immediately telephoned Capt. Frederick Harper-Shove, a recruiter for Hounslow spy school – and Col Walter Wilson's right hand man in Dublin District Special Branch. Harper-Shove, based in Dublin Castle, took the call. He then organised a car to pick up the three policemen while he quickly assembled a squad of intelligence operatives.

At 2 a.m. the RIC officer and his two men arrived at Dublin Castle to find twelve men in military caps and black trench coats awaiting. Among them were Capt. Baggallay, Lt Henry Angliss, Lt Charles Peel and Major George Osbert Smyth. Major Smyth, thirty years old, had recently arrived in Ireland to avenge his gunned down brother, Col Bryce Ferguson Smyth. Lts Peel and Angliss were in charge of the raiding party.

Within minutes, they were positioned outside the hotel. The three policemen were instructed to remain outside while the military effected the arrest. They then rang the hotel bell and rattled the night gate impatiently. This brought the night porter, William Barrett, rushing to the door where he noticed the large group outside with their officers' caps pulled down over their eyes. Barrett asked them their business, insisting he had no accommodation. He was told abruptly to open up, that they were the military and were not there for a room. When he complied a revolver was shoved into his face while another officer demanded the register. Barrett obliged. It was quickly scanned for the information the officers sought – Lynch's room number. Capt. Baggallay was then left covering the porter while the rest crept upstairs to the third floor, and Room 6.

They knocked on the door several times before Lynch answered in his pyjamas, groggy after having just awoken. He was then shoved back into the room. Lts Peel and Angliss followed him. Peel began to question Lynch – startled and wide awake – impassively, as if to settle him. Lynch, however, was not fooled. He saw Angliss wrap bedclothes tightly around his revolver.[1] Suspecting he was about to be killed he then attempted to force his way past Peel, but there was no escape. Peel grappled him and threw him forcefully back onto the bed. Then, a muffled shot rang out. Lynch was shot through the jaw. The bullet shattered his spinal cord, killing him instantly. Angliss then placed his smoking revolver on the floor next to the bed, then he and Peel led the rest of the men out of the hotel and back to the Castle. The shot had been so muffled that nobody else in the hotel had heard it.

Soon afterwards a telephone call was received at Great Brunswick Street barracks from yet another one-legged British intelligence officer, twenty-six-year-old Capt. Jocelyn Lee Hardy (prosthetic legs being a common feature among veteran British officers since the war). Hardy had been seconded to F Company Auxiliaries. He reported that a joint raid had just been carried out on the Royal Exchange Hotel and that a man had been shot dead by the RIC after the man himself had first fired. Ten minutes later a unit of the DMP arrived at the hotel from Brunswick Street and told William Barrett they were there to investigate the shooting of a man named Lynch. Barrett was at a loss. He told them he knew nothing of a shooting and queried the source of their claim. 'The military' was the reply. Barrett then informed them of the recent raid, but added that raids were all too common in the city. He led them to Lynch's room. He knocked, then with no answer he opened the door. Lynch's corpse lay before them sprawled on the blood-soaked bed. Spatters stained the wallpaper, ceiling, carpet and furniture.

The following day's official reports of Lynch's killing were met with cynicism. This sentiment was aggravated by the subsequent revelation that no coroner's inquest would be allowed; a military court of inquiry would take place instead behind closed doors. Arthur Griffith expressed fury.

Michael Collins' intelligence department, sensing a new enemy strategy, wasted no time. David Neligan and Lily Mernin were instructed to get any information they could about Lynch's killing, particularly units and personnel involved. Their efforts soon bore fruit. It became apparent that new players were operating out of Dublin Castle who shot first and did not ask questions. New names such as Baggallay, Hardy, Peel, Angliss and Smyth appeared on growing lists of those to be found and watched.

Among those stalking such enemy players was twenty-one-year-old William Beaumont, a British Army veteran. William's brother, twenty-six-year-old Seán, was a member of Trinity College's OTC, but was also a secret republican sympathiser. Dan McDonnell, who had worn his mother's stockings over his face at the previous year's Collinstown raid, had been recruited to IRA intelligence in August 1920, and knew Seán Beaumont. McDonnell had suggested that Seán employ his connections to tease out among his university associates anyone willing to gather information on the recently arrived Auxiliaries. Many of them frequented the same establishments such as Kidd's Back pub in nearby Nassau Street. Beaumont had spoken of the indignation felt by his college fellows from the growing countrywide reprisals.

Seán's brother, William, had recently witnessed the Auxiliaries' brutality on a tram in Dawson Street. Several cadets had boarded and verbally abused its passengers, including himself, until one of them found an old army notebook in his pocket. It contained details of campaigns William had fought in, which were recognised by one of the Auxiliaries. The result was warm-hearted backslapping. William feigned a cordial response, but was quietly furious. He later told Seán he would happily shoot one of them. Seán's unexpected response was that William should utilise his recently established rapport to gain information for others willing and able to shoot them.

A meeting was arranged with Michael Collins, Tom Cullen and Frank Thornton. Ironically, Collins had already received word of a less reassuring aspect to William Beaumont's character; he had been overheard boasting while drinking that he would 'catch Michael Collins' and attain a £20,000 reward for doing so. Collins took a chance, casually revealing that: 'I am the fellow that is worth £20,000'.[2] Beaumont was impressed. The upshot was his agreement to work for IRA intelligence by cavorting with his newly found Auxiliary friends and picking up loose talk in the process.

Beaumont was successful in fostering a fruitful bonhomie with the cadets despite being rarely in a fit state to recollect their interactions. Night after night he was brought back to the Castle after Kidd's Back for more drink, then, in the early hours, driven by armoured car to his home at 175 Strand Road in Sandymount, where Seán tried to write down any information he had while his drunken sibling could recount it.[3] Nevertheless, it was a nerve-racking game for William.

It was equally trying for Thornton, Cullen and Frank Saurin. Beaumont soon introduced them to his widening circle of castle agents at Kidd's Back. The three had also made contact with other secret service agents, posing as touts, and spent hour-upon-hour in the company of men such as Capt. George Bennett and Lt Peter Ames, and several others who would happily tear them limb from limb if they discovered their true identities, or found them during a raid.

After one occasion when the conversation inevitably veered towards Michael Collins and his assassins, Tom Cullen was asked by one of them: 'Surely you fellows know these men – Liam Tobin, Tom Cullen and Frank Thornton, these are Collins' three officers and if you can get these fellows we would locate Collins himself'.[4] Thornton could not have been more surprised if the ground opened up and swallowed him.[5] The three IRA men's poker faces concealed a mixture of acute anxiety and relief at the revelation that the enemy obviously possessed no photographs or descriptions of them. Nonetheless, it would only have taken one of the other enemy agents they had previously met in Rabiatti's Saloon alongside Det. Neligan to wander in and confer with the likes of Bennett and Ames, and reveal the fact that they had previously identified themselves to them as fellow English agents, and not touts – with potentially dire consequences.

Meanwhile, the Cork town of Mallow was next on the list of British reprisals. On Tuesday 28 September Liam Lynch and Ernie O'Malley led an audacious IRA raid on the town's army barracks. Using deception to gain entry its guard detail were overpowered and held captive while a huge quantity of weapons, including two Hotchkiss light machine guns and ammunition, were captured. It was the first successful IRA seizure of a military barracks. Vengeance was unleashed upon the town that night. Flames lit up the surrounding countryside for miles. A local priest later broke down in tears when he described women and children banging on the door of his parochial house at midnight desperately seeking refuge as streams of bullets ripped through the air. Two days later it was the turn of Tubbercurry in Sligo following the shootings of more policemen. Black and Tans went berserk burning several buildings and the local creamery. The same day, 30 September, Hamar Greenwood made a speech to the RIC in the Phoenix Park appealing for an end to reprisals, whilst acknowledging the unbearable pressure affecting the police. However, he also spoke of widespread press exaggeration of their ferocity. The *Manchester Guardian* derided such deflection. The liberal newspaper accused the authorities in Ireland of wreaking a campaign of revenge upon a population simply because they shared nationality with insurgents; 'exactly what the German commanders in Belgium said'.[6]

***

As September ended, world attention was still focused on Terence MacSwiney's hunger strike, in its forty-ninth day. Expecting imminent death, MacSwiney wrote impassioned correspondences to IRA GHQ, referring to powerful but unseen influences from those already dead lending their weight to watch over them, alluding to himself soon taking his place among their ethereal ranks. Singling out Collins, Brugha, McKee, Mulcahy, O'Hegarty, Stack and Leo Henderson for praise he also wrote of the spirit of Cork exorcising the spectre of its inactivity in 1916. Conflicting messages from Dublin had seen the Cork Brigade sitting on its hands during the Rising while Dublin burned; a cause of consternation and shame among the Cork Brigade since.[7]

PEACE OFFERINGS AND TRAGEDY FOR THE DUBLIN BRIGADE

On 1 October Arthur Griffith took centre-stage once again among a gathering of international journalists. In the wake of John Lynch's killing Griffith stated that a list existed of Sinn Féin leaders marked out by crown agents for assassination. He added, referring to black propaganda: 'I am the first on the list, and the story is to be circulated, as it was in the case of the Lord Mayor of Cork, that I was assassinated because I was urging moderate action'.[8] Griffith had recently advocated a treaty – as had De Valera 3,000 miles away – that would provide Irish self-government while protecting Britain's strategic security concerns.[9]

Griffith spoke forebodingly of the same tools being used on him that had been employed to kill Councillor Lynch. He also claimed that reprisals were a calculated strategy orchestrated by the crown. Subsequently, orders were issued to the military and police not to arrest Griffith, a move the authorities feared would fuel enemy propaganda, despite a recent directive to prosecute those encouraging opposition or issuing inflammatory statements.[10] Ironically, five days earlier, a secret meeting had been scheduled at the offices of Corrigan's Solicitors in 3 St Andrew Street between Griffith and Sir John Anderson. Acting as intermediaries were William Corrigan for Griffith and William Wylie for Anderson. Both intermediaries, former colleagues, had last met on opposing sides in Richmond barracks four years earlier when Corrigan had been a prisoner facing his own court martial and possible execution; Wylie had spoken up for him. Nevertheless, the meeting was fruitless. Griffith had insisted on Anderson recognising the Dáil before discussions, which Anderson refused.

Back in Westminster, with the enactment of the Government of Ireland Bill looming large, no less furtive machinations were under way to quarantine the six unionist Ulster counties. The bill had been formulated to keep them under the remit of Dublin Castle and the over-arching Council of Ireland. Walter Long, James Craig and others had, however, recently contrived to ensure otherwise. The bill had contained stipulations in the form of financial and administrative sweeteners to be provided to Ireland following any eventual reunification under the bill's terms. Long strove instead to ensure separate financial and authoritative controls within each administration, free from such preconditions. Craig, meanwhile, had insisted upon a separate assistant under secretary for Northern Ireland, to be vetted for approval by a committee to ensure – among other factors – he was not Catholic. Craig also put forward a proposition of building an armed constabulary around the existing UVF.[11] This had horrified General Macready who recognised the armed threat posed to the British government by the UVF during the 1914 Home Rule crisis. Sir John Anderson backed Macready, warning of civil war in the country should it be allowed. Nevertheless, Lloyd George was more tolerant of the UVF, and sidestepped Macready's threat to resign if the organisation was officially recognised by presenting Craig with the authority to build the bones of such a force under the guise of the 'Ulster Special Constabulary'. Macready would disparaged this as the 'raising of Carson's army from the grave'.[12]

Meanwhile, former Prime Minister Asquith was once again calling for dominion status in Ireland in the wake of the escalating reprisals. Éamon de Valera, with his hands full in the USA trying to overcome insurmountable divisions between Irish political factions there, rejected Asquith's proposition during a subsequent interview in New York. Lloyd George, rubbing his hands with glee at revelations of such bitter divisions within Irish America, also rejected the idea, and spoke hawkishly instead of 'breaking up the murder gangs'.[13] Hitting back at Griffith, he also claimed that reprisals were the inevitable consequences of war which Sinn Féin had sought, further retorting that the police had every right to defend themselves.

Four miles south of Westminster, on 7 October, flowers arrived at Brixton Prison from the mother of a victim – Rose Gibbons – of Dublin's most notorious reprisal, in Balbriggan. Both cavalry and foot soldiers heavily guarded the prison itself. Terence MacSwiney, terribly emaciated, his teeth protruding, cheeks hollow and eyes sunken, received a note with the flowers.[14] The note was a gesture of solidarity and expressed prayers for 'The Mayor and the boys' and the success of Irish freedom.[15]

Still also showing solidarity with the freedom struggle were Ireland's rail workers. On 9 October two loaded military railway wagons – stationary due to the embargo – in Kingsbridge station were successfully burned in an IRA raid overseen by Peadar Clancy. The wagons had been packed to the brim with cargo a week earlier. Railwaymen, accordingly, refused to operate the train.[16] A succession of replacement drivers and stokers were then brought in. Each, in turn, refused to operate it. Eventually, word reached Dublin Brigade HQ of the consignment, and a plan was put in place to destroy it.

PEACE OFFERINGS AND TRAGEDY FOR THE DUBLIN BRIGADE

Two dozen men of D Company 1st Battalion were initially detailed to carry out the attack on Saturday 7 October. However, due to the weekend there were too few staff members and commuters to camouflage the Volunteers as they prepared to strike, so it was postponed until the following Monday morning, but instead with only eleven Volunteers due to the remainder having work commitments.[17] Charlie Byrne was in command. Pat McCrea was at hand with a car to transport any captured arms and ammunition.

Despite the wagons being isolated in the open, away from the rest of the rolling stock, the IRA men moved inconspicuously enough to successfully launch their attack. They were assisted by the yard's lacklustre guard detail – two half-alert sentries; the remainder either playing cards, cleaning equipment or cooking. Byrne assigned one man per enemy soldier as they got to within striking distance and all enemy positions were revealed. Then they struck. Pistols and knives were shoved into faces. A sentry was knocked out with a blow to the head from a pistol handle. Several sharp surrender commands followed. The engagement was brief. The ten British soldiers were disarmed, then locked in an empty wagon after their webbing and helmets were commandeered. Then, the two cargo wagons were doused with petrol and set alight. Within minutes, it was all over and the Volunteers escaped back through the station's concourse, cheered by railway staff and spectators who looked on as the distant wagons blazed, with mini-explosions resounding as ammunition ignited and thick black smoke soared into the morning sky.

When the Volunteers dispersed, Pat McCrea drove towards Fitzwilliam Place to dump the captured haul. He had a narrow escape on College Green when several Crossley Tenders containing Auxiliaries approached from College Street. Luckily for him, a policeman on point duty outside Trinity College stopped the Auxiliaries to let him pass. The arms and equipment were successfully dumped. The military reported afterwards that the IRA had tried but failed to set alight the rail carriage containing the surrendered soldiers. This was scoffed at.

The opposite side of the city also saw action on the railways. Paddy Daly and Joe Leonard had left 10 Bessborough Avenue to make their way to 100 Seville Place, a recently established HQ for Squad members, when they saw a roadblock spring up on Newcomen Bridge at North Strand.[18] They filtered through along the railway, avoiding the road, and successfully made

Seville Place where they dismissed some Squad members who had guarded the building overnight. With a subsequent appointment in Glasnevin, Daly and Leonard took to the railway lines again and made their way as far as Drumcondra Bridge where they saw another roadblock. After they had crept stealthily northbound under the bridge they spotted an opportunity – the soldiers were exposed on the bridge. Both then opened fire with their Mauser semi-automatics. The soldiers at the roadblock dashed for cover and dispersed, assuming they were under attack from a large IRA unit. Daly and Leonard relished their small victory and continued towards Phibsboro. Mountjoy Prison – both men's former lodgings – sat to their left, the Royal Canal to their right.

Another former Mountjoy inmate, Seán Treacy, and his close friend Dan Breen, had been letting their hair down in recent evenings playing cards at the Flemings' Drumcondra residence. They had been ordered by GHQ to remain in Dublin for planned operations that, for various reasons, were cancelled. Both were keen to return to Tipperary. Treacy would soon do so – in a coffin.

Joseph Lawless was a nightly visitor there. He relished Treacy's devilish humour and banter with Breen. Lawless noticed how Breen looked up to Treacy and that the latter was the brains of the combative pair. Breen had won a small amount of money at cards and had then placed the winnings on a horse, an outsider which subsequently also won. He and Treacy, recognising that their days could end momentarily with the squeeze of a trigger finger, set out to enjoy their good fortune.

On the night of 11 October they treated two Fleming sisters, Dot and Kay, to an evening at recently opened La Scala Theatre in Lower Sackville Street, despite the accompanying and commonplace risks that its patrons could be searched on the way out. The previous night Breen had been followed by enemy agents from another pub in Great Britain Street offering sanctuary to IRA men – Kirwan's in No. 49 – but had eluded them.

Leaving the theatre, Breen observed a suspicious-looking man watching people. Then, as the four companions walked towards Nelson's Pillar to board a tram back to Drumcondra, Kay Fleming told Breen: 'There's a friend following', referring to the same individual, clearly an enemy agent.[19] Breen turned and dauntlessly stared him down. He backed off. Soon they alighted the tram on Lower Drumcondra Road and made for Flemings, on the western side of the road between Hollybank Road and Botanic Avenue.

Once inside, however, Joseph Lawless told them that word had come from Michael Collins of an expected raid on Flemings that night. Breen and Treacy had no time to lose, it was approaching curfew. They walked to the two-storey house of Professor John Carolan, situated in nearby Upper Drumcondra Road – named 'Fernside'. The professor was a lecturer in nearby St Patrick's College. They had been given a latchkey to the house by Carolan and told they could stay any time. He had also shown them how to escape quickly out the house's rear. Richard Mulcahy was also a regular resident as he too moved ceaselessly between safe houses.

It was a bright moonlit night. In the stillness the pair heard distant rumblings of military patrols. On arrival just before midnight, with no one awake, they went upstairs to a bedroom overlooking the back garden. Sharing the same bed, they stripped down to underclothes, their loaded pistols close to hand. Both were initially unable to sleep, their senses alerted for reasons unknown, until eventually, exhaustion took its merciful hold and they dozed.

Their slumbers were brief. As a nearby church bell chimed for 1 a.m. on Tuesday 12 October a succession of loud bangs and knocks followed by the sound of breaking glass from the house's front jolted them. A raid was in progress. Searchlights suddenly shone at the back of the house. Professor Carolan rushed to the front door. It came crashing open on him. He was then pinned against a wall in the wide hallway by an infantryman while officers approached from outside shouting a rapid succession of questions. Soldiers rushed in and began fanning throughout the ground floor.

Upstairs, Breen and Treacy desperately sought to dress and escape. Two intelligence officers, recently arrived Major Smyth and Capt. Alfred White, entered and rushed for the staircase followed by a corporal. Commanding the section of nervous infantrymen behind them were fellow intelligence officers Lts Philip Atwood and Robert Jeune. Professor Carolan remained pinned to the wall downstairs, barely able to breathe as profanities were barked in his face.

Major Smyth paused on the staircase and was overtaken by the corporal, who then, with Capt. White, rushed around upstairs, disturbing an elderly lodger. Then just as White paused outside Breen and Treacy's door at the back of the large landing, a sudden hail of shots came from behind it. White instantly slumped, the thirty-eight-year-old mortally wounded. A second succession of shots rang out from the room where muzzles flashed again like strobe lights, wounding the corporal. Enraged, Major Smyth, his pistol primed, then rushed the rest of the staircase and ran straight into Breen, on the landing, his blood boiling. Breen fired first. Smyth jerked, twisted and fell at his feet. He joined his brother in death.

At this point Treacy, behind Breen and desperately scanning for an escape, saw in the moonlight two soldiers detailed to cover the building's rear running along adjacent Home Farm Road to reinforce the frontal assault. Their semi-automatic fire had fooled them into thinking there were more enemy than they had bargained for to the house's front. Breen implored Treacy to escape, saying he would cover him and follow. Treacy climbed barefoot out the window, then through an open window in the house's conservatory. Exiting the conservatory he then scrambled for the back wall at the end of the long narrow garden, scaled it, before opening fire and badly wounding two other soldiers, one of whom had just raised his Lee Enfield to shoot. Panting, he then waited for Breen but with no sign of him, he disappeared into the night, fearing the worst for him.

Breen had been wounded several times by a rapid burst of return fire from the hallway. Blood flowed down his right arm as he slammed and locked the door behind him. Another fusillade of lead smashed into timber and plaster around him just as he did. One bullet had grazed his forehead, another two wounded his leg while another struck his chest. Breen's angry and defiant shouts kept his blood up nonetheless, and were matched by groans from the wounded corporal, as well as Professor Carolan's teenage son Robert, also in the house and wounded.

Pumping with adrenalin, Breen, wide-eyed, scanned the rear of the house for Treacy and an escape, but saw no sign of Treacy. He climbed barefoot out the window, barely able to focus, and collapsed through the conservatory, breaking his big toe and landing amid a cascade of shattering glass. Now weaponless, grimacing and struggling to breathe, he escaped out the back, past the two wounded British soldiers. He called out unsuccessfully for his comrade, then made his own escape, staggering away into the darkness.

Professor Carolan, forty-six years old, was wrenched upstairs by one of the British lieutenants and questioned furiously. Names were demanded and

PEACE OFFERINGS AND TRAGEDY FOR THE DUBLIN BRIGADE

locations of nearby safe houses. The officer demanded to know where a man named Mulcahy was. Then another shot rang out. Carolan was shot through the neck. The professor slumped helplessly as Smyth and White's adjacent bodies were moved.

The house reeked of cordite. Wafts of smoke emanated from dozens of spent rounds and the smouldering carpet and rugs onto which they had tumbled. Blood was smeared and spattered all over the landing, stairs and hallway walls and floors, the back bedroom and its window. Carolan's horrified wife, Bridget, rushed to her husband, screaming and demanding an ambulance while she stemmed the flow of his blood. The house was then thoroughly searched. Neighbours in the middle-class suburb stayed back from their curtained windows, terrified, as the military took stock outside Fernside. Reinforcements arrived to secure the area and search for the fugitives. Sniffer dogs were summoned, as was an ambulance to take Professor Carolan, his wife and son to the Mater Hospital. His son was not badly wounded.

Breen, now delirious from blood loss and shock, teetered and lurched his way around the back of St Patrick's College, crossed Millbourne and Millmount Avenue, and then waded across the shallow Tolka river, a move which later put paid to the efforts of the sniffer dogs. Soaking wet and shivering, he faced a

Auxiliaries with bloodhounds used as sniffer dogs to track IRA suspects. Luckily for Dan Breen, the Tolka River enabled him to elude enemy sniffer dogs as he desperately sought escape. (*Courtesy of Mercier Archive*)

terrace of two-storey town houses on Botanic Avenue, all but one of which – the home of Frederick and Kathleen Holmes, No. 77 – were in darkness. About to lapse into unconsciousness, he knocked on the door, his only hope.

Breen's astonishing luck was, however, still with him. Despite Frederick's initial reservations Breen was taken into the house and treated. Kathleen defied the curfew and made her way to fetch a nearby district nurse named Long.[20] She promptly arrived and, with Mrs Holmes, stemmed Breen's bleeding. Breen was now unconscious.

The military departed Fernside at 5 a.m. Flemings, as earlier predicted, was also ransacked and several occupants arrested. Nurse Long, knowing them, went there at 7.30 a.m. to convey news of Breen's whereabouts but saw the raid and kept walking to nearby 120 Lower Drumcondra Road, the terraced home of the Dillon family, cousins of the Flemings.[21] There she found Joseph Lawless. He had slept there peacefully despite the brutal skirmish half-a-mile away. He sprung to action.

He cycled to his rental garage in St Ignatius Road, procured a Rover touring car and drove to the western end of Botanic Avenue. From there he walked to No. 77, was admitted, and saw Breen lying delirious on a mattress in a downstairs back room calling out for Treacy. Realising the situation's urgency, he then sped by car to Brennan & Walsh outfitters in Sackville Street. Both proprietors were Volunteers and the shop acted as a hub. Dick McKee, staying nearby, was sent for and soon arrived. McKee then ordered Joe Vize, Maurice Brennan and Tom Kelly – the three already there on other business – to accompany Lawless and rescue Breen. McKee then arranged for Breen's admission to Geraldine O'Donel's private nursing home in 62 Eccles Street. There he would be secure.

Half-an-hour later Lawless dropped his comrades off at the Holmes in Botanic Avenue, and while they fetched him, he drove up Drumcondra Road to observe Fernside, where everything appeared normal again. He returned, and after Breen was carefully loaded into the car, it was driven with the roof down to avoid suspicion given the fine weather.[22] Breen, by now inebriated with brandy to ease his agony, was propped up between Vize and Kelly. However, to everyone's alarm he started trashing about deliriously just as they approached Doyle's Corner in Phibsboro. He was restrained just in time to avoid the attentions of a policeman on point duty there who raised his hand for Lawless to stop and allow a Crossley Tender full of Auxiliaries to pass along the North Circular Road. Lawless' hand caressed his pistol as the Auxiliaries passed slowly and stared suspiciously at the car's passengers. A collective sigh of relief was felt in the car when the vehicle finally passed.

Minutes later, as Lawless approached 62 Eccles Street, he saw policemen on the pavement just outside the Mater Hospital. He then noticed McKee and Mick McDonnell walking towards him and McKee beckoning him on. He slowed down to allow McKee and McDonnell to jump onto his running board. McKee told him that the hospital was being searched, and that McDonnell would hide them until arrangements were made to get Breen back into No. 62 without drawing attention. McDonnell squeezed into the car which then turned left onto Dorset Street only to run into the same Tender bristling with Auxiliaries again. Lawless' pulse raced, but the enemy passed again without interfering.

McDonnell directed them to his dump on North Great Charles Street. Then, to everyone's exasperation, he revealed that he could not find the key to open it. McDonnell then departed to fetch alternative keys, instructing Lawless to proceed instead to a disused coach house in Mountjoy Square. By now Breen had been given more brandy to counter his increasingly uncontrollable rants and gesticulations. These were beginning to attract the attentions of curious and quick-witted youths who mockingly speculated about the cause of the peculiar-looking passenger's troubles as the car meandered through the city's back streets.[23] He was unconscious again as the car pulled into the coach house. There they waited silently, wondering what had happened the previous night. They feared for Treacy.

Half-an-hour later they heard the welcome sound of McDonnell's distinctive voice. Even more welcome was the unexpected sight of Treacy, standing before them in ridiculous-looking oversized clothes. Jibes quickly followed. He was cut in several places, clearly exhausted, but otherwise in good spirits, as was Breen who suddenly woke, alerted by Treacy's voice. Treacy quickly detailed the others about the gunfight and his subsequent escape across country barefoot and barely clothed to Phil Ryan's safe house in Finglas where he was fed, sheltered, and provided with his ill-fitting clothes.

At 11 a.m. word was received that Eccles Street was secure. Breen was driven to No. 62. McKee stood once again in the street, as did Treacy and a large IRA security detail. Breen was seen safely into the nursing home, content despite his half-delirium and excruciating pain that the friend he loved like a brother was safe, though unaware that he would never set eyes on him again.

Treacy had ensured Breen had a pistol. Professor Carolan, meanwhile, later made a statement in the Mater Hospital detailing the night's events. Damning of the raiding party's conduct it was subsequently published in *The Freeman's Journal*. He eventually succumbed to his wound on 27 October.

Rapidly dying from his wounds in the same hospital that morning was Matt Furlong. The twenty-eight-year-old veteran of, among other operations, the London mission in 1918 to assassinate cabinet members, and a prominent member of GHQ munitions staff, as well as the 5th Battalion engineers, had been testing a new mortar planned to rival the British Stokes Mortar.[24] Operating it in Co. Meath, a shell had exploded in its barrel as Furlong prepared to fire it. He was horrifically wounded and died in agony soon after admission to hospital. He was the sixth IRA member to accidentally die that day; five others were killed in Wexford when explosives they were manufacturing blew up.

***

Two days after Fernside's ferocious fracas filled Dublin's newspapers D Company 1st Battalion were in action again. It had recently been brought to Brigadier McKee's attention that a weekly army payroll collection in cash was made by the military each Thursday at 11 a.m. in a Rolls-Royce armoured car from the Munster and Leinster Bank at Doyle's Corner.[25] An ambush was prepared.

Nine Volunteers under Charlie Byrne took positions around the corner and waited, primed to pounce shortly before 11 a.m. only to fear they were on a fool's errand when there was no sign of the car. Then, eventually, it lumbered from the North Circular Road and pulled up outside the bank. The morning was mild but overcast. After an officer alighted the remaining two guards appeared just as uninspired as their comrades had in Kingsbridge three days earlier. After the officer had entered the bank they remained within the car, visible through small hatches left open to cool them. The engine was left running. Bernard Byrne had been detailed to jam the vehicle's turret which contained a Vickers machine gun from its rear. As soon as this was accomplished the rest would rapidly converge.

PEACE OFFERINGS AND TRAGEDY FOR THE DUBLIN BRIGADE

With no one watching the car's rear Byrne was able to approach unchallenged, until a pistol shot rang out from within Charlie Byrne's coat pocket; he had loaded his pistol but negligently left its safety off. The two guards reacted instantly, the gunner suddenly spraying fire at the Volunteers to the vehicle's front. They closed rapidly, having mistaken the accidental discharge as an attack signal. Bernard Byrne scrambled up the back of the car desperately and unsuccessfully trying to jam its turret. The gunner maintained fire. Short controlled bursts of shots flew from the machine gun barrel at a rate of ten-per-second and whizzed through the air striking concrete, metal and glass. Civilians throughout the bustling area scrambled for cover. Some, more distant, momentarily feared a return to the destruction wrought in 1916, having not heard such abrasive staccato fire from a machine gun since the Easter Rising, others from their recent military service.

Volunteer Bill O'Connell sprinted towards the car.[26] A bullet through the forehead sent him tumbling to the ground, killed before his body crashed to the cobblestones. His brains splattered the street. This did not prevent the remaining IRA men from quickly surrounding the car. They jumped on its running boards while Bernard Byrne managed to insert his pistol barrel into a gap in a hatch which the car's two occupants fought ferociously to close. He fired several shots, their deafening echoes reverberated along with the ricocheting bullets inside smashing against metal and into flesh to the sound of terrified screams and shouts from those being cut, gashed and blinded by bullet and metal fragments. The machine gun was silent. In the chaos, Charlie Byrne inserted his revolver through a vision slit at the vehicle's front, only to have the gunner wrench and wrestle the barrel away.

Charlie Byrne, seeing no other option, ordered a retreat. Bernard Byrne, then sprinting away, came suddenly face to face with the British officer. He raised his pistol to fire, but it clicked harmlessly, to the officer's relief. Byrne needed to reload but had no time. The officer reached for his own sidearm but Byrne punched him full force in the face, knocking him flat, and then sped past him, only to run into a local butcher who threatened him with a cleaver. Byrne's pointing pistol quickly persuaded the butcher to back away.[27]

All the surviving IRA men then escaped. Whatever chance Charlie Byrne had of concealing his part in the disaster faded when two smouldering holes were seen in his coat pocket from the accidentally discharged pistol that had alerted the guards. Back in Phibsboro an ambulance arrived to remove Connolly's body and the wounded soldiers to King George V Hospital. Replacement soldiers soon moved the armoured car.

***

Just after the failed ambush, less than a mile from Phibsboro, in the Republican Outfitters on Talbot Street, Liam Tobin, Frank Thornton and Tom Cullen spoke with Dick McKee, Peadar Clancy, and Frank and Leo Henderson. They had an ambitious operation in mind: General Tudor and Hamar Greenwood were due to attend Capt. White's funeral procession that day as it made its sombre way along Dublin's quays with a ship awaiting to take his remains to England. Smyth, on the other hand, was to be interred in Banbridge. Dublin Brigade members were being deployed in small units to assassinate Tudor and Greenwood from a succession of vantage points. IRA Intelligence officers were also dispersed along the route. However, the job was called off when news then arrived that neither target would be attending the procession. Most of the officers in Talbot Street then departed to recall their men, leaving Clancy and McKee behind.

Just minutes later, shortly after noon, Seán Brunswick, of the 1st Battalion, arrived breathless at the outfitters and informed both officers of the failed Phibsboro ambush. He added that Auxiliaries had just surrounded the Mater Hospital, which he had passed on his way, in their search for Dan Breen and Seán Treacy. Clancy ordered Brunswick to position a man at the hospital to observe developments and to report back him every fifteen minutes with updates. Brunswick then warned McKee and Clancy that the shop was being monitored. This was nothing new, nonetheless he described the watcher's appearance to them. He left and subsequently instructed Volunteer Bernard Ryan to keep his eye on the hospital, others, summoned by Byrne, soon discreetly reinforced Ryan.

McKee later sent word to brigade officers to prepare their men for a different job. Word was sent to Paddy Daly to report to 94 Talbot Street, positioned on the street's southern side between Gardiner Street and Marlborough Street.

Daly arrived at 3 p.m. followed by Tom Keogh and Joe Leonard. They were told of the enemy search still under way in the Mater and instructed to stay local and have the rest of the Squad on standby in case Breen's whereabouts was discovered. A short while later Seán Treacy arrived by bicycle, oblivious to the presence of the watcher spoken of by Brunswick – Sgt Francis Christian – a British intelligence operative. But Christian recognised Treacy. He quickly telephoned Major Frank Carew at Dublin Castle. The major was equally quick to action; one officer, Lt Gilbert Price, and twenty other ranks from the 1st Lancashire Fusiliers were rapidly detailed to two lorries backed up by a formidable twin-turret Peerless armoured car. Talbot Street was to be raided. Troops, operating on continuous rotational alerts, were quickly briefed. Vehicles, in a similar state of constant readiness, were mounted. Christian remained in Talbot Street ready to telephone again of further developments, huddling under his civilian overcoat as a cold wind blew and a shower of rain pelted down. He was seen several times by Brunswick as the IRA man updated McKee and Clancy inside the outfitters.

At 3.30 p.m. Paddy Daly tried to convince Treacy to join himself and the other two elsewhere for dinner. Treacy declined, citing business with McKee. The others tried to persuade him with the lure of a nice meal and hot tea, but they eventually left him alone; it was a decision they would soon regret.

Just before 4 p.m., the two Castle lorries and armoured car turned into North Earl Street from Sackville Street. The rain had stopped. 94 Talbot Street was 200 yards to their front and right. A sudden alarming shout of 'Raid!' from the street brought McKee rushing to the shop's doorway from where he glanced left and saw the enemy vehicles speeding from Nelson's Pillar. He shouted back inside: 'They're coming!' Get out!'[28] McKee and Clancy had a well-rehearsed plan. McKee stepped casually away from the building, mingling quickly with pedestrians. Clancy ensured nothing incriminating was lying around, then dashed out the back, calling Treacy to follow. Moments later, the three military vehicles screeched and skidded to a halt on the road's opposite side.

Seán Treacy had other plans. Fearing capture – a fate he had professed he would prefer death to – he rushed out the front reaching for his handgun just as soldiers were forming a cordon, but accidentally mounted McKee's bicycle, too large for him, instead of his own. He stumbled, providing time for Sgt Christian to rush in and wrench him from it. Both men grappled viciously for their lives until Christian, a champion boxer, began to overpower Treacy. Then, two shots rang out. Christian's face changed suddenly from a fierce scowl to a confused look of sudden deflation, disbelief, and terror. Two bullets had just ripped through his torso. He went limp.

KILLING AT ITS VERY EXTREME

Lt Price then opened fire at Treacy with his revolver, but Treacy's aimed response was sharper and Price fell dead. Civilians scattered for safety. Shopkeepers crouched behind counters. Office workers in upper floors distanced themselves from windows; others, unable to resist, glanced out at the spectacle. Then the armoured car suddenly spewed fire from one of its Hotchkiss machine guns, its distinctive hissing echoes reverberating. A succession of rapid bursts spat redhot .303 rounds at Treacy, killing him instantly. Also struck were fifteen-year-old messenger boy Peter Carroll and fifty-seven-year-old Joseph Cunningham, the latter knocked from his bicycle as bullets cut through him like a scythe.[29] A policeman was also shot through the arm.

By now the military cordon had widened following the arrival of army reinforcements. Seán Brunswick had been returning to No. 94 – being ransacked – with another update when he became trapped within the cordon. Having taken cover from the machine gun fire, and emerged as their echoes faded, he saw three men sprawled on the footpath: Christian, Price and Treacy.[30]

Brunswick observed a number of civilians approach a recently arrived army officer, claiming to be ambulance men and seeking permission to assist the wounded. The officer approved. Brunswick availed of the opportunity, presenting as a medical student. Christian was moaning desperately in a pool of blood on the wet pavement as Brunswick passed him and went straight to Treacy, clearly dead, with blood all over his face from a gaping head wound.[31]

The bodies of Seán Treacy and Lt Price outside Spiedl's Butchers in Talbot Street. (*Courtesy of Mercier Archive*)

With no time to waste, he quickly searched his pockets. He found ammunition, pens, dispatches and – most importantly – a field message book.³² He sneaked them into his own pockets.

Soon the crowds started to return. Treacy's body was picked up and hauled into the back of a lorry, thrown to its wooden floor like a butchered animal carcass. A recently arrived movie cameraman filmed it. His and Lt Price's

British soldiers and civilians carrying Seán Treacy's body (*Courtesy of Mercier Archive*)

British soldiers lifting Seán Treacy's body into a lorry.
(*Courtesy of Mercier Archive*)

KILLING AT ITS VERY EXTREME

Talbot Street on 14 October 1920, following the shooting of Seán Treacy, Sergeant Christian, Lieutenant Price and two civilians, including a fifteen-year-old messenger boy. (*Courtesy of Mercier Archive*)

Outside Peadar Clancy's Republican Outfitters on the day of the shootings. (*Courtesy of Mercier Archive*)

bodies were then driven to Dublin Castle. Sgt Christian was rushed to King George V Hospital. He survived. Both machine gunned civilians died soon afterwards, while the wounded policeman needed his arm amputated, but survived.

Meanwhile, seventeen-year-old 2nd Battalion Volunteer Charlie Dalton was among those watching the Mater Hospital as soldiers and Auxiliaries came and went. McKee soon joined them, looking subdued and pensive at the sight of another armoured car. Dalton approached and asked him if they were to attack them. McKee replied: 'I am afraid we can do nothing now. I cannot allow the men to throw away their lives, and if only the armoured cars will go away we will get a chance'.³³ He then broke the news of Seán Treacy's death and his own narrow escape. Word filtered through the ranks of those keeping watch, prompting calls for enemy blood as Auxiliaries began departing the hospital looking satisfied – they had discovered the body of a badly wounded man in the hospital morgue and thought it was Breen. McKee ordered his men to restrain themselves as the enemy drove away.

That evening in Dublin Castle David Neligan noticed Col Winter and several army officers stood around the back of the covered lorry recently returned from Talbot Street. Neligan peered under the waterproof cover and saw two corpses. Winter rasped: 'That is Treacy and one of my men'.³⁴ He added that, to be sure, they would soon have someone up from Tipperary to identify Treacy and Breen's bodies, still under the impression that Breen's remains were by safely in King George V Hospital. Treacy's and Lt Price's bodies were soon transported there.

Dick McKee was vexed by the presence of British armoured cars in the city. There was little he or his men could do against them. Here two twin-turret armoured cars are pictured together in the distance in Kildare Street during a raid. To their front is a military lorry carrying a 60 centimetre searchlight.
(*Courtesy of Mercier Archive*)

A British officer poses next to an Austin armoured car.
(*Courtesy of Mercier Archive*)

17

INCREASED BRITISH PRESSURE AND PROPAGANDA DISASTERS

'Give my love to the boys in the company'

Two days after Col Winter had summoned them, Det. Sgt Daniel Roche and Det. Const. Fitzmaurice of the Tipperary RIC arrived in Dublin Castle. Unfortunately for them, David Neligan was detailed to escort them to King George V Hospital to identify Treacy's remains, as well as those they still thought were Breen's – but were actually Matt Furlong's, his remains having since been transported there. Roche identified Treacy's body as soon as he saw it, but looking at Furlong, sneered: 'That is not Breen, I would know his bulldog face anywhere'.[1]

When this information was relayed to Col Winter he requested that Roche and Fitzmaurice remain in Dublin and trawl the city's hospitals for Breen. Meanwhile, Neligan contacted Liam Tobin and informed him of this development, and also that he was due to meet Roche the following day at lunchtime. Tobin set out to ensure that Roche, in particular, would not be breathing during his return journey to Tipperary. That night, 16 October, as Seán Treacy's remains were moved to the pro cathedral, four miles away in Rathgar a conclave of senior IRA personnel and police spies took place in Julia O'Donovan's home.

However, there was still more killing to be done on the British side. At 2 a.m. the following morning, sixty-year-old locksmith Peter O'Carroll was shot dead in his shop premises in 92 Manor Street, above which was his home. O'Carroll had, for several years, been employing his shop as a weapons hub and three of his four sons, Liam, Michael and Seán, were 1st Battalion Volunteers.

Just before 2 a.m. both ends of Manor Street had been sealed off by the military.[2] With the area secured, there was a knock on O'Carroll's door. When he answered several soldiers shoved him into his shop and began interrogating him, demanding to know where his sons were. O'Carroll, speaking from beneath a thick hanging moustache, refused to answer despite repeated threats. He was shot in the head. His wife and twelve-year-old son Gerard, upstairs, never heard the muffled shot, and eventually found the body in a pool of blood after the soldiers had departed with a card attached to it saying: 'Spies beware, IRA'.[3] O'Carroll was the second victim of Dublin Castle within a month to be shot in his pyjamas. Such pitiless gestures were soon to be repaid by the IRA – with interest.

However, his killer, clearly attempting to mask the assassination as a result of IRA in-fighting – the strategy previously castigated by Arthur Griffith – had been easy to identify, owing to a detailed description provided by Mrs O'Carroll afterwards; a tall well-spoken officer, walking with a pronounced limp, a thin moustache and dimpled chin had recently been making direct threats against her husband in front of her. It was Capt. Lee Hardy.

Sunday 17 October saw the grieving O'Carroll family embroiled in a struggle to see that a public inquiry was held into Peter's killing. Michael Staines, a council alderman, called an urgent meeting of Dublin Corporation and demanded the city coroner took charge, only to be ignored by the authorities who pressed for a military inquiry.[4] Later, when policemen called to the Manor Street premises requesting family members to identify the body at the nearby Richmond Hospital, they refused – not recognising the military's jurisdiction.

Matters escalated. Twelve-year-old Gerard was later seized by the police and brought to the hospital.[5] When Mrs O'Carroll got wind of this, she and several locals beat the police to the hospital's huge metal gates and a fracas broke out. The police were joined by army officers who insisted that they could not release Peter's body for burial without formal identification by the family, adding that they were only there to ensure justice. Mrs O'Carroll erupted, accusing the military of operating their own type of justice – sealing off streets to facilitate murder; worse, with the forged note left on the body, they had 'maligned the living and defamed the dead'.[6] Later that evening, Peter's three Volunteer sons and several A Company comrades held up the hospital guard at pistol point and retrieved the body, only to be told that a directive had just been received there to hand it over anyway.

That Sunday morning David Neligan had received a note from Liam

Tobin, written by Michael Collins. The note said: 'Concentrate on Hardy'.[7] Neligan then also received instructions from Tobin that he was to rendezvous with Frank Thornton at Capel Street's adjacent quayside before his scheduled lunchtime meeting with Dets Roche and Fitzmaurice.

When they met just before lunchtime Thornton was accompanied by Charlie Dalton. Thornton told Neligan that Roche and Fitzmaurice were to be shot there and then. Hearing this, Neligan informed the pair that both detectives were having lunch in the nearby Ormond Hotel. They would soon be leaving to continue trawling hospitals. Thornton instructed Neligan to signal them by blowing his nose when he met with them and to do his best to point out Roche – their priority. Neligan noticed four men hanging around on the corner of Capel Street and Grattan Bridge.

Just then, Neligan turned to see Roche and Fitzmaurice walking from the hotel's front door towards him. Thornton and Dalton made themselves scarce, joining the Squad nearby. Neligan approached and spoke to the RIC men. Thornton, Dalton, Joe Dolan, Vinny Byrne, Jim Slattery and Tom Keogh, then looked on as Neligan blew his nose; the first signal – these were the men.

Neligan and his two police colleagues strolled to the corner of Capel Street and Ormond Quay. Then, just as they turned left into Capel Street building works forced the three to walk single file on the pavement, shadowed from the road's opposite side by the closing four-man Squad; Thornton and Dalton had stayed put. This presented Neligan with the opportunity to hold back a few paces and point out Roche, his burly figure just ahead of him. Dolan let them pass the protruding scaffolding and stepped ahead of his following Squad accomplices while they themselves crossed the road in pursuit. At the corner of Strand Street, Dolan levelled his pistol at Roche. Keogh and Slattery were just behind.

Dolan fired first, but missed. Neligan, Fitzmaurice and Roche scattered with the loud cracks. Dolan fired again at Roche who eventually collapsed mid-sprint, wounded. Nearby a young girl and an elderly man were also hit by Dolan's ragged fire. Keogh and Slattery were more clinical, finishing Roche off with a shot each as he struggled like a hooked fish, writhing and twisting in anguish. Det. Const. Fitzmaurice raced away up Capel Street. The Squad pursued him but were outrun.[8]

Neligan vanished into the side-streets before returning on foot to Dublin Castle, as did Fitzmaurice. There, Neligan faced questioning from his superiors, having been seen by Fitzmaurice speaking to suspicious-looking men before the shooting. Neligan, concealing his sudden anxiety, protested innocence and expressed indignation at such conjecture. He insisted that he had merely spoken to a passer-by who had been awaiting a Phoenix Park tram. It was almost a fatal mistake; the tram for the park ran on the river's opposite side. Nonetheless, luck was on Neligan's side – the matter went no further.

Civilians being searched for arms in Dublin. As well as raids, street searches for weapons and incriminating documents were, at this point, rampant in the capital. (*Courtesy of Mercier Archive*)

A civilian is questioned by British soldiers in a Dublin Park. (*Courtesy of Mercier Archive*)

Seán Treacy's death had sent a shockwave through the IRA leadership, but Sgt Roche's subsequent killing sent a resounding message to the RIC similar to that conveyed by force to DMP's G-Division whose members refused to assist in the continued search for Dan Breen. No RIC officer took Roche's place.

The following day, Monday 18 October, Treacy's remains were buried

A British officer searches a civilian for arms. (*Courtesy of Mercier Archive*)

Auxiliaries in Westland Row train station.
(Courtesy of Kilmainham Gaol Museum OPW, 19PC-1B51-03)

in Kilfeacle Cemetery in Tipperary. Tens of thousands attended his funeral procession. The atmosphere was volatile, with scuffles breaking out between mourners and the police and some military units. Notably, however, one army unit stood to attention and presented arms in salute as his remains, held within a Tricolour-draped coffin, had passed them on its way from Limerick Junction train station to a waiting hearse.[9]

Treacy's funeral took place the day after General Macready advised the British cabinet that unrelenting reprisals in Ireland needed to be constrained, again citing martial law as the only alternative. The prime minister expressed willingness to accede to this, but – fearing too much of a backlash from the powerful Irish-American lobby in Washington – not before that year's looming American presidential elections were concluded.[10]

It was also the day after Michael Fitzgerald died on hunger strike in Cork Gaol. His sacrifice was, however, soon to be eclipsed.

British soldiers are brought to attention by their officer in front rendering a salute as Michael Fitzgerald's remains are removed from St Peter and Paul's church in Cork for burial following his death after a sixty-seven-day hunger strike. *(Courtesy of Mercier Archive)*

***

In Dublin, military raids were taking place at a rate of ten-per-day. Col Winter was busily laying the groundwork for a Central Raid Bureau (CRB) to ratchet up the pressure, employing Scotland Yard screened clerical staff to circumvent enemy infiltration.[11] Col Winter aggressively sought 'hot' intelligence from recently captured prisoners and documents for which counter-measures could be rapidly enacted after the documents and information were passed to the bureau.[12] As a consequence of the growing resistance to raids, epitomised at Fernside and Talbot Street, and increased levels of ingenuity in arms and document concealment, raiding parties were increased in size on 19 October from twelve to twenty men and ordered to anticipate resistance, particularly from snipers.[13]

Ironically, the military frequently found themselves welcomed during such raids by householders relieved not to be visited instead by the Black and Tans or Auxiliaries. IRA members found themselves harried from pillar to post, forced into billets with little in the way of comfort and facilities as winter approached. Volunteers in North County Dublin, the area flush with Black and Tans, were often forced to billet in barns or improvised dug outs.[14]

Raiding parties themselves were frequently horrified at the filthy conditions in city tenements; sometimes finding a dozen people sharing a single room and five or six to a bed. Troops, hardened by trench warfare, frequently picked up infections from trawling through such unfamiliar squalor.[15] Nonetheless, infections of the far more detrimental kind were being administered with increasing regularity by raiding parties on unfortunate female victims, subjected to sexual assault and rape by some troops with little to fear in the way of consequence owing to, among other factors, the terrible stigma bestowed upon victims, a circumstance seen as advantageous not only by the British military.

Meanwhile, back-channel communications were once again in play between both warring sides. Patrick Moylett, a forty-two-year-old senior IRB figure with strong London business connections, was dispatched in early October by Arthur Griffith to contact John Steele, a journalist colleague of Carl Ackerman's. Steele was the London correspondent for the *Chicago Tribune*. He now acted as a go-between.

Moylett was a major facilitator of IRA arms imports, employing sheds in Sheriff Street purchased by the 'Irish Shipping and Trading Company' of which he was a director. The business was, astonishingly, the Irish agent for Nobel Explosives. His warehouse regularly received concealed shipments of Russian rifles and Czech pistols. Cathal Brugha was notified of each consignment before their subsequent distribution. The company kept offices in 19 Eustace Street and 7 Fleet Street.[16]

Moylett eventually took a chance when the opportunity presented itself by speaking with Herbert A. L. Fisher at the Foreign Office in 15–16 Downing Street. Despite fearing being perceived as a double agent if spotted on his way there, he nevertheless enjoyed a revealing joust with Fisher, Liberal Minister for Education and chairman of the Cabinet Committee for Ireland.[17] Fisher – having initially been parried by Moylett over accusations of murder gangs with the retort that the British were also employing them – had asked about

INCREASED BRITISH PRESSURE AND PROPAGANDA DISASTERS

Moylett's commitment to a republic, seeking room for negotiation. Moylett had replied metaphorically that as a self-respecting fisherman, he would not boast of catching a trout, or even a dozen trout, if he had set out to land a salmon. Fisher's response: 'What about a salmon trout?' floored him momentarily until he replied that it would be better than a trout, but eventually insisting: 'we will fish until we get the salmon'.[18] In other words, they would hold out for a republic.

Moylett's conclusion upon initially reporting back to Griffith in Dublin on 15 October had been that if the British were not as hard up as Sinn Féin to discuss a settlement he would not have been entertained. These developments were discussed during a Dáil session over the next couple of days which marked the end of Sinn Féin meetings for the time being; the risk of enemy raids too high.

Just days later, on 20 October, adjacent to Phoenix Park, Kevin Barry's family and friends, including his sister Katherine, arrived at Marlborough barracks and awaited the start of his long-anticipated court martial. The barracks and surrounding area teemed with military. At 10 a.m. the court doors opened, and the family entered with the defence solicitor, Seán Woods. At an elevated table in front sat ten court-martial officers. The presiding officer, fifty-one-year-old Brigadier General Cranley Charlton Onslow of the 25th Provisional Brigade, sat in the centre with officers on either side. The family took their seats and waited anxiously. On the North Circular Road a heavily escorted armoured transport bringing Barry to the court had broken down and a replacement had been dispatched. Barry was to be tried under ROIA, with a sentence of hanging if convicted.

Katherine Barry's employer, Mr E. Aston, was a Freemason, and had managed to petition Hamar Greenwood, a fellow Mason, facilitated by Masonic intermediaries. Aston had ridiculed the charge against Barry of being a murderer, protesting that he was only a child. Greenwood, however, had insisted: 'He may be a child in years, but he is a long time mixed up with that crowd'.[19]

Barry entered the courtroom at 10.45 a.m. surrounded by his military escort, smiling at his family. His smile disappeared when he saw the 'brass-hat' senior officers presiding. As soon as he sat his lawyer requested an adjournment, pleading that the case had been handed to him at the last minute without adequate time to prepare his client's defence. General Onslow agreed. Barry scowled.

When court eventually resumed Barry's charges were read out; three counts of murder over the deaths of Private Marshall Whitehead and his two comrades. Then, the judge advocate officer contended that despite the fact that the accused had been carrying a .38 calibre pistol and the bullet removed from Whitehead's body was a .45, he was nonetheless one of the ambushers; therefore, as a party to the murders he was liable to be charged for them.

Barry's turn to address proceedings was met with a tense pause, following which he declared dismissively: 'As a soldier of the Irish Republic, I refuse to recognise the court'.[20] This prompted General Onslow to emphasise to him the gravity of his situation. In response, Barry nonchalantly pulled out a copy of the previous day's *Evening Telegraph* newspaper and began reading it.

Woods then addressed the court again, explaining officially that his client refused to recognise the court, meaning he could no longer act for him. He asked, however, to be allowed to remain as a family friend. This was agreed to. He then sat quietly with Barry's family.

Military witnesses were brought in one by one to present testimony. Following each, Onslow asked Barry if he had any questions for them, to be told 'no' each time. The process continued until Barry eventually lost his patience and protested: 'I don't recognise the court. I have no interest in what anybody says here. You are only wasting your time asking me'. Onslow's face reddened, before he retorted: 'It is my duty to ask you. I think as a soldier you can appreciate that'.[21] The unexpected acknowledgement of this status disarmed Barry. Remaining defiant, but now respectful, he answered: 'Righto (*sic*). If it facilitates you, I have no questions'.[22] The court then broke for lunch. When it reconvened Mr Aston spoke at length on Barry's character. Following this, the general adjourned proceedings, announcing that Barry's sentence would be promulgated in due course. He was then escorted back to Mountjoy Prison.

At 8 p.m. a district courts-martial officer entered Barry's cell. Pausing momentarily, he then read Barry his sentence: 'You, Kevin Barry, have been found guilty of murder, and sentenced to death by hanging'. He then asked him if he understood. Barry replied 'yes'. The cell door was closed and locked.

20 October was also the day Terence MacSwiney slipped into a coma in Brixton Prison. Tensions were already high in England's capital following violent clashes between tens of thousands of protesting miners, trade unionists, and unemployed activists, many calling for revolution. Now it escalated further.

INCREASED BRITISH PRESSURE AND PROPAGANDA DISASTERS

This growing volatility and industrial unrest was not wasted on senior players in Irish separatism. Arthur Griffith appealed in the *Irish Bulletin* that day for the civilised world to rally behind appeals for mercy for Kevin Barry, while Erskine Childers began to pen a series of similar letters for the British press, employing the opportunity to also castigate the crown over the continuing hunger strikes. Childers also took the opportunity to highlight again the continuing reprisals; the same month had already seen further such atrocities in Roscommon, Galway, Clare, Tipperary, and Kerry. In Kerry, however, far worse was still to come.

Then, on 25 October, Terence MacSwiney's seventy-four-day ordeal ended with his death at 5.40 a.m. in Brixton. It was also the day twenty-five-year-old

Terence MacSwiney's coffin in Southwark cathedral.
(*Courtesy of Mercier Archive*)

MacSwiney's huge funeral procession in London, 28 October 1920.
(*Courtesy of Mercier Archive*)

Joseph Murphy joined his comrades in death following his own seventy-six-day fast in Cork. Murphy's passing, like Michael Fitzgerald's, was completely overshadowed by events in London.

MacSwiney's demise was met with reverence for his sacrifice from newspapers in Ireland, Britain and throughout the world. From all nationalities, creeds and races there was praise, admiration and condemnation of Britain for portraying a stance of callous disregard for him and his cause. A thirty-year-old kitchen hand from Indo-China working in London, driven to tears by MacSwiney's sacrifice wrote: 'A nation that has such citizens will never surrender'. His name was Ho Chi Minh. Huge processions took place in Dublin where Cumann na mBan were out in force, among them Rose McNamara, feeling indignation to match that when she had heard the dawn volleys over four years earlier from Kilmainham Gaol's Stonebreaker's Yard during the 1916 executions. Winston Churchill later spoke of MacSwiney, saying: 'He was a brave man! They are a fine people, we cannot afford to lose them. We shall be shaking hands together in three months'.[23]

Meanwhile, back in Dublin on Thursday 28 October, Dick McKee had arranged for an affidavit to be taken from Kevin Barry, detailing his brutal treatment following his capture. Kathleen Barry, Dr Myles Keogh, and Seán Woods, there to obtain it, were ushered into Mountjoy Prison's boardroom where Barry sat flanked by two Auxiliaries. As the affidavit was then taken the Auxiliaries surprised Barry and the others by assisting him with phrasing military terms, as well as – less astonishingly – displaying a keen interest in the ambush. They betrayed no surprise at Barry's sworn allegations of his mistreatment.

Later, as Barry sat reflecting in his cell, comforted by shouts in support from his wing-mates, the same courts-martial officer as before returned with news that his death sentence had been confirmed. This triggered a series of appeals from, among others, Dublin's archbishop and lord mayor. These were to fall on deaf ears nonetheless.

Protestations regarding Barry's youth were deflected with references to the similar youth of the soldiers slain at the Monk's Bakery ambush. RIC Chief Insp. Smith threatened to resign if Barry was reprieved. Given that Smith was by now little more than a figurehead General Macready's insistence that the execution went ahead carried more weight. Macready feared uncontrollable military reprisals in the event of a reprieve. Barry was the first prisoner to be convicted of murder under ROIA.

INCREASED BRITISH PRESSURE AND PROPAGANDA DISASTERS

Commuting his sentence, in Macready's mind, would be received with similar disdain by loyal police and soldiers as the 'surrender' to the Mountjoy hunger strikers in April; he reckoned it would push them over the edge. However, clemency appeals also came from Westminster. Prominent Labour Party member J. H. Thomas spoke of a brave, educated and much loved boy. He then produced Barry's recently sworn affidavit, read from it, and then, finally, echoing Macready in July, laid the blame for all Ireland's recent tribulations on Ulster's resistance to Home Rule since 1914.

Patrick Moylett had been back in London for several days conducting further high-level talks by the time Terence MacSwiney's remains were taken on 28 October for the first part of their final journey from Brixton to Euston train station – bound for Holyhead, then Dublin, and finally Cork – followed by a procession of mourners one-and-a-half miles long, some in full Volunteer uniforms. Metropolitan police officers wearing black gloves saluted the coffin on its way through London's packed streets.[24]

General Macready anticipated a different reaction in Dublin, however, and unexpectedly decreed that the remains were not to be landed there, fearing 'rioting on a scale difficult to foresee', but brought directly instead to Cork.[25] Scuffles broke out that night in Holyhead as mourners, receiving the news, reacted angrily. They opted to cross to Dublin themselves regardless, knowing the public indignation that would follow their arrival the following morning without MacSwiney's remains would only further his, and Ireland's, cause. MacSwiney was then transported to Cork on board the *Rathmore*.[26]

Dublin was in mourning the following day, as was most of the country, with shops and businesses closed in respect and the city silent save for the noises of ramped-up military and Auxiliary patrols. Following a requiem mass in the pro cathedral a huge procession made its way along Dublin's quays towards Kingsbridge station, part of the original planned route for the late lord mayor's final journey, where there were clashes with the military. Cumann na mBan at one point, through sheer weight of numbers, forced an army formation back from Capel Street Bridge when they tried to interrupt the procession.[27]

On Friday 29 October Patrick Moylett set off for Dublin with a letter from Lloyd George asking if the Dáil could nominate three or four men to speak on its behalf if a conference to discuss peace terms could be arranged. MacSwiney's funeral had had a profound effect on prominent Westminster politicians who called out for dialogue.²⁸ Moylett had suggested posting the letter; Lloyd George, however, insisted on Moylett bringing it himself to ensure safe delivery. When Griffith saw it two days later he broke down in tears of joy; the letter represented a tacit acknowledgement by the prime minister of the Dáil. Moylett had previously pointed out to his Westminster counterparts that recognition of Dáil Éireann would be a prerequisite to any such talks. Griffith was overcome. When they later spoke of potential delegates Michael Collins was proposed. Moylett suggested otherwise, citing Collins as being too impulsive, but added additionally that Collins had a reputation as an inflexible hardliner, and that this could be used to their advantage.²⁹

***

That same day, Sunday 31 October, Katherine Barry, her brother, Michael, and their mother, Mary, arrived at Mountjoy Prison for what would be their last visit with Kevin. Entering the prison – surrounded by thousands of protesters – they found the pathways swarming with soldiers and Black and Tans, the latter brought into the city as added protection in case of a rescue attempt. Inside the main reception Auxiliaries were present in force.

The previous day had seen Lloyd George assure Mr Aston, Katherine's employer, who had travelled to see the prime minister on her behalf, that he would grant her brother a last-minute reprieve. Katherine, later hearing this, was sceptical. She was right to be; during a subsequent discourse, Field Marshal Wilson had warned Lloyd George that he could not be responsible for the inevitable breakdown of discipline within the army if Barry was reprieved. Barry would face the hangman.

The family were then brought to the boardroom where Kevin waited again with his two Auxiliary guards. Five armed warders provided extra security. The family took their seats, lost for words initially until their reticence was punctuated with news

Three Auxiliaries in Mountjoy Prison. (*Courtesy of Kilmainham Gaol Museum OPW, KMGLM 2010.0019*)

of visits Kevin had received from supportive fellow students. Conversation then began to flow until, eventually, the deputy governor, Mr Meehan, stepped in and regretfully told them their time was up. Barry's mother struggled to maintain composure as they said their farewells. Finally, Kevin kissed his sister goodbye, smiled, and said: 'Give my love to the boys in the company'.[30] The family turned for one last departing look, Barry stood straight and saluted.

Fr Albert visited the condemned man after the family had walked sorrowfully away from his cell. Afterwards he left the prison to be swamped by the huge crowds gathered in protest and in prayer; the latter not just for Barry, but also for Terence MacSwiney – buried in Cork that same day. The Barry family remained with them. Fr Albert heralded to them that Kevin was in good spirits and that he had given him a message for them; a simple one: 'Hold on and stick to the Republic'.[31]

Jack Plunkett had been given orders by Dick McKee to prepare an explosive mine earlier that day at a dump in Denzille Lane. He and several others had begun fabricating a 200-pound device to blow up a huge section of Mountjoy's outer wall. Following this, Volunteers led by McKee himself, Tom Ennis, Tom Keogh, Frank Flood and several others, planned to storm in and rescue him – they were desperate to save him.[32] The plan was eventually called off, however; it was feared that Barry would be killed 'while attempting to escape' along with the rescue party, but more importantly, many civilians.[33]

Meanwhile, Barry's mother still held out hope for a last-minute reprieve. Michael Collins had commented pessimistically on the unlikely prospect of Barry getting out alive with such a rescue, declaring: 'If Kevin is to be killed, it should not be through any act of ours'. Collins felt acute despondency for Barry's fate, which followed him to a meeting with Griffith and Moylett that night. It added to the melancholy that had beset him with the death of the hunger strikers, as well as the untimely passing of Det. Joe Cavanagh from an embolism the previous week.

The three met less than a mile from the prison in 3 Mountjoy Square to discuss Lloyd George's recent proposal. Collins, despite his despondency, expressed satisfaction at Moylett's work. Their conversation then veered between Barry's imminent execution and divisions within Irish factions in the USA and recent criticisms there of proposed solutions articulated by De Valera; namely that Ireland could bear a similar relationship with Britain as the USA to Cuba under the Monroe Doctrine – effectively a protectorate. Collins was highly critical of De Valera. Griffith insisted, however, that they knew their president better than those opposing him in America and that they would stand by him.[34] Soon afterwards Moylett would return to London for more talks.

***

On Monday 1 November 1920 Dublin city was enveloped in an atmosphere of oppressive silence in anticipation of the first execution of an Irish republican prisoner by the crown since 1916. Thousands of civilians were already gathered again outside Mountjoy Prison. As the church bells began to sound out for 7 a.m. on 'All Saint's Day' Canon John Waters of the Holy Cross College, and a priest, Fr MacMahon, entered Kevin Barry's cell and said mass with him. As they murmured in prayer the cell door's spyhole went ominously dark. An eye – that of forty-six-year-old John Ellis, a hangman brought from England to perform the execution – looked through at the prisoner. Within seconds Ellis had the information he needed – the condemned man's size and approximate weight.

Shortly before 8 a.m., with Barry sitting on an old stool, having knelt in prayer for the best part of an hour, his cell door opened, a tall, well-dressed man – the executioner's assistant – stepped inside and asked Barry to stand and hold out his hands. Barry complied. The assistant then tied them behind Barry's back, trying to reassure him with the words: 'I won't hurt you'.[35] Canon Waters had attended several hangings up to this point, but had never heard the condemned man being spoken to like this before.

They walked slowly out of the cell, along a succession of silent prison corridors with Canon Waters and Fr MacMahon on either side of Barry, until they arrived at the prison's hang-room where a hood was placed over Barry's head. Guards stood silently around inside as they then entered. The scaffold stood before them, surrounded by whitewashed walls and lit

Kevin Barry, the first republican prisoner to be executed in Dublin since May 1916. He was convicted of murder following the deaths of the first British soldiers in action in Dublin since the Rising (*Courtesy of Kilmainham Gaol Museum OPW, 19PD-1A17-26*)

INCREASED BRITISH PRESSURE AND PROPAGANDA DISASTERS

up by skylights in the room's centre with the hanging rope dangling from its horizontal beam. Barry and the clergymen were led up on to a creaking wooden floor just under the rope.

At this point Executioner Ellis stood behind Barry and, in a sudden single move, fixed the rope in place around his neck, ensuring the right amount of slack in the noose. He then positioned Barry at the centre of a trap door already beneath his feet. The room was silent apart from the muttered hum of prayers. Ellis then stepped away, then, from behind a rail, drew back a safety bolt before reaching for a lever and pulling on it. The lever, attached to a hinge mechanism in the wooden floor, opened the trapdoor suddenly with a loud mechanical clunk, followed instantaneously by the dull snap of the rope breaking Barry's fall, and his neck and spinal cord, ending his life.

The prison bell tolled as Barry's body, following confirmation of his death, was then carried out to the prison garden for burial. Four warders carried a recently made coffin from the nearby prison workshop. Barry's body was placed in the coffin as a small procession of warders and clergymen made their way towards the freshly dug grave to pay respects. British soldiers on duty there, their weapons secured momentarily elsewhere, joined them. Prison inmates strained to see the sad procession from overlooking cell windows. A gloom descended. No one spoke. The North Circular Road outside the prison was also silent, then, thousands took to their knees once again in prayer. A note was placed on the prison gate announcing Barry's execution.

Mark Sturgis wrote in his diary that day: 'Barry hanged this morning in Mountjoy. Would have been better to have shot him as a rebel after Drumhead Court Martial at the time rather than hanging him as a murderer after a month.'[36] The *Irish Independent* carried a far more favourable description of Barry as a brave young man who had not flinched in the face of death.

***

Later that day, events in the country saw Britain's plummeting international profile sink to new depths when Ellen Quinn, a twenty-four-year-old mother of three, was shot dead by Black and Tans in Gort, Co. Galway, while she held one of her children in her arms. Then, Tralee was next.

With a population of 10,000, the town was subjected to an onslaught by Black and Tans and Auxiliaries that resulted in a siege. Following several shootings of police and the abductions of two more who were never seen again, they went berserk. They fired into crowds of church goers, set fire to several premises and the town hall, and ordered all businesses and public buildings, including schools, closed until the missing RIC men were found. Rumours abounded that the policemen had been shot and their bodies incinerated in a gas furnace.

The subsequent siege drew international press reporters and made front page news throughout the world. A strict curfew was enforced. Inevitably, civilians were forced to venture outside, resulting in numerous shootings. Amid reports of near starvation in the town Hamar Greenwood ordered the siege lifted on 9 November when the British army were sent in in force to do so. This was the same day that Lloyd George announced in London's Guildhall while toasting the Auxiliaries: 'We have taken steps by which we have murder by the throat'.[37]

This propaganda disaster was then aggravated when the Auxiliaries in Dublin's Killiney filmed a staged ambush and tried to portray it as the first successfully filmed engagement with the IRA in which the Auxiliaries prevailed, dubbing it 'the Battle of Tralee' to coincide with recent skirmishing there. Republican propagandists successfully ridiculed it. Notably, events soon to materialise highlighted just how far removed from reality the film was in its depiction of an unprofessional IRA unit presenting easy pickings for Auxiliary cadets. Even more noteworthy was the pending IRA response to Lloyd George's boastful assertions in the Guildhall. He would soon regret speaking such words.

Ballinalee in Longford was successfully defended from a large force of RIC and Black and Tans on 4 November. Nearby Granard was not so lucky; it too burned, attacked following the killing of an RIC district inspector in the Greville Arms hotel, owned by the family of Kitty Kiernan, whose relationship with Michael Collins amounted to far more than the strong affections she had shared with Harry Boland. Collins, meanwhile, had his work cut out in Dublin; plans were being made by IRA Intelligence, GHQ, and the Dublin Brigade to shatter the British military establishment once and for all, as Dublin's War of Independence was about to reach unprecedented levels of brutality.

EPILOGUE

Bloody Sunday – 21 November 1920

'The Lord have mercy on your souls'

We proceeded into Holles St., into Merrion Square, and turned into Up. Mount St. When we came to No. 28, I detailed four or five men to keep guard outside. I then went to the hall door, along with Tom Ennis, and rang the bell. A servant girl opened the door. I asked her could I see Lieutenant Bennett or Lieutenant Aimes, at the same time jamming the door with my foot. As I entered the hall, I beckoned to the remainder of my men to follow. When inside, I asked the girl where did the two officers sleep. She replied: 'Lieutenant so-and-so sleeps in there', pointing to the front parlour, 'the other officer sleeps in the back room down there'. I detailed Tom Ennis to take the back room and said I would look after the other one.

I gently tried the handle to open the door, and found that it was locked. The servant then said to me: 'You can get in by the back parlour. The folding doors are open'. I said: 'Thank you'. I went into the back parlour, with Sean Doyle and Herbie Conroy each side of me. As I opened the folding doors, the officer, who was in bed, was in the act of going for his gun under his pillow. Doyle and myself dashed into the room, at the same time ordering him to put up his hands, which he did. Doyle dashed around by the side of the bed, and pulled a Colt.45 from beneath the pillow. Right behind us came Frank Saurin and he started collecting from papers, etc. which was his job. I remember looking into a drawer and seeing a Sinn Féin tie there and, if I am not mistaken, photographs of the 1916 leaders. I ordered the British officer to get out of the bed. He asked me what was going to happen and I replied: 'Ah, nothing'. I then ordered him to march in front of me.

As we were entering the back of the hall, I heard the hell of a row going on somewhere outside – very heavy revolver fire. My next surprise was hearing a ring on the door. The man covering the door looked at me, but did not speak a word. I said to him: 'Open the door', and in walked a British Tommy, a dispatch rider. Ordering him to put up his hands, which he did, I left him under guard in the hall. I marched my officer down to the back room where the other officer was. He was standing up in the bed, facing the wall. I ordered mine to do likewise. When the two of them were together, I said to myself 'The Lord have mercy on your souls!' I then opened fire with my Peter. They both fell dead.[1]

'This Irish St Bartholomew' as Sir Nevil Macready, commander of the British forces in Ireland, labelled Bloody Sunday morning, exemplifies the type of face to face killing at its very extreme.[2]

ENDNOTES

Prologue
1 Frank Henderson, Bureau of Military History Witness Statement (hereafter BMH WS) 821, p. 25.
2 *Ibid.*, p. 26.
3 Harry Colley, BMH WS 1687, p. 35.
4 *Ibid.*

1 New Leaders Emerge
1 The quote comes from the same source as footnote 15 in this chapter. All quotes at the beginning of subsequent chapters are taken from within that chapter.
2 Fianna: a militant nationalist youth organisation formed by Constance Markievicz and Bulmer Hobson in 1909. Cumann na mBan, translating as 'Women's Council', was founded in April 1914 as a women's republican organisation to operate in tandem with the Irish Volunteers.
3 During spring 1914 Ulster unionist leaders had conspired with Imperial Germany to procure and land thousands of weapons and armaments in Ulster to resist constitutional Home Rule, by force if necessary. A provisional government had lain in wait in case hostilities commenced.
4 Fr O'Flanagan frequently clashed with his clerical superiors over his political stance.
5 John F. Shouldice, BMH WS 679, p. 16.
6 Maryann Gialanella Valiulis, *Portrait of a Revolutionary General Richard Mulcahy*, p. 27.
7 The deeds of this building had been given to the Volunteers following the Rising.
8 Risteárd Mulcahy, *My Father, The General: Richard Mulcahy and the Military History of the Revolution*, p. 37.
9 Dominic Price, *We Bled Together: Michael Collins, The Squad and The Dublin Brigade*, p. 56.
10 The gaol also hosted a clandestine wedding between prominent Volunteer officer Diarmuid Lynch, incarcerated a month before McKee, and Kathleen Quinn.
11 Or *Kaiserschlacht*: Kaiser's Battle.
12 Over a million shells were fired into a 150-square-mile defensive and communication zone of the British lines in just five hours. It was the most concentrated barrage of the entire war.
13 A large part of this line consisted of the 36th Ulster Division, as well as the 16th Irish Division, both of which were effectively destroyed as fighting forces in spite of dauntless resistance. The rapidly advancing Germans, surging forward from thick clouds of fog and poison gas, and wearing gas-masks, fought with unprecedented aggression, employing 'Stormtrooper' tactics, using hand-grenades, sub-machine guns, flamethrowers, a handful of tanks, bayonets, and all backed up by further massed artillery strikes. Their supreme commander, General Erich Ludendorff, was desperate to break the deadlock before the vast numbers of recently arrived troops from the United States under General John J. Pershing, which had entered the war against them in April 1917, could take up their battle stations and tip the balance against Germany. They were also in a race against time – food and war materials were running out in Germany and her allies were in disarray.
14 David Lloyd George, *War Memoirs*, Vol. 5, p. 2669.
15 *Ibid.*, p. 2665.
16 Influenced by the recent arrival of the United States into the war given the huge Irish diaspora there.
17 The Earl of Longford and Thomas O'Neill, *Éamon de Valera*, p. 72.
18 This was not down to the fact that the party's vice-president was clergyman Michael

O'Flanagan. Their positioning was instead primarily down to the fact that, by 1918, the mutual grievances of church and nationalists in general over the repeated Home Rule debacles, the repressive British responses to the Rising, the pending prospect of partition, and the clergy's growing ambivalence towards the Great War – not to mention their repugnance at the imminent prospect of being compelled to participate in it – had done nothing to check this trend. Additionally, and pivotally, Sinn Féin were seen as a party with little interest in separating church and state.

19 Richard Holmes, *The Little Field Marshal: Sir John French*, p. 326.
20 21 April also saw the Volunteers lose another man. This time in Dublin when James Gallagher was accidentally shot during target practice with his company in Templeogue; this was just hours after adding his own name to the pledge. He died of shock and blood loss. His father, a Corkman, spoke at his funeral days later, stating that he was the first casualty in the new struggle for liberation, and asked people, therefore, not to sympathise.
21 In Belfast, dominated by unionists, potential strikers were warned that they would be locked out of their jobs if they participated. Most unionist employers saw resistance to conscription as treachery against those already fighting and dying in their droves in British Army uniforms, and there was plenty of hard-line support for this sentiment among the populace. In Derry, where the unionist influence was formidable but less prevalent than Belfast, the strike was dismissed as simply an increased prevalence of absenteeism.
22 Under a 'dual monarchy' each of the British Isles would have separate parliaments under the nominal sovereignty of the crown of England. The IPP had, under John Redmond, advocated enlistment in 1914 to fight in the Great War and had become viewed increasingly as a party of appeasement. This contrasted with the proven efficacy of the adoption of radically less compliant strategies, as proven in Ulster during the Home Rule Crisis of 1912–14 when Sir Edward Carson and James Craig's sabre-rattling and brinkmanship vis-a-vis the Ulster Covenant, subsequent gun-running, and threat of armed rebellion was seen to hold sway in seeing off Home Rule. This was also seen in the rest of Ireland after 1916, when it became clear that despite its failings, the Rising had, at the very least, placed nationalist Ireland's desire for independence – whatever degree that might be – back on the agendas of British politicians.
23 South Armagh in February, Waterford in March, and East Tyrone in April.
24 Seán McLoughlin, BMH WS 290, p. 41.

2 Planned Assassinations

1 In March 1914, several prominent British Army officers had threatened to resign or accept dismissal for refusing to obey commands to mobilise against the Ulster Volunteers who had threatened to support under arms a provisional government in Ulster against Home Rule. French had attached his name to a document pledging not to deploy the British Army against them if instructed to do so.
2 French had rigorously re-jigged Britain's home defences against invasion while simultaneously campaigning for the detachment of a specific force for home air defence.
3 Holmes, *The Little Field Marshal*, p. 335.
4 John Crowley, Donal Ó Drisceoil, Mike Murphy, John Borgonovo, *Atlas of the Irish Revolution*, p. 327.
5 Holmes, *The Little Field Marshal*, p. 338.
6 Joseph Good, BMH WS 388, p. 38.
7 Ibid., p. 39.
8 Ibid.
9 The City of Dublin Steam Packet Company provided round-the-clock service, originally with four twin-screw steamships named after each of Ireland's provinces. These boats were generally – up to that point, at least – considered fast enough to minimise their vulnerability to submarine attacks in the Irish Sea compared with some slower naval vessels. Unsuccessful U-boat attacks had been made. The mail boats were camouflaged and each carried a twelve-

ENDNOTES

pounder deck gun. Unfortunately six months after French's crossing, the tragic deaths of 565 passengers on board the RMS *Leinster* in one such attack proved that they were, nonetheless, still vulnerable to the submarine menace.

10 Holmes, *The Little Field Marshal*, p. 338.
11 Richard Bennett, *The Black and Tans*, p. 11.
12 Casement had been captured by the British, tried for treason and executed in Pentonville Prison in London on 3 August 1916, an occasion that further cemented anti-British sentiment in Ireland.
13 The Germans hoped, following contact with more senior Volunteer figures, to land arms at a later date and create an additional front for the British to contend with. This had, been a German initiative. On a strategic level, they were anticipating the isolation of Great Britain during their spring offensives by driving a wedge between her forces and her allies before neutralising them and then bringing Britain to terms. Therefore, the more unrest they could foster in Ireland – effectively Britain's 'back yard' – the better the possibility of facilitating this.
14 Holmes, *The Little Field Marshal*, p. 340.
15 Darrell Figgis, *Recollections of the Irish War*, p. 210.
16 Principally, Regulation 14B provided for 'Executive Detention' of enemies within the realm's borders.
17 T. Ryle Dwyer, *De Valera: The Man & The Myths*, p. 24.
18 Lorcan Collins, *Ireland's War of Independence 1919–21: The IRA's Guerrilla Campaign*, p. 50.
19 Cal McCarthy, *Cumann na mBan and the Irish Revolution*, p. 96.
20 *Ibid.*, p. 94.
21 Frank Henderson, BMH WS 821, p. 35.
22 Derek Molyneux and Darren Kelly, *When the Clock Struck in 1916: Close Quarter Combat in the Easter Rising*, p. 297.
23 Charles Townshend, *The British Campaign in Ireland 1919–1921: The Development of Political and Military Policies*, p. 18.
24 Frank Henderson, BMH WS 821, p. 35.
25 Joseph O'Connor, BMH WS 487, p. 9.
26 James L. O'Donovan, BMH WS 1713, p. 3.
27 Joseph Good, BMH WS 388, p. 42.
28 John Gaynor, BMH WS 1447, p. 9.
29 William Whelan, BMH WS 369, p. 7.
30 *Ibid*.
31 Having initially made some considerable but strategically insignificant territorial gains, huge numbers of exhausted and demoralised German soldiers, normally disciplined beyond question, were unable to forego the luxuries they pillaged, foraged, and looted *en masse* while advancing. As they pressed forward from buffer to bulwark, many gorged themselves on the captured booty and supplies considered all too common for the allied soldiers but denied to the half-starved Germans for so long. Drunkenness was rampant. The discipline necessary to maintain their advancing momentum could not be maintained as they extended themselves further from their tenuous supply lines. Losses were huge, reinforcements were scant, equipment and ammunition ran short. At home, many of their families were starving as a result of the four-year-old British naval blockade; furthermore, morale was buckling and revolution was in the air.
32 The first began on 8 August and was centred around the strategic city of Amiens, the flat, hard ground surrounding it was ideal for the hundreds of British Army tanks launched at the Germans, and backed up by squadron after squadron of airplanes and massed artillery which itself was deployed with devastating effect in earth-shattering creeping-barrages. The no-less-debilitated French Army also counter-attacked *en masse* to the south and south-east with similarly calamitous results to the Kaiser's army as well as to themselves, while simultaneously the fresh American troops joined the fray in their hundreds of thousands, and died in their tens of thousands. The Germans were caught completely off balance.

33 Fewer than 15,000 Irishmen enlisted in the British Army voluntarily between March and November 1918. Conscription had, nonetheless, worked effectively as a placating measure elsewhere. The perception that it was at least 'on the way' had helped stem the hostility and expected unrest.
34 Bennett, *The Black and Tans*, p. 5.
35 Crowley, Ó Drisceoil, Murphy and Borgonovo, *Atlas of the Irish Revolution*, p. 329.
36 December 1918 also saw a wing of Belfast's Crumlin Road Prison destroyed in a well-organised revolt organised by Austin Stack. The Volunteer deputy chief of staff had been transported and incarcerated there since his arrest the previous May. The revolt had been preceded by hunger strikes over the gradual rescinding of political status among the seventy republican prisoners incarcerated there, and came to a head when a Volunteer prisoner, John Doran, was forcefully placed among the prison's criminal inmates. The revolt lasted for a number of days over the Christmas period; food had been stockpiled by the protesters in the weeks beforehand under Stack's watch. The prison wing was badly damaged. Eventually the prison was surrounded by several hundred RIC men, British soldiers, and a large loyalist mob. Order was subsequently restored and Doran was placed among his comrades.
37 The epidemic originated in an army training camp in the USA, and was subsequently transported to Europe on troop ships.

3 Shooting at Soloheadbeg and the First Dáil

1 Piaras Béaslaí, *Michael Collins and the making of a new Ireland*, Vol. 1, p. 256.
2 William Murphy, *Political Imprisonment and the Irish*, p. 125.
3 Major-General Sir Frederick Maurice, *The Life of Viscount Haldane of Cloan*, p. 64.
4 This was a result of the departure of his unpopular predecessor, Edward Shortt. The chief secretary was nominally subordinate to the lord lieutenant, but was, however, a cabinet and Commons member with effective responsibility for governance. Macpherson spent little time in Ireland. His under secretary, James MacMahon, was, nominally, in charge on the ground most of the time. However, his appointment had been something of a sop to the Catholic church, and MacMahon had little real power, and his narrow-minded assistant under secretary, Sir John Taylor, really held the reins.
5 Maurice, *The Life of Viscount Haldane of Cloan*, p. 66.
6 Richard Burdon, *Haldane, An Autobiography*, p. 816.
7 Holmes, *The Little Field Marshal*, p. 348.
8 The evidence for this was flimsy: Haldane had been educated in Germany during his youth. He was also a student of German philosophy. His grasp of the Teutonic had seen him taking part in pre-war naval negotiations with Imperial Germany, which had ultimately failed. However, in spite of this, Long, who viewed events through a particularly conservative unionist prism, would have done well to consider that it was Haldane's armed force reforms that had, in no small part, underpinned the efficient deployment of the BEF against Germany in 1914 – under the command of Field Marshal French. The vastly outnumbered BEF, which also comprised many Irish units, had proved itself a hugely effective force. The tactical skill displayed during its 200-mile fighting retreat had helped stall the German advances long enough to facilitate an eventual allied counter-strike that staved off defeat.
9 Joseph O'Carroll, BMH WS 728, p. 1–2.
10 Dan Breen, *My Fight for Irish Freedom*, p. 33.
11 Diarmuid Ferriter, *A Nation and Not a Rabble: The Irish Revolution 1913–1923*, p. 191.
12 Seamus Robinson, BMH WS 1721, p 27.
13 Breen, *My Fight for Irish Freedom*, p. 35.
14 Máire Comerford, *The First Dáil*, p. 51.
15 The Irish Volunteers had been formed in November 1913 as a reaction to the founding of the UVF as a force to fight against Home Rule in 1912. In doing so they had, ostensibly at least, been preparing to defend the policy of the British government they now – just over five years later – sought to subvert. Home Rule had been acceptable to the majority of Irish

people in 1913. When the Great War broke out the Volunteers had split into two camps, one of which flocked to the military to, effectively, fight for Home Rule by proxy, while the more radical other camp prepared for insurrection. Now, in 1919, Ireland – like the world – was a vastly different place. Former conservative nationalists were far more receptive to the protestations of Sinn Féin regarding both their recent grievances over Home Rule, the aftermath of the Rising, the appalling Great War casualties and, of course, conscription; notwithstanding their less conspicuous disgruntlements, such as the almost halving of Ireland's population during the past eighty years compared with its doubling elsewhere on average within the British Isles, or the disproportionate taxation levels that had existed to Ireland's detriment since the passing of the Act of Union. These and other issues were compounded with their general resentment over their culture's historic decimation over centuries, an issue that had been brought to the forefront of the Irish psyche in the late nineteenth century by organisations such as the Gaelic League, the GAA, and others.

16 Londonderry was the official name for the constituency during the 1918 election.
17 Charles Townshend, *Political Violence in Ireland: Government and Resistance Since 1848*, p. 328.
18 Máire Comerford, *The First Dáil*, p. 52.
19 Arthur Mitchell, *Revolutionary Government in Ireland: Dáil Éireann 1919–1922*, p. 17.
20 Irish nationalism largely became adopted by the re-emerging Catholic hurch, particularly during the previous century when, in the aftermath of the 1798 Rebellion and the subsequent Act of Union, 'divide and rule' had become the order of the day and non-Catholic 'dissenters' such as Presbyterians and Methodists became, generally, less aggrieved with direct colonial rule from Westminster. Emancipation had improved the lot of long-suffering Catholics – particularly the better off – but the Great Hunger that had then ravaged and traumatised Ireland left millions of its less well off Catholics – the majority of the decimated population – with little in the way of comfort from their desperate circumstances other than their entrenched religious beliefs, which were fostered from a very young age through the church's growing influence in education and which, in the main, they clung to like wreckage. The series of small rebellions that followed in the latter part of the century and the widespread land agitations, coupled with the overall Gaelic revival among all classes while Home Rule loomed on the horizon, suggested that the wind was changing in terms of the power base becoming more equitable towards the increasingly nationalist Catholic majority. Furthermore, during the 1880s and afterwards Westminster sought to increasingly placate the Catholic church as a means of keeping Ireland's more conservative moderates onside, while simultaneously undermining the IRB. Recruitment of clergymen and women accelerated dramatically following the turn of the twentieth century as the Catholic church continued, almost in tandem with the nationalists, to grow in confidence and stature. A backlash was feared among many unionists based upon the ascendancy of Irish nationalism inevitably elevating the position of a church that they themselves saw as a powerful and increasingly arrogant threat.
21 John F. Shouldice, BMH WS 679, p. 22.
22 Holmes, *The Little Field Marshal*, p. 348.
23 *Ibid*.
24 *Ibid*.
25 It must be borne in mind that Volunteer groups throughout Ireland were already under instructions from GHQ to employ initiative regarding offensive weapons and ammunition procurement operations. Additionally, Séamus Robinson had authorised the ambush fearing that by the time permission had been sought and received from GHQ that the opportunity would have already passed.
26 Maurice, *The Life of Viscount Haldane of Cloan*, p. 66.

4 Escape from Lincoln and Collinstown Arms Raid
1 Longford and O'Neill, *Éamon de Valera*, p. 85.
2 Béaslaí, *Michael Collins*, Vol. 1, p. 267.

3   Longford and O'Neill, *Éamon de Valera*, p. 86
4   Béaslaí, *Michael Collins*, Vol. 1, p. 270.
5   David Fitzpatrick, *Harry Boland's Irish Revolution*, p. 117.
6   T. Ryle Dwyer, *The Squad and the Intelligence Operations of Michael Collins*, p. 26.
7   Fitzpatrick, *Harry Boland*, p. 116.
8   *Ibid.*
9   Béaslaí, *Michael Collins*, Vol. 1, p. 281.
10 Longford and O'Neill, *Éamon de Valera*, p. 90.
11 The Royal Flying Corps (RFC) was the British Army's air arm. In April 1918 the RFC merged with The Royal Naval Air Service, and became The Royal Air Force.
12 Various, *Dublin's Fighting Story 1916–21, Told By The Men Who Made It*, p. 242.
13 Price, *We Bled Together*, pp. 57–58.
14 Daniel McDonnell, BMH WS 486, p. 2.
15 Patrick O'Connor, BMH WS 608, p. 4.
16 Joseph V. Lawless, BMH WS 1043, p. 255.
17 Michael Lynch, BMH WS 511, p. 68.
18 Daniel McDonnell, BMH WS 486, p. 3.
19 Patrick McCrea, BMH WS 413, p. 7.

5 G-Division Penetrated and Tensions Escalate

1   Paddy Daly later referred to himself as Paddy O'Daly. However, during 1916 and immediately afterwards, he identified as Daly. For continuity we have maintained it as Paddy Daly, as he is known in our earlier books.
2   Paddy Daly, BMH WS 387, p. 5.
3   Michael Noyk, BMH WS 707, p. 23.
4   *Príomh Aire* actually translates as prime minister. The title Uachtaráin na hÉireann was later adopted as president of Ireland.
5   With the advent of the Ministry of Defence, added to the formation of GHQ the previous year, the Volunteer National and Resident Executives continued to exist, but only on a nominal basis until 1920.
6   Fergus O'Farrell, *Cathal Brugha*, p. 48.
7   Terence de Vere White, *Kevin O'Higgins*, p. 28.
8   Seán Saunders, BMH WS 817, p. 3.
9   www.oireachtas.ie/en/debates/debate/dail/1919-04-04/10/
10 O'Farrell, *Cathal Brugha*, p. 51.
11 www.oireachtas.ie/en/debates/debate/dail/1919-04-04/12/
12 Eamon Broy, BMH WS 1280, p. 97.
13 *Ibid.*, p. 98.
14 Price, *We Bled Together*, p. 76.
15 Tim Pat Coogan, *Michael Collins*, p. 107.
16 Eamon Broy, BMH WS 1280, p. 80.
17 *Ibid.*
18 *Ibid.*
19 Dwyer, *The Squad*, p. 45.
20 www.oireachtas.ie/en/debates/debate/dail/1919-04-10/2/.
21 *Ibid.*
22 *Ibid.*, translated from Irish to English.
23 www.oireachtas.ie/en/debates/debate/dail/1919-04-10/4/.
24 *Ibid.*
25 Mitchell, *Revolutionary Government*, p. 114
26 The 'Scarlett Pimpernel' was the fictional aristocratic and secretive Englishman who consistently wrong-footed the authorities in post revolutionary France, while operating a secret society to rescue French counterparts from the guillotine.

27 Interestingly, when the inquest into the policemen's deaths took place the jury placed the blame for their deaths on the government – not the rescuers.
28 Charles Townshend, *The British Campaign*, p. 25.
29 Price, *We Bled Together*, p. 68.

6 Shootings, Ambush and Assassination

1 Dept. of Foreign Affairs and Trade: Documents on Irish Foreign Policy No. 9.
2 *Ibid.*, No. 12.
3 Very Rev. T. J. Stanley, BMH WS 913, pp. 1–2.
4 Frank Robbins, BMH WS 585, pp. 158–59. Robbins had recently returned from the USA where he had been working alongside Liam Mellows in procuring arms.
5 Seamus Kavanagh, BMH WS 1053, pp. 8–9.
6 The first republican court was set up in Ballinrobe Co. Mayo on 17 May. 1920.
7 Townshend, *The British Campaign in Ireland*, p. 26.
8 Michael Lynch, BMH WS 511, p. 71.
9 *Ibid.*, p. 71.
10 *Ibid.*
11 *Ibid.*, p. 72.
12 *Ibid.*
13 Vincent Byrne, BMH WS 423, p. 10.
14 http://johnny-doyle.blogspot.com/2013/01/victory-parade-dublin-1919.html.
15 James J. Slattery, BMH WS 445, p. 2.
16 *Ibid.*, p. 4.
17 Dwyer, *The Squad*, p. 47.
18 Joseph V. Lawless, BMH WS 1043, p. 287.
19 *Ibid.*
20 James J. Slattery, BMH WS 445, p. 5.
21 Michael Lynch, BMH WS 511, p. 73.
22 *Ibid.*
23 Townshend, *The British Campaign in Ireland*, p. 29.
24 White, *Kevin O'Higgins*, p. 32.
25 www.oireachtas.ie/en/debates/debate/dail/1919-08-20/12/.
26 Townshend, *The British Campaign in Ireland*, p. 30.
27 Breen, *My Fight for Irish Freedom*, p. 98.

7 Formation of 'Squad'

1 Dwyer, *The Squad*, p. 49.
2 Sr Eithne (E. Lawless), BMH WS 414, p. 2.
3 *Ibid.*, p. 3.
4 Seamus Ua Caomhanaigh, BMH WS 889, p. 104.
5 *Ibid.*, p. 106.
6 James J. Slattery, BMH WS 445, p. 5.
7 *Ibid.*, p. 6.
8 *Ibid.*
9 Price, *We Bled Together*, p. 81.
10 Pádraig Yeates, *A City in Turmoil: Dublin 1919–21*, p. 52.
11 James Scannell, 'DMP Casualties During the War of Independence', *Dublin Historical Record*, Vol. 61, No.1, p. 9.
12 George Fitzgerald, BMH WS 684, p. 10.
13 Paddy Daly, BMH WS 387, p. 10. Joe Leonard, BMH WS 547, p. 1.
14 Paddy Daly, BMH WS 387, p. 10.
15 Joe Leonard, BMH WS 547, p. 2.
16 Paddy Daly, BMH WS 387, p. 11.

17 Michael McDonnell, BMH WS 225, pp. 2–3.
18 https://scholarworks.gsu.edu/cgi/viewcontent.cgi?article=1045&context=history_theses, p. 8.
19 Townshend, *The British Campaign in Ireland 1919–1921*, p. 32.
20 Mitchell, *Revolutionary Government*, p. 60.
21 http://humphrysfamilytree.com/OMara/republican.loan.html.
22 Mitchell, *Revolutionary Government*, p. 60.
23 Michael McDonnell, BMH WS 225, p. 3.
24 Patrick Egan, BMH WS 327, p. 51.
25 Michael Foley, *The Bloodied Field: Croke Park. Sunday 21 November 1920*, p. 87.
26 *Ibid.*, p. 56.
27 Annie Farrington, BMH WS 749, p. 2.
28 George Fitzgerald, BMH WS 684, p. 11.
29 Patrick O'Donoghue, BMH WS 847, p. 10.
30 Townshend, *The British Campaign in Ireland*, p. 35.
31 Michael McDonnell, BMH WS 225, p. 3.
32 *Ibid.*, p. 4.
33 Paddy Daly, BMH WS 387, p. 12.
34 *Ibid.*, p. 12.
35 Dwyer, *The Squad*, p. 61.
36 Laurence Nugent, BMH WS 907, p. 175.
37 Mitchell, *Revolutionary Government*, p. 53.
38 Dáithí O'Donoghue, BMH WS 548, p. 8.
39 Béaslaí, *Michael Collins*, Vol. 1, p. 373.
40 Seán McCluskey, BMH WS 512, p. 4.
41 Dwyer, *The Squad*, p. 59.
42 Bennett, *The Black and Tans*, p. 86.
43 Joseph E. A. Connell Jnr, *Michael Collins: Dublin 1916–1922*, p. 280.
44 Breen, *My Fight for Irish Freedom*, p. 81.

8 G-Division under Pressure

1 Townshend, *The British Campaign*, p. 42.
2 Mitchell, *Revolutionary Government*, p. 55
3 *Ibid.*, p. 54.
4 Hurley was later court-martialled and imprisoned. He was released in 1921, only to be shot dead tending to a wounded soldier in Dublin during the Civil War in 1922.
5 Derek Molyneux & Darren Kelly, *Those of us Who Must Die: Execution, Exile and Revival After the Easter Rising*, p. 95.
6 Vincent Byrne, BMH WS 423, p. 12.
7 *Ibid.*
8 *Ibid.*
9 *Ibid.*, p. 13.
10 Dwyer, *The Squad*, p. 68.
11 Vincent Byrne, BMH WS 423, p. 13.
12 Dwyer, *The Squad*, p. 70.
13 Frank O'Connor, *The Big Fellow*, p. 81.
14 Connell Jnr, *Michael Collins: Dublin 1916–1922*, p. 101.
15 Holmes, *The Little Field-Marshal*, p. 346.
16 Vincent Byrne, BMH WS 423, p. 15.
17 *Ibid.*
18 *Ibid.*
19 Joe Ambrose, *Seán Treacy and the Tan War*, p. 112.
20 Paddy Daly, BMH WS 387, p. 16.

21 Price, *We Bled Together*, p. 94.
22 Michael McDonnell, BMH WS 225, p. 4.
23 *Ibid.*, p. 5.
24 Breen, *My Fight for Irish Freedom*, p. 87.
25 *Ibid.*
26 Paddy Daly, BMH WS 387, p. 18.
27 Vincent Byrne, BMH WS 423, p. 17.
28 *Ibid.*
29 Breen, *My Fight for Irish Freedom*, p. 89.
30 Patrick Daly, BMH WS 387, p. 19.
31 Price, *We Bled Together*, p. 98.
32 *Ibid.*
33 Michael Lynch, BMH WS 511, p. 80.
34 *Ibid.*, p. 80–1.
35 *Ibid.*, p. 82.
36 Joe Leonard, BMH WS 547, p. 3.
37 Cathal Liam, *Fear Not the Storm: The Story of Tom Cullen, An Irish Revolutionary*, p. 23.
38 Mitchell, *Revolutionary Government*, p. 55.

9 War Declared, Elections and Raids

1 Holmes, *The Little Field-Marshal*, p. 354.
2 *Ibid.*
3 Townshend, *The British Campaign*, p. 37.
4 Foley, *The Bloodied Field*, p. 64.
5 http://treaty.nationalarchives.ie/wp-content/uploads/2011/11/Barton.pdf, p. 2.
6 Mitchell, *Revolutionary Government*, p. 86.
7 Dáithí O'Donoghue, BMH WS 548, p. 19.
8 Breen, *My Fight for Irish Freedom*, p. 93.
9 Michael Lynch, BMH WS 511, p. 86.
10 *Ibid.*
11 Ian Kenneally, *The Paper Trail: Newspapers and Propaganda in Ireland 1919–1921*, p. 105.
12 Gearóid Ua h-Uallacháin, BMH WS 336, p. 12.
13 Bennett, *The Black and Tans*, p. 18.
14 Foley, *The Bloodied Field*, p. 71
15 Bennett, *The Black and Tans*, p. 23
16 Yeates, *A City in Turmoil*, p. 45.
17 Crowley, Ó Drisceoil, Murphy and Borgonovo, *Atlas of the Irish Revolution*, p. 351.
18 William Sheehan, *Fighting for Dublin: The British Battle For Dublin 1919–1921*, p. 9.
19 Frank Thornton, BMH WS 615, p. 39.
20 *Ibid.*
21 *Ibid.*
22 Dwyer, *The Squad*, p. 75.
23 Crowley, Ó Drisceoil, Murphy, Borgonovo, *Atlas of the Irish Revolution*, p. 374.
24 Holmes, *The Little Field-Marshal*, p. 354.
25 W. H. Kautt, *Ground Truths: British Army Operations in the Irish War of Independence*, p. 31; Townshend, *The British Campaign*, p. 49.
26 *Ibid.*, p. 50.
27 David Neligan, BMH WS 380, p. 5.
28 O'Connor, *The Big Fellow*, p. 87.
29 *Ibid.*
30 *Ibid.*, p. 88.
31 Bennett, *The Black and Tans*, p. 52.
32 W. T. Cosgrave, BMH WS 449, p. 2.

33 Mitchell, *Revolutionary Government*, p. 121.
34 Michael Laffan, *Judging WT Cosgrave*, p. 64.
35 Mitchell, *Revolutionary Government*, p. 123.

10 G-Division Decimated and British Intelligence

1   Joseph Dolan, BMH WS 663, pp. 1–2.
2   David Neligan, BMH WS 380, p. 5.
3   Paddy Daly, BMH WS 387, p. 23.
4   *Ibid.*, p. 24.
5   *Ibid.*
6   Joseph Dolan, BMH WS 663, p. 2; Scannell, *DMP Casualties during the War of Independence*, p. 13.
7   Kautt, *Ground Truths*, p. 26.
8   Bennett, *The Black and Tans*, p. 26.
9   Townshend, *The British Campaign*, p. 57.
10 *Ibid.*, p. 54.
11 Vincent Byrne, BMH WS 423, p. 22.
12 http://theirishrevolution.ie/cork-spy-files-1/.
13 www.bloodysunday.co.uk/castle-intelligence/thomson/isham/isham.html.
14 Sheehan, *Fighting for Dublin*, p. 11.
15 Kautt, *Ground Truths*, p. 39.
16 https://trove.nla.gov.au/newspaper/article/63848590.
17 *The Mail* (Australia), 28 February 1920.
18 Joseph Dolan, BMH WS 663, p. 10.
19 *Ibid.*
20 Paddy Daly, BMH WS 387, p. 26.
21 O'Connor, *The Big Fellow*, p. 92.
22 Paddy Daly, BMH WS 387, p. 27.
23 Evans, Gary, *The Raising of the First Internal Dáil Éireann Loan and the British Responses to it, 1919–1921*, p.110.
24 *Ibid.*, p. 111–2.
25 Evans, *The Raising of the First Internal Dáil Éireann Loan*, p.119.
26 Michael Noyk, BMH WS 707, p. 27.
27 www.dail100.ie/en/long-reads/eamon-de-valeras-st-patricks-day-message.
28 Vincent Byrne, BMH WS 423, p. 22.
29 Fionnuala Mac Curtain, *Remember It's For Ireland: A Family Memoir of Tomás Mac Curtáin*, p. 126.
30 *Ibid.*, p. 128.
31 *Ibid.*, p. 132.

11 The Black and Tans Arrive

1   O'Connor, *The Big Fellow*, p. 92.
2   Coogan, *Michael Collins*, p. 133.
3   Dwyer, *The Squad*, p. 97.
4   Vincent Byrne, BMH WS 423, p. 37.
5   *Ibid.*, p. 38.
6   Bennett, *The Black and Tans*, p. 37.
7   White, *Kevin O'Higgins*, p. 39.
8   Bennett, *The Black and Tans*, p. 37.
9   Townshend, *The British Campaign*, p. 56.
10 Yeates, *A City in Turmoil*, p. 108.
11 Joseph Dolan, BMH WS 663, p. 6.
12 O'Connor, *The Big Fellow*, p. 102.

13 Joseph Dolan, BMH WS 663, p. 7.
14 Vincent Byrne, BMH WS 423, p. 41.
15 www.bloodysunday.co.uk/castle-intelligence/thomson/bell/bell.html.
16 Vincent Byrne, BMH WS 423, p. 41.
17 Paddy Daly, BMH WS 387, p. 28.
18 *Ibid.*
19 http://mural.maynoothuniversity.ie/4012/1/MLitt_-_Gary_Evans.pdf, p. 130.
20 Laurence Nugent, BMH WS 907, p. 184.
21 Bennett, *The Black and Tans*, p. 32.
22 Townshend, *The British Campaign*, p. 74.
23 Bennett, *The Black and Tans*, p. 36.
24 Since November 1919, among the challenges accompanying Macpherson's brief, he had been endeavouring to reform the education system and oversee school funding through local authorities. A side effect of this would have been a significant dilution of the Catholic church's influence in education. The Dáil had been noticeably reticent regarding its education policy, principally because its hands were full with overseeing a revolution fundamental to which was Catholic church support. The same church was, in the main, repelled by the assassinations, affray and violence with which it was associated and it was deemed unwise to antagonise it further over something that could best be tackled at a more convenient date, notwithstanding the fact that many TDs embraced church involvement in schooling. Others, including Collins, Brugha and Stack, discreetly saw merit in Macpherson's proposition and advocated a similar future policy under the Dáil. The Catholic church saw things differently, dismissing the bill with which such reforms would be enacted as sacrilege and subsequently oversaw a host of nationwide assemblies damning such a proposition. Macpherson stepped aside under the onslaught.
25 Mitchell, *Revolutionary Government*, p. 128.
26 *Ibid.*, p. 129.
27 George Fitzgerald, BMH WS 684, p. 17.
28 Liz Gillis, *May 25: The Burning of the Custom House Dublin*, p. 60.
29 Frank Gallagher, *Days of Fear: Diary of a 1920s Hunger Striker*, p. 15.
30 Andrew McDonnell, BMH WS 1768, p. 44.
31 *Ibid.*
32 Gillis, *May 25*, p. 60.
33 Michael Biggs, *Hunger Strikes by Irish Republicans*, p. 9.
34 Andrew McDonnell, BMH WS 1768, p. 44.
35 *Ibid.*, p. 46.
36 Gallagher, *Days of Fear*, p. 117.
37 *Ibid.*
38 *Ibid.*, p. 117–8.
39 *Ibid.*, p. 118.
40 Lorcan Collins, *Ireland's War of Independence 1919–21*, p. 108.
41 Paddy Daly, BMH WS 387, p. 32.
42 White, *Kevin O'Higgins*, p. 38.
43 Andrew McDonnell, BMH WS 1768, p. 46.
44 Gallagher, *Days of Fear*, p. 132.
45 Molyneux and Kelly, *When the Clock Struck in 1916*, p. 302.
46 Laffan, *Judging W. T. Cosgrave*, p. 65.

12 New Players at Dublin Castle

1 Ronan Fanning, *Fatal Path*, p. 223.
2 Townshend, *The British Campaign*, p. 78.
3 *Ibid.*, p. 77.
4 *Ibid.*, p. 98.

5   Ibid.
6   White, *Kevin O'Higgins*, p. 39.
7   Collins, *Ireland's War of Independence*, p. 100.
8   Joseph Dolan, BMH WS 663, p. 12.
9   Dwyer, *The Squad*, p. 103.
10 Bennett, *The Black and Tans*, p. 42.
11 *An t-Óglách*, Vol. 11. No. 10, 1 May 1920.
12 Seán Prendergast, BMH WS 755, p. 320.
13 Sheehan, *Fighting for Dublin*, p. 17.
14 Kautt, *Ambushes and Armour*, p. 54.
15 Mitchell, *Revolutionary Government*, p. 158.
16 Vincent Byrne, BMH WS 423, p. 42.
17 Paddy Daly, BMH WS 387, p. 30.
18 Harry Colley, BMH WS 1687, p. 44.
19 Fanning, *Fatal Path*, p. 226.
20 Townshend, *The British Campaign*, p. 84.
21 Bennett, *The Black and Tans*, p. 45.
22 Townshend, *The British Campaign*, p. 93.
23 Ibid.
24 Fanning, *Fatal Path*, p. 227.
25 Ibid., p. 228.
26 Ibid., p. 229.
27 Christopher Byrne, BMH WS 642, p. 3.
28 Price, *We Bled Together*, p. 133.
29 Ibid., p. 135.
30 Townshend, *The British Campaign*, p. 95.
31 Ibid., p. 94.
32 Yeates, *A City in Turmoil*, p. 136.
33 Kautt, *Ambushes and Armour*, p. 61.
34 O'Connor, *The Big Fellow*, p. 98.
35 Mitchell, *Revolutionary Government*, p. 148.
36 T. J. McElligott, BMH WS 472, p. 14.
37 Ibid.
38 Townshend, *The British Campaign*, p. 92.
39 Ibid.
40 Tim Pat Coogan, *Michael Collins*, p. 157.

13 Intelligence War Intensifies

1   Seán Prendergast, BMH WS 755, p. 321.
2   Joseph Dolan, BMH WS 663, p. 8.
3   Seán Prendergast, BMH WS 755, p. 325.
4   George Fitzgerald, BMH WS 684, p. 24.
5   Collins, *Ireland's War of Independence*, p. 114.
6   Mitchell, *Revolutionary Government*, p. 126.
7   Ibid.
8   Liam O'Leary, BMH WS 1276, p. 6.
9   Seán Whelan, BMH WS 1085, p. 6.
10 David Neligan, BMH WS 380, p. 1.
11 Connell, *Michael Collins*, p. 61.
12 David Neligan, BMH WS 380, p. 2.
13 Ibid., p. 3.
14 Jeremiah Mee, BMH WS 379, p. 3.
15 Ibid., p. 11.

16 Mitchell, *Revolutionary Government*, p. 149.
17 *Ibid.*, p. 150.
18 Frank Henderson, BMH WS 821, p. 65.
19 Townshend, *The British Campaign*, p. 69.
20 Yeates, *A City in Turmoil*, p. 127.
21 Nicholas Laffan, BMH WS 703, p. 8.
22 Collins, *Ireland's War of Independence*, p. 120.
23 Joseph Good, BMH WS 388, p. 55.

14 Shootings, Reprisals and Auxiliaries Deployed

1 Jeremiah Mee, BMH WS 379, p. 19.
2 Erskine Childers, *Military Rule in Ireland*, p. 38.
3 Meghan Elizabeth Menard, *Reporting for the State Department: Carl W. Ackerman's Cooperation with Government During WW1*, p. 46.
4 Mitchell, *Revolutionary Government*, p. 217.
5 Frank Henderson, BMH WS 821, p. 76.
6 Dywer, *The Squad*, p. 133.
7 Seán Culhane, BMH WS 746, p. 6.
8 G. R. Kenna, *Facts and Figures of the Belfast Pogrom 1920–1922*, p. 16.
9 Carson and James Craig's oversight of the Larne gun running in spring 1914 in tandem with the 'Curragh incident', threatened to de-stabilise the entire British Army at a very inopportune time, considering that the Great War was just months away. Bennett, *The Black and Tans*, p. 70.
10 Townshend, *The British Campaign*, p. 101.
11 *Ibid.*, p. 102.
12 Alphonsus Sweeney, BMH WS 1147, p. 6.
13 Townshend, *The British Campaign*, p. 109.
14 *Ibid.*, p. 110.
15 Paul O'Brien, *Havoc: The Auxiliaries in Ireland's War of Independence*, p. 28.
16 *Ibid.*, p. 31.
17 Christopher Fitzsimons, BMH WS 581, p. 2.
18 Bennett, *The Black and Tans*, p. 67.
19 Yeates, *A City in Turmoil*, p. 142; Bennett, *The Black and Tans*, p. 80.
20 Sheehan, *Fighting for Dublin*, p. 23.
21 Bennett, *The Black and Tans*, p. 81.
22 www.bloodysunday.co.uk/castle-propaganda/civil-pib/clarke/clarke-basil.
23 Dave Hannigan, *Terence MacSwiney*, p. 24.
24 Joseph V. Lawless, BMH WS 1043, p. 310.
25 Price, *We Bled Together*, p. 134.
26 Kenna, *Facts and Figures*, p. 36.
27 Bennett, *The Black and Tans*, p. 85.
28 *Ibid*.
29 *Ibid.*, p. 86.
30 James MacGuill, BMH WS 353. p. 85.
31 Mitchell, *Revolutionary Government*, p. 200.
32 *Ibid.*, p. 208.
33 Hannigan, *Terence MacSwiney*, p. 63.

15 Auxiliaries Take on IRA and Propaganda Disasters for Britain

1 O'Connor, *The Big Fellow*, p. 104.
2 Menard, *Reporting for the State Department*, p. 46.
3 Mitchell, *Revolutionary Government*, p. 163.
4 *Ibid.*, p. 164.

5   Frank Thornton, BMH WS 615, p. 7.
6   *Ibid.*, p. 6.
7   *Ibid.*, p. 7.
8   *Ibid.*, p. 21.
9   Breen, *My Fight For Irish Freedom*, p. 129.
10 Foley, *The Bloodied Field*, p. 85.
11 Townshend, *The British Campaign*, p. 112.
12 *Ibid.*, p. 113.
13 Mitchell, *Revolutionary Government*, p. 209.
14 Michael Knightly, BMH WS 834, p. 2.
15 *Ibid.*, p. 3.
16 Dwyer, *The Squad*, p. 138.
17 Michael Knightly, BMH WS 834, p. 3.
18 *Ibid.*
19 John Plunkett, BMH WS 865, p. 32.
20 *Ibid.*
21 Seán O'Neill, BMH WS 1154, p. 7.
22 A colloquial term for sweet fizzy drinks.
23 Seamus Kavanagh, BMH WS 493, p. 6.
24 *Ibid.*, p. 14.
25 Price, *We Bled Together*, p. 149.
26 Hannigan, *Terence MacSwiney*, p. 107.
27 John Gaynor, BMH WS 1447, p. 19.
28 Joseph V. Lawless, BMH WS 1043, p. 318.
29 Michael Rock, BMH WS 1398, p. 12.
30 John Gaynor, BMH WS 1447, p. 21.
31 Hopkinson, *The Irish War of Independence*, p. 149.
32 Townshend, *The British Campaign*, p. 115.
33 Townshend, *The Republic: The Fight for Irish Independence*, p. 163.
34 Mitchell, *Revolutionary Government* p. 217.
35 Kautt, *Ambushes and Armour*, p. 91.
36 Collins, *Ireland's War of Independence*, p. 136.
37 Bennett, *The Black and Tans*, p. 102.
38 *Ibid.*, p. 96.
39 Bennett, *The Black and Tans*, p. 79.

16 Peace Offerings and Tragedy for the Dublin Brigade

1   Kevin O'Shiel, BMH WS 1170, p. 1024.
2   Frank Thornton, BMH WS 615, p. 22.
3   Laurence Nugent, BMH WS 709, p. 3.
4   Frank Thornton, BMH WS 615, p. 23.
5   *Ibid.*
6   Townshend, *The British Campaign*, p. 119.
7   Hannigan, *Terence MacSwiney*, pp. 166–7.
8   Bennett, *The Black and Tans*, pp. 102–3.
9   Mitchell, *Revolutionary Government*, p. 218.
10 *Ibid.*, p. 213.
11 Fanning, *Fatal Path*, p. 234.
12 Townshend, *The British Campaign*, p. 124.
13 Bennett, *The Black and Tans*, p. 104.
14 Hannigan, *Terence MacSwiney*, p. 179.
15 *Ibid.*, p. 180.
16 Patrick McCrea, BMH WS 413, p. 11.

17 Bernard Byrne, BMH WS 631, p. 7.
18 Joseph Leonard, BMH WS 547, p. 10.
19 Breen, *My Fight For Irish Freedom*, p. 138.
20 Joseph V. Lawless, BMH WS 1043, p. 324.
21 *Ibid.*
22 *Ibid.*, p. 326.
23 *Ibid.*, p. 328.
24 *Ibid.*, p. 340.
25 Bernard Byrne, BMH WS 631, p. 8.
26 *Ibid.*, p. 10.
27 *Ibid.*, p. 11.
28 Various, *Dublin's Fighting Story*, p. 275.
29 Yeates, *A City in Turmoil*, p. 183.
30 Seán Brunswick, BMH WS 898, p. 6.
31 *Ibid.*
32 *Ibid.*
33 Charles Dalton, *With The Dublin Brigade*, p. 107.
34 David Neligan, BMH WS 380, p 9.

17 Increased British Pressure and Propaganda Disasters

1   David Neligan, BMH WS 380, p 10.
2   Liam O'Carroll, BMH WS 594, p. 12.
3   David Neligan, BMH WS 380, p 7.
4   Liam O'Carroll, BMH WS 594, p. 11.
5   *Ibid.*, p. 12.
6   Yeates, *A City in Turmoil*, p. 184.
7   David Neligan, BMH WS 380, p 7.
8   Paddy Daly, BMH WS 387, p. 40.
9   Ambrose, *Seán Treacy*, p. 153.
10 Fanning, *Fatal Path*, p. 239.
11 Townshend, *The British Campaign*, p. 127.
12 *Ibid.*
13 *Ibid.*, p. 128.
14 Yeates, *A City in Turmoil*, p. 176.
15 *Ibid.*, p. 177.
16 Patrick Moylett, BMH WS 767, p. 20.
17 *Ibid.*, p. 51.
18 *Ibid.*, p. 52.
19 Katherine Barry-Moloney, BMH WS 731, p. 12.
20 *Ibid.*, p. 16.
21 *Ibid.*, p. 17.
22 *Ibid.*
23 Mitchell, *Revolutionary Government*, p. 214.
24 Hannigan, *Terence MacSwiney*, p. 255.
25 Bennett, *The Black and Tans*, p108.
26 Hannigan, *Terence MacSwiney*, p. 262.
27 *Ibid.*, p. 263.
28 Patrick Moylett, BMH WS 767, p. 60.
29 *Ibid.*, p. 62.
30 Katherine Barry-Moloney, BMH WS 731, p. 44.
31 *Ibid.*, p. 46.
32 Collins, *Ireland's War of Independence*, p. 157.
33 John Plunkett, BMH WS 865, p. 46.

34 Patrick Moylett, BMH WS 767, p. 63.
35 Rev. Fr Laurence, ODC, BMH WS 899, p. 1.
36 Mitchell, *Revolutionary Government*, p. 214.
37 Bennett, *The Black and Tans*, p. 115.

Epilogue

1 Vincent Byrne, BMH WS 423, p. 54–5.
2 Anne Dolan, 'Killing and Bloody Sunday, November 1920', *The Historical Journal* 49, 3 (2006) pp. 789–810.

BIBLIOGRAPHY

Books

Abbott, Richard, *Police Casualties in Ireland 1919–1922* (Mercier Press, Cork, 2019)

Addison, R. T. Hon. Christopher, *Politics From Within 1911–1918*, Vols 1 and 2 (Herbert Jenkins Limited, London, 1924)

Ambrose, Joe, *Seán Treacy and the Tan War* (Mercier Press, Cork, 2007)

Andrew, Christopher, *The Defence of the Realm: The Authorized History of MI5* (Penguin books, London, 2010)

Andrew, Christopher and Dilks, David, *The Missing Dimension: Government and Intelligence Communities in the Twentieth Century* (Palgrave, London, 2014)

Andrews, C. S., *Dublin Made Me* (Lilliput Press, Dublin, 2001)

Asquith, Margot, *The Autobiography of Margot Asquith*, Vol. 2 (Thornton Butterworth Ltd., London, 1922)

Augusteijn, Joost, *The Irish Revolution 1913–1923* (Palgrave, Hampshire, 2002)

Barry, Tom, *Guerilla Days in Ireland* (Mercier Press, Cork, 2013)

Béaslaí, Piaras, *Michael Collins and the Making of a New Ireland*, Vol. 1 (Phoenix Publishing Co. Ltd., Dublin, 1922)

Bennett, Richard, *The Black and Tans* (Four Square Books, London, 1961)

Bew, Paul, *Churchill & Ireland* (Oxford University Press, Oxford, 2016)

Boyle, Andrew, *The Riddle of Erskine Childers: A Biography* (Hutchinson & Co. Ltd., London, 1977)

Breen, Dan, *My Fight for Irish Freedom* (Anvil Books, Dublin, 1993)

Bromage, Mary C., *Churchill in Ireland* (University of Notre Dame Press, Indiana, 1964)

— *De Valera: The Rebel Gunman Who Became President of Ireland* (Four Square, London, 1967)

Buckland, Patrick, *James Craig: Irish Lives* (Gill, Dublin, 1981)

Byrne, Myles, *The Memoirs of Myles Byrne Vol. 1* (Maunsel & Co., Limited, Dublin 1907)

Carey, Tim, *Mountjoy – The Story of a Prison* (The Collins Press, Cork, 2000)

Carroll, Denis, *They Have Fooled You Again: Michael Flanagan (1876–1942) Priest, Republican, Social Critic* (Columba Press, Dublin, 1993)

Clarke, Kathleen, *Kathleen Clarke – Revolutionary Woman* (The O'Brien Press, Dublin, 1991)

Collier, Basil, *Brasshat: A Biography of Field-Marshal Sir Henry Wilson 1864–1922* (Secker & Warburg, London, 1961)

Collins, Lorcan, *Ireland's War of Independence 1919–21: The IRA's Guerrilla Campaign* (O'Brien Press, Dublin, 2019)

Collins, Michael, *The Path to Freedom* (The Talbot Press, Dublin, 1922)

Colum, Padraic, *Arthur Griffith* (Browne & Nolan Ltd, Dublin, 1959)

Comerford, Marie, *The First Dáil* (Joe Clarke, Dublin, 1969)

Connell Jnr, Joseph E. A., *Michael Collins: Dublin 1916–1922* (Wordwell Ltd., Dublin, 2017)

Coogan, Tim Pat, *De Valera: Long Fellow, Long Shadow* (Random House, London, 1993)

— *Ireland in the Twentieth Century* (Arrow Books Ltd, London, 2003)

— *Michael Collins, A Biography* (Arrow Books Ltd, London, 1991)

Corbett, Jim, *Not While I have Ammo: A History of Captain Connie Mackey, Defender of the Strand* (Nonsuch Publishing, Dublin, 2008)

Costello, Francis (ed), *In His Own Words: Michael Collins* (Gill & Macmillan Ltd., Dublin 1997)

Cottrell, Peter, *The Anglo-Irish War: The Troubles of 1913–1922* (Osprey Publishing, Oxford, 2006)

Crowley, John, Ó Drisceoil, Donal, Murphy, Mike, Borgonovo, John (eds.), *Atlas of the Irish Revolution* (Cork University Press, Cork, 2017)

Crozier, Brig. General F. P., *A Brass Hat in No Man's Land* (Johnathan Cope & Harrison Smith, New York, 1930)

— *The Men I Killed* (Createspace Independent Publishing, Amazon, 2016)

Dagg, George A. de M. Edwin, *The Road Route Guide of the Royal Irish Constabulary* (Hodges, Figgis & Co. Ltd., Dublin, 1993)

Dalton, Charles, *With the Dublin Brigade, Espionage and Assassination with Michael Collins' Intelligence Unit* (Mercier Press, Cork, 2014)

Dangerfield, George, *The Damnable Question: A History of Anglo-Irish Relations* (Barnes & Noble Inc., New York, 1999)

Dawson, Richard, *Red Terror and Green: The Sinn Fein–Bolshevist Movement* (E. P. Dutton & Company, New York, 1920)

De Burca, Padraig, & Boyle, John F., *Free State Or Republic?* (Talbot Press, Dublin, 1922)

De Vere White, Terence, *Kevin O'Higgins* (Anvil Books, Kerry, 1948)

Deasy, Liam, *Towards Ireland Free: The West Cork Brigade in the War of Independence 1917–21* (Mercier Press, Cork, 1973)

Dorney, John, *Peace After The Final Battle: The Story of the Irish Revolution 1912–1924* (New Island Books, Dublin, 2013)

Dwyer, T. Ryle, *De Valera: The Man and the Myth* (Poolbeg Press Ltd., Dublin, 1992)

— *Éamon de Valera* (Gill & Macmillan, Dublin, 1980)

— *The Squad and the Intelligence Operations of Michael Collins* (Mercier Press, Cork, 2005)

— *Michael Collins: The Man Who Won the War* (Mercier Press, Cork, 2009)

Enright, Seán, *After the Rising: Soldiers, Lawyers and Trials of the Irish Revolution* (Merrion Press, Kildare, 2016)

Evans, Gary, *The Raising of the First Internal Dáil Éireann Loan and the British Responses to It, 1919–1921* (NUI Maynooth, February 2012)

BIBLIOGRAPHY

Fanning, Ronan, *Fatal Path: British Government and Irish Revolution 1910–1922* (Faber & Faber, London, 2013)

Ferriter, Diarmuid, *A Nation and Not a Rabble: The Irish Revolution 1913–1923* (Profile Books, London, 2015)

— *Judging Dev* (Royal Irish Academy, Dublin, 2007)

— *The Transformation of Ireland 1900–2000* (Profile Books, London, 2005)

Figgis, Darrell, *Recollections of the Irish War* (Doubleday, Doran & Company Inc., New York, 1928)

— *The Historic Case for Irish Independence* (Maunsel & Company Ltd., Dublin, 1918)

Finlay, Ken & Roche, Tom, *Dublin 4, Sandymount – Donnybrook – Ballsbridge – Ringsend* (Cottage Publications, Donaghadee, 2006)

Finlay, Ken, *Dublin Day by Day: 366 Days of Dublin History* (Nonsuch Publishing Limited, Dublin, 2005)

Fitzpatrick, David, *Harry Boland's Irish Revolution* (Cork University Press, Cork, 2004)

Foley, Michael, *The Bloodied Field: Croke Park. Sunday 21 November 1920* (O'Brien Press, Dublin, 2014)

Foster, R. F., *Vivid Faces: The Revolutionary Generation in Ireland 1890–1923* (Penguin Books, London, 2015)

Foy, Michael T., *Michael Collins's Intelligence War: The Struggle Between the British and the IRA 1919–1921* (Sutton Publishing, Gloucestershire, 2006)

Gallagher, Frank, *Days Of Fear: Diary of a 1920s Hunger Striker* (Mercier Press, Cork, 2008)

Galligan, Kevin, *Peter Paul Galligan: 'One of the Most Dangerous Men in the Rebel Movement'* (The Liffey Press, Dublin, 2012)

George, David Lloyd, *War Memoirs*, Vol. 5 (Ivor Nicholson & Watson, London, 1936)

George, Earl Lloyd, *My Father, Lloyd George* (Crown Publishers Inc., New York, 1961)

Gillis, Liz, *May 25: The Burning of the Custom House Dublin* (Kilmainham Tales, Dublin, 2017)

— *Women of the Revolution* (Mercier Press, Cork, 2014)

— *The Fall of Dublin: Military History of the Irish Civil War* (Mercier Press, Cork, 2011)

Gleeson, James, *Bloody Sunday* (Four Square books, London, 1963)

Gregory, Adrian & Paseta, Senia, *Ireland and the Great War: A War to Unite Us All?* (Manchester University Press, Manchester, 2002)

Guevara, Ernesto 'Che', *Guerrilla Warfare* (BN Publishing, California, 2013)

Haldane, Richard Burdon, *Richard Burdon Haldane: An Autobiography* (Hodder and Stoughton, London, 1929)

Hannigan, Dave, *Terence MacSwiney: The Hunger Strike That Rocked an Empire* (O'Brien Press, Dublin, 2010)

Hart, Peter (ed.), *Irish Narratives: British Intelligence in Ireland, 1920–21. The Final Reports* (Cork University Press, Cork, 2011)

Haverty, Anne, *Constance Markievicz Irish Revolutionary* (Pandora, London, 1988)

KILLING AT ITS VERY EXTREME

Henry, Robert Mitchell, *The Evolution of Sinn Féin* (The Talbot Press, Dublin, 1920)

Herlihy, Jim, *The Dublin Metropolitan Police 'A Short History and Genealogical Guide'* (Four Courts Press, Dublin, 2001)

Hinkson, Pamela, *Seventy Years Young – Memories of Elizabeth Countess of Fingal* (The Lilliput Press, Dublin, 1991)

Hittle, J. B. E., *Michael Collins and the Anglo-Irish War: Britain's Counterinsurgency Failure* (Potomac Books, Nebraska, 2015)

Holmes, Richard, *The Little Field-Marshal Sir John French* (Jonathan Cape, London, 1981)

Hopkinson, Michael, *Green Against Green: The Irish Civil War* (Gill & Macmillan, Dublin, 2004)

— *The Irish War of Independence* (Gill & Macmillan, Dublin, 2002)

Jeffery, Keith (ed.), *The Military Correspondence of Field Marshal Sir Henry Wilson 1918–1922* (The Army Records Society, London, 1985)

Jeffery, Keith, *MI6: The History of the Secret Intelligence Service 1909–1949* (Bloomsbury Paperbacks, London, 2011)

Johnstone, Tom, *Orange Green & Khaki: The Story of the Irish Regiments in the Great War 1914–1918* (Gill & Macmillan, Dublin, 1992)

Kautt, W. H. (ed.), *Ground Truths: British Army Operations in the Irish War of Independence* (Irish Academic Press, Kildare, 2014)

— *Ambushes and Armour: The Irish Rebellion 1919–1921* (Irish Academic Press, Dublin, 2011)

Kee, Robert, *Green Flag Volume 3: 'Ourselves Alone'* (Penguin Books, London, 1989)

Keegan, John, *A History of Warfare* (Vintage, New York, 1994)

Kenna, G. R., *Facts and Figures of the Belfast Pogrom 1920–1922* (The O'Connell Publishing Company, Dublin, 1922)

Kenneally, Ian, *Courage and Conflict, Forgotten Stories of the Irish at War* (The Collins Press, Cork, 2010)

— *The Paper Wall: Newspapers and Propaganda in Ireland 1919–1921* (The Collins Press, Cork, 2008)

Laffan, Michael, *Judging W.T. Cosgrave* (Royal Irish Academy, Dublin, 2014)

Lawlor, Sheila, *Britain & Ireland 1914–1923* (Rowman & Littlefield Publishers, Maryland, 1983)

Leeson, D. M., *The Black & Tans: British Police and Auxiliaries in the Irish War of Independence* (Oxford University Press, Oxford, 2013)

Liam, Cathal, *Fear not the Storm: The Story of Tom Cullen An Irish Revolutionary* (St Pádraic Press, Ohio, 2011)

Longford, The Earl of, & O'Neill, Thomas P., *Éamon de Valera* (Arrow Books, London, 1974)

MacSwiney, Terence, *Principles of Freedom* (Mercier Press, Cork, 2020)

Maher, Jim, *Harry Boland: A Biography* (Mercier Press, Cork, New Edition 2020)

Mac Curtain, Fionnuala, *Remember It's for Ireland: A Family Memoir of Tomás Mac Curtáin* (Mercier Press, Cork, 2006)

BIBLIOGRAPHY

Macardle, Dorothy, *The Irish Republic* (Farrar, Straus and Giroux, New York, 1965)

MacLaren, Roy, *Empire and Ireland: The Transatlantic Career of the Canadian Imperialist Hamar Greenwood, 1870–1948* (McGill, Queen's University Press, Canada, 2015)

MacLellan, Anne, *Dorothy Stopford Price: Rebel Doctor* (Irish Academic Press, Dublin, 2014)

Macready, General the Rt. Hon. Sir Neville, *Annals of an Active Life,* Vols 1 & 2 (Hutchinson & Co., London, 1925)

Marreco, Anne, *The Rebel Countess: The Life and Times of Constance Markievicz* (Phoenix Press, London, 2000)

Matthews, Ann, *Renegades: Irish Republican Women 1900-1922* (Mercier Press, Cork, 2010)

Maurice, Major-General Sir Frederick, *Haldane 1915–1928: The Life of Viscount of Cloan. K. T., O. M.* (Faber And Faber Limited, London, 1939)

McCall, Ernest, *The Auxiliaries: Tudor's Toughs. A Study of the Auxiliary Division Royal Irish Constabulary 1920–1922* (Red Coat Publishing, Newtownards, 2010)

McCann, John, *War by the Irish* (The Kerryman Limited, Tralee, 1946)

McCarthy, Cal, *Cumann na mBan and the Irish Revolution* (revised edition, The Collins Press, Cork, 2014)

McConville, Seán, *Irish Political Prisoners, 1848–1922: Theatres of War* (Routledge, Abingdon, 2002)

McCullagh, David, *De Valera, Volume 1: Rise 1882–1932* (Gill Books, Dublin, 2017)

McDonnell, Vincent, *Michael Collins: Most Wanted Man* (The Collins Press, Cork, 2015)

McGee, Owen, *The IRB: The Irish Republican Brotherhood, from the Land League to Sinn Féin* (The Four Courts Press, Dublin, 2007)

McGough, Eileen, *Diarmuid Lynch: A Forgotten Irish Patriot* (Mercier Press, Cork, 2013)

McGreevy, Ronan, *Wherever the Firing Line Extends: Ireland and the Western Front* (The History Press, Dublin, 2017)

McGuire, Charlie, *Seán McLoughlin, Ireland's Forgotten Revolutionary* (Merlin Press, Pontypool, 2011)

McMahon, Sean, *Great Irish Heroes* (Mercier Press, Cork, 2008)

— *Rebel Ireland, from Easter Rising to Civil War* (Mercier Press, Cork, 2001)

— *The War of Independence* (Mercier Press, Cork, 2019)

Messenger, Charles, *Broken Sword: The Tumultuous Life of General Frank Crozier 1879–1937* (The Praetorian Press, Barnsley, 2013)

Mitchell, Arthur, *Revolutionary Government in Ireland: Dáil Éireann 1919–1922* (Gill & MacMillan, Dublin, 1995)

Molyneux, Derek & Kelly, Darren, *Those of Us Who Must Die: Execution, Exile and Revival After the Easter Rising* (The Collins Press, Cork , 2017)

— *When the Clock Struck in 1916: Close Quarter Combat in the Easter Rising* (The Collins Press, Cork, 2015)

Moran, May, *Executed for Ireland: The Patrick Moran Story* (Mercier Press, Cork, 2010)

Mulcahy, Risteárd, *My Father the General: Richard Mulcahy and the Military History of the Revolution* (Liberties Press, Dublin, 2009)

— *Richard Mulcahy (1886-1971): A Family Memoir* (Aurelian Press, Dublin, 1999)

Murphy, Brian P., *John Chartres: Mystery Man of the Treaty* (Irish Academic Press, Dublin, 1995)

Murphy, William, *Political Imprisonment and the Irish* (Oxford University Press, Oxford, 2014)

Naughton, Lindie, *Markievicz: A Most Outrageous Rebel* (Irish Academic Press, Kildare, 2016)

Norman, Diana, *Terrible Beauty, A Life of Constance Markievicz* (Poolbeg Press Ltd., Dublin, 1988)

Ó Comhraí, Cormac and Ó Comhraí, Stiofán, *Peadar Clancy: Easter Rising Hero, Bloody Sunday Martyr* (Cranny Publications, Galway, 2016)

Ó Duibhir, Liam, *Prisoners of War: Ballykinlar Internment Camp 1920–1921* (Mercier Press, Cork, 2013)

O'Brien, Paul, *Havoc: The Auxiliaries in Ireland's War of Independence* (The Collins Press, Cork, 2017)

O'Brien, Stan D., *John Joe's Story: Commandant Joe O'Brien* (self-published, 2016)

O'Connor, Batt, *With Michael Collins in the Fight for Irish Independence* (Peter Davies Ltd, London, 1929)

O'Connor, Frank, *The Big Fellow* (Mercier Press, Cork, 2018)

O'Farrell, Fergus, *Cathal Brugha* (University College Dublin Press, Dublin, 2018)

O'Farrell, Padraic, *Who's Who in the Irish War of Independence and Civil War 1916–1923* (The Lilliput Press, Dublin, 1997)

O'Hegarty, P. S., *A Short Memoir of Terence MacSwiney* (P. J. Kenedy & Sons, New York, 1922)

— *Sinn Féin an Illumination* (Maunsel & Co. Ltd, Dublin, 1919)

O'Malley, Ernie, *On Another Man's Wound* (Mercier Press, Cork, 2013)

— *The Men will Talk to Me: Galway Interviews* (Mercier Press, Cork, 2013)

— *The Men Will Talk to Me: Kerry Interviews* (Mercier Press, Cork, 2012)

— *The Men Will Talk to Me: West Cork Interviews* (Mercier Press, Cork, 2015)

O'Reilly, Terence (ed.), *Our Struggle for Independence: Eyewitness Accounts from the Pages of An Cosantóir* (Mercier Press, Cork, 2009)

Pakenham, Frank, *Peace By Ordeal* (Jonathan Cope, London, 1935)

Phillips, W. Alison, *The Revolution in Ireland 1906–1923* (Longmans, Green and Co. Ltd., London, 1926)

Price, Dominic, *We Bled Together: Michael Collins, The Squad and the Dublin Brigade* (The Collins Press, Cork, 2017)

Raymond, E. T., *Mr Lloyd George: A Biography* (W. Collins Sons & Co. Ltd., Glasgow, 1922)

Regan, John X., *What made Ireland Sinn Féin* (Washington Press, Boston, 1921)

Ryan, Annie, *Comrades: Inside the War of Independence* (Liberties Press, Dublin, 2007)

Ryan, Meda, *Irish Revolutionaries – Liam Lynch: The Real Chief* (Mercier Press, Cork, 2012)

BIBLIOGRAPHY

— *Michael Collins and the Women Who Spied For Ireland* (Mercier Press, Cork, 2006)

Scannell, James, *DMP Casualties During the War of Independence* (Dublin Historical Record, Dublin, 2008)

Sheehan, Captain D. D., *Ireland Since Parnell* (Daniel O'Connor, London, 1921)

Sheehan, William, *British Voices From the Irish War of Independence 1918–1921: The Words of British Servicemen Who Were There* (The Collins Press, Cork, 2007)

— *Fighting For Dublin: The British Battle For Dublin 1919–1921* (The Collins Press, Cork, 2007)

— *Hearts & Mines: The British 5th Division, Ireland, 1920–1922* (The Collins Press, Cork, 2009)

Shouldice, Frank, *Grandpa the Sniper: The Remarkable Story of a 1916 Volunteer* (The Liffey Press, Dublin, 2015)

Stewart, A. T. Q., *Edward Carson: Irish Lives* (Gill, Dublin, 1981)

Strachan, Hew, *The First World War* (Penguin Books, London, 2005)

Taber, Robert, *War of the Flea: The Classic Study of Guerrilla Warfare* (Potomac Books Inc., Nebraska, 2002)

Talbot, Hayden, *Michael Collins' Own Story* (Hutchinson & Co., London, 1923)

Townshend, Charles, *The British Campaign in Ireland 1919–1921: The Development of Political and Military Policies* (Oxford Historical Monographs, Oxford, 1975)

— *The Republic: The Fight for Irish Independence* (Penguin Books, London, 2014)

Turner, Edward Raymond, *Ireland and England in the Past and at Present* (The Century Co., New York, 1919)

Valiulis, Maryann Gialanella, *Portrait of a Revolutionary-General Richard Mulcahy and the Founding of the Irish Free State* (Irish Academic Press, Dublin, 1993)

Various, *Dublin's Fighting Story 1916–21: Told by the Men Who Made It* (Mercier Press, Cork, 2009)

Various, *Limerick's Fighting Story 1916–1921: Told by the Men Who Made It* (Mercier Press, Cork, 2009)

Various, *IRA Jailbreaks: 1918–1921* (Mercier Press, Cork, 2010)

Various, *The Anglo-Irish War* (Belfast Historical and Educational Society, Belfast, 2010)

Various, *With the IRA in the Fight for Freedom, 1919 to the Truce: The Red Path of Glory* (Mercier Press, Cork, 2010)

Von Clausewitz, Carl, *On War* (Wordsworth Editions Limited, Hertfordshire, 1997)

Von Spohn, Colonel, *The Art of Command* (Herr A. Bath, Berlin, 1907)

Walsh, Maurice, *Bitter Freedom: Ireland in a Revolutionary World* (Faber & Faber, London, 2016)

— *The News from Ireland: Foreign Correspondents and the Irish Revolution* (I. B. Tauris, London, 2011)

Ward, Margaret, *In Their Own Voice: Women and Irish Nationalism* (Attic Press, Dublin, 1995)

Wells, Warre B., *An Irish Apologia* (Maunsel & Co. Ltd, Dublin, 1917)

White, G. & O'Shea, B., *Irish Volunteer Soldier 1913–23* (Osprey Publishing, Oxford, 2003)

Woodcock, Caroline, *An Officer's Wife in Ireland* (Parkgate Publications Ltd, London, 1994)
Yeates, Pádraig, *A City in Turmoil: Dublin 1919–1921* (Gill & Macmillan, Dublin, 2012)
Younger, Calton, *A State of Disunion: Griffith, Collins, Craig, De Valera* (Muller, London, 1972)

E-books

Eddleston, John, *British Executions, Volume Four, 1916 to 1920* (Bibliofile Publishers, 2012)
Igoe, Mark, *Nemo & The White Snake* (Marco Books, 2016)
Marques, Major Patrick D., *Guerrilla Warfare Tactics in Urban Environments* (War College Series, 2015)

Primary Source

Bureau of Military History Witness statements, 1913–1921

Theses

Biggs, Michael, 'Hunger Strikes by Irish Republicans, 1916–1923' (University of Illinois, 2004)
Evans, Gary, 'The Raising of the First Internal Dáil Éireann Loan and the British Responses to It, 1919–1921' (NUI Maynooth, February 2012)
Leeson, David, 'The Black And Tans: British Police in the First Irish War, 1920–21' (McMaster University Ontario, 2003)
Menard, Meghan Elizabeth, 'Reporting for the State Department: Carl W. Ackerman's Cooperation with Government During WW1' (Louisiana State University, 2015)
Rast, Mike, 'Tactics, Politics, and Propaganda in the Irish War of Independence, 1917–1921' (Georgia State University, 2011)
Reynolds, John, 'Divided Loyalties: The R.I.C. in County Tipperary 1919–1922' (University of Limerick)

Websites

http://1914-1918.invisionzone.com
http://annual.capuchinfranciscans.ie
http://hansard.millbanksystems.com
https://irishconstabulary.com
http://irishvolunteers.org
https://issuu.com
http://kilmainhamgaolmuseum.ie
http://kilmainhamtales.ie
www.bl.uk
www.bloodysunday.co.uk
www.bureauofmilitaryhistory.ie
www.communistpartyofireland.ie
www.dublin-fusiliers.com

BIBLIOGRAPHY

www.heritageireland.ie

www.historyireland.com

www.irishmedals.org

www.irishnewsarchive.com

www.iwm.org.uk

www.mi5.gov.uk/history

www.militaryarchive.co.uk

www.militaryarchives.ie

www.nli.ie

www.oireachtas.ie

www.paperspast.natlib.govt.nz

www.policehistory.com/museum

www.rcpi.ie

www.richmondbarracks.ie

www.royalirishconstabulary.com

www.royal-irish.com

www.sis.gov.uk/our-history

www.theauxiliaries.com

www.thegazette.co.uk

www.westernfrontassociation.com

ACKNOWLEDGEMENTS

Darren: To my wife, Joanne, and my children, Aaron, Liam and Adele – I could not have done this without you by my side. Thank you for all the support and, most importantly, the fun, the joy and laughter. All I can say is I love you all.

Derek: My most profound thanks must go, once again, to my beautiful wife, Lisa, and my gorgeous two girls, Shannon and Catriona. You are an endless source of inspiration. Your encouragement (occasional eye-rolling), love and support has seen me over the countless hurdles that come hand in hand with work such as this. Thank you again so much.

Thanks yet again to both our parents and families for your inexhaustible support. It has been amazing to uncover our shared family histories relating to this period and your patience and support has been an inspiration and a godsend.

The authors would like to express tremendous gratitude to Pat Rooney and Paul Greene for going the extra miles – again! – thanks so much – you made things so much easier. Thanks also to Marcus Howard, Jean O'Donnell, Frances Howard for working alongside us. Getting to know you has been one of the best things about this incredible journey – long may it continue. We must also thank Johnny Doyle for all your help, encouragement and expertise. Thanks also to Claudine, Max and Axel Meyer, Una Molyneux, Colin Crawford, Cain and Jack, Dolores, Sarah and Ben Quinlan, Colin O'Reilly, Maurice and Alison Moran, Angela and Tommy Lawless, Dick and Collette Sweetman, Larry and Gráinne Murphy, Don Doyle, Anthony O'Reardon, Conor Forde, Derek Jones, Terry Crosbie, Proinsias Ó Rathaille, Joe Mooney, Sinead Crowley at RTÉ, Ronan McGreevy of *The Irish Times*, Anne Dolan of Trinity College, Niall MacDonagh, Diane Butler, Jill Corish, Shane McMenamin and Greg Simons (Department of Foreign Affairs and Trade Library), Niamh McDonald, Garbhan de Paor, Tanith Conway, Robert

ACKNOWLEDGEMENTS

Dooley, Jim and Yvonne Barrett, Michelle, Vitor and Alex Gonsalves, Aidan Gorman, as well as Steve & Mia Doyle. We would also like to thank all the staff at registry and corporate services of the Department of Foreign Affairs and Trade, as well as everyone else in the department for all their assistance and encouragement, especially Matthew McFarland, Linda Collins, James Searson, Darragh O'Neill, Michael Ryan, Jenny McStay, Seán Breen and Deirdre Greene, everybody at the Office of Public Works (OPW) for all your help and support, particularly Philip Early. A further thanks to all at registry, facilities management, and property management – especially Dr Luke Diver – an excellent military historian, Aoife Torpey of Kilmainham Gaol (OPW); thank you so much – again.

A big thanks must also go to Johnny O'Dwyer, Jimmy Sheridan, Richie Ellis, Shane Doyle, Jim McDermott, Finnian O'Dowd, Ant Dennehy and all the players and members of the Thomas McCurtain GAA Club East London & Essex, also to Marc and Mags Ó Dalaigh, Breda and Cormac Grannell, Conor and Caroline O'Mahony, Martin and Siobhan McGovern and all the children at Thomas MacCurtains' Underage Hurling, Camogie and Gaelic Football, Dave and Nev from *Claidheamh Soluis*, Con and Niamh O'Connor, Wayne Jenkins, Teresa Culleton, Kevin Brennan, Bróna, Mel, Diarmuid, Bart and all the Moore Street crew, the Royal Irish Academy, Kevin Street Library, Liz Gillis, Las Fallon, Kieran and Christina McMullen, Rick and Carolyn Styron, Declan Woolhead, Maria Poole, Sinclair Dowey, Mick and John O'Brien yet again for such valuable military input, Paul O'Brien, Joseph E. A. Connell Jnr, Lorcan Collins, Niamh Hassett and everyone from Comóradh na n'Óglách – 'Where Tipperary leads …' National Library of Ireland, Military Archives, Petesy Burns, Liam Beattie, Stevie McLoughlin, Anne Campbell, Cathy O'Sullivan and the old Belfast Crew. Liam Ó Briain, Stef Thompson and everyone at Raw Combat International, Tommy and Billy Allen and everyone at Resistance PT, Paul, Joe, Bren and everyone at Self-Protection Ireland.

Thanks so much again to all the followers of the Facebook page 'Dublin 1916–1923 Then and Now'. We hope to count on your continuing support and feedback, which is an endless source of inspiration. Meeting with so many of you has enhanced this adventure so much. The same goes for everyone who has helped and encouraged us in our previous works and gave them such a fantastic response.

Finally, the authors would also like to express our sincerest gratitude to Mary, Patrick, Deirdre, Noel, Wendy, Sarah and all at Mercier Press for your boundless enthusiasm. Your interest in this work has been way beyond the commercial and was a tonic to us at a testing time. We look forward so much to working with you on our next work and into the future. We would also like to express our thanks to Con and Anna Collins, Paula Elmore, Gillian Hennessy and all at The Collins Press for everything you did to help set us on this journey some years back, and to Gill Books.

INDEX

A

Ackerman, Carl 259, 275, 324
Adelaide Hospital 227
Adelaide Road 284
Ailesbury Road 201, 202
Airfield Road 184
America 6, 67, 68, 82, 99, 111, 115, 126, 127, 145, 167, 191, 218, 234, 235, 257, 267, 281, 288, 302, 331
Ames, Peter 299, 300
Amiens Street 126, 157, 192
Anderson, John 229, 232, 234, 236, 254, 263, 268, 301, 302
Andrews, Todd 209
Angliss, Lt Henry 297, 298
Arbour Hill 13
Archer, Liam 283
Ashe, Thomas 5, 14, 15, 17, 45, 52, 73, 92, 120
Ashtown 6, 102, 103, 146, 149, 150, 161, 162, 167, 172, 186, 204, 205, 207, 226
Asquith, Herbert 22, 28, 220, 230, 288, 302
Aston, E. 325, 330
Aston Quay 170
Atwood, Philip 305
Aungier Street 38, 96, 121, 185
Auxiliaries (Auxies) 6, 7, 256, 266, 269, 278, 279, 280, 282, 284, 287, 293, 295, 297, 298, 303, 307, 309, 312, 316, 317, 322, 324, 328, 330, 333, 334

B

Bachelors Walk 26, 90, 158, 170
Bachelor, William 139
Baggallay, Geoffrey 296, 297, 298
Baggot Street 82, 101, 204, 205
Balbriggan 7, 40, 207, 288, 289, 291, 292, 293, 294, 295, 302
Baldonnell 272, 289
Ballinalee 334
Ballinrobe (Mayo) 232
Ballisodare 165
Ballybough 108
Ballybrack 230
Ballycanew 244
Ballycarney 243
Ballytrain, Co. Monaghan 183
Banbridge (Co. Down) 247, 261, 262, 312
Banks, Arthur 286
Bantry 272
Barrett, Ben 121, 140, 142, 143, 149, 150, 188, 189
Barrett, Daniel 87, 121, 122, 189
Barrett, William 297, 298
Barry, Katherine 325, 330

Barry, Kathleen 328
Barry, Kevin 7, 241, 284, 285, 286, 287, 288, 325, 326, 327, 328, 329, 330, 331, 332, 333
Barry, Mary 330
Barry, Michael 330
Barton, Johnny 26, 90, 110, 139, 140, 141, 142, 143, 166
Barton, Robert 58, 78, 79, 80, 82, 83, 94, 123, 161, 162, 180, 182, 190
Béaslaí, Piaras 47, 58, 80, 81, 82, 83, 84, 94, 95, 106, 124, 126, 127, 128, 137, 274
Beaumont 10
Beaumont, Seán 298
Beaumont, William 298, 299
Beggar's Bush 280, 282
Belfast 24, 26, 52, 58, 67, 94, 124, 127, 167, 171, 172, 175, 176, 179, 213, 217, 230, 261, 262, 267, 271, 272, 295
Belgium 46, 134, 160, 252, 288, 300
Belgrave Square 201
Bell, Alan 144, 167, 169, 175, 187, 190, 191, 201, 202, 203, 204, 205, 213, 281
Bellewstown 249
Bell, James 69, 144
Bennett, George 299, 300, 335
Beresford Place 208
Berkeley Road 182, 221
Berry, Joe 79, 80
Bessborough Avenue 122, 303
Birmingham 124
Black and Tans 6, 195, 200, 206, 223, 229, 230, 236, 242, 249, 262, 266, 267, 268, 269, 271, 276, 288, 289, 290, 291, 292, 293, 294, 295, 300, 324, 330, 333, 334,
Blackpool 193
Blythe, Ernest 83, 117
Boast, Frederick 166
Boland, Gerry 63
Boland, Harry 6, 9, 34, 36, 42, 43, 44, 48, 58, 59, 62, 63, 64, 65, 66, 67, 68, 69, 93, 104, 126, 234, 235, 236, 334
Boland, Jim 63
Boland, Ned 63
Bonar Law, Andrew 40, 207, 220, 228
Bond Loan Scheme 167
Booterstown 202
Borris 244
Botanic Avenue 108, 305, 308
Botanic Road 226
Bow Lane 181, 182
Bow Street 201, 217
Breen, Dan 51, 52, 53, 54, 66, 96, 125, 126, 135, 137, 148, 149, 150, 151, 152, 153, 154, 156, 158, 160, 182, 183, 197, 207, 208, 226, 265,

365

278, 279, 304, 305, 306, 307, 308, 309, 310, 312, 317, 318, 321
Brendan Road 79, 173
Brennan, Maurice 308
Brennan, Michael 185
Brennan, Robert 130
Breslin, Peadar 71, 72, 73, 74
Brind, John 169, 281
British Expeditionary Force (BEF) 28, 48
Broadstone 146, 147, 148, 149, 165, 221
Brooke, Frank 264, 265
Browne, John 27
Broy, Eamon (Ned) 33, 85, 86, 87, 88, 89, 90, 94, 116, 145, 170, 171, 207, 245, 277, 280
Brugha, Cathal 16, 30, 31, 32, 34, 39, 40, 41, 44, 48, 57, 58, 59, 62, 66, 67, 83, 84, 86, 92, 102, 104, 105, 106, 107, 111, 112, 120, 124, 125, 131, 140, 171, 188, 271, 300, 324
Brunswick, Seán 312, 314
Brunswick Street 33, 86, 88, 89, 129, 142, 209, 213, 217, 245, 271, 281, 285, 297, 298
Bruton, John 145, 245
Bryan, Thomas 283
Burke, Head Const. Peter 289, 290
Burke, Michael 289
Butt Bridge 184
Byrne, Bernard 310, 311
Byrne, Charlie 303, 310, 311
Byrne, Eddie 197
Byrne, Insp. 146, 147, 166, 180
Byrne, Matt 277
Byrne, Robert 86
Byrnes, John Charles 'Jack' (Jameson) 144, 146, 147, 189, 190, 195
Byrne, Tom 36, 71
Byrne, Vinny (Vincent) 9, 141, 142, 143, 147, 148, 149, 150, 151, 152, 153, 155, 156, 177, 178, 181, 182, 184, 185, 192, 197, 198, 199, 201, 202, 203, 204, 222, 225, 226, 227, 264, 265, 320

C

Cabinteely 230
Cabra 85, 86, 149, 155, 163, 164
Cairo Café 195, 196, 197, 198
Caldwell, Patrick 121, 196, 198, 199, 204
Camden Street 39, 112, 169, 200, 215
Campbell, Henry Joseph 191
Canada 22, 288
Capel Street 101, 320, 329
Carbery, Chris 84
Carew, Frank 313
Carlisle Pier 234, 282
Carlow 225, 244, 284
Carolan, Bridget 307
Carolan, Prof. John 305, 306, 307, 310
Carolan, Robert 306
Carrigan, Jimmy 285
Carroll, Peter 314
Carson, Edward 22, 33, 42, 49, 57, 58, 221, 261, 262, 267, 302
Casement, Roger 32, 134
Castleisland 248
Castleknock 102
Castletownbere 125
Cavan 25, 161, 213
Cavanagh, Det. Joseph 33, 170, 245, 331
Ceannt, Áine 162, 186
Chancery Street 10
Chesterton, G. K. 274
Childers, Erskine 78, 123, 162, 185, 235, 236, 256, 257, 267, 327
Christian, Francis 313, 314, 316
Churchill, Winston 69, 112, 113, 200, 228, 231, 236, 254, 263, 328
Church Street 268, 284, 285, 286, 287
Churchtown 253
City Hall 14, 36, 47, 180, 280
Clancy, Peadar 30, 42, 81, 82, 121, 124, 146, 163, 164, 181, 182, 184, 185, 209, 210, 213, 214, 216, 239, 240, 241, 252, 285, 302, 312, 313
Clare 15, 16, 19, 32, 83, 111, 113, 121, 174, 254, 294, 327
Clarke, Basil 269
Clarke, Joe 42
Clarke, Kathleen 26, 34
Clarke, Tom 26, 243
Clonmel Street 133, 178
Clontarf 58, 64, 80, 126, 235
Colbert, Con 46
Coleman, Richard 45
Cole, Walter 167
College Green, Dublin 59, 106, 128, 129, 131, 141, 142, 185, 191, 199, 264, 303
College Street 80, 118, 119, 129, 142, 303
Colley, Harry 260
Collins, Michael 5, 6, 13, 16, 17, 18, 26, 33, 34, 41, 44, 47, 51, 58, 59, 62, 63, 64, 65, 66, 67, 68, 69, 70, 78, 79, 80, 82, 83, 84, 85, 86, 87, 88, 89, 90, 93, 94, 95, 96, 100, 104, 105, 106, 111, 112, 113, 115, 116, 117, 120, 121, 122, 123, 124, 125, 126, 127, 131, 132, 133, 134, 137, 139, 140, 144, 145, 146, 158, 159, 162, 169, 170, 171, 172, 173, 174, 177, 178, 179, 180, 183, 187, 188, 189, 190, 191, 195, 196, 197, 214, 218, 234, 235, 243, 244, 245, 248, 256, 259, 274, 275, 276, 280, 281, 282, 296, 298, 299, 300, 305, 320, 330, 331, 332, 334
Collinstown 63, 70, 71, 73, 77, 78, 81, 86, 97, 102, 103, 121, 176, 255, 284, 289, 298
Connaught Street 156, 225
Connolly, Gus 184
Connolly, James 100, 233
Connolly, Joseph 110, 140
Conroy, Herbie 335
Constitution Hill 239, 240, 285
Coolidge, Calvin 191
Coolock 9
Cooney, Annie 46, 184, 212
Cooney, Eileen 184

INDEX

Cope, Alfred (Andy) 229, 232, 234, 268, 293
Corcoran, William 30, 289
Cork 13, 17, 27, 33, 53, 58, 62, 81, 82, 90, 96, 114, 115, 122, 125, 127, 137, 174, 183, 193, 194, 218, 223, 228, 242, 253, 258, 260, 261, 262, 268, 269, 270, 271, 288, 294, 300, 301, 323, 328, 329, 331
Corrigan, William 301
Cosgrave, William 34, 83, 95, 123, 139, 218
Couch, Ralph 67
Craig, Insp. 261
Craig, James 49, 161, 221, 301
Creel, George 68, 161, 221
Croke Park 15, 33
Cross Guns Bridge 226
Crowe, Tim 52, 54
Crow Street 141, 158, 159, 176, 188, 189, 191, 197, 201, 222, 242, 260, 276, 277
Crozier, Frank Percy 266, 267
Crumlin 67, 217, 230
Culhane, Seán 261, 271
Cullen, Owen 73, 76, 102, 124, 274, 276, 278, 279
Cullenswood House 39, 81, 82, 177, 186, 187
Cullen, Tom 86, 145, 158, 159, 170, 171, 176, 177, 187, 189, 195, 196, 198, 199, 249, 274, 277, 278, 299, 312
Cumann na mBan 14, 27, 35, 36, 41, 44, 46, 114, 138, 139, 184, 208, 212, 252, 293, 328, 329
Cunningham, Joseph 314
Curragh 28, 30, 180, 200, 266, 267, 280
Custom House, Dublin 38, 208, 242

D

Dáil Éireann 5, 6, 47, 48, 54, 55, 56, 57, 58, 59, 60, 61, 62, 66, 67, 68, 69, 70, 79, 82, 83, 84, 90, 91, 92, 93, 99, 100, 102, 104, 105, 112, 113, 114, 115, 117, 121, 123, 130, 131, 132, 134, 137, 139, 145, 161, 162, 167, 168, 170, 171, 173, 174, 175, 177, 187, 190, 191, 194, 196, 199, 204, 205, 225, 232, 234, 242, 249, 250, 267, 275, 276, 277, 301, 325, 329, 330
Dalkey 201
Dalton, Charlie 197, 260, 316, 320
Dalton, Det. Laurence 221, 222, 223, 225
Daly, Edward 47, 243
Daly, Paddy 9, 79, 80, 81, 82, 120, 121, 122, 128, 129, 137, 140, 142, 143, 148, 149, 150, 151, 152, 153, 154, 155, 177, 178, 179, 183, 185, 188, 189, 201, 202, 204, 214, 215, 222, 226, 227, 265, 303, 304, 312, 313
Dame Street 84, 141, 176, 178
Dawson Street 14, 54, 55, 94, 100, 101, 209, 298
de Valera, Éamon 5, 6, 13, 14, 15, 16, 23, 24, 34, 36, 49, 52, 57, 59, 63, 64, 65, 66, 67, 68, 69, 70, 71, 73, 83, 91, 92, 93, 94, 95, 99, 100, 104, 111, 112, 191, 195, 234, 235, 236, 301, 302, 331, 332
de Valera, Sinéad 16, 99, 289
Deansgrange 113, 205
Defence of the Realm Act (DORA) 34

DeLoughry, Peter 64
Denham, G. C. 238
Dennis, Patrick 185
Denzille Lane 331
Derham, James 289, 290
Derry 24, 56, 251, 258
D'Espard, Charlotte 35, 182, 293
Devlin, Joe 262
Devlin, Liam 274, 275, 276
Dicker, Madeleine ('Dilly') 146
Dillon, John 23, 24
Dingle 248, 270
DMP 9, 26, 33, 41, 53, 55, 56, 85, 86, 89, 97, 100, 101, 116, 123, 137, 138, 139, 143, 150, 155, 166, 167, 181, 185, 186, 218, 225, 231, 236, 244, 255, 277, 297, 321
Dolan, Joe 176, 177, 178, 188, 189, 198, 201, 202, 203, 208, 222, 223, 239, 240, 241, 260, 320
D'Olier Street 118, 142, 164, 188, 189
Dominick Street 222
Donegal 116, 161
Donegan, Séamus 38
Donnelly, Simon 42, 43, 55
Donnybrook 79, 204, 277
DORA (Defence of the Realm Act) 268
Doran, William 197
Dorset Street 221, 222, 309
Dowling, Joseph 32, 33
Downing, Michael 125, 143, 166
Downing Street, London 68, 160, 220, 228, 324
Doyle, Alderman Peadar 283
Doyle's Corner 225, 226, 308, 310
Doyle, Seán 72, 121, 122, 150, 177, 178, 283, 335
Dromore 261
Drumcondra 15, 68, 70, 80, 82, 102, 108, 110, 117, 126, 134, 148, 157, 227, 255, 304, 305, 308
Drumcondra Bridge 108, 304
Dublin Castle 6, 9, 24, 33, 43, 48, 51, 55, 70, 84, 86, 90, 97, 106, 112, 114, 115, 130, 139, 141, 143, 145, 159, 160, 163, 168, 169, 170, 171, 172, 177, 179, 180, 183, 191, 196, 198, 201, 204, 205, 207, 213, 219, 220, 221, 223, 225, 229, 232, 234, 237, 242, 245, 249, 250, 258, 259, 266, 268, 277, 278, 279, 284, 296, 298, 301, 313, 316, 317, 318, 319, 320
Dudley, George Vernon 282, 283, 295
Duffy, George Gavan 78, 99
Duffy, William 283
Duggan, Eamonn 18, 67, 84, 86, 190
Dundalk 20, 36, 52, 272
Dundalk Gaol 20, 52
Dunleavy, James 185
Dunne, Edward 93
Dunne, Thomas 231
Dwyer, Thomas 243

E

Eccles Street 145, 250, 308, 309
Edgeworth-Johnstone, Walter 55, 138, 167, 245
Ellis, John 332

Emmet, Robert 124
Ennis 118
Enniscorthy 243
Ennis, Patrick 192
Ennis, Tom 107, 108, 110, 118, 120, 122, 140, 146, 148, 149, 157, 192, 331, 335
Ennistymon 111, 294
Etchingham, Seán 83
Eustace Street 324
Exchange Street 278

F

Fagan, Brian 117
Fairview 255, 270
Falls Road 262
Farnan, Robert 67, 195
Farrell Boyd, Gerard 168
Farrell, Thomas 268
Farrington, Annie 126
Fermanagh 243, 264
Fermoy 114, 253, 254, 258
Fernside (Drumcondra) 305, 307, 308, 310, 323
Fingal 73, 76, 77, 96, 197
Finglas 19, 309
Finnegan, Const. Luke 180
Fisher, Herbert A. L. 324
Fisher, Warren 220, 229, 230
Fitzgerald, Billy 241
Fitzgerald, Desmond 102, 107, 130, 181, 259, 281
Fitzgerald, George 72, 73, 74, 75, 121, 122, 123, 127, 197, 206, 207, 208, 214, 218, 239, 240, 241, 242
Fitzgerald, James 241
Fitzgerald, Michael 253, 269, 323, 328
Fitzgibbon Street 277
Fitzmaurice, Det. Const. 320, 321
Fitzwilliam Place 242, 303
Flanagan, Michael 253
Flanagan, Paddy 43, 50, 56, 101, 102
Flanagan, Thomas 248
Fleet Street 324
Fleming, Cyril Francis 172, 270
Fleming, Dot 304
Fleming, Kay 304
Fleming, Mick 126, 148, 266
Fleming, Monica 270
Fleming, Pádraig 80, 81, 82
Flood, Frank 286, 331
Flynn, Patrick 53
Fogarty, Michael 123
Foran, Tom 233
Forbes-Redmond, Ass. Com. William 167, 171, 172, 173, 176, 177, 178, 179, 180, 184, 245
Four Courts 135, 137, 201, 244
France 46, 59, 68
French, John 5, 6, 21, 28, 29, 32, 33, 34, 35, 44, 48, 49, 50, 55, 58, 60, 61, 62, 68, 69, 82, 94, 96, 97, 104, 106, 107, 113, 114, 123, 124, 127, 128, 131, 135, 136, 137, 138, 143, 144, 146, 147, 148, 149, 150, 151, 152, 153, 154, 155, 156, 157, 158, 160, 161, 166, 172, 180, 181, 182, 205, 206, 213, 216, 219, 220, 221, 258, 260, 263, 264, 265, 281, 295
Friends of Irish Freedom (FOIF) 67
Frongoch 17, 20, 26, 36, 80, 87, 126
Furlong, Matt 30, 39, 40, 96, 97, 310, 318

G

Gaelic Athletic Association (GAA) 15, 17, 44, 63
Gaelic League 44, 114, 121, 139, 144, 164
Galbally 27
Gallagher, Frank 130, 214, 216
Galway 24, 114, 174, 262, 268, 327, 333
Gardiner Place 167
Gardiner Row 177
Gardiner Street 126, 188, 312
Gaynor, John 30, 40, 289
Gay, Thomas 33, 86
General Headquarters (GHQ) 5, 9, 16, 17, 18, 19, 23, 26, 27, 30, 31, 34, 36, 37, 38, 44, 47, 53, 66, 70, 71, 77, 83, 96, 103, 104, 106, 107, 111, 120, 121, 127, 135, 140, 146, 162, 163, 165, 166, 168, 169, 174, 181, 182, 183, 187, 191, 197, 206, 207, 208, 212, 230, 244, 250, 251, 252, 253, 264, 268, 272, 275, 281, 292, 300, 304, 310, 334
General Post Office (GPO), Dublin 52, 102, 105, 244
George V hosiptal, King 37, 155, 185, 284, 312, 316, 317, 318
Geraghty, Dr 156
Germany 20, 29, 32
Gibbons, Joseph 291, 295
Gibbons, Rose 302
Gibney, May 36
Ginnell, Laurence 83, 84, 102, 200
Glasgow 55, 172, 200
Glasnevin 14, 45, 114, 188, 304
Gleeson, Frank 227
Glendoo 101
Gloucester Jail 69
Godfrey, James 53
Golden, Davy 241, 285
Gonne, Maud 34
Gooding, John Henry 281
Good, Joe 30, 31, 32, 34, 37, 40, 41, 254
Gordon, Lionel Smith 162
Gorey 243, 244
Gormanston 289, 290, 292, 293
Gough, Sir Hubert 295
Government of Ireland Bill 167, 220, 221, 224, 242, 263, 301
Grafton Street 42, 55, 129, 141, 142, 176, 177, 178, 185, 195, 198, 199
Granard 334
Grantham Street 158, 160
Grattan Bridge 135, 320
Great Britain Street 73, 96, 102, 107, 201, 274, 304
Great Denmark Street 36, 251

INDEX

Greenwood, Thomas Hamar 206, 207, 218, 224, 228, 232, 254, 257, 259, 263, 264, 280, 293, 300, 312, 325, 334
Gresham hotel 68, 126, 155
Greystones 16, 99
Griffith, Arthur 15, 23, 24, 25, 26, 34, 35, 57, 70, 83, 84, 99, 100, 102, 114, 122, 123, 127, 130, 172, 182, 190, 259, 281, 282, 298, 301, 302, 319, 324, 325, 327, 330, 331, 332
Grosvenor Road 274
Guilfoyle, Joe 197, 198, 199, 201, 202, 203, 239
Gwynn, Stephen 293

H

Hacketstown 284
Haldane, Richard 48, 49, 50, 61, 68, 104, 221
Halley, Det. Sgt 90, 151, 155
Hall, William 33
Ha'penny Bridge 201
Harcourt Street 42, 43, 115, 117, 128, 129, 131, 134, 135, 145, 172, 176, 177, 178, 196, 199, 264
Hardy, Frank Digby 281, 282
Hardy, Jocelyn Lee 297, 298, 319, 320
Harper-Shove, Frederick 296
Harrington, Timothy 162, 163, 164
Hayes, Seán 134
Henderson, Frank 9, 10, 11, 36, 52, 165, 200, 213, 259, 312
Henderson, Leo 300, 312
Henrietta Street 239, 240, 241
Henry, Attorney General 207
Henry, Denis 190
Henry Place 163
Heron, Archie 96
Heuston, Seán 45
Heytesbury Street 148, 157
Higgins, Maurice 285, 287
Hill-Dillon, Stephen 169, 195, 196, 238, 239
Hoey, Daniel 94, 95, 96, 97, 116, 117, 118, 119, 120, 129, 140, 143, 166
Hoey, Patricia 134
Hogan, Seán 51, 52, 53, 54, 66, 96, 125, 135, 137, 149, 151, 152, 156, 197
Holland, Robert 147
Hollybank Road 305
Holmes, Frederick 308
Holmes, Kathleen 308
Holohan, Garry 71, 163
Holohan, Patrick 70, 71, 72, 73, 74, 75, 76, 77, 79, 103, 163, 164, 208
Holyhead 32, 34, 69, 329
Home Farm Road 306
Home Rule 14, 22, 23, 29, 32, 33, 55, 127, 206, 257, 263, 302, 329
House of Commons 23, 35, 40, 112, 167, 257, 261, 340
Howth 78, 234, 270
Hughes, Annie 199
Humphries, Thomas 288

Hunger strikes 14, 52, 80, 82, 86, 123, 124, 209, 210, 212, 213, 214, 216, 217, 224, 227, 228, 233, 239, 247, 254, 269, 273, 288, 300, 323, 327, 329, 331
Hunter, Tom 121, 214
Hunt, Michael 103
Hurley, James 139
Hyde Park 144

I

Inchicore 233
India 8, 124, 237, 238, 254
Irish Citizen Army (ICA) 16, 36, 42, 43, 100, 110, 233
Irish National Aid and Volunteer Dependants' Fund (INAVDF) 26
Irish Parliamentary Party (IPP) 22, 23, 24, 44, 45, 48, 57, 162, 262
Irish Republican Brotherhood (IRB) 15, 18, 19, 26, 51, 52, 63, 65, 70, 84, 87, 99, 104, 106, 112, 113, 115, 121, 145, 194, 222, 234, 274, 324
Irish Self Determination League) ISDL 144, 182, 271
Irish Women's Workers Union (IWWU) 35, 36, 200
Isham, Ralph 184
Islandbridge 102, 106

J

Jameson, John [Alias John Byrnes] 144, 169, 170, 173, 184, 187, 188
Jeune, Robert 305
John Rogerson's Quay 184
Johnson, Thomas 58, 256, 257
Jones, Thomas 259
Jones, William 114

K

Kavanagh, Capt. 288
Kavanagh, James 117
Kavanagh, Séamus 285, 286, 287
Kells 214
Kells, Det. 215
Kells, Henry 213, 214, 215, 218
Kelly, Bartholomew 154
Kelly, Edward 36, 94
Kelly, Frank 64, 66
Kelly, Henry 182, 183
Kelly, Mick 185
Kelly, Thomas 48, 180
Kelly, Tom 204, 308
Kenmare 248
Kennedy, Laurence 166
Kennedy, Mick 108, 110, 197
Kennedy, Tadhg 244, 245
Keogh, Myles 217, 328
Keogh, Tom 107, 108, 109, 120, 121, 131, 140, 141, 142, 143, 150, 152, 157, 177, 178, 179, 181, 192, 198, 201, 202, 204, 222, 226, 227,

369

239, 240, 241, 264, 265, 312, 320, 331
Kerry 27, 47, 128, 139, 143, 172, 174, 244, 245, 268, 270, 289, 327
Kevin Street 181, 277
Kiernan, Kitty 234, 235, 334
Kilcoyne, Tom 188, 189
Kildare 23, 33, 38, 55, 200
Killarney 128, 248
Killiney 230, 231, 334
Kill o' the Grange 230
Kilmainham Gaol 13, 37, 78, 100, 184, 216, 273, 328
Kilmallock 296
Kilmashogue 282, 284
Kiltyclogher 95
Kingsbridge 30, 69, 302, 310, 329
King's County (Offaly) 96, 120
Kingstown (Dún Laoghaire) 137, 172, 186, 230, 233, 234, 277, 282
Kissane, Tom 285, 287
Knightly, Michael 191, 202, 281
Knocklong 96, 103, 125, 126, 160

L

Laffan, Nicholas 252
Lahinch 294
Laide, Richard 27
Land Bank 161, 162, 167
Larkin, Joe 230
Lawless, Eithne 116, 117, 133, 234
Lawless, Frank 134
Lawless, James 291
Lawless, Joseph 73, 75, 76, 96, 97, 102, 110, 116, 158, 270, 295, 304, 305, 308, 309
Lawson, Patrick 76
Leddy, Phil 185
Leitrim 95, 248
Lennox Street 200
Leonard, Joe 81, 120, 121, 122, 128, 129, 140, 142, 143, 147, 148, 149, 156, 177, 178, 188, 189, 206, 215, 226, 227, 303, 304, 312
Limerick 27, 86, 96, 133, 174, 221, 223, 254, 265, 268, 269, 296, 322
Lime Street 184
Lincoln Jail 63, 64, 66
Lindsay Road 226
Lisburn 270, 271
Liscannor 294
Lismore 254, 258
Listowel 245, 246, 248, 256, 257
Liverpool 47, 55, 93, 99, 100, 127, 172, 200, 217
Lloyd George, David 22, 23, 28, 29, 32, 40, 49, 160, 161, 206, 221, 254, 257, 261, 263, 271, 282, 302, 329, 330, 331, 334
London 17, 28, 30, 31, 32, 34, 39, 45, 63, 66, 68, 78, 87, 120, 122, 123, 124, 125, 127, 128, 137, 144, 158, 159, 161, 168, 169, 171, 180, 182, 200, 205, 217, 218, 232, 233, 238, 243, 254, 257, 259, 263, 269, 293, 310, 324, 328, 329, 332, 334

Longford 17, 29, 105, 157, 158, 174, 334
Long, Walter 22, 32, 33, 50, 60, 97, 113, 161, 172, 190, 220, 250, 263, 301
Loughlinstown 230
Love, Michael 122
Lucan 166, 284
Lucas, Cuthbert 253, 254, 265
Lynch, Christie 10, 11
Lynch, Fionán 124
Lynch, John 296, 297, 298, 301
Lynch, Liam 27, 71, 72, 96, 102, 104, 105, 106, 111, 114, 158, 163, 253, 300
Lynch, Michael 19, 77, 114, 138, 181
Lynch, Sgt 110
Lynch, Vice-Brigadier 71, 72, 96, 102, 104, 111, 156, 157, 158
Lynn, Kathleen 46, 200, 230
Lyons, Ned 82
Lyster, Seán 281

M

MacBride, John 34, 37
MacCurtain, Elizabeth 193
MacCurtain, Tomás 137, 193, 194, 196, 218, 228, 242, 243, 270
MacDermott, Seán 94, 95, 140, 273
MacDonagh, John 123
MacDonagh, Joseph 267
MacDonagh, Thomas 123
MacMahon, Under Secretary James 84, 99, 180, 229, 332
MacNeill, Eoin 51, 56, 62, 83, 92, 215
MacNeill, Hugo 215
Macpherson, Ian 48, 68, 69, 96, 97, 112, 146, 160, 172, 206, 207, 220
Macready, Cecil Frederick Nevil 161, 206, 213, 216, 220, 221, 223, 224, 225, 228, 229, 230, 231, 233, 234, 245, 254, 262, 263, 267, 280, 284, 294, 302, 322, 329, 336
MacSwiney, Mary 273
MacSwiney, Terence 7, 228, 269, 271, 273, 288, 300, 302, 326, 327, 328, 329, 331
Magee, Mick 75
Maguire, Sam 63, 123
Mahon, Bryan 30
Mallow 300
Malone, Áine 160
Malone, Brigid 182
Malone, Michael 69, 160
Malone, William 160
Manchester 59, 66, 67, 124, 127, 134, 195, 295, 300
Mannix, Daniel 267
Mannix, Jerry 277
Manor Street 43, 318, 319
Mansion House 14, 23, 24, 42, 47, 54, 55, 56, 59, 60, 62, 69, 79, 89, 91, 93, 94, 95, 96, 100, 101, 112, 167
Markievicz, Countess 34, 45, 57, 83, 95, 177, 196, 256

INDEX

Marlborough barracks 155, 325
Marlborough Street 185, 277, 312
Maryborough (Portlaoise) prison 80
Mater hospital 110, 114, 156, 183, 189, 212, 223, 227, 231, 307, 309, 310, 312, 316
Maxwell, John Grenfell 28
Maynooth 23, 104
Mayo 41, 53, 102, 120, 195, 232, 254
McCabe, William 231
McCan, Pierce 69
McCarthy, Michael 223
McCluskey, Seán 132
McCormack, Patrick 52
McCrea, Patrick 73, 76, 102, 303
McDonnell, Andrew 209, 210, 215, 216, 217
McDonnell, Dan 72, 74, 75, 298
McDonnell, James 53, 54, 62
McDonnell, Mick 77, 106, 107, 108, 110, 111, 117, 118, 120, 121, 122, 123, 124, 125, 127, 128, 131, 140, 141, 142, 143, 146, 147, 148, 149, 150, 154, 155, 156, 157, 177, 181, 182, 183, 192, 193, 198, 199, 201, 202, 203, 205, 222, 226, 309
McElligott, Thomas (T.J.) 144, 235, 236
McFeely, Insp. 87, 116, 133
McGarry, Seán 34, 65, 68
McGowan, Josie 41, 100
McGrath, Gabriel 185, 186
McGrath, Paddy 163, 164, 184, 185, 187
McGrath, Patrick 284
McGuinness, Joseph 17, 34
McKee, Dick 5, 9, 10, 11, 13, 17, 18, 19, 20, 27, 36, 37, 38, 39, 42, 45, 47, 52, 67, 71, 72, 77, 84, 87, 89, 103, 104, 105, 106, 107, 111, 117, 120, 121, 122, 126, 128, 131, 132, 134, 138, 157, 182, 183, 184, 193, 197, 208, 209, 230, 231, 239, 240, 241, 249, 252, 253, 259, 285, 288, 300, 308, 309, 310, 312, 313, 316, 317, 328, 331
McKenna, Kathleen 130
McLoughlin, Seán 26, 27, 51, 80, 82, 95, 150, 151, 154, 268
McMahon, Joseph 244
McMahon, Liam 66, 67, 127
McMahon, Seán 18, 38
McNamara, Det. Jim 170, 171, 172, 173, 177, 245, 278
McNamara, Rose 184, 212, 328
McNaughton, James Scott 189
McNulty, Frederick 195, 199, 205, 235
Meaney, Patrick 231
Meath 38, 107, 214, 215, 294, 310
Mee, Jeremiah 246, 247, 248, 256, 261
Melbourne 267
Mercer Street 181
Mernin, Elizabeth 'Lily' 84, 169, 195, 196, 249, 298
Merrigan, Tom 74, 75
Merrion Road 201, 204
Merrion Square 67, 335
Middle Abbey Street 43, 164, 169

Millbourne Avenue 108, 307
Millmount Avenue 108, 109, 110, 307
Millmount Terrace 108, 109
Milner, Alfred 28, 29
Milroy, Seán 65, 68, 123
Miltown Malbay 294
Molesworth Street 94, 95
Molloy, Brian Fergus 195, 196, 197, 198, 199, 235
Molony, Helena 36
Monaghan 161, 183
Monkstown 201
Montague Street 178, 179
Mooney, James 30
Moore, George 60, 61
Moore Lane 163, 274
Moore Street 63
Morehampton Road 173
Mountjoy Prison 11, 14, 19, 52, 78, 79, 80, 82, 90, 120, 123, 138, 167, 182, 209, 211, 212, 213, 215, 217, 218, 221, 284, 304, 309, 326, 328, 329, 330, 331, 332, 333
Mountjoy Street 34, 95, 134, 182, 222, 235
Mount Street 69, 101, 130, 160, 217
Moylett, Patrick 324, 325, 329, 330, 331
Moynihan, Patrick 259
Mulcahy, Richard 5, 13, 16, 17, 18, 19, 27, 30, 31, 33, 34, 39, 44, 47, 52, 58, 61, 62, 67, 79, 81, 83, 84, 87, 89, 95, 104, 105, 111, 112, 117, 120, 121, 122, 124, 125, 126, 140, 163, 165, 169, 177, 186, 190, 200, 249, 250, 273, 283, 292, 300, 305, 307
Munroe, Charles 82
Munro, Major 209
Munster Street 274
Murphy, Fintan 66, 134
Murphy, Francis 113
Murphy, Joseph 328
Murray, Patrick 30
Murtagh, Joseph 194

N

Nassau Street 55, 93, 141, 142, 185, 195, 208, 298
Naul 73, 76, 188, 289
Neligan, David 133, 171, 223, 244, 245, 277, 278, 298, 300, 317, 318, 319, 320, 321
Nelson Street 182
Newcomen Bridge 70, 303
New Ross 243
North Circular Road 11, 147, 212, 252, 309, 310, 325, 333
North Great Charles Street 148, 309
North King Street 284, 285, 286, 287
North Strand 70, 122, 155, 157, 255, 303
Northumberland Road 69
North Wall 67, 185, 200, 233
Noyk, Michael 83, 191
Nunan, Seán 57, 87, 88, 89, 100, 105

371

O

Oakley Road 39, 162, 177, 180
O'Brien, Arthur (Art) 145, 190, 233, 257
O'Brien, Denis 90
O'Brien, Martin 86
O'Brien, Nancy 84
O'Brien, Patrick 90
O'Brien, William 58, 232, 256
O'Carroll, Gerard 319
O'Carroll, Liam 43, 318
O'Carroll, Michael 318
O'Carroll, Peter 318, 319
O'Carroll, Seán 318
O'Connell, Bill 311
O'Connell Bridge 119
O'Connell, Jeremiah J. (Ginger) 115
O'Connell, Patrick 53, 54, 62
O'Connor, Batt 79, 80, 127, 131, 134, 170, 173, 195
O'Connor, Joe 184
O'Connor, Joseph 36, 67
O'Connor, Patrick 75, 76
O'Connor, Rory 18, 79, 124, 283
O'Donel, Geraldine 251, 308
O'Donoghue, Dáithí 131, 132, 133, 134, 162
O'Donoghue, Paddy 66, 124, 127
O'Donovan, James 253
O'Donovan, Julia 184, 277, 318
O'Duffy, Eoin 183
O'Dwyer, Patrick 52, 53, 54
O'Flanagan, Bob 287
O'Flanagan, Michael 15, 55, 57, 129, 286, 287
Ó Foghludha, Michael 85
O'Hanlon, Gertrude 130
O'Hanrahan, Harry 33
O'Hegarty, Bríd 163
O'Hegarty, Diarmuid 115, 123, 134, 137, 167, 274
O'Higgins, Kevin 139, 215, 218, 225
O'Keefe, Patrick 117
O'Kelly, Séamus 43
O'Kelly, T. Seán 59, 78, 83, 90, 99
O'Leary, Liam 243
O'Mahony, Eddie 10, 11
O'Mahony, Seán 84, 134
O'Malley, Ernie 183, 300
O'Mara, Peadar 231
O'Meara, Jack 52
O'Neill, James 100
O'Neill, Laurence 23, 180
O'Neill, Seán 286, 287
Onslow, Cranley Charlton 325, 326
O'Reilly, Joe 82, 86, 94, 95, 127, 128, 133, 134, 158, 159, 169, 170, 173, 187, 245, 274
Oriel Place 192, 193
Ormond Quay 16, 320
O'Shea, James 100, 101
O'Shea, Power 246
O'Shiel, Kevin 296
O'Sullivan, Gearóid 184, 236, 274, 296

O'Toole, Laurence 165

P

Parkgate Street 30, 106, 169, 195
Parliament Street 137, 145, 176, 284, 296
Pearse, Pádraig 13, 29
Pearson, Alfred 70
Peel, Charles 297, 298
Pershing, John J. 191
Peter Street 227
Phibsboro 155, 156, 158, 181, 200, 225, 226, 304, 308, 312
Phoenix Park 29, 71, 102, 146, 147, 149, 151, 166, 289, 296, 300, 321, 325
Pleasants Street 213, 215
Plunkett, George Noble 56, 57, 62, 83, 99, 185, 196, 242
Plunkett, Horace 271
Plunkett, Jack 283, 331
Plunkett, John 242
Plunkett, Joseph 274
Poland 59, 232
Poolbeg Street 142
Poole, Christopher 'Kit' 43
Portobello 129, 200, 215
Portumna 114
Prendergast, Seán 240, 241
Price, Gilbert 313, 314, 317
Purfield, Vincent 73, 207, 208

Q

Queenstown (Cobh) 268
Quigley, May 278
Quinlisk, Timothy 134, 145, 146, 183
Quinn, Ellen 333

R

Rafter, Seamus 43
Raheny 270
Ranelagh 39, 162
Rathfarnam 50, 123
Rathgar 16, 184, 277, 318
Rathmines 185, 200, 274, 277
Reading Gaol 25
Redmond, John 22, 23, 44
Reilly, Sam 30
Restoration of Order in Ireland Act (ROIA) 268, 275, 281, 325, 328
Revell, Richard 225, 226, 227
Richmond barracks 13, 26, 63, 73, 78, 79, 94, 105, 106, 140, 301
Richmond hospital 217, 319
Richmond Road 70, 97, 110, 156
Roberts, Andrew 9, 10, 50, 61
Robinson, Mick 287
Robinson, Séamus 51, 52, 53, 54, 66, 96, 125, 148, 149, 151, 155, 156, 157, 197, 207, 208
Roche, Det. Daniel 318, 320
Rockbrook 270

INDEX

Rock, Michael 76, 289, 290, 292
Rooney, William 76
Roosevelt, Franklin D. 191
Roscommon 28, 56, 58, 64, 137, 146, 147, 149, 268, 327
Rotunda 16, 105, 243, 259, 263, 264
Royal Air Force (RAF) 38, 70, 71, 106, 215
Royal City of Dublin Hospital 101, 204
Royal Irish Constabulary (RIC) 9, 10, 17, 19, 27, 39, 43, 50, 51, 52, 53, 55, 85, 88, 89, 92, 96, 97, 101, 103, 113, 114, 123, 143, 144, 146, 155, 165, 166, 167, 171, 172, 183, 194, 200, 206, 207, 218, 220, 224, 225, 229, 230, 231, 235, 236, 241, 243, 244, 247, 248, 251, 256, 258, 260, 262, 263, 265, 266, 269, 270, 278, 280, 289, 290, 291, 293, 294, 295, 296, 297, 300, 318, 320, 321, 328, 334
Rumble, Sgt George 152
Russell, Seán 165, 260
Russell, Thomas 19
Russia 20, 232
Rutland Place 252
Rutland Square 16, 18, 30, 73, 76, 77, 87, 121, 146, 162, 164, 239, 249, 275, 292
Ryan, Bernard 312
Ryan, Dr 156, 158
Ryan, Michael 52, 93
Ryan, Min 95
Ryan, Phil 309
Ryan, P. J. 75
Ryder's Row 285

S

Sackville Street 16, 19, 52, 63, 105, 119, 126, 135, 155, 157, 169, 188, 285, 287, 304, 308, 313
Saunderson, Edward 32
Saurin, Frank 195, 299, 335
Savage, Martin 9, 10, 148, 150, 152, 153, 154, 155, 156, 157, 164, 165
Schoolhouse Lane 94
Scotland 32, 120, 127, 144, 169, 171, 190, 266, 272, 274, 275, 276, 323
Sears, Private 255
Secret service 123, 168, 229, 256, 276, 277, 282, 299
Seville Place 165, 192, 303, 304
Shanahan, Phil 126, 200
Shankill Road 262
Sharkey, Paddy 146, 147, 148
Shaw, Frederick 30
Shaw, General 70, 77, 98, 113, 205
Shaw, Jack 185
Sheehan, Paddy 133
Sheehy Skeffington, Hanna 93, 123
Sheriff Street 192, 324
Ship Street 182, 296
Simmonscourt Road 202, 203
Sinn Féin 5, 6, 14, 15, 16, 23, 24, 25, 32, 33, 34, 35, 42, 43, 44, 45, 46, 47, 48, 49, 56, 57, 58, 59, 60, 61, 64, 65, 67, 68, 69, 70, 78, 79, 81, 83, 85, 86, 88, 90, 104, 112, 114, 115, 116, 117, 129, 131, 132, 134, 135, 139, 143, 144, 147, 161, 162, 167, 168, 174, 175, 178, 180, 181, 190, 221, 223, 224, 225, 230, 235, 236, 237, 242, 247, 248, 250, 255, 257, 258, 261, 263, 272, 275, 280, 285, 290, 296, 301, 302, 325, 335
Sir Patrick Dun's Hospital 265
Skerries 270, 292
Slattery, James 107, 108, 109, 110, 111, 117, 118, 120, 121, 122, 140, 141, 142, 143, 150, 181, 192, 198, 199, 201, 202, 203, 222, 239, 240, 241, 265, 320
Sligo 34, 90, 165, 246, 295, 300
Sligo Jail 34
Smith-Cumming, Mansfield 238
Smith, Insp. 144, 166, 205, 328
Smith, Insp. Gen. 146, 220, 229, 236
Smith, Thomas 138, 144, 231
Smyth, Bryce Ferguson 246, 247, 248, 256, 257, 260, 261, 262, 297, 298, 305
Smythe, Private 255
Smyth, Eugene 106
Smyth, George Osbert 297, 305, 306, 307, 312
Smyth, Mary 289
Smyth, Patrick 90, 105, 106, 108, 109, 110, 117, 197, 222
Smyth, Thomas 109
Snow, Capt. 218
Soloheadbeg 5, 47, 50, 61, 66, 96, 125, 126, 265
South Anne Street 184
South Frederick Street 184
South Great George's Street 177
South King Street 198
Special Duties Unit 107, 117, 120, 121, 128, 182, 198
Special Duties Units 6, 146, 177, 197
Spencer, Robert 221, 222
Squad, the 6, 197, 198, 201, 203, 214, 215, 222, 225, 226, 239, 259, 260, 264, 303, 304, 312, 320, 344
SS *Baltic* 268
Stack, Austin 18, 67, 94, 124, 126, 173, 244, 300
Stafford 87
Staines, Michael 319
St Andrew Street 112, 199, 301
Stapleton, William 255, 260
Steele, John 324
Stepaside 50, 270
Stephen's Green 42, 54, 55, 117, 132, 176, 178
St Ignatius Road 102, 308
St Mary's Place 222
Straw, William 291, 292
Strickland, Peter 294
Sturgis, Mark 229, 232, 234, 237, 263, 265, 266, 268, 280, 293, 333
Swanzy, Oswald 270
Sweeney, Capt. Pat 182
Sweeney, Patrick 10, 11
Switzerland 58
Swords 45, 73, 76, 258

373

Synott, Michael 244

T

Talbot Street 121, 267, 312, 313, 314, 316, 317, 323
Tallaght 289
Tannam, Liam 82
Taylor, Assistant Under Secretary John 144, 180, 200, 219, 220, 229
Tegart, Charles 238
Templemore 269
Terenure 236
Thompson, Basil 32, 33, 144, 168, 169, 170, 174, 177, 183, 184, 187, 188, 189, 238, 239, 258, 275, 282
Thornton, Frank 157, 158, 159, 170, 171, 172, 173, 176, 177, 196, 197, 198, 223, 243, 244, 274, 275, 276, 277, 281, 299, 312, 320
Thurles 96, 103, 111, 180, 233, 243
Tipperary 26, 27, 50, 62, 69, 80, 90, 103, 104, 114, 126, 174, 197, 207, 243, 265, 268, 269, 278, 304, 317, 318, 322, 327
Tobin, Liam 86, 121, 122, 123, 127, 158, 159, 170, 171, 173, 184, 188, 189, 191, 195, 196, 197, 198, 200, 201, 202, 203, 205, 218, 222, 225, 226, 243, 244, 245, 274, 276, 278, 279, 299, 312, 318, 319, 320
Toomey, Jack 156, 226
Townsend Street 142
Tracy, Patrick 33
Tralee 27, 39, 244, 248, 333, 334
Traynor, Oscar 9, 10, 11, 52, 165, 177, 259, 260
Treacy, Seán 51, 52, 53, 54, 66, 69, 96, 125, 135, 137, 148, 149, 150, 155, 156, 157, 160, 197, 265, 278, 304, 305, 306, 308, 309, 310, 312, 313, 314, 315, 317, 318, 321, 322
Trinity College 22, 42, 106, 128, 131, 135, 137, 142, 178, 201, 264, 298, 303
Tuam 262
Tubbercurry 300
Tudor 234, 280
Tudor, Henry Hugh 231, 232, 246, 248, 263, 266, 279, 280, 312
Tyrone 243

U

Ulster 14, 22, 23, 24, 36, 49, 50, 51, 68, 78, 138, 160, 161, 172, 175, 183, 206, 213, 221, 251, 252, 261, 263, 266, 271, 272, 301, 302, 329
Ulster Volunteer Force (UVF) 161, 282, 302
University College Dublin (UCD) 16, 17, 83, 284
Upper Abbey Street 245
Upper Gardiner Street 188
Upper Oriel Street 192

V

Vaughan's hotel 87, 93, 158, 191, 197, 274
Vize, Joe 308

W

Waldron, Lawrence Ambrose 231
Wales 13, 17, 40, 45, 70, 206
Walsh, Const. 185
Walsh, Frank 93
Walsh, J. J. 81, 82, 137, 221
Walsh, John 185
Washington, Pte Henry 287
Waterford 17, 57, 80, 174, 254
Waterford Street 185
Waterloo Road 173
Waters, Canon John 332
Westland Row 45, 233, 265
Westminster 21, 25, 40, 44, 46, 47, 60, 138, 167, 168, 172, 174, 190, 220, 256, 257, 261, 266, 301, 302, 329, 330
Westmoreland Street 118, 143, 264
Wexford 43, 55, 59, 129, 134, 144, 243, 244, 245, 253, 310
Wexford Street 55, 129, 253
Wharton, Thomas 128, 129, 130, 132, 139
Whelan, Seán 244
Whelan, William 30, 31, 32, 34, 40
White, Capt. Alfred 305, 307, 312, 323
Whitehall 73, 123, 127, 207
Whitehead, Matthew 288, 326
Whitehead, Pte Marshall 326
Whitworth Road 81
Wicklow 38, 51, 58, 78, 79, 82, 83, 106, 162, 174, 188, 197, 198, 264
Wilson, Field Marshal Henry 29, 30, 180, 228, 234, 264, 273, 295, 296, 330
Wilson, Percival Lea 243, 244
Wilson, Walter 238, 239, 296
Wilson, Woodrow 59, 67, 68, 93, 221
Winter, Ormonde de L'Épée 236, 237, 239, 265, 317, 318, 323
Woods, Robert 57
Woods, Seán 325, 328
Wormwood Scrubs 180, 217, 218, 233
Wylie, William 221, 230, 263, 301

Y

Young, Thomas 96, 97